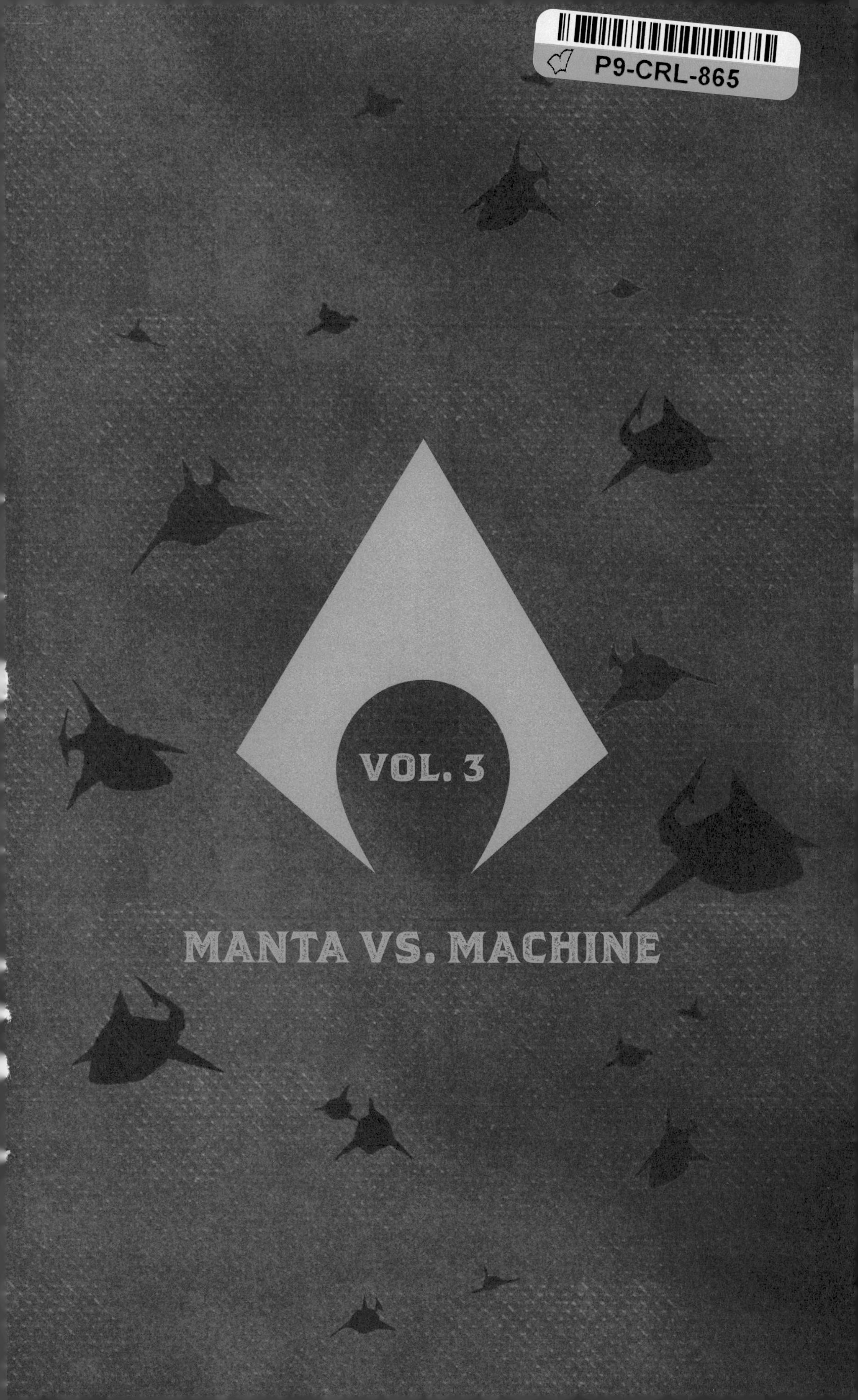
VOL. 3
MANTA VS. MACHINE

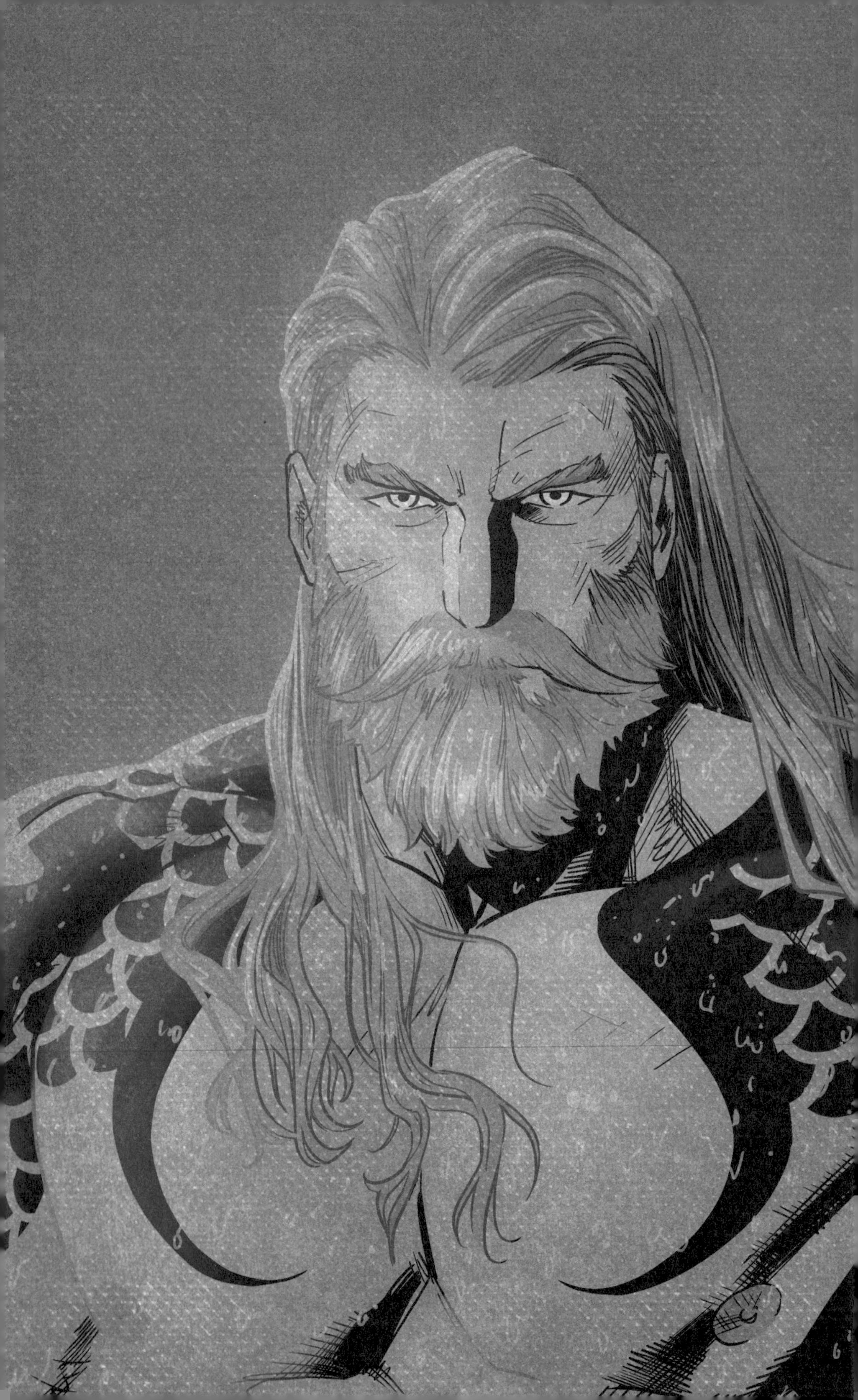

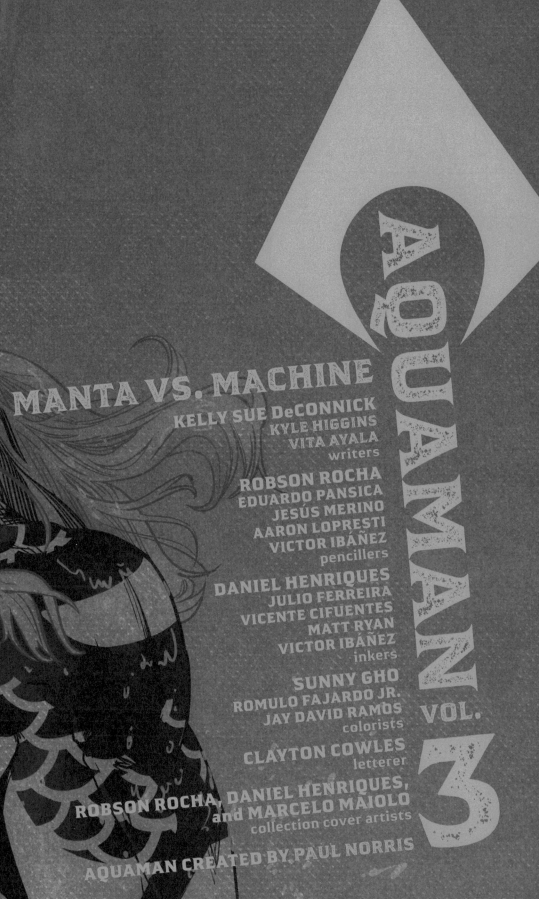

MANTA VS. MACHINE

KELLY SUE DeCONNICK
KYLE HIGGINS
VITA AYALA
writers

ROBSON ROCHA
EDUARDO PANSICA
JESÚS MERINO
AARON LOPRESTI
VICTOR IBÁÑEZ
pencillers

DANIEL HENRIQUES
JULIO FERREIRA
VICENTE CIFUENTES
MATT RYAN
VICTOR IBÁÑEZ
inkers

SUNNY GHO
ROMULO FAJARDO JR.
JAY DAVID RAMOS
colorists

CLAYTON COWLES
letterer

ROBSON ROCHA, DANIEL HENRIQUES,
and MARCELO MAIOLO
collection cover artists

AQUAMAN CREATED BY PAUL NORRIS

AQUAMAN VOL. 3

ALEX ANTONE ALEX R. CARR Editors – Original Series
ANDREA SHEA Associate Editor - Original Series
JEB WOODARD Group Editor – Collected Editions
ROBIN WILDMAN Editor – Collected Edition
STEVE COOK Design Director – Books
GABRIEL MALDONADO Publication Design
ERIN VANOVER Publication Production

BOB HARRAS Senior VP – Editor-in-Chief, DC Comics

DAN DiDIO Publisher
JIM LEE Publisher & Chief Creative Officer
BOBBIE CHASE VP – New Publishing Initiatives
DON FALLETTI VP – Manufacturing Operations & Workflow Management
LAWRENCE GANEM VP – Talent Services
ALISON GILL Senior VP – Manufacturing & Operations
HANK KANALZ Senior VP – Publishing Strategy & Support Services
DAN MIRON VP – Publishing Operations
NICK J. NAPOLITANO VP – Manufacturing Administration & Design
NANCY SPEARS VP – Sales
JONAH WEILAND VP – Marketing & Creative Services
MICHELE R. WELLS VP & Executive Editor, Young Reader

AQUAMAN VOL. 3:
MANTA VS. MACHINE

DC Comics, 2900 West Alameda Ave.,
Burbank, CA 91505. Printed by LSC Communications,
Owensville, MO, USA. 5/22/20. First Printing.
ISBN: 978-1-77950-281-0

Library of Congress Cataloging-in-Publication Data
is available.

PEFC Certified
This product is from
sustainably managed
forests and controlled
sources
PEFC/29-31-337   www.pefc.org

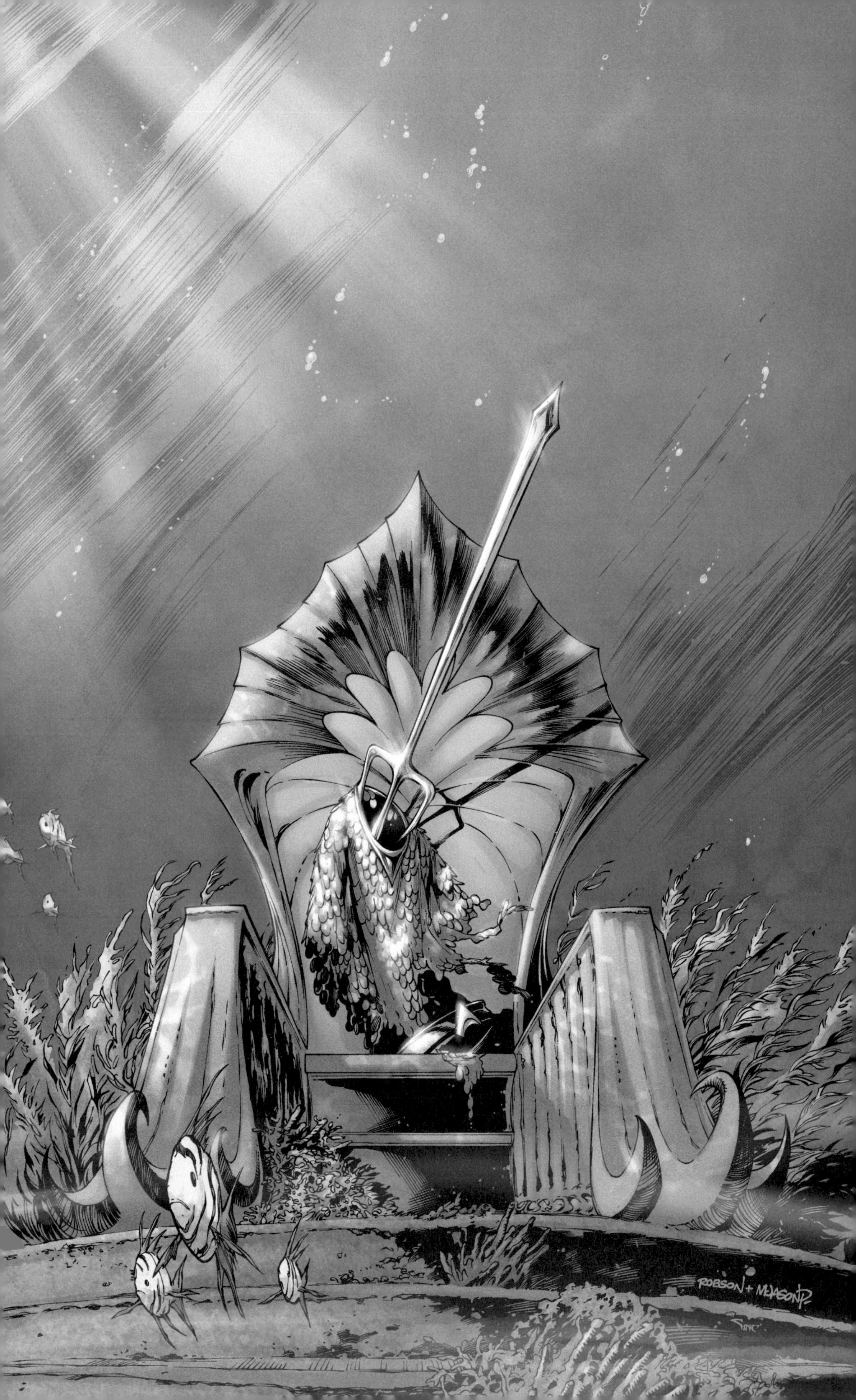
ROBSON + McJASON P.

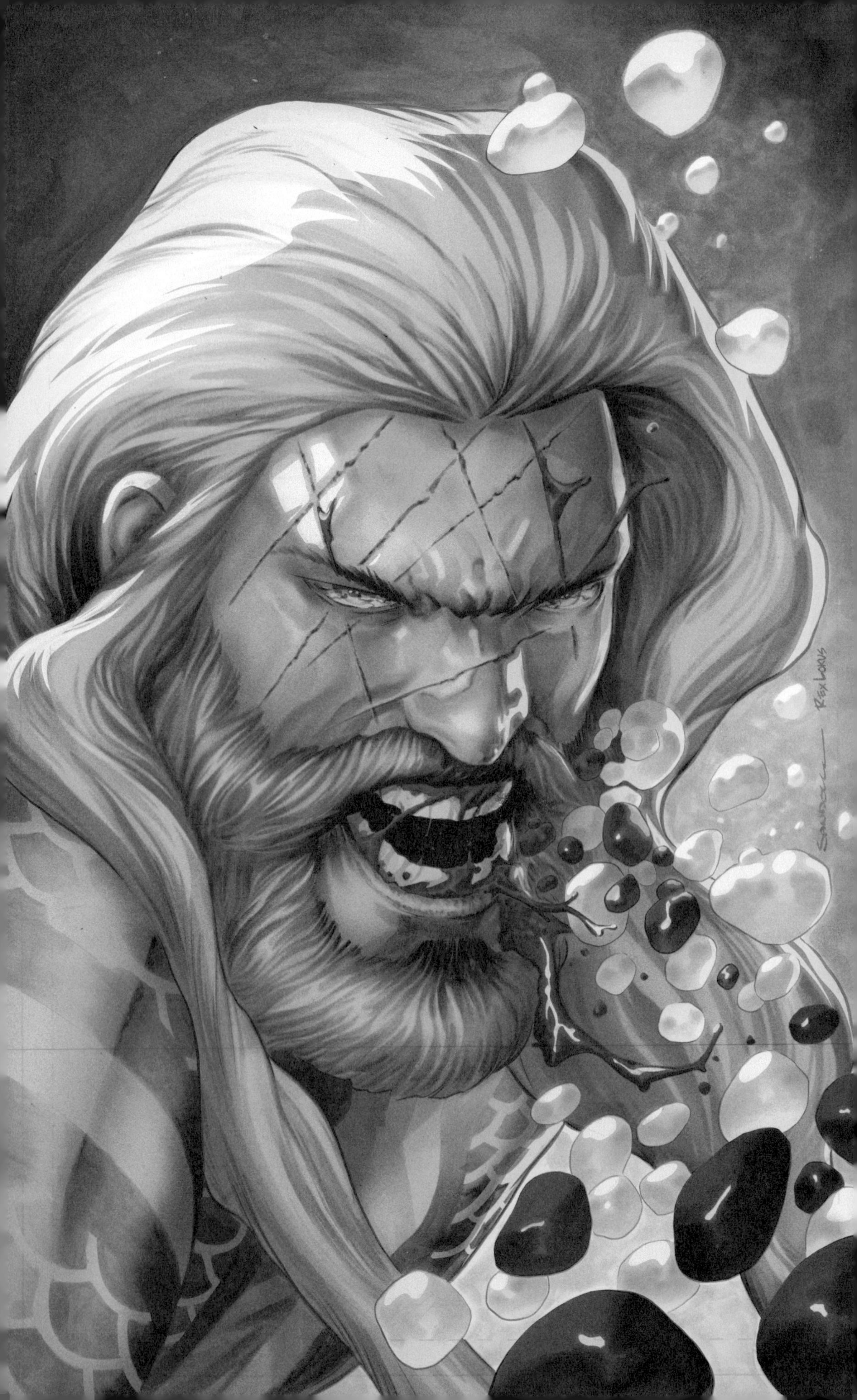
REX LOKUS

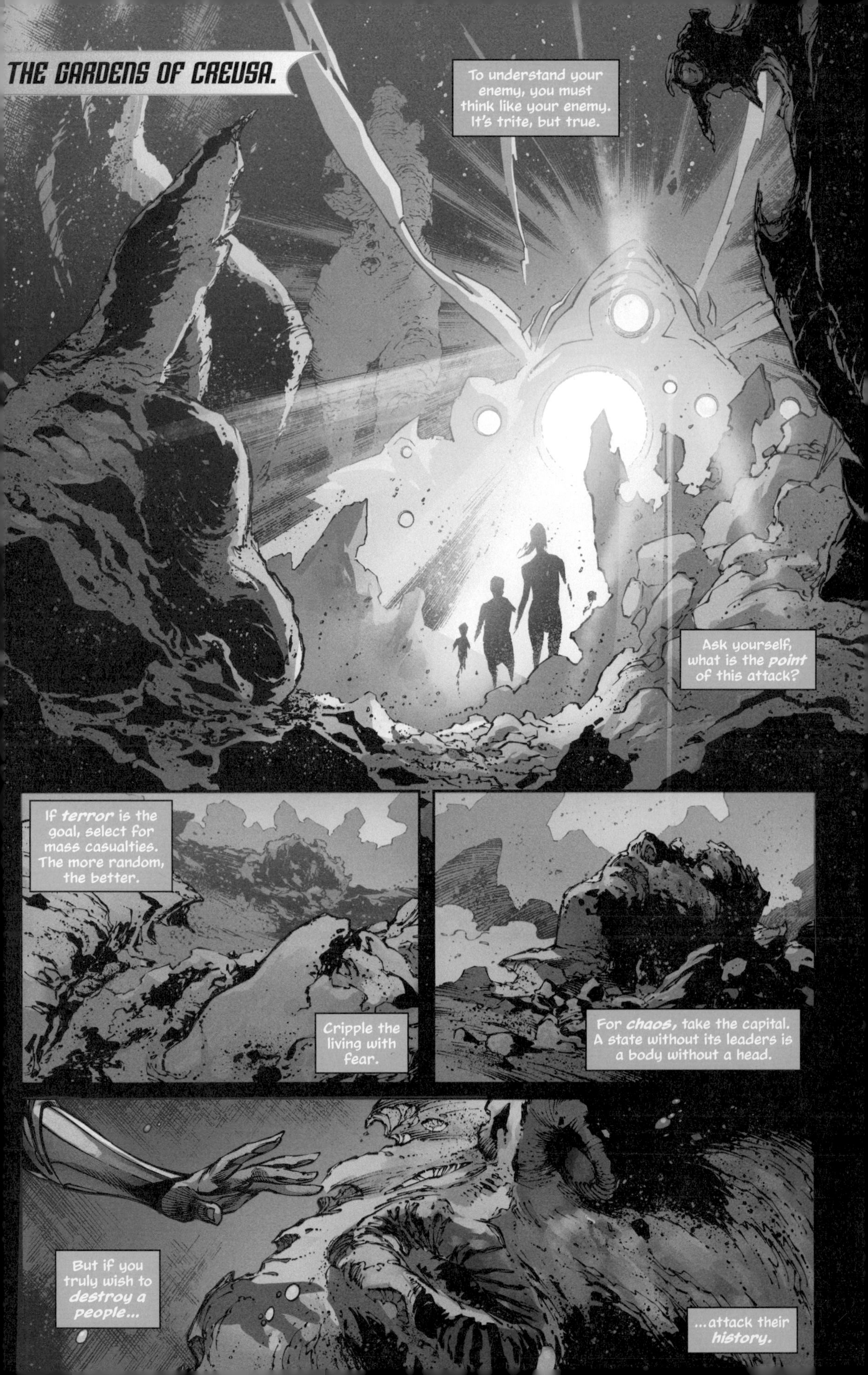
THE GARDENS OF CREUSA.
To understand your enemy, you must think like your enemy. It's trite, but true.
Ask yourself, what is the *point* of this attack?
If *terror* is the goal, select for mass casualties. The more random, the better.
Cripple the living with fear.
For *chaos,* take the capital. A state without its leaders is a body without a head.
But if you truly wish to *destroy a people...*
...attack their *history.*

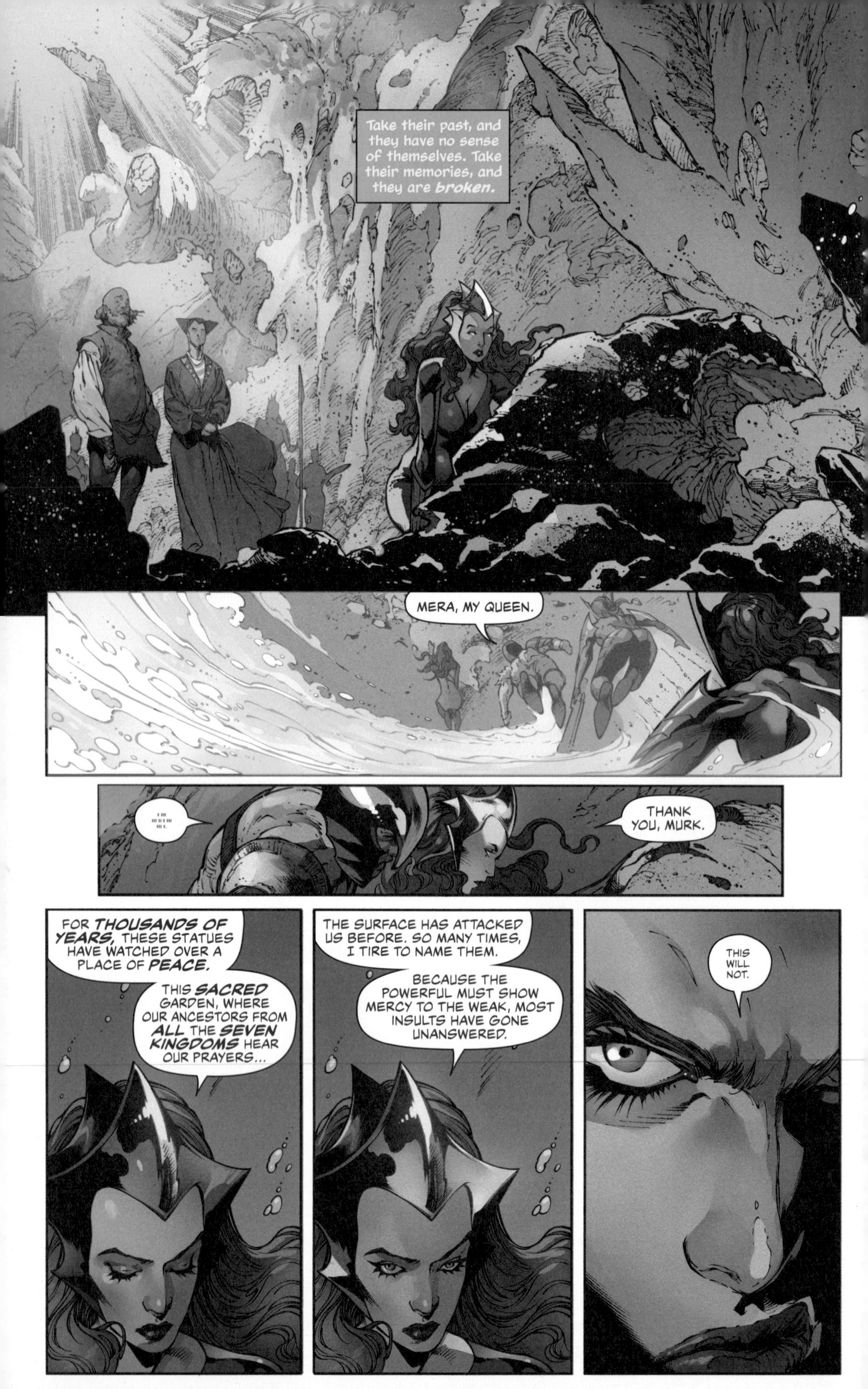
Take their past, and they have no sense of themselves. Take their memories, and they are *broken.*
MERA, MY QUEEN.
THANK YOU, MURK.
FOR **THOUSANDS OF YEARS,** THESE STATUES HAVE WATCHED OVER A PLACE OF **PEACE.**
THIS **SACRED** GARDEN, WHERE OUR ANCESTORS FROM **ALL** THE **SEVEN KINGDOMS** HEAR OUR PRAYERS...
THE SURFACE HAS ATTACKED US BEFORE. SO MANY TIMES, I TIRE TO NAME THEM.
BECAUSE THE POWERFUL MUST SHOW MERCY TO THE WEAK, MOST INSULTS HAVE GONE UNANSWERED.
THIS WILL NOT.

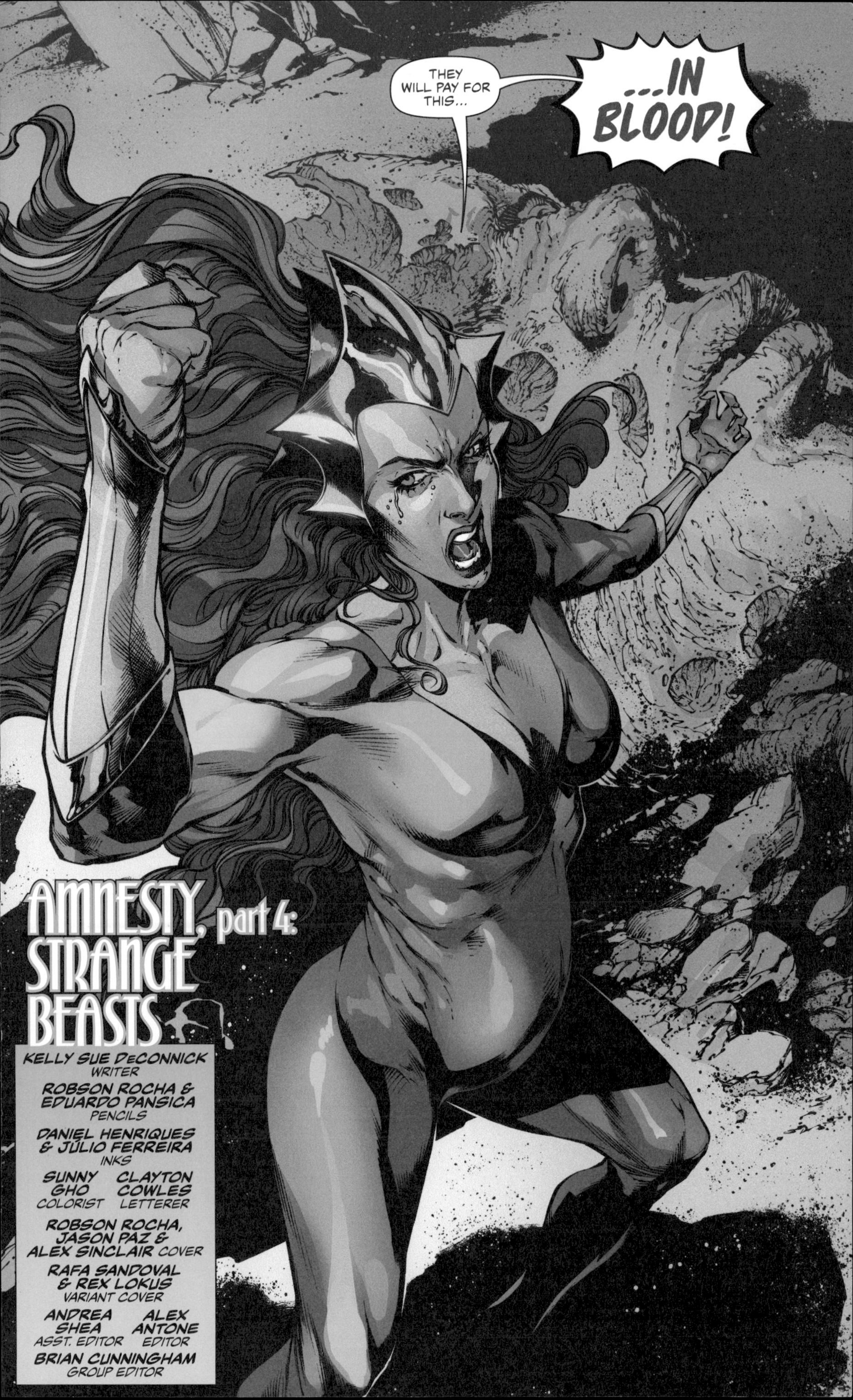
THEY WILL PAY FOR THIS...
...IN BLOOD!
AMNESTY, part 4: STRANGE BEASTS
KELLY SUE DeCONNICK WRITER
ROBSON ROCHA & EDUARDO PANSICA PENCILS
DANIEL HENRIQUES & JÚLIO FERREIRA INKS
SUNNY GHO COLORIST
CLAYTON COWLES LETTERER
ROBSON ROCHA, JASON PAZ & ALEX SINCLAIR COVER
RAFA SANDOVAL & REX LOKUS VARIANT COVER
ANDREA SHEA ASST. EDITOR
ALEX ANTONE EDITOR
BRIAN CUNNINGHAM GROUP EDITOR

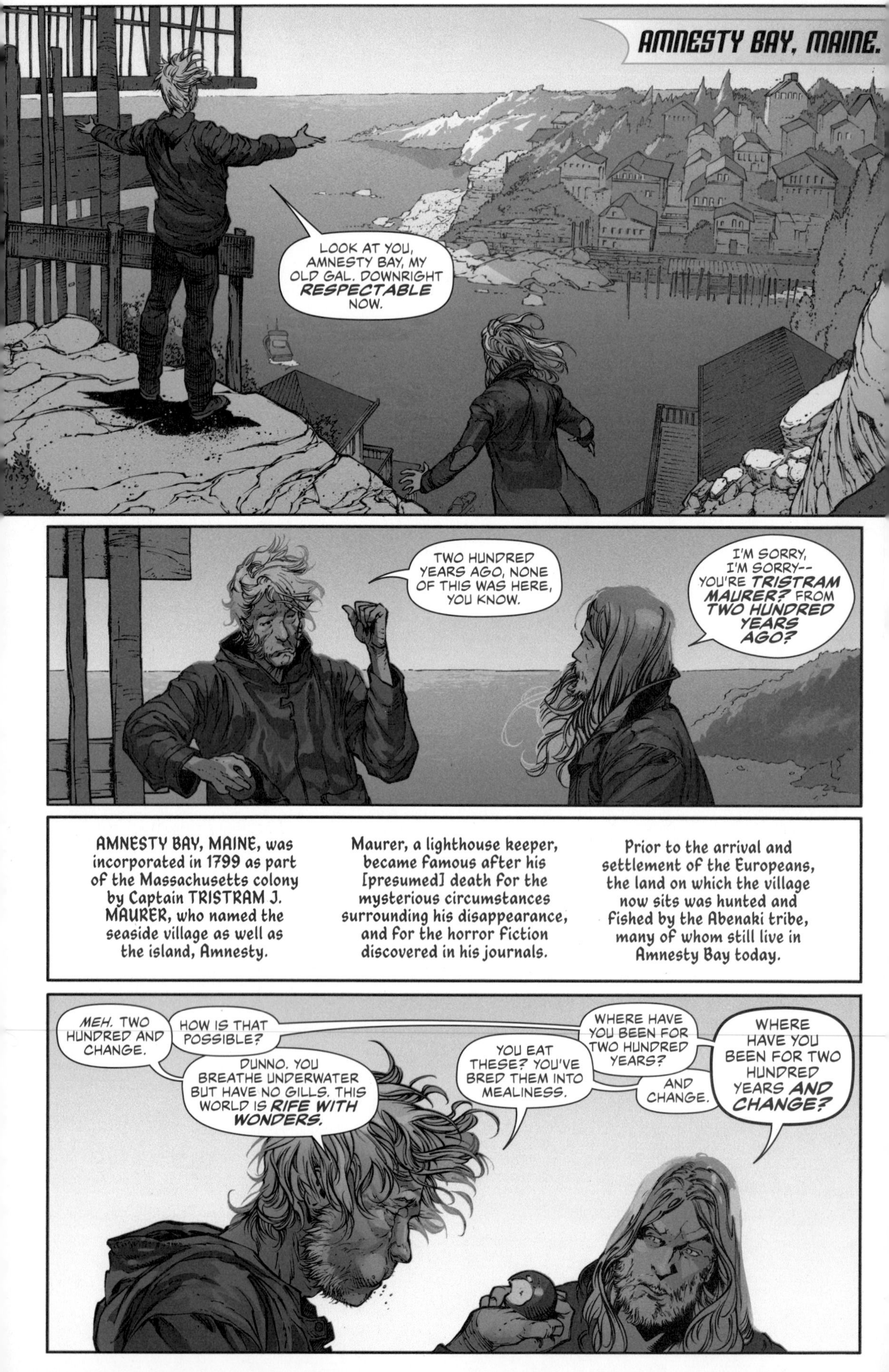
AMNESTY BAY, MAINE.
LOOK AT YOU, AMNESTY BAY, MY OLD GAL. DOWNRIGHT RESPECTABLE NOW.
TWO HUNDRED YEARS AGO, NONE OF THIS WAS HERE, YOU KNOW.
I'M SORRY, I'M SORRY-- YOU'RE TRISTRAM MAURER? FROM TWO HUNDRED YEARS AGO?
AMNESTY BAY, MAINE, was incorporated in 1799 as part of the Massachusetts colony by Captain TRISTRAM J. MAURER, who named the seaside village as well as the island, Amnesty.
Maurer, a lighthouse keeper, became famous after his [presumed] death for the mysterious circumstances surrounding his disappearance, and for the horror fiction discovered in his journals.
Prior to the arrival and settlement of the Europeans, the land on which the village now sits was hunted and fished by the Abenaki tribe, many of whom still live in Amnesty Bay today.
MEH. TWO HUNDRED AND CHANGE.
HOW IS THAT POSSIBLE?
DUNNO. YOU BREATHE UNDERWATER BUT HAVE NO GILLS. THIS WORLD IS RIFE WITH WONDERS.
YOU EAT THESE? YOU'VE BRED THEM INTO MEALINESS.
WHERE HAVE YOU BEEN FOR TWO HUNDRED YEARS?
AND CHANGE.
WHERE HAVE YOU BEEN FOR TWO HUNDRED YEARS AND CHANGE?

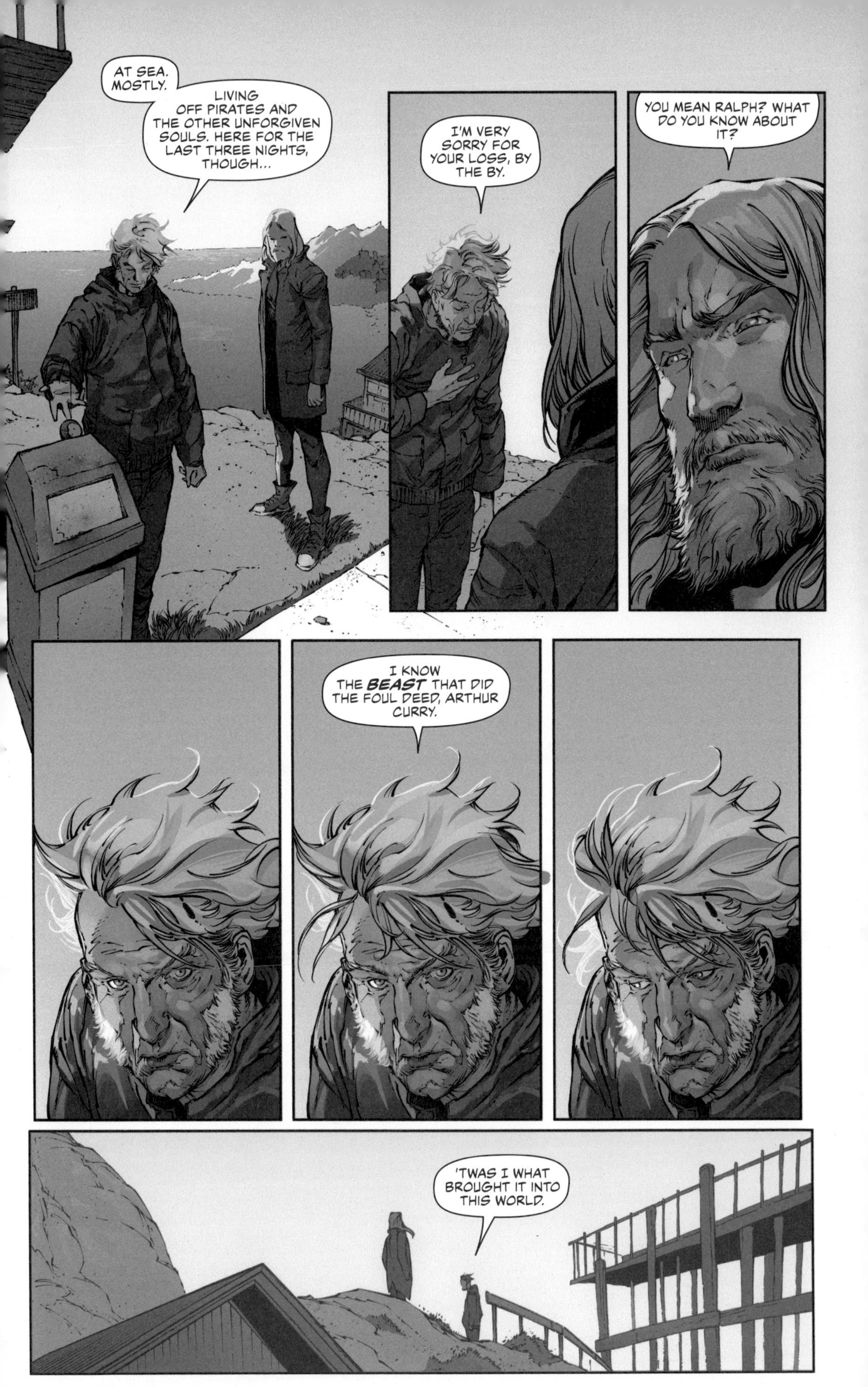

AT SEA. MOSTLY.
LIVING OFF PIRATES AND THE OTHER UNFORGIVEN SOULS. HERE FOR THE LAST THREE NIGHTS, THOUGH...
I'M VERY SORRY FOR YOUR LOSS, BY THE BY.
YOU MEAN RALPH? WHAT DO YOU KNOW ABOUT IT?
I KNOW THE BEAST THAT DID THE FOUL DEED, ARTHUR CURRY.
'TWAS I WHAT BROUGHT IT INTO THIS WORLD.

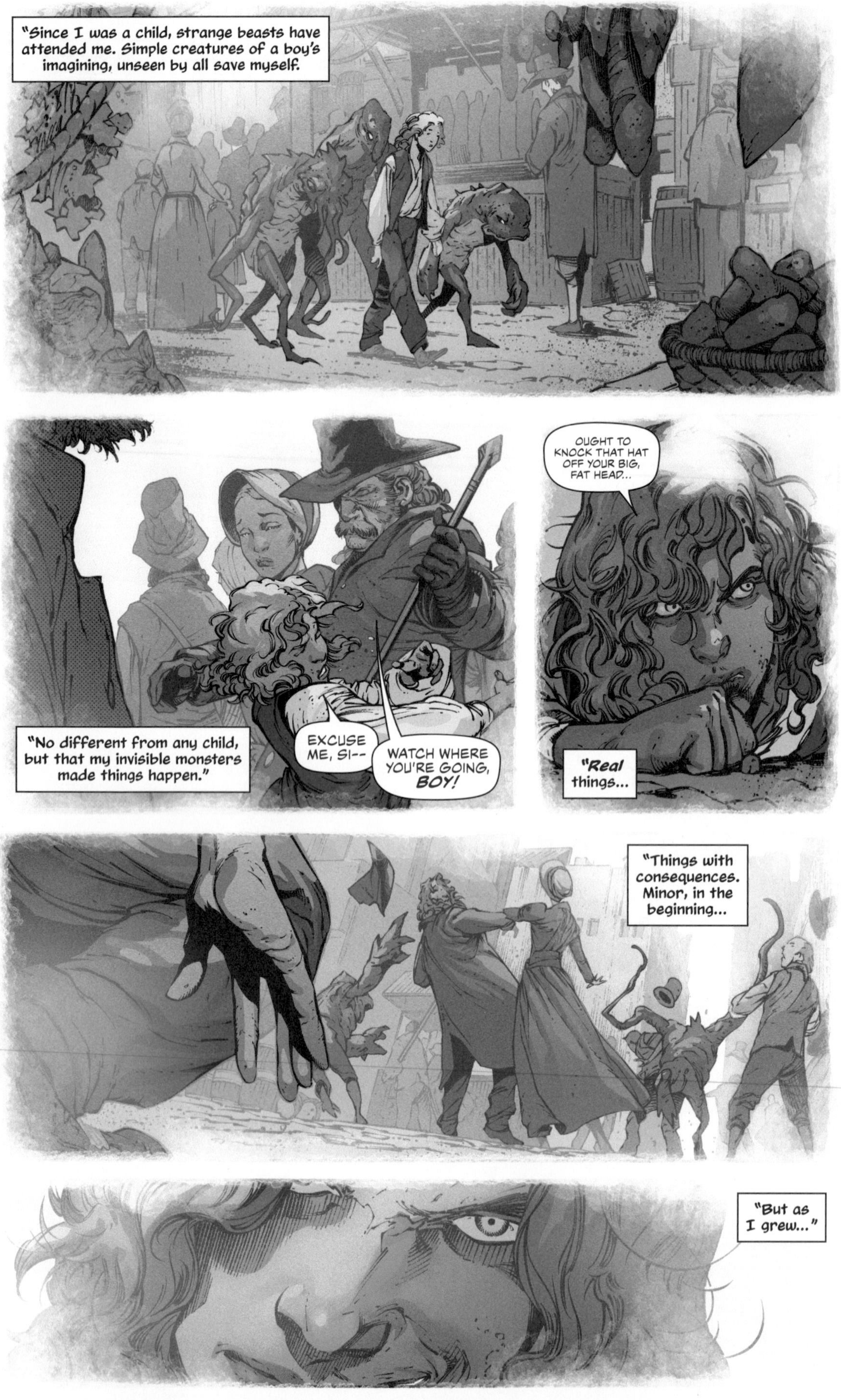
"Since I was a child, strange beasts have attended me. Simple creatures of a boy's imagining, unseen by all save myself.
"No different from any child, but that my invisible monsters made things happen."
EXCUSE ME, SI--
WATCH WHERE YOU'RE GOING, BOY!
OUGHT TO KNOCK THAT HAT OFF YOUR BIG, FAT HEAD...
"Real things...
"Things with consequences. Minor, in the beginning...
"But as I grew..."

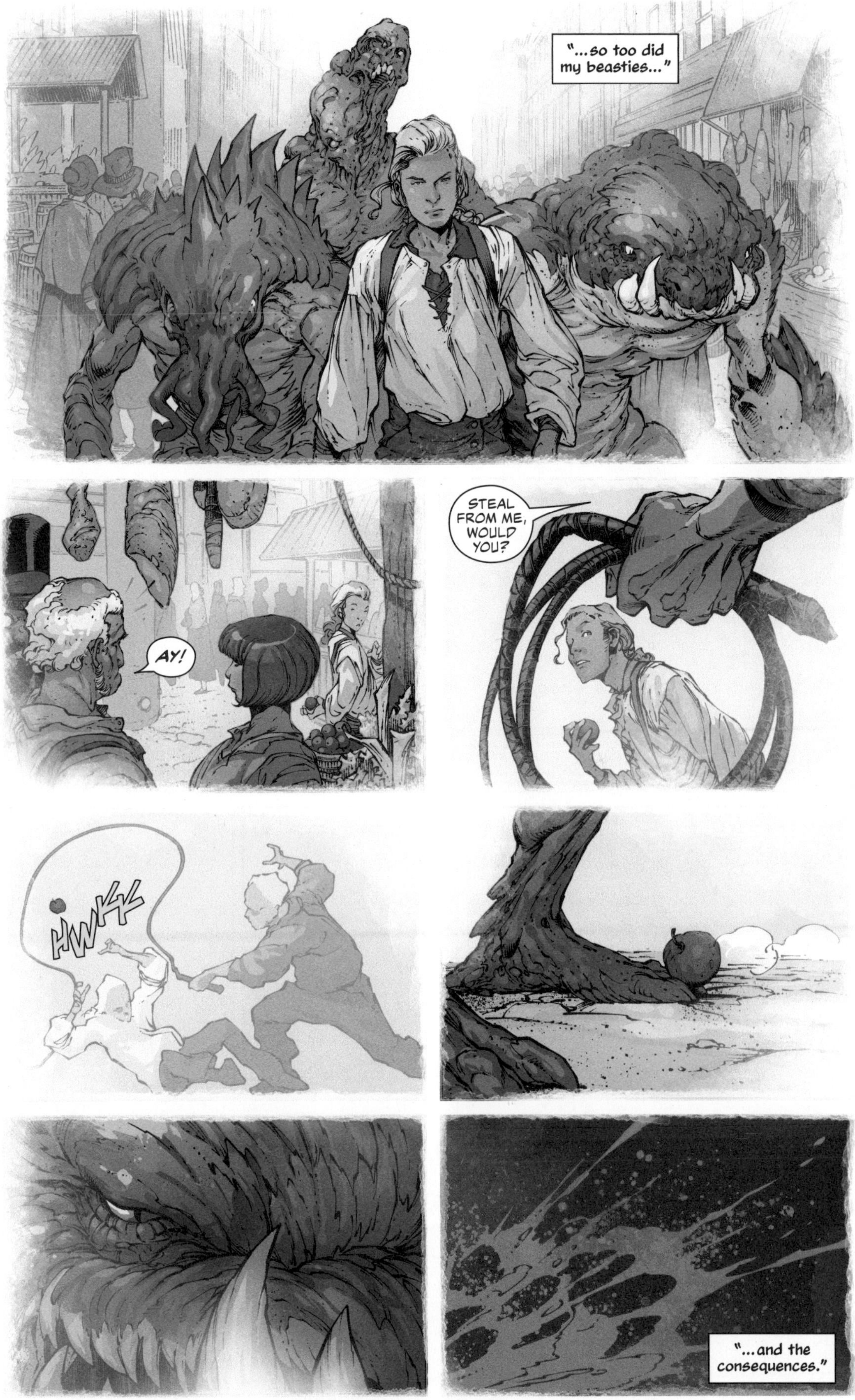

"...so too did my beasties..."
AY!
STEAL FROM ME, WOULD YOU?
HWKK
"...and the consequences."

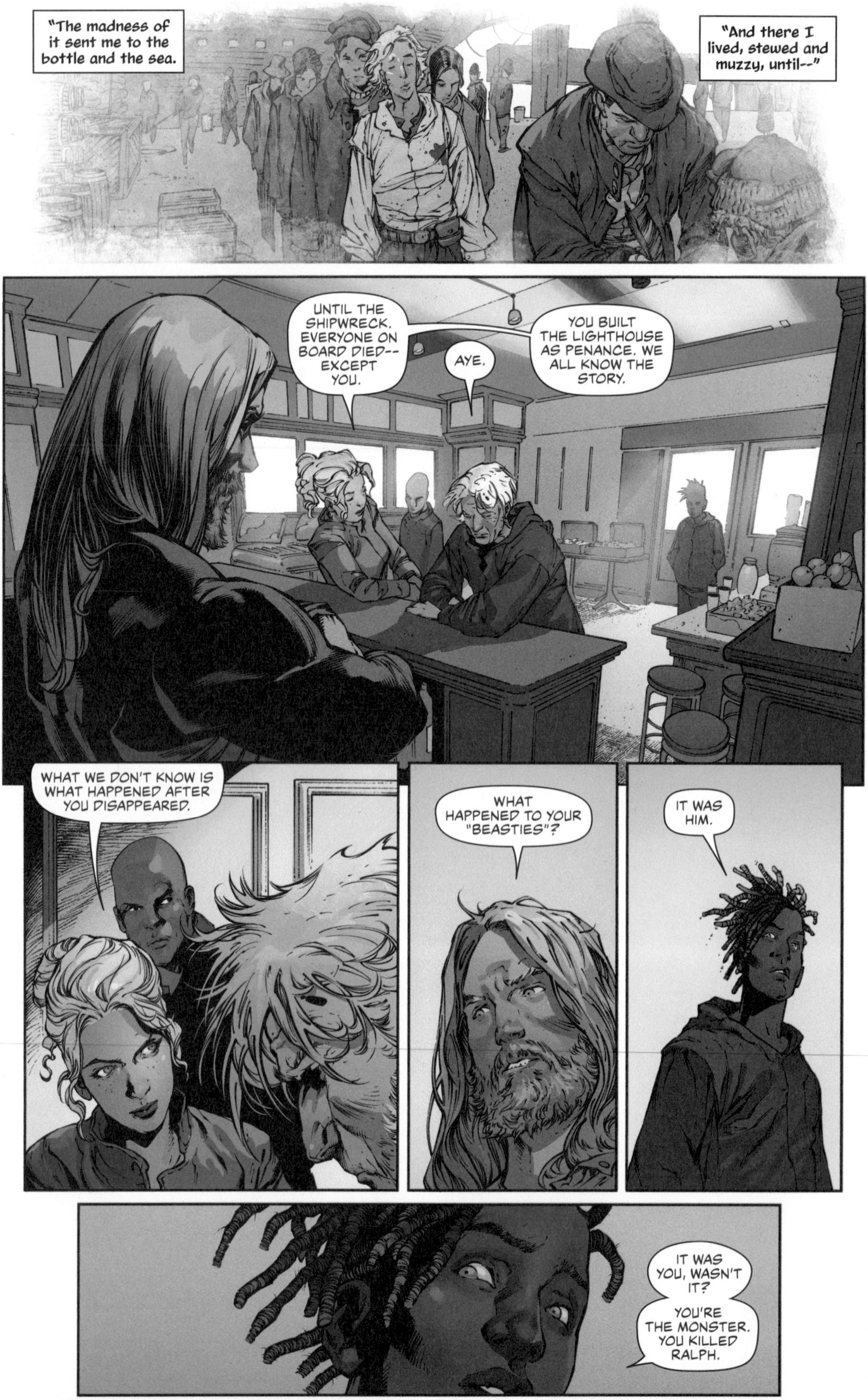
"The madness of it sent me to the bottle and the sea.
"And there I lived, stewed and muzzy, until--"
UNTIL THE SHIPWRECK. EVERYONE ON BOARD DIED-- EXCEPT YOU.
AYE.
YOU BUILT THE LIGHTHOUSE AS PENANCE. WE ALL KNOW THE STORY.
WHAT WE DON'T KNOW IS WHAT HAPPENED AFTER YOU DISAPPEARED.
WHAT HAPPENED TO YOUR "BEASTIES"?
IT WAS HIM.
IT WAS YOU, WASN'T IT?
YOU'RE THE MONSTER. YOU KILLED RALPH.

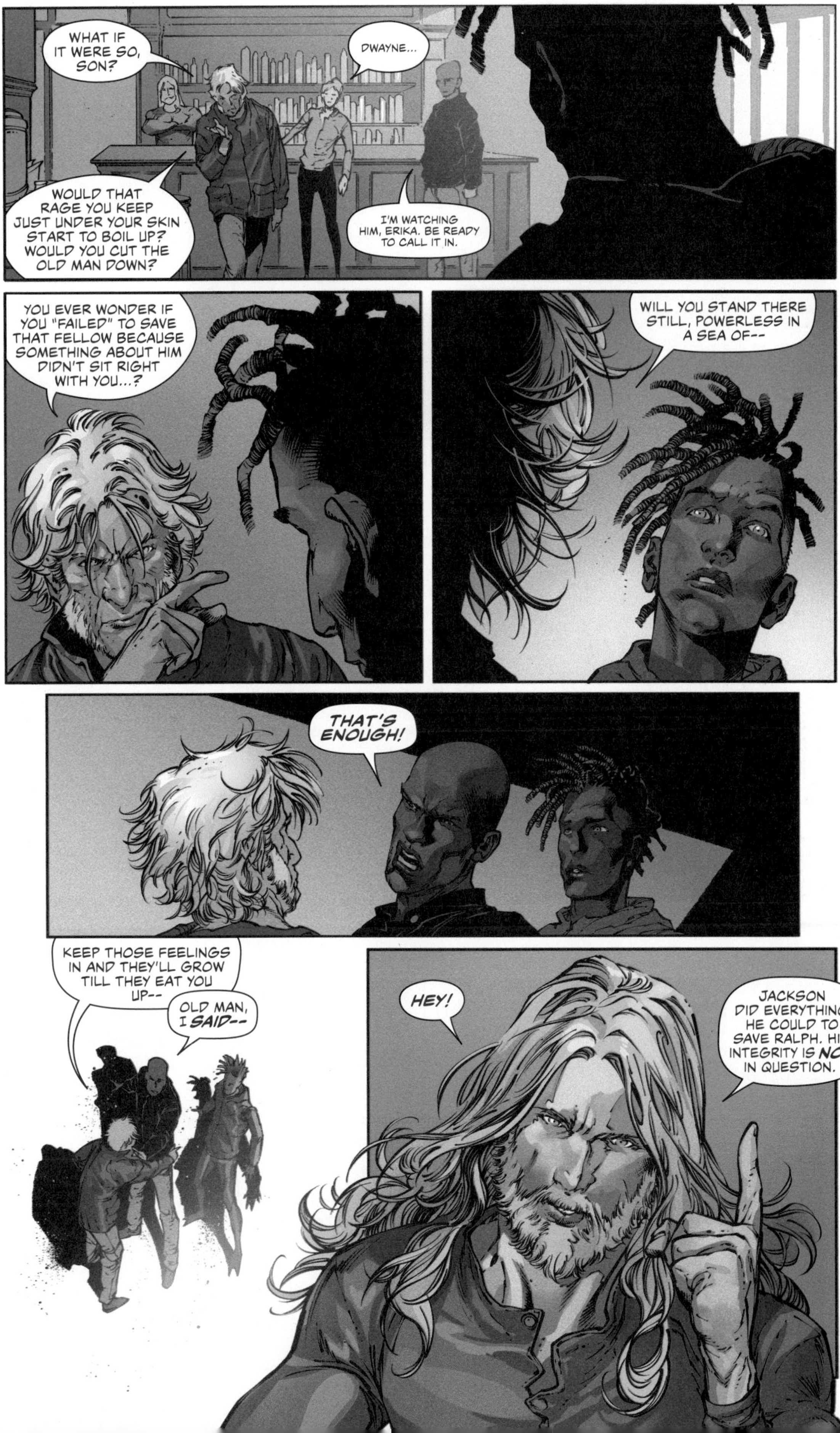
WHAT IF IT WERE SO, SON?
WOULD THAT RAGE YOU KEEP JUST UNDER YOUR SKIN START TO BOIL UP? WOULD YOU CUT THE OLD MAN DOWN?
DWAYNE...
I'M WATCHING HIM, ERIKA. BE READY TO CALL IT IN.
YOU EVER WONDER IF YOU "FAILED" TO SAVE THAT FELLOW BECAUSE SOMETHING ABOUT HIM DIDN'T SIT RIGHT WITH YOU...?
WILL YOU STAND THERE STILL, POWERLESS IN A SEA OF--
THAT'S ENOUGH!
KEEP THOSE FEELINGS IN AND THEY'LL GROW TILL THEY EAT YOU UP--
OLD MAN, I SAID--
HEY!
JACKSON DID EVERYTHING HE COULD TO SAVE RALPH. HIS INTEGRITY IS NOT IN QUESTION.

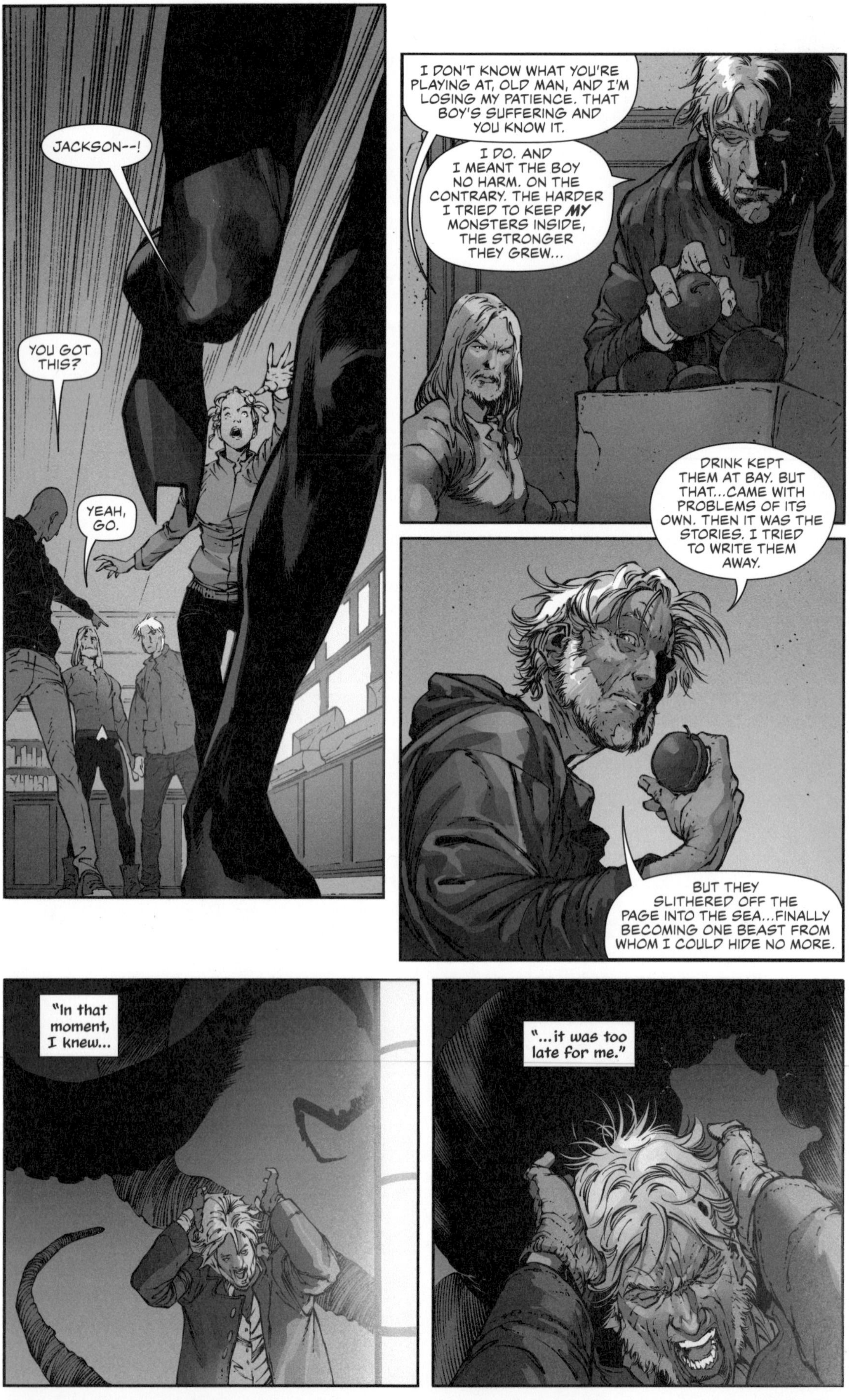
JACKSON--!
YOU GOT THIS?
YEAH, GO.
I DON'T KNOW WHAT YOU'RE PLAYING AT, OLD MAN, AND I'M LOSING MY PATIENCE. THAT BOY'S SUFFERING AND YOU KNOW IT.
I DO. AND I MEANT THE BOY NO HARM. ON THE CONTRARY. THE HARDER I TRIED TO KEEP MY MONSTERS INSIDE, THE STRONGER THEY GREW...
DRINK KEPT THEM AT BAY. BUT THAT...CAME WITH PROBLEMS OF ITS OWN. THEN IT WAS THE STORIES. I TRIED TO WRITE THEM AWAY.
BUT THEY SLITHERED OFF THE PAGE INTO THE SEA...FINALLY BECOMING ONE BEAST FROM WHOM I COULD HIDE NO MORE.
"In that moment, I knew...
"...it was too late for me."

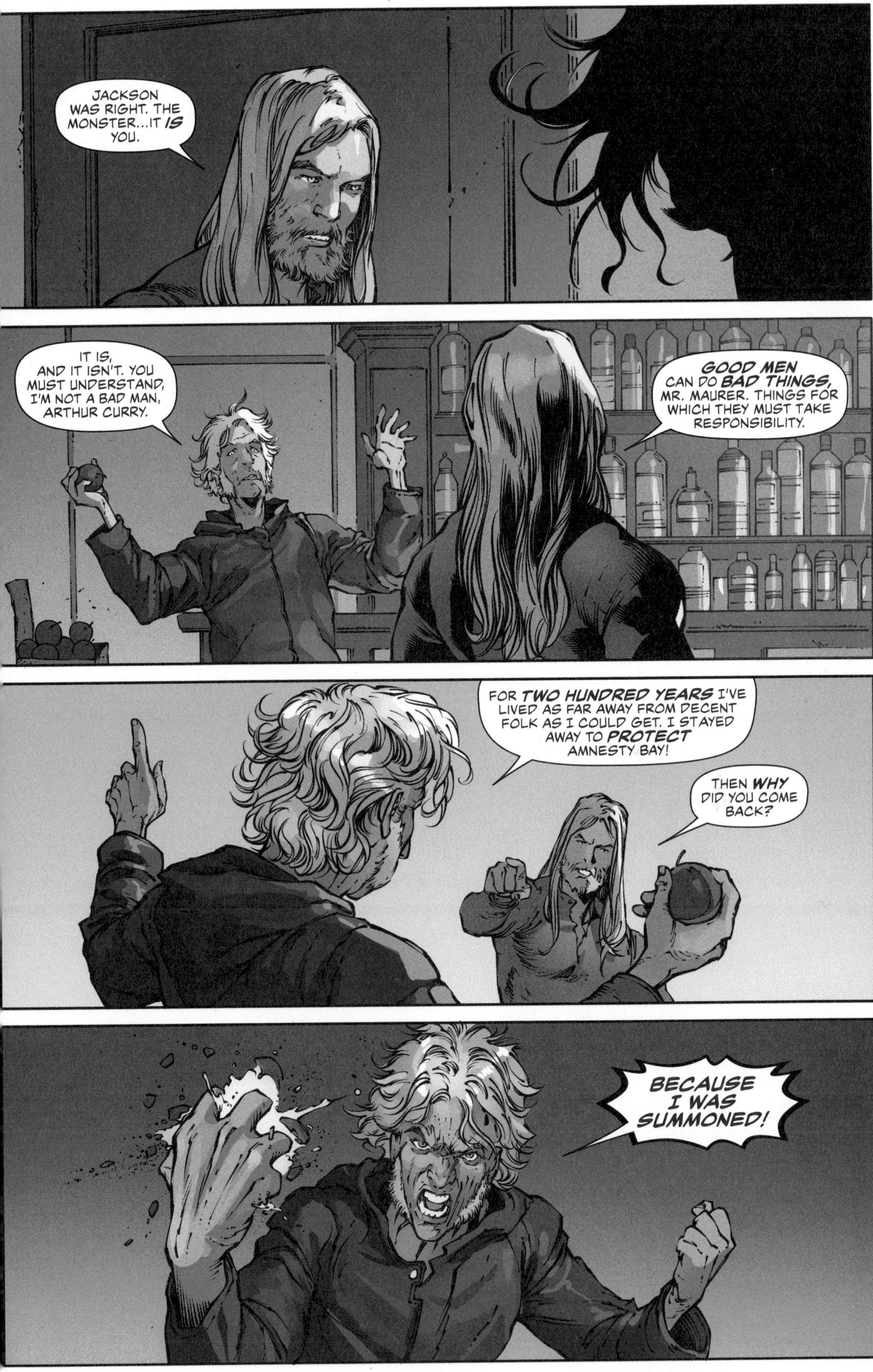
JACKSON WAS RIGHT. THE MONSTER...IT *IS* YOU.
IT IS, AND IT ISN'T. YOU MUST UNDERSTAND, I'M NOT A BAD MAN, ARTHUR CURRY.
GOOD MEN CAN DO *BAD THINGS,* MR. MAURER. THINGS FOR WHICH THEY MUST TAKE RESPONSIBILITY.
FOR *TWO HUNDRED YEARS* I'VE LIVED AS FAR AWAY FROM DECENT FOLK AS I COULD GET. I STAYED AWAY TO *PROTECT* AMNESTY BAY!
THEN *WHY* DID YOU COME BACK?
BECAUSE I WAS SUMMONED!

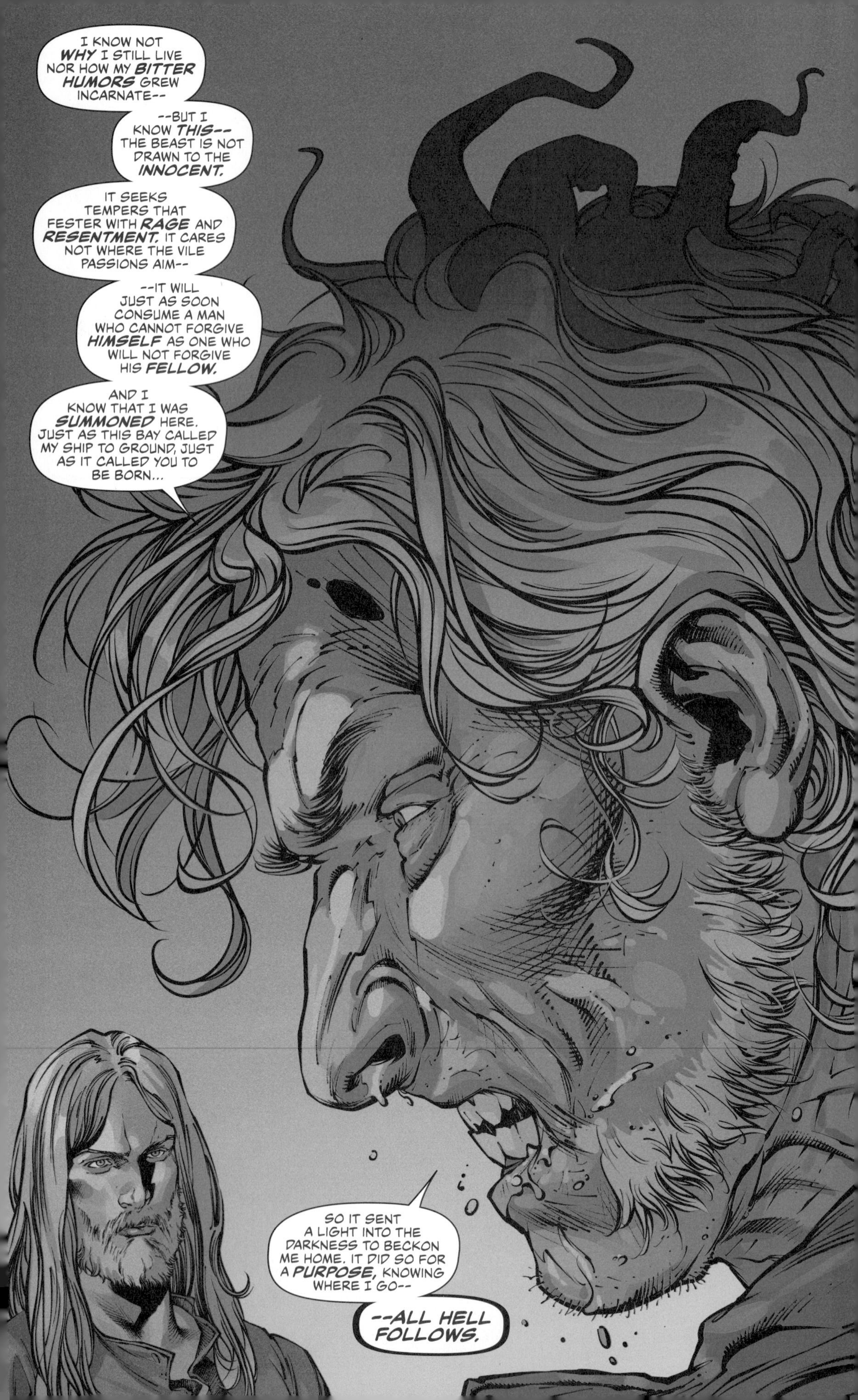
I KNOW NOT WHY I STILL LIVE NOR HOW MY BITTER HUMORS GREW INCARNATE--
--BUT I KNOW THIS-- THE BEAST IS NOT DRAWN TO THE INNOCENT.
IT SEEKS TEMPERS THAT FESTER WITH RAGE AND RESENTMENT. IT CARES NOT WHERE THE VILE PASSIONS AIM--
--IT WILL JUST AS SOON CONSUME A MAN WHO CANNOT FORGIVE HIMSELF AS ONE WHO WILL NOT FORGIVE HIS FELLOW.
AND I KNOW THAT I WAS SUMMONED HERE. JUST AS THIS BAY CALLED MY SHIP TO GROUND, JUST AS IT CALLED YOU TO BE BORN...
SO IT SENT A LIGHT INTO THE DARKNESS TO BECKON ME HOME. IT DID SO FOR A PURPOSE, KNOWING WHERE I GO--
--ALL HELL FOLLOWS.

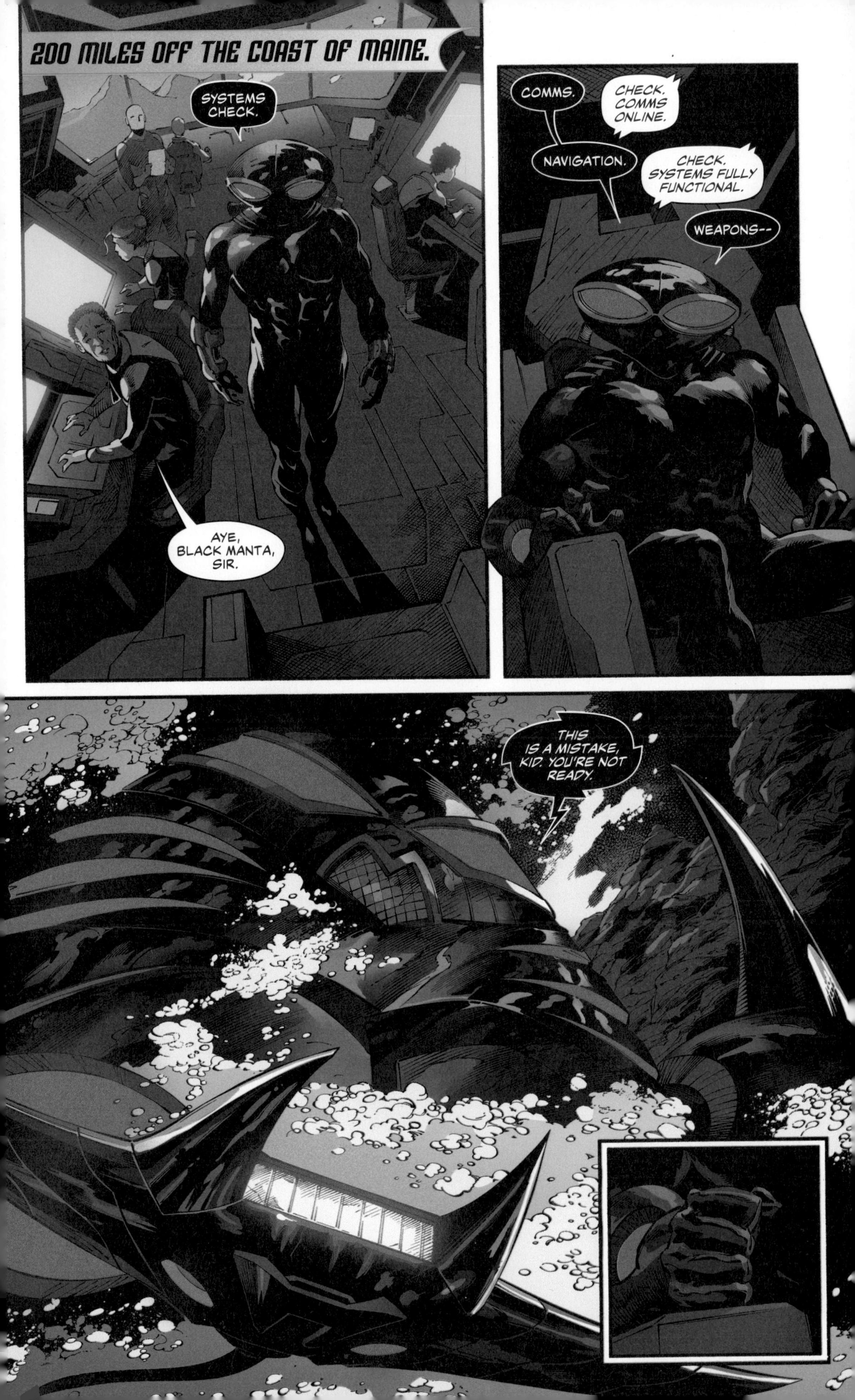
200 MILES OFF THE COAST OF MAINE.
SYSTEMS CHECK.
AYE, BLACK MANTA, SIR.
COMMS.
CHECK. COMMS ONLINE.
NAVIGATION.
CHECK. SYSTEMS FULLY FUNCTIONAL.
WEAPONS--
THIS IS A MISTAKE, KID. YOU'RE NOT READY.

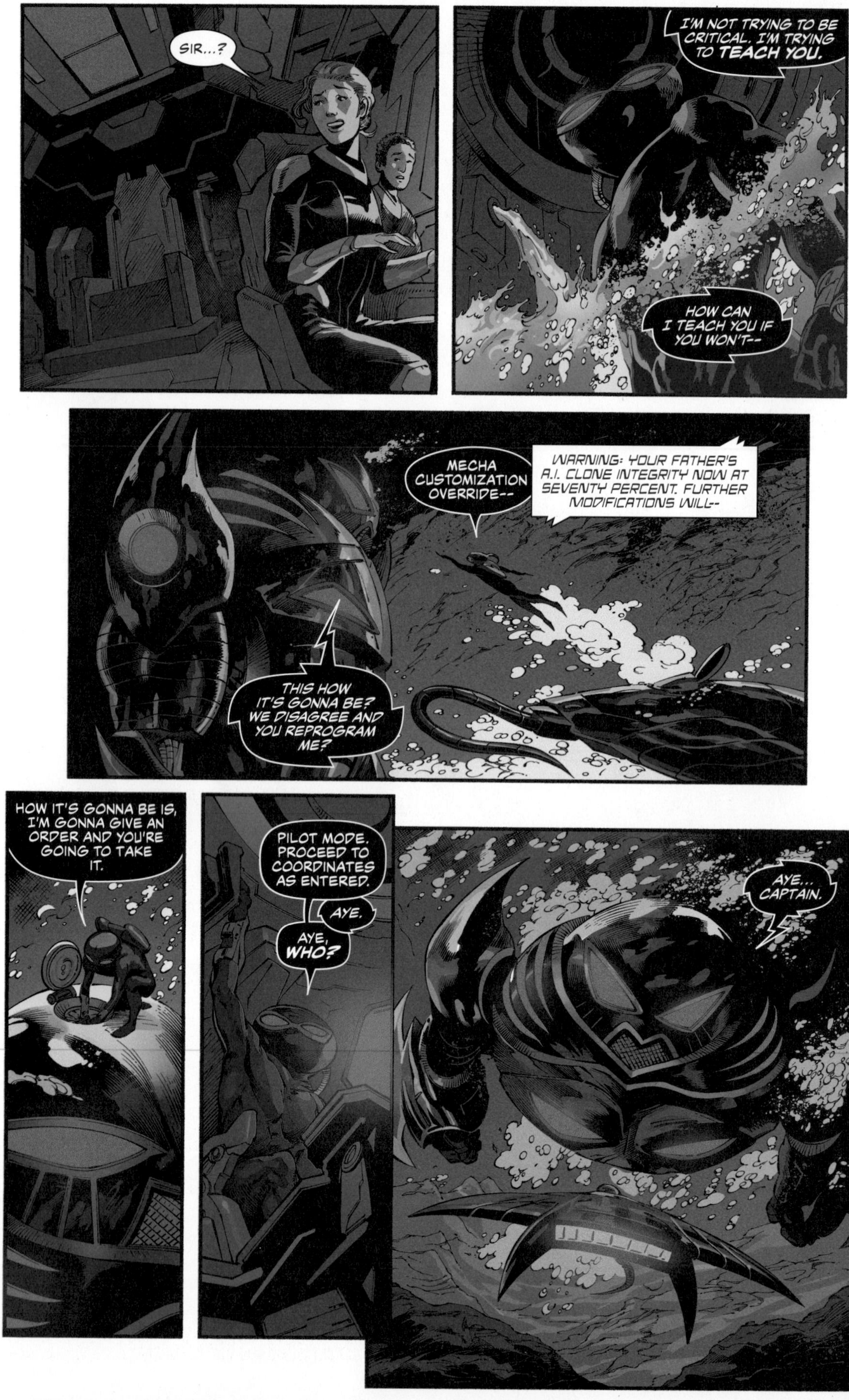
SIR...?
I'M NOT TRYING TO BE CRITICAL. I'M TRYING TO TEACH YOU.
HOW CAN I TEACH YOU IF YOU WON'T--
MECHA CUSTOMIZATION OVERRIDE--
WARNING: YOUR FATHER'S A.I. CLONE INTEGRITY NOW AT SEVENTY PERCENT. FURTHER MODIFICATIONS WILL--
THIS HOW IT'S GONNA BE? WE DISAGREE AND YOU REPROGRAM ME?
HOW IT'S GONNA BE IS, I'M GONNA GIVE AN ORDER AND YOU'RE GOING TO TAKE IT.
PILOT MODE. PROCEED TO COORDINATES AS ENTERED.
AYE.
AYE, WHO?
AYE... CAPTAIN.

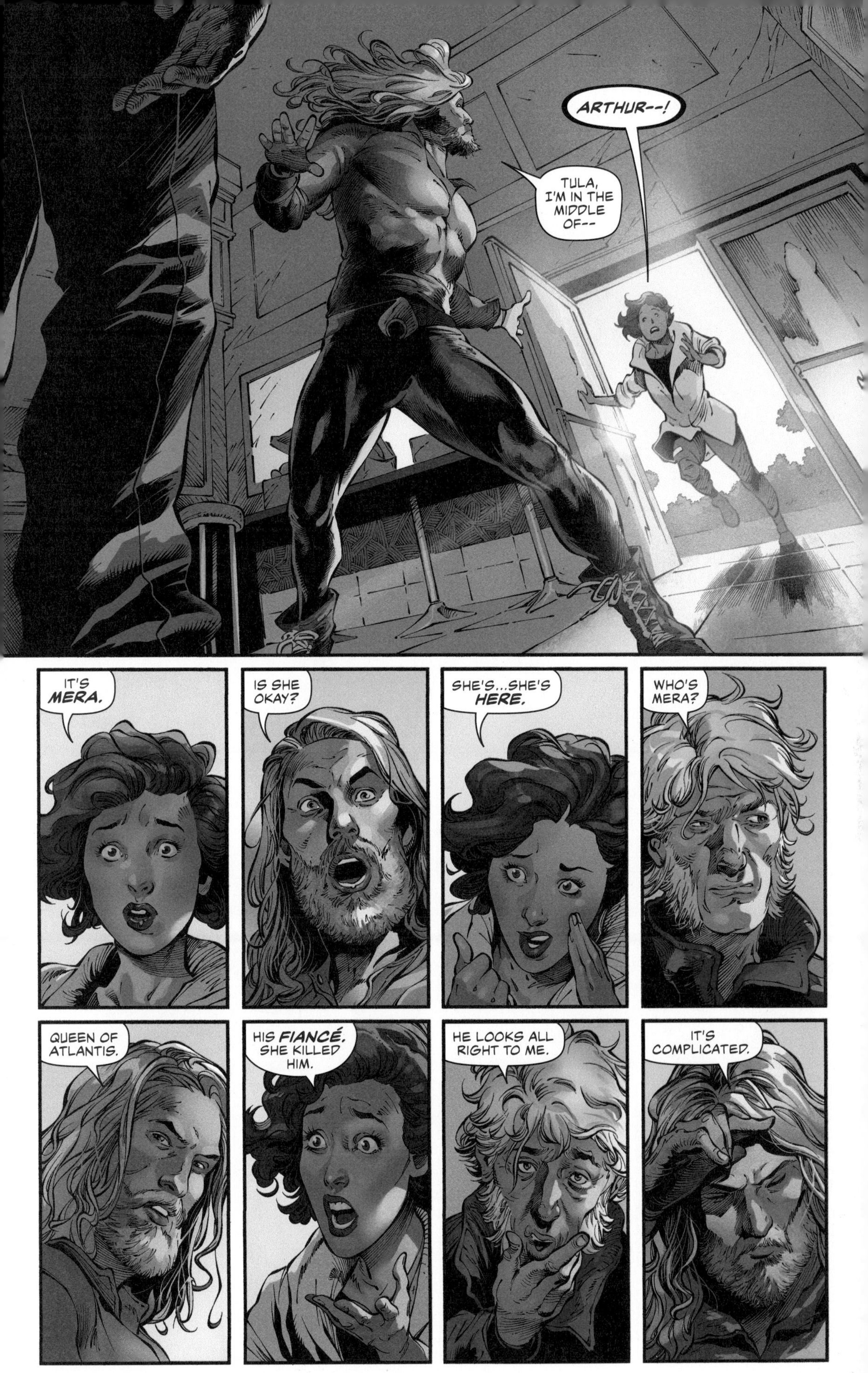
ARTHUR--!
TULA, I'M IN THE MIDDLE OF--
IT'S MERA.
IS SHE OKAY?
SHE'S...SHE'S HERE.
WHO'S MERA?
QUEEN OF ATLANTIS.
HIS FIANCÉ. SHE KILLED HIM.
HE LOOKS ALL RIGHT TO ME.
IT'S COMPLICATED.

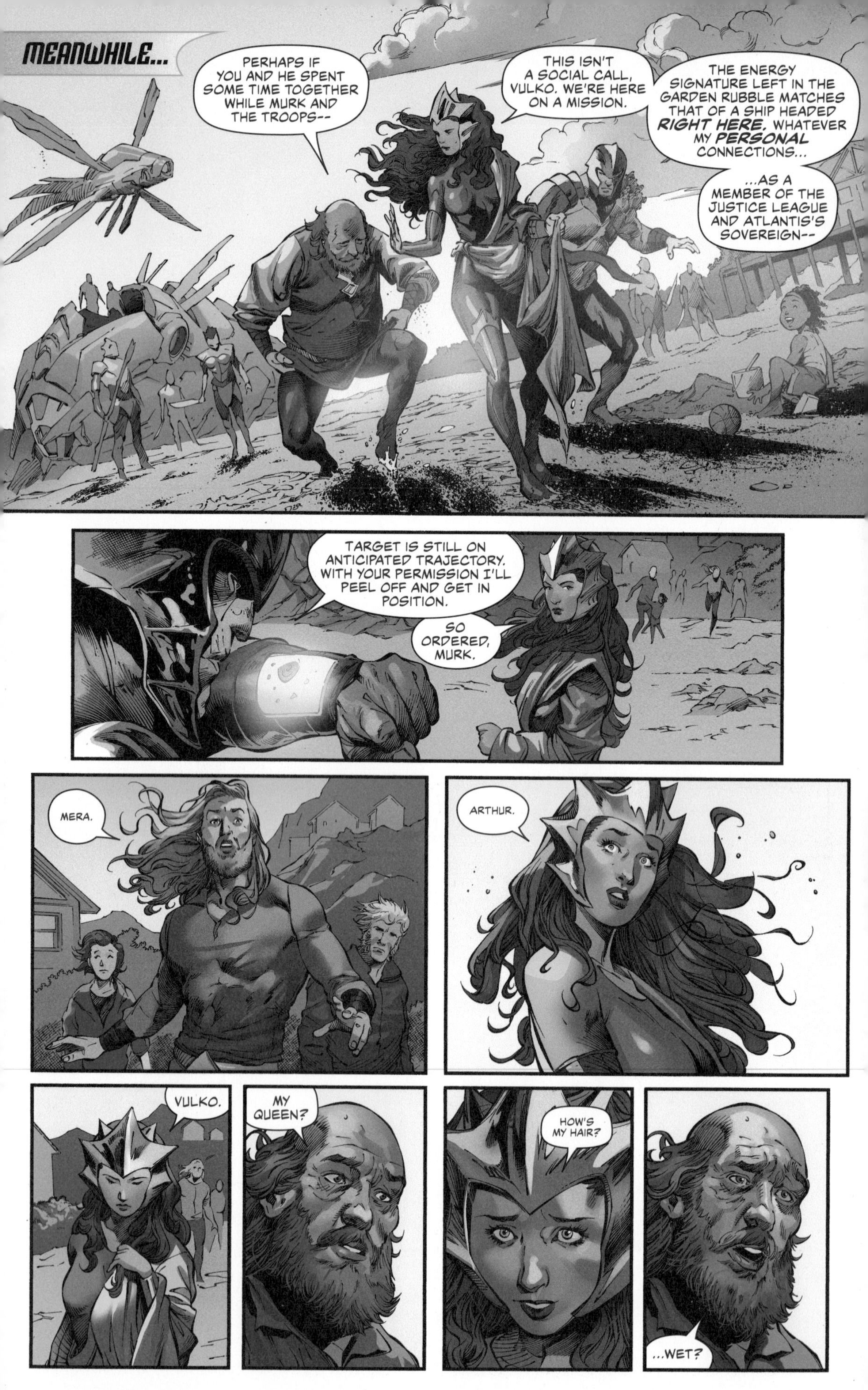
MEANWHILE...
PERHAPS IF YOU AND HE SPENT SOME TIME TOGETHER WHILE MURK AND THE TROOPS--
THIS ISN'T A SOCIAL CALL, VULKO. WE'RE HERE ON A MISSION.
THE ENERGY SIGNATURE LEFT IN THE GARDEN RUBBLE MATCHES THAT OF A SHIP HEADED RIGHT HERE. WHATEVER MY PERSONAL CONNECTIONS...
...AS A MEMBER OF THE JUSTICE LEAGUE AND ATLANTIS'S SOVEREIGN--
TARGET IS STILL ON ANTICIPATED TRAJECTORY. WITH YOUR PERMISSION I'LL PEEL OFF AND GET IN POSITION.
SO ORDERED, MURK.
MERA.
ARTHUR.
VULKO.
MY QUEEN?
HOW'S MY HAIR?
...WET?

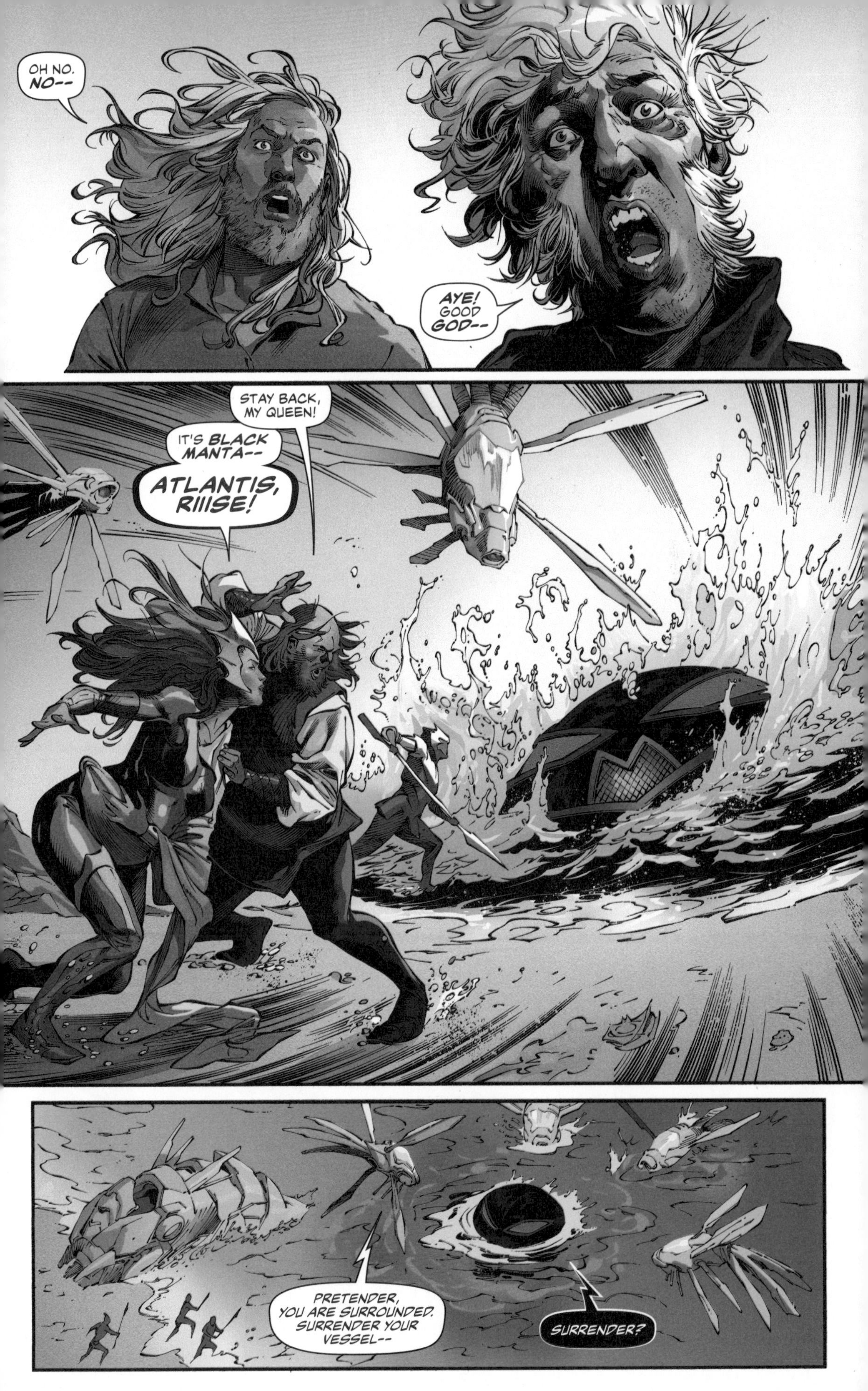

OH NO. NO--
AYE! GOOD GOD--
STAY BACK, MY QUEEN!
IT'S BLACK MANTA--
ATLANTIS, RIIISE!
PRETENDER, YOU ARE SURROUNDED. SURRENDER YOUR VESSEL--
SURRENDER?

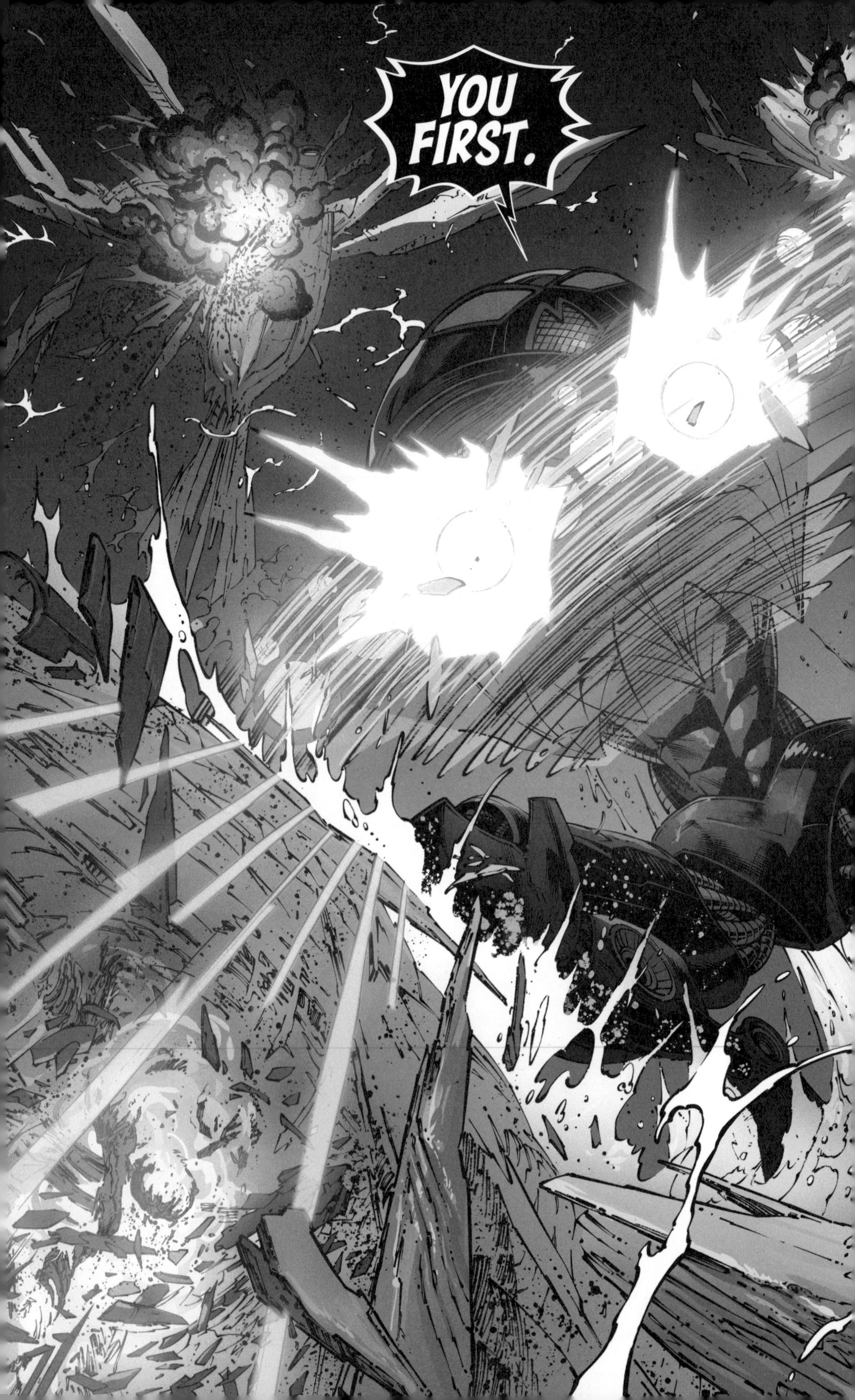
YOU FIRST.

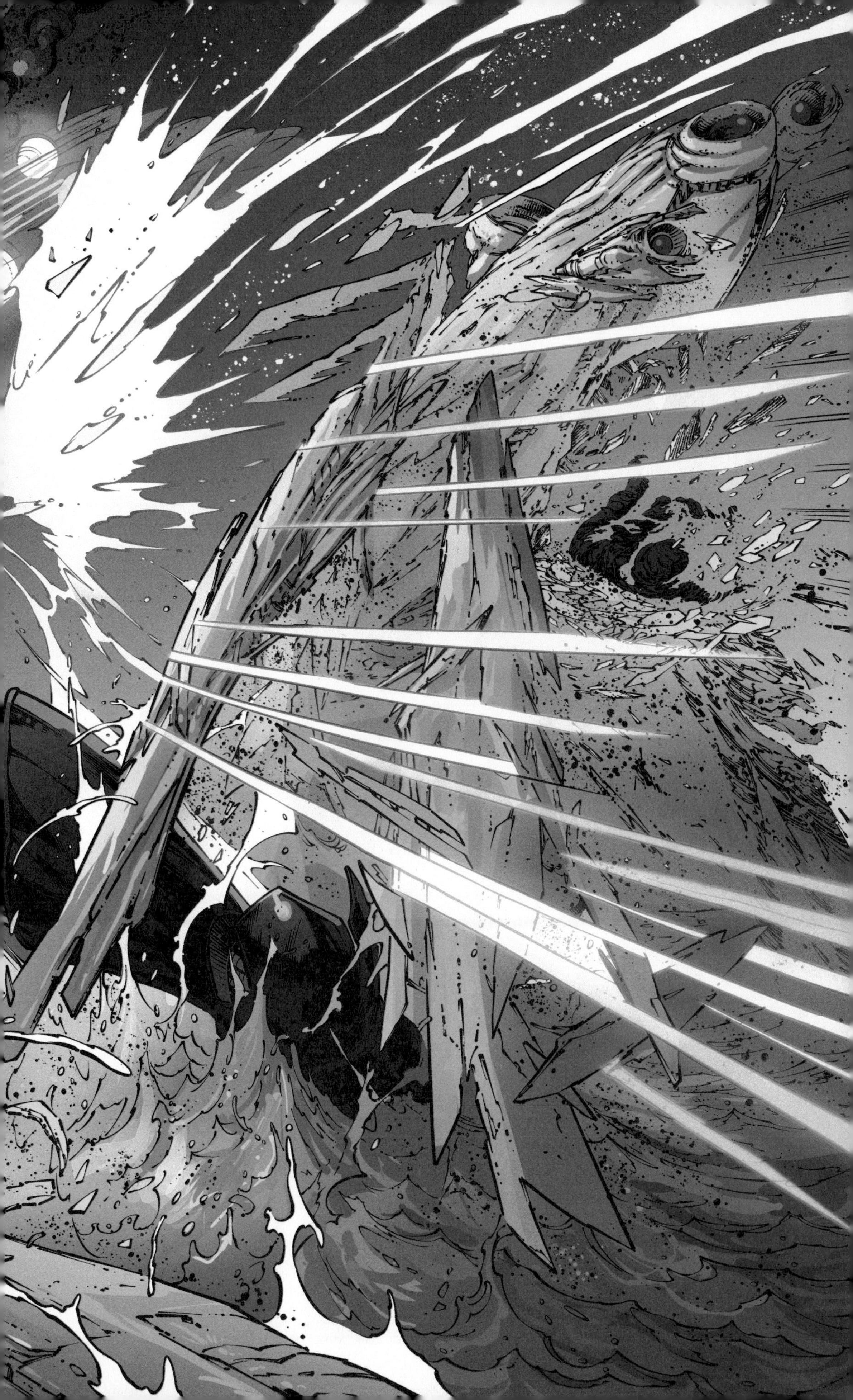

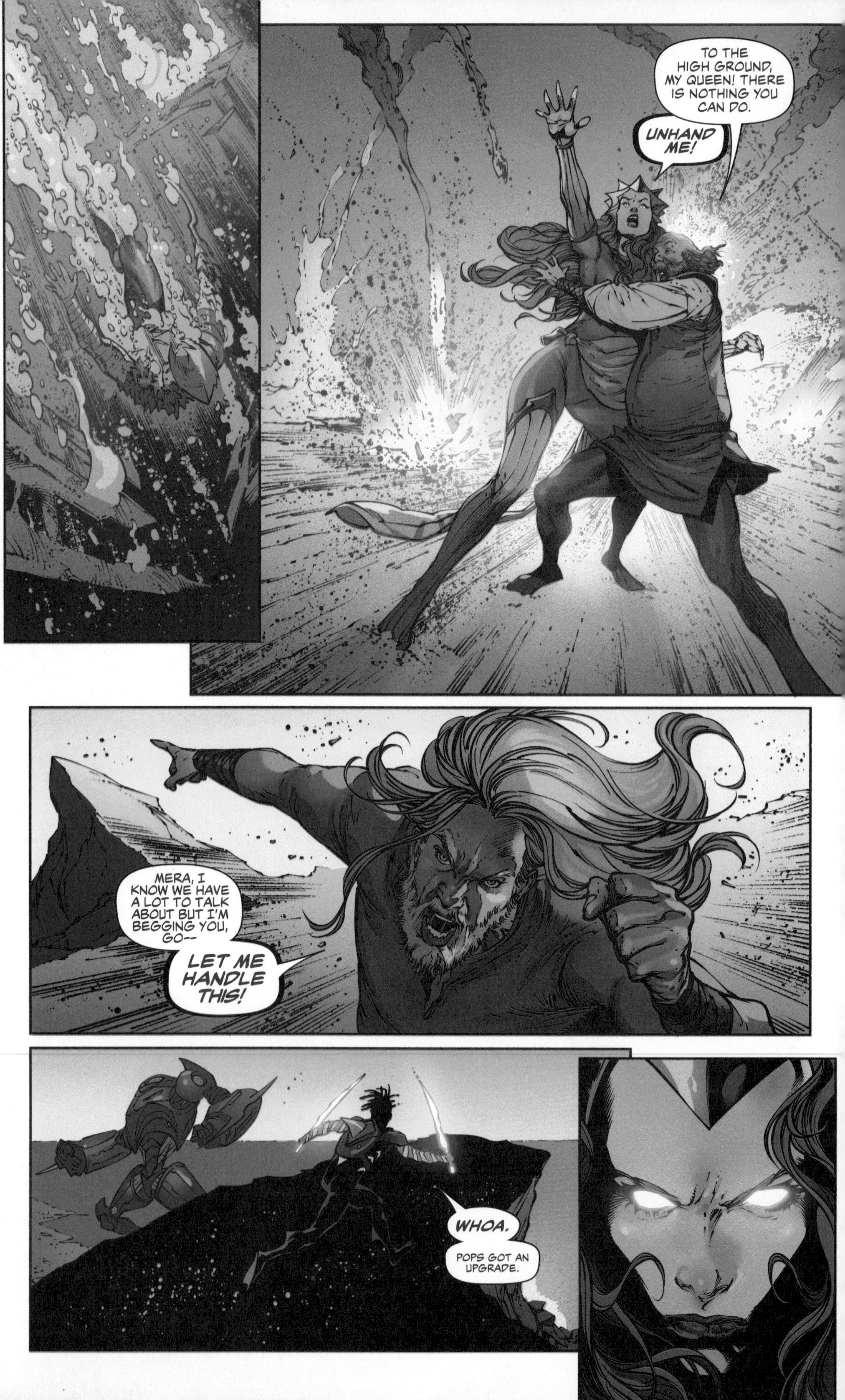
TO THE HIGH GROUND, MY QUEEN! THERE IS NOTHING YOU CAN DO.
UNHAND ME!
MERA, I KNOW WE HAVE A LOT TO TALK ABOUT BUT I'M BEGGING YOU, GO--
LET ME HANDLE THIS!
WHOA.
POPS GOT AN UPGRADE.

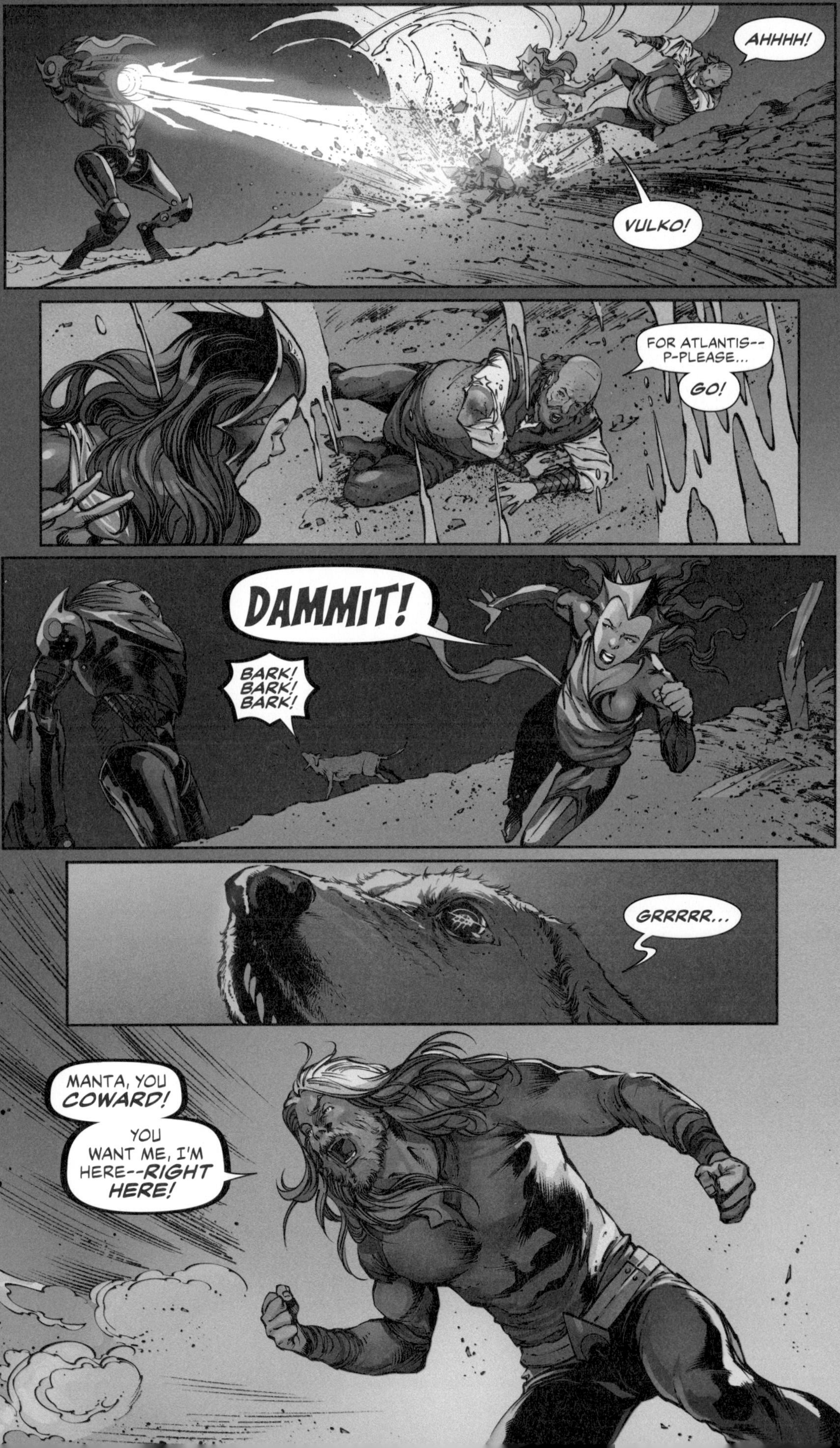
AHHHH!
VULKO!
FOR ATLANTIS-- P-PLEASE...
GO!
DAMMIT!
BARK! BARK! BARK!
GRRRRR...
MANTA, YOU COWARD!
YOU WANT ME, I'M HERE--RIGHT HERE!

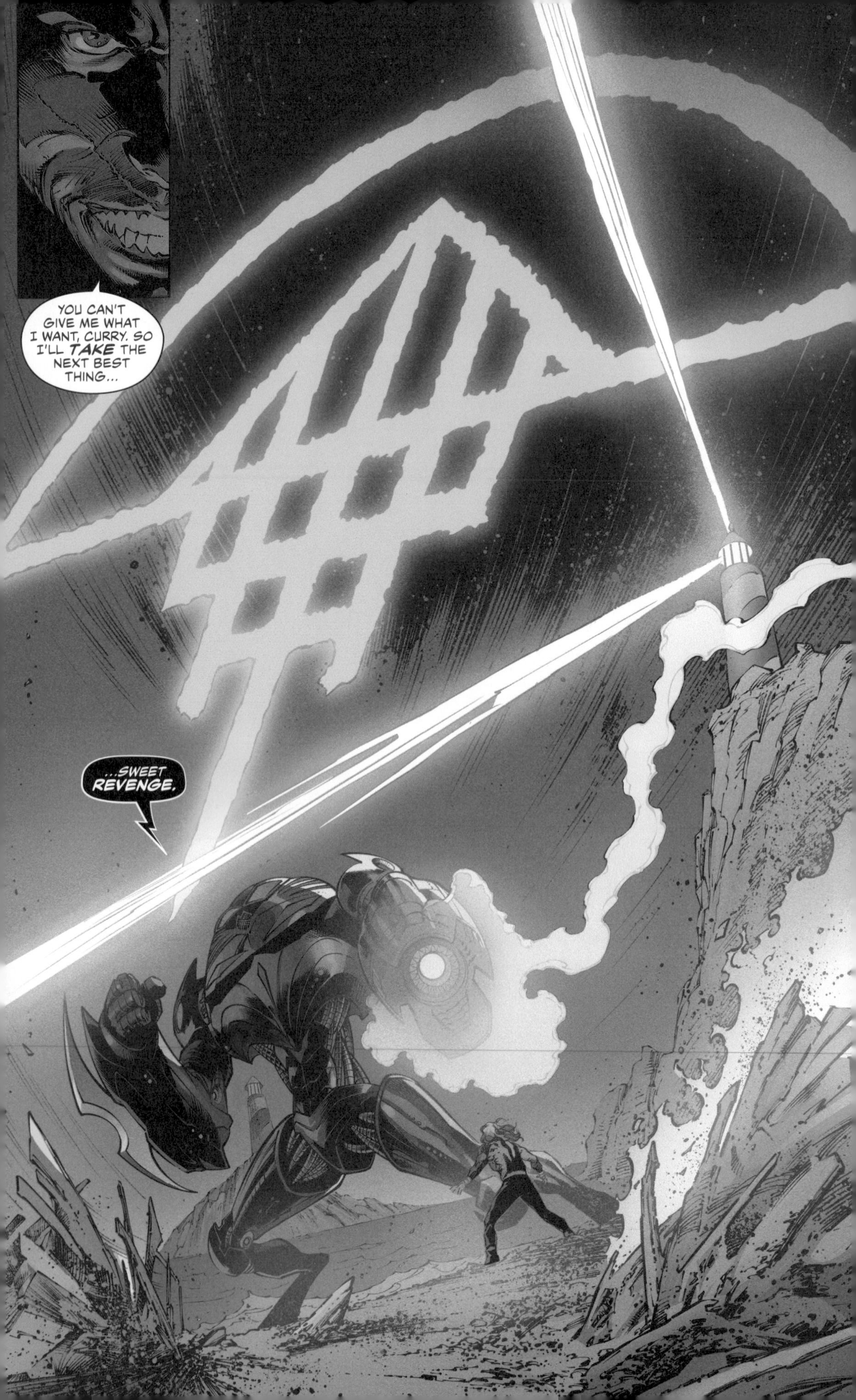
YOU CAN'T GIVE ME WHAT I WANT, CURRY. SO I'LL TAKE THE NEXT BEST THING...
...SWEET REVENGE.

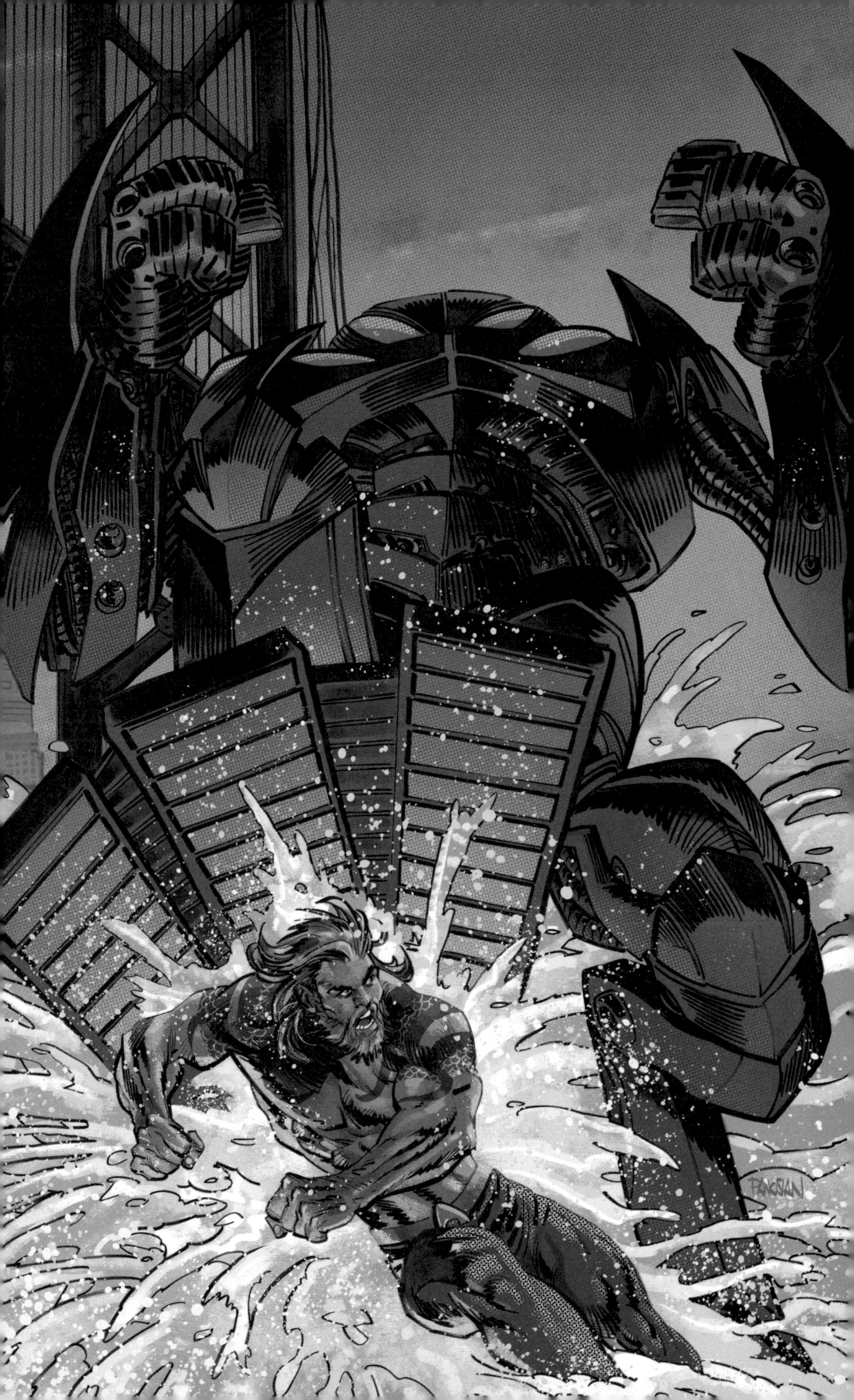
PANOSIAN

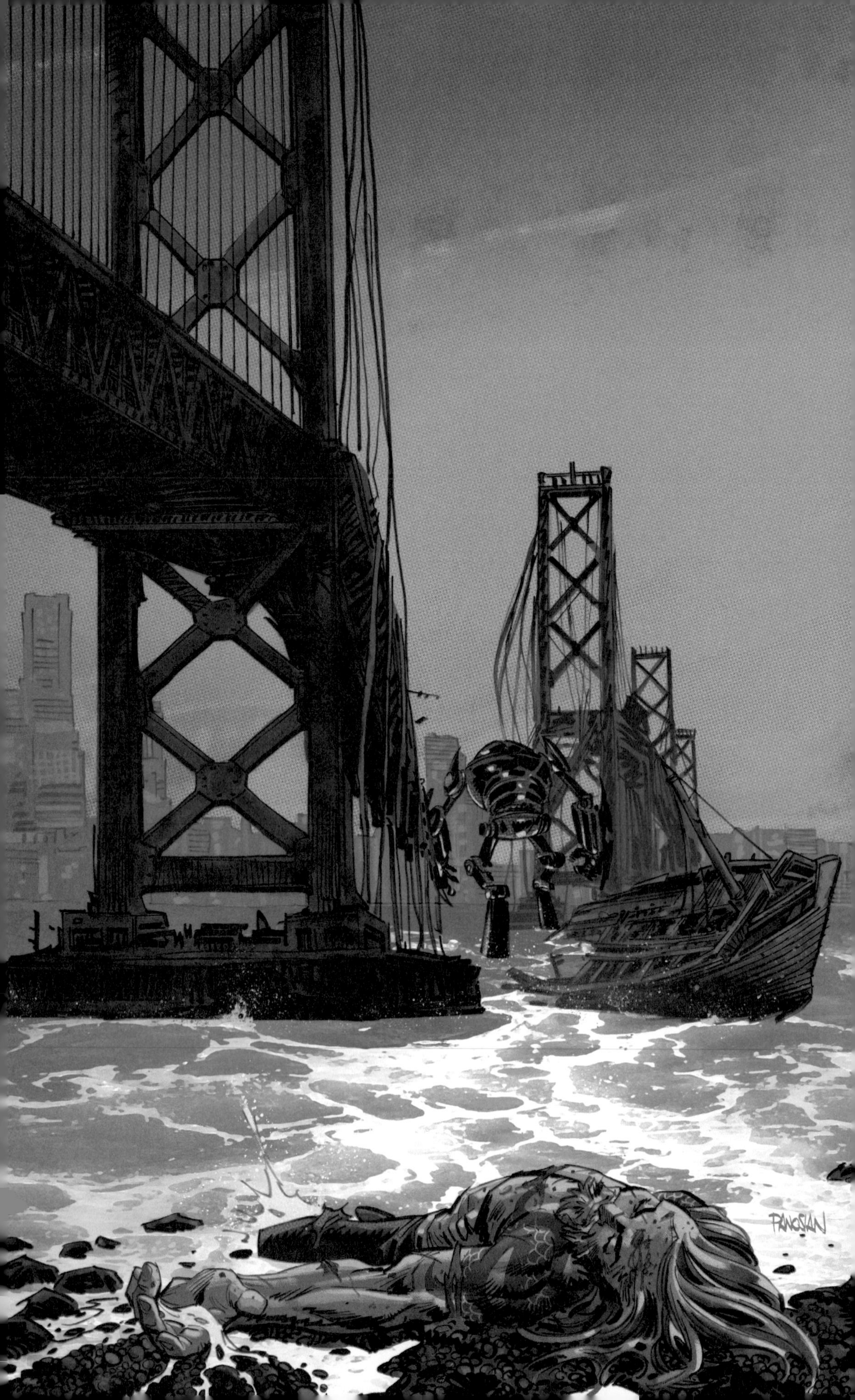
PANOSIAN

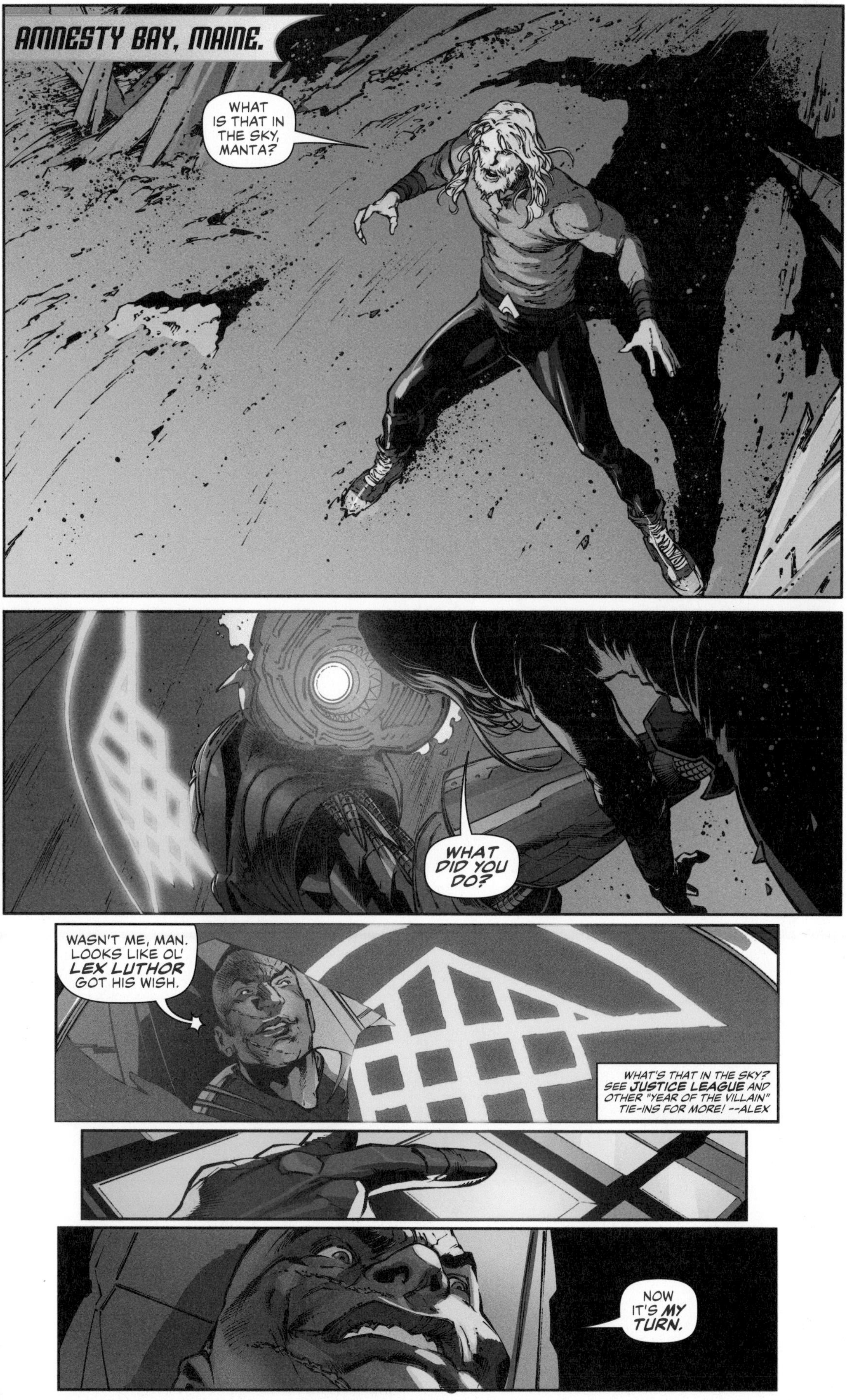
AMNESTY BAY, MAINE.
WHAT IS THAT IN THE SKY, MANTA?
WHAT DID YOU DO?
WASN'T ME, MAN. LOOKS LIKE OL' LEX LUTHOR GOT HIS WISH.
WHAT'S THAT IN THE SKY? SEE JUSTICE LEAGUE AND OTHER "YEAR OF THE VILLAIN" TIE-INS FOR MORE! --ALEX
NOW IT'S MY TURN.

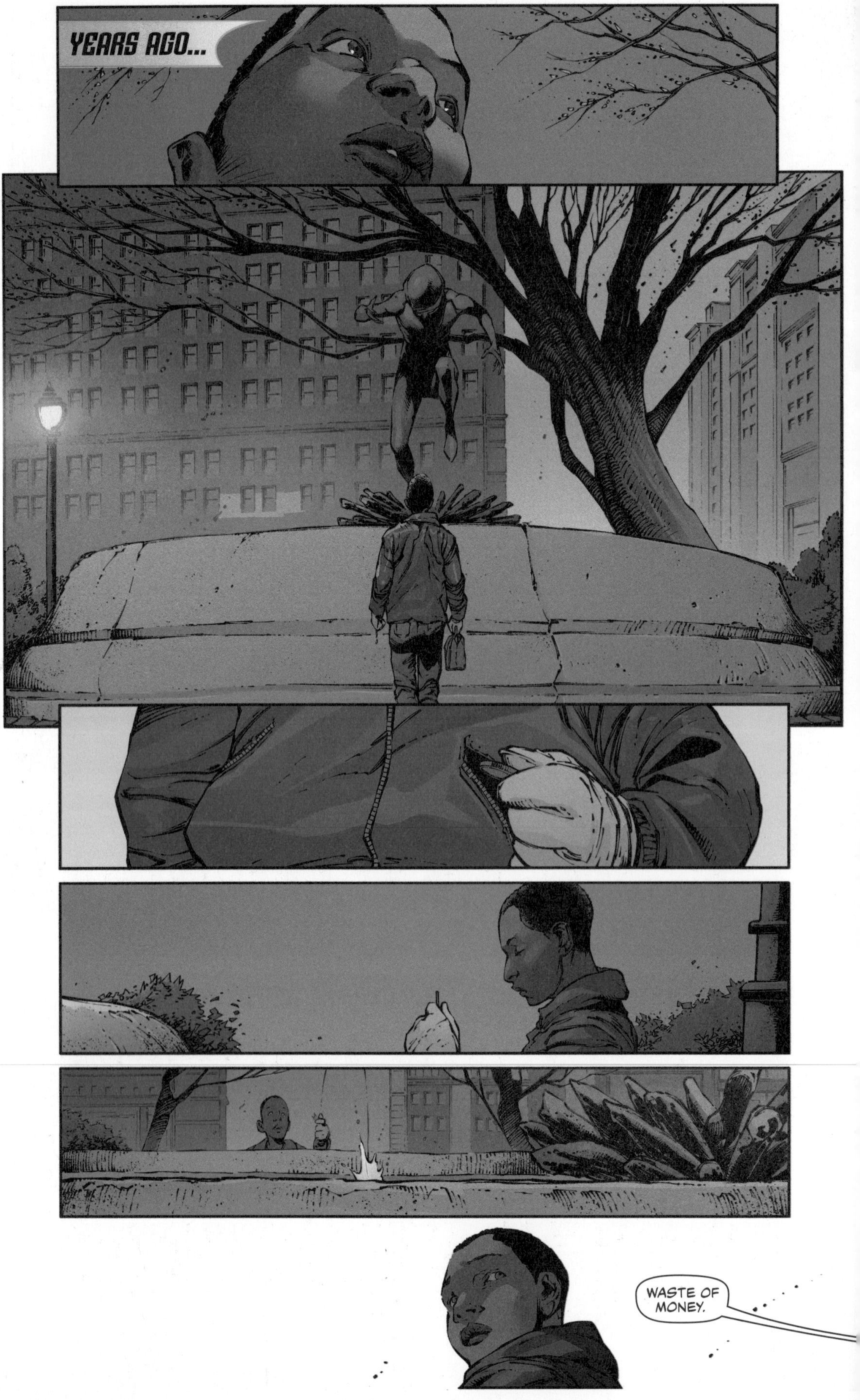
YEARS AGO...
WASTE OF MONEY.

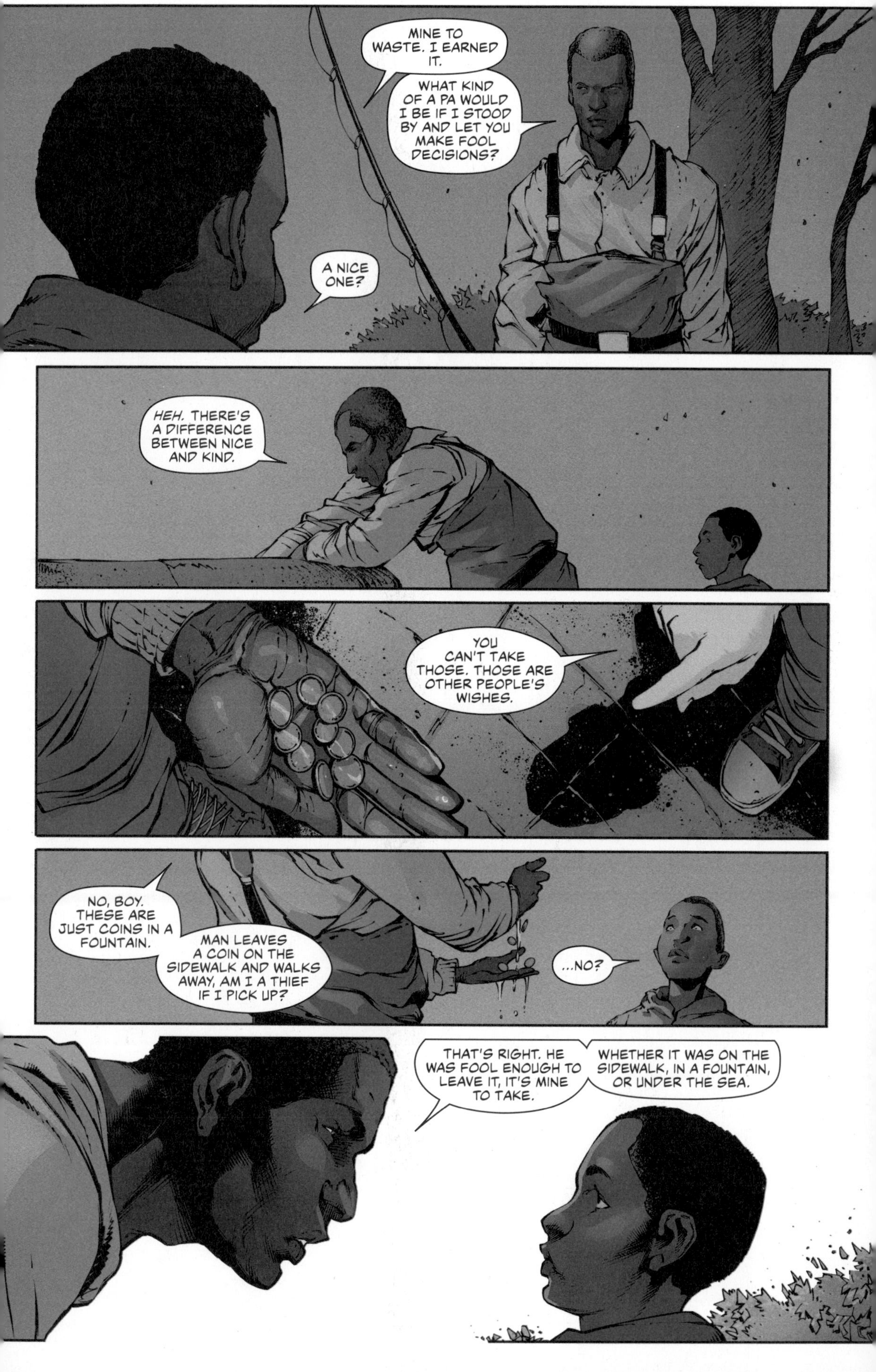
MINE TO WASTE. I EARNED IT.
WHAT KIND OF A PA WOULD I BE IF I STOOD BY AND LET YOU MAKE FOOL DECISIONS?
A NICE ONE?
HEH. THERE'S A DIFFERENCE BETWEEN NICE AND KIND.
YOU CAN'T TAKE THOSE. THOSE ARE OTHER PEOPLE'S WISHES.
NO, BOY. THESE ARE JUST COINS IN A FOUNTAIN.
MAN LEAVES A COIN ON THE SIDEWALK AND WALKS AWAY, AM I A THIEF IF I PICK UP?
...NO?
THAT'S RIGHT. HE WAS FOOL ENOUGH TO LEAVE IT, IT'S MINE TO TAKE.
WHETHER IT WAS ON THE SIDEWALK, IN A FOUNTAIN, OR UNDER THE SEA.

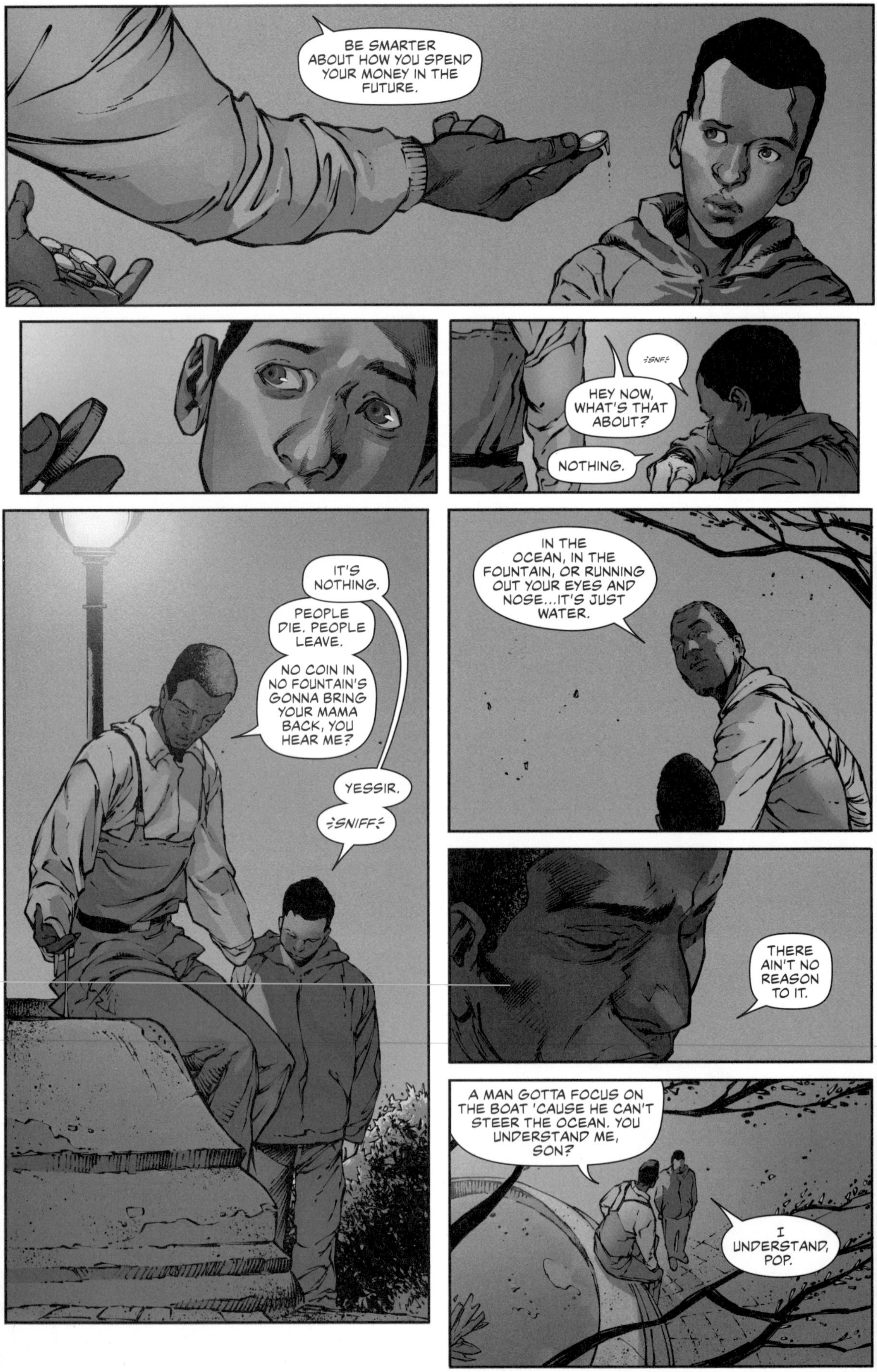
BE SMARTER ABOUT HOW YOU SPEND YOUR MONEY IN THE FUTURE.
SNF
HEY NOW, WHAT'S THAT ABOUT?
NOTHING.
IT'S NOTHING.
PEOPLE DIE. PEOPLE LEAVE.
NO COIN IN NO FOUNTAIN'S GONNA BRING YOUR MAMA BACK, YOU HEAR ME?
YESSIR.
SNIFF
IN THE OCEAN, IN THE FOUNTAIN, OR RUNNING OUT YOUR EYES AND NOSE...IT'S JUST WATER.
THERE AIN'T NO REASON TO IT.
A MAN GOTTA FOCUS ON THE BOAT 'CAUSE HE CAN'T STEER THE OCEAN. YOU UNDERSTAND ME, SON?
I UNDERSTAND, POP.

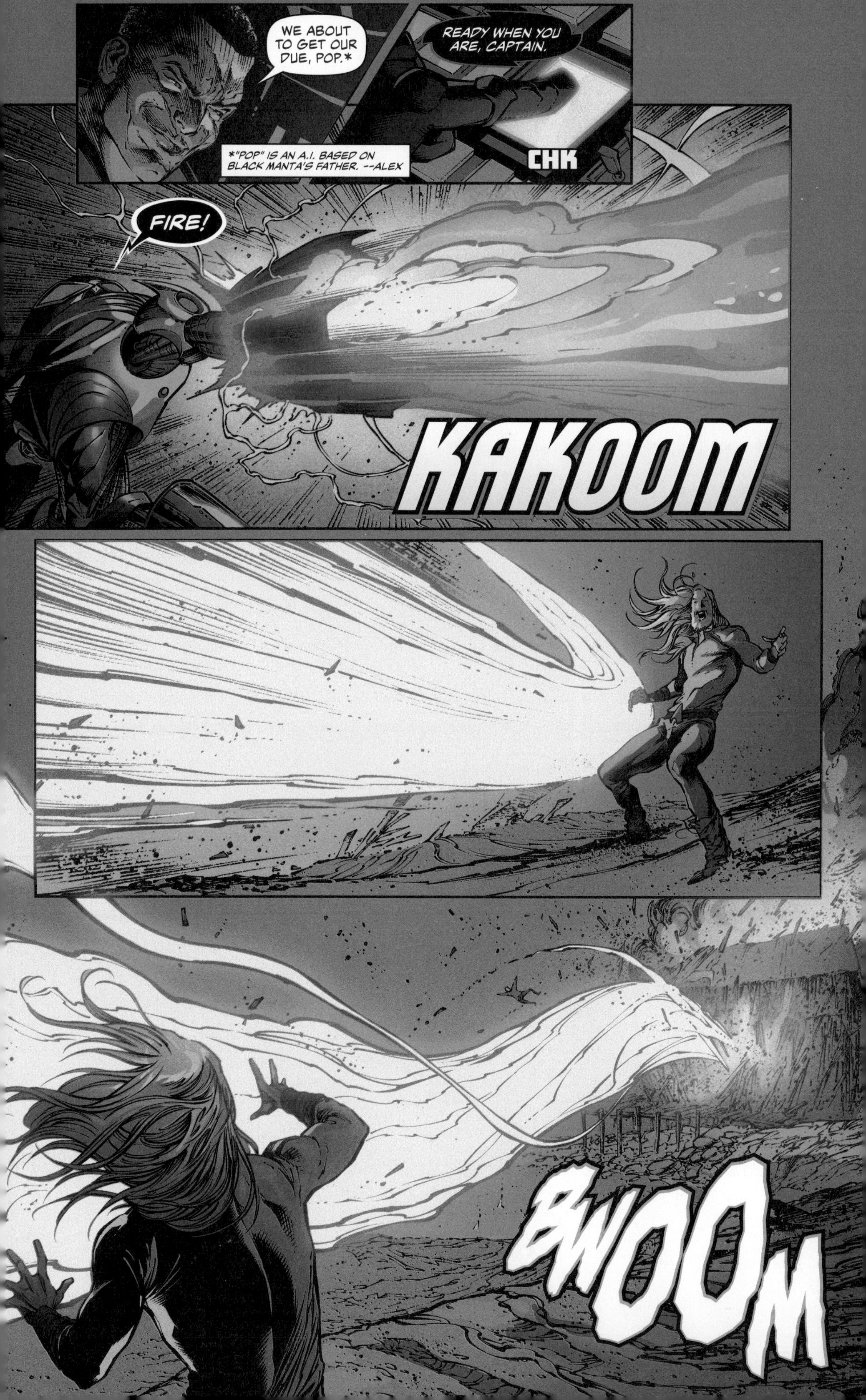
WE ABOUT TO GET OUR DUE, POP.*
*"POP" IS AN A.I. BASED ON BLACK MANTA'S FATHER. --ALEX
READY WHEN YOU ARE, CAPTAIN.
CHK
FIRE!
KAKOOM
BWOOM

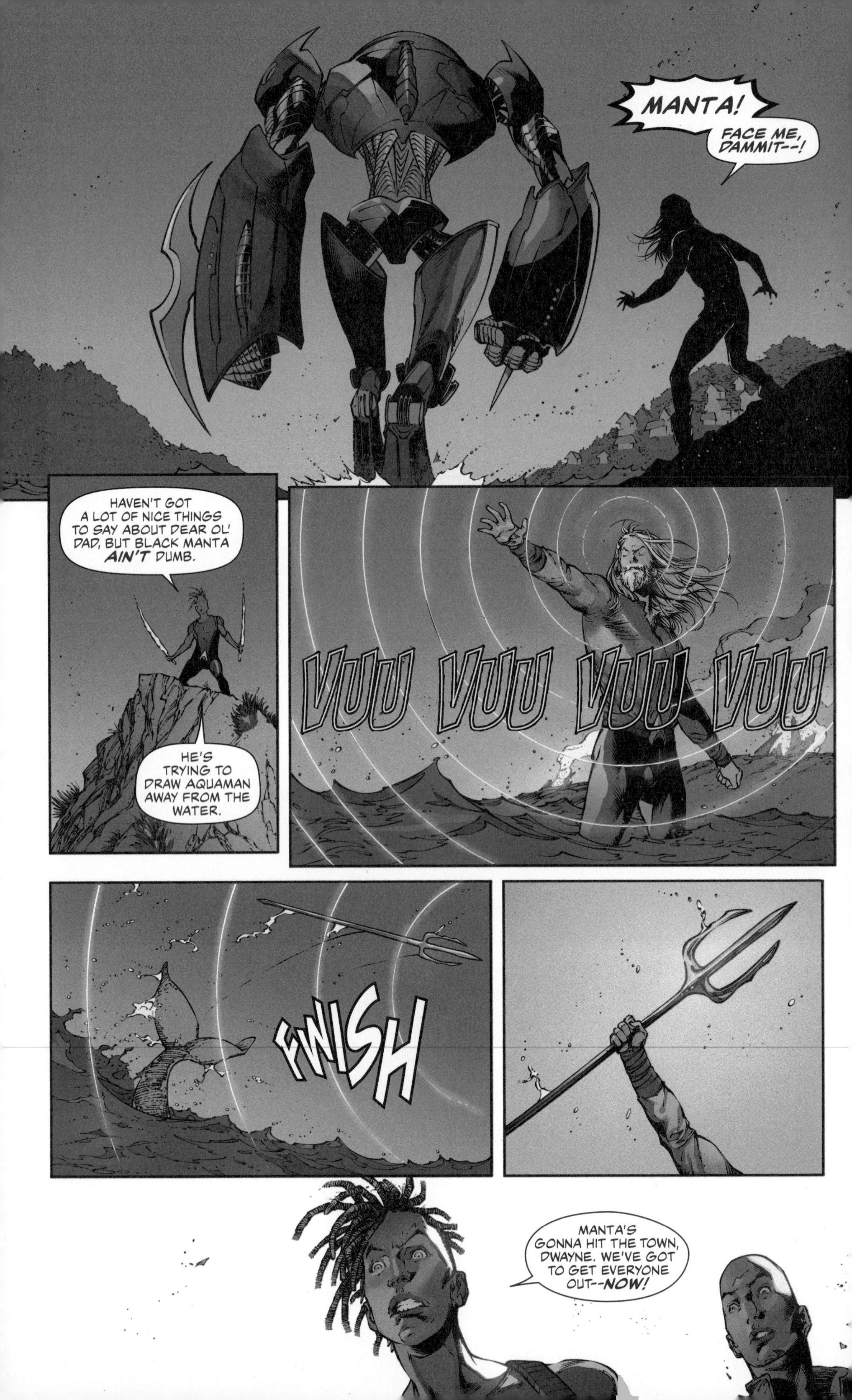
MANTA!
FACE ME, DAMMIT--!
HAVEN'T GOT A LOT OF NICE THINGS TO SAY ABOUT DEAR OL' DAD, BUT BLACK MANTA AIN'T DUMB.
HE'S TRYING TO DRAW AQUAMAN AWAY FROM THE WATER.
VUU VUU VUU VUU
FWISH
MANTA'S GONNA HIT THE TOWN, DWAYNE. WE'VE GOT TO GET EVERYONE OUT--NOW!

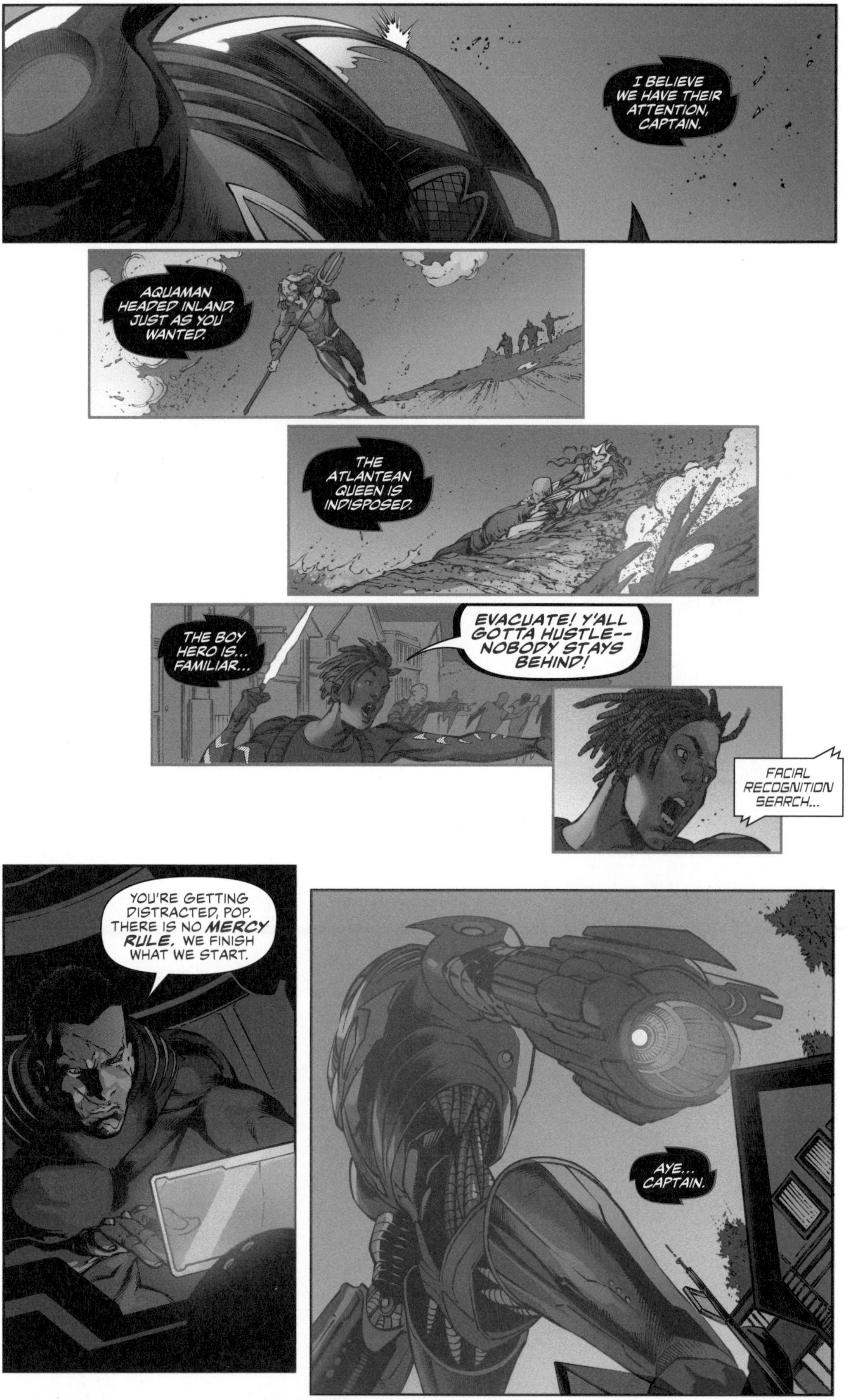
I BELIEVE WE HAVE THEIR ATTENTION, CAPTAIN.
AQUAMAN HEADED INLAND, JUST AS YOU WANTED.
THE ATLANTEAN QUEEN IS INDISPOSED.
THE BOY HERO IS... FAMILIAR...
EVACUATE! Y'ALL GOTTA HUSTLE-- NOBODY STAYS BEHIND!
FACIAL RECOGNITION SEARCH...
YOU'RE GETTING DISTRACTED, POP. THERE IS NO MERCY RULE. WE FINISH WHAT WE START.
AYE... CAPTAIN.

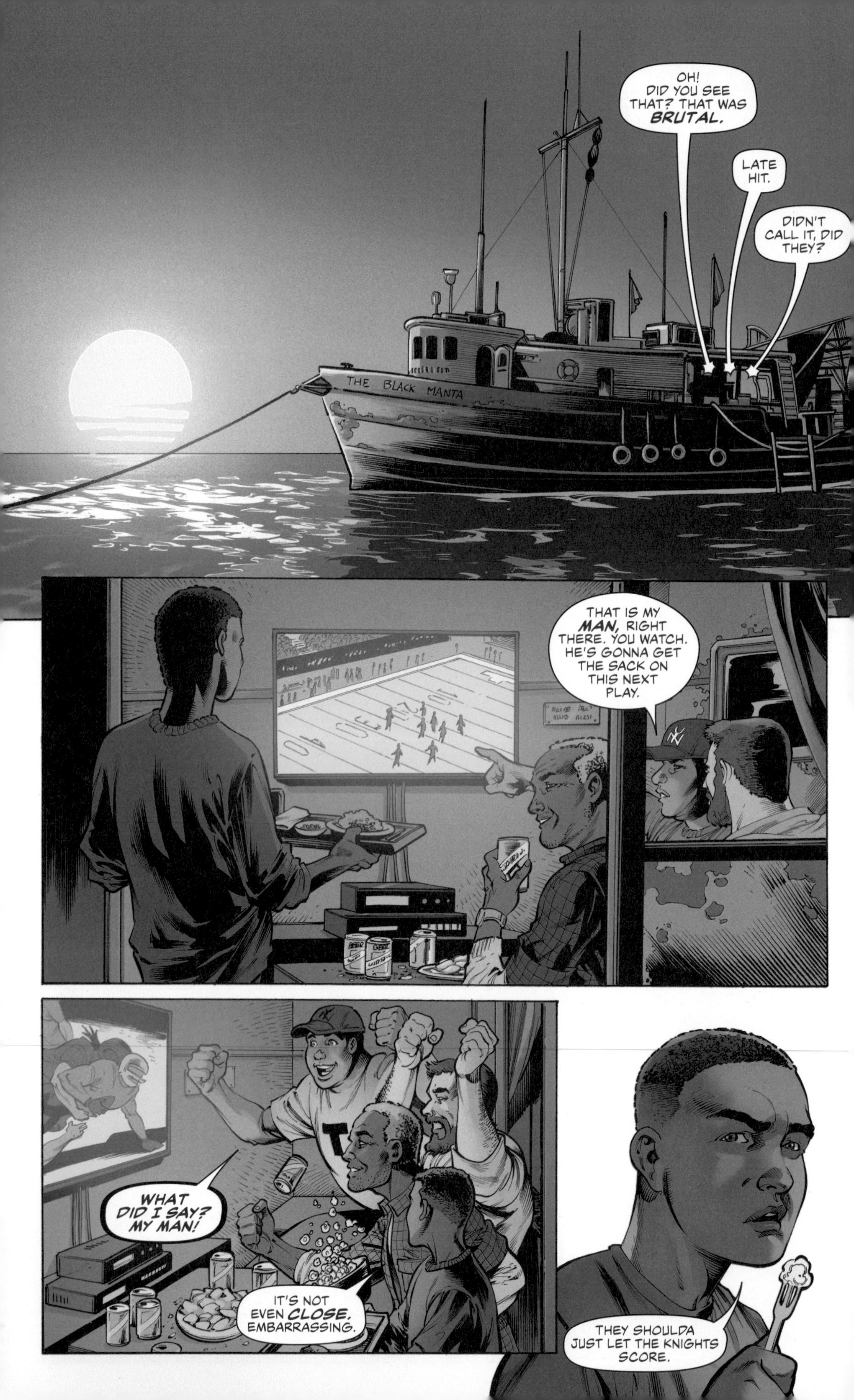
OH! DID YOU SEE THAT? THAT WAS BRUTAL.
LATE HIT.
DIDN'T CALL IT, DID THEY?
THE BLACK MANTA
THAT IS MY MAN, RIGHT THERE. YOU WATCH. HE'S GONNA GET THE SACK ON THIS NEXT PLAY.
WHAT DID I SAY? MY MAN!
IT'S NOT EVEN CLOSE. EMBARRASSING.
THEY SHOULDA JUST LET THE KNIGHTS SCORE.

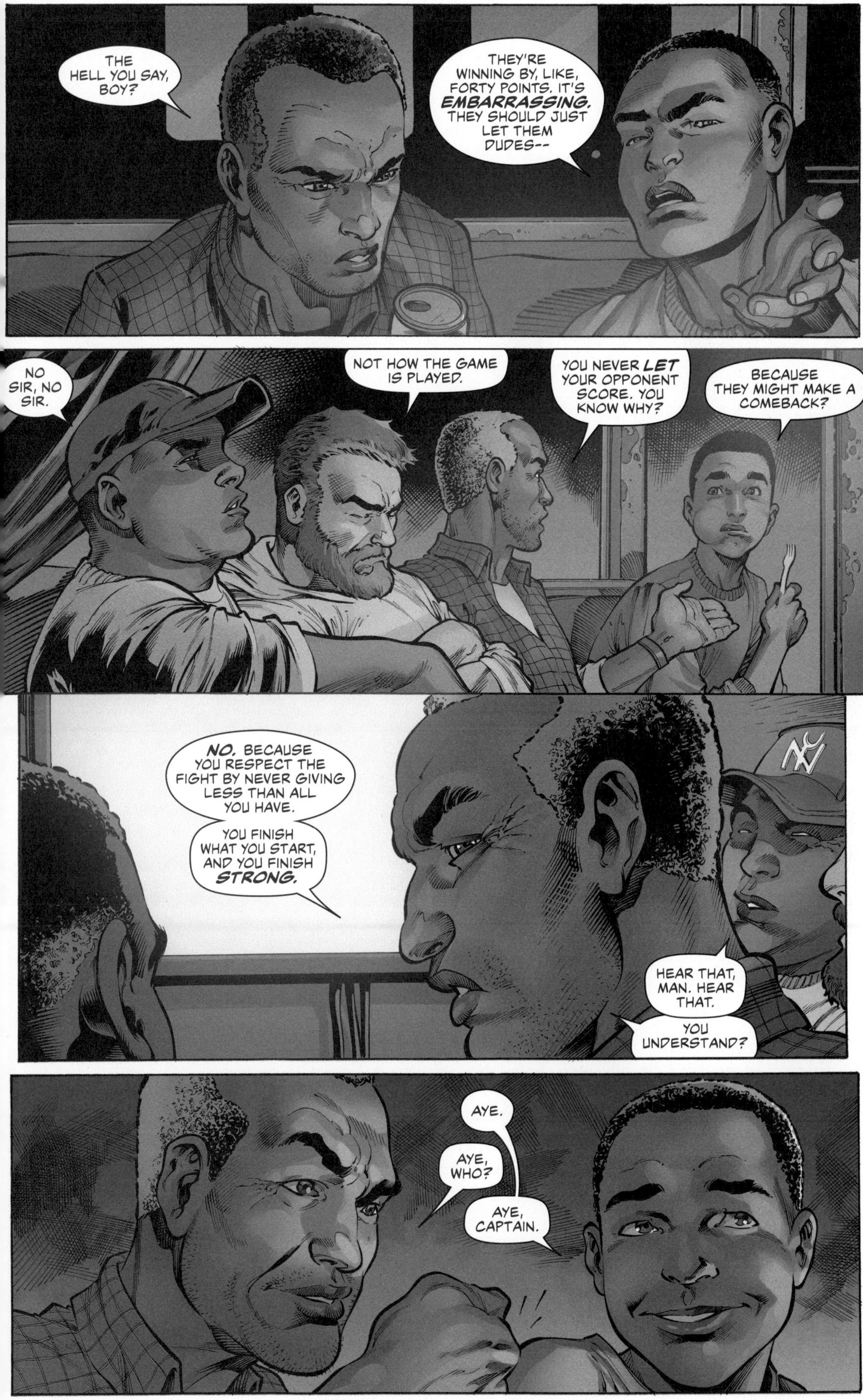
THE HELL YOU SAY, BOY?
THEY'RE WINNING BY, LIKE, FORTY POINTS. IT'S EMBARRASSING. THEY SHOULD JUST LET THEM DUDES--
NO SIR, NO SIR.
NOT HOW THE GAME IS PLAYED.
YOU NEVER LET YOUR OPPONENT SCORE. YOU KNOW WHY?
BECAUSE THEY MIGHT MAKE A COMEBACK?
NO. BECAUSE YOU RESPECT THE FIGHT BY NEVER GIVING LESS THAN ALL YOU HAVE.
YOU FINISH WHAT YOU START, AND YOU FINISH STRONG.
HEAR THAT, MAN. HEAR THAT.
YOU UNDERSTAND?
AYE.
AYE, WHO?
AYE, CAPTAIN.

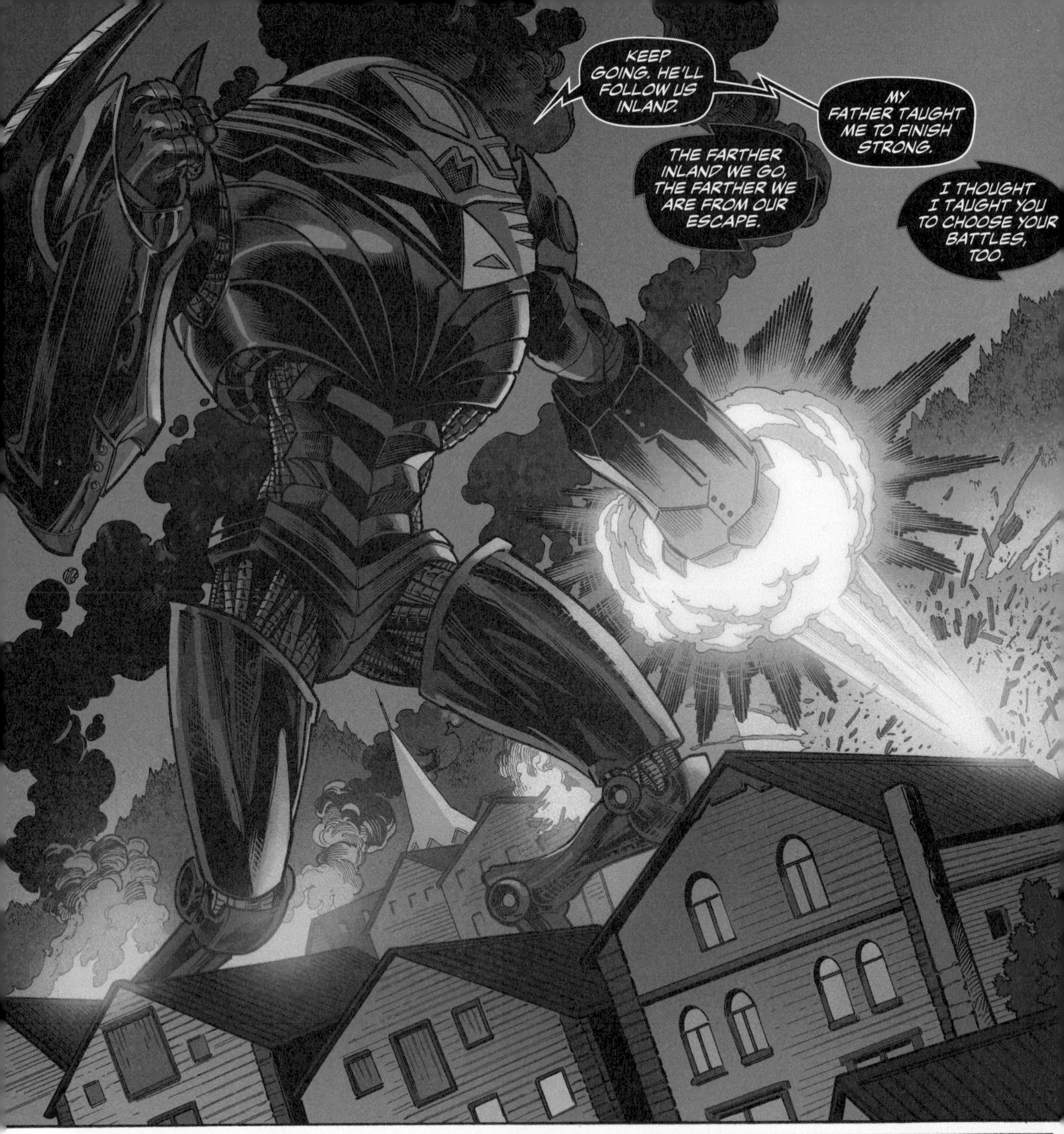
KEEP GOING. HE'LL FOLLOW US INLAND.
MY FATHER TAUGHT ME TO FINISH STRONG.
THE FARTHER INLAND WE GO, THE FARTHER WE ARE FROM OUR ESCAPE.
I THOUGHT I TAUGHT YOU TO CHOOSE YOUR BATTLES, TOO.

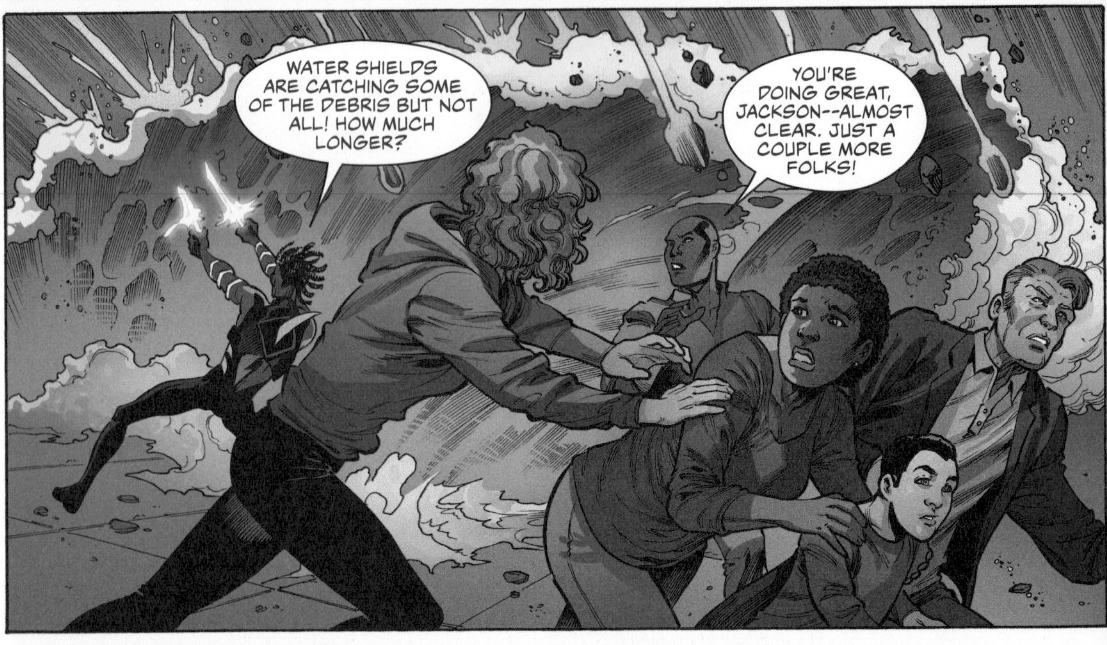
WATER SHIELDS ARE CATCHING SOME OF THE DEBRIS BUT NOT ALL! HOW MUCH LONGER?
YOU'RE DOING GREAT, JACKSON--ALMOST CLEAR. JUST A COUPLE MORE FOLKS!

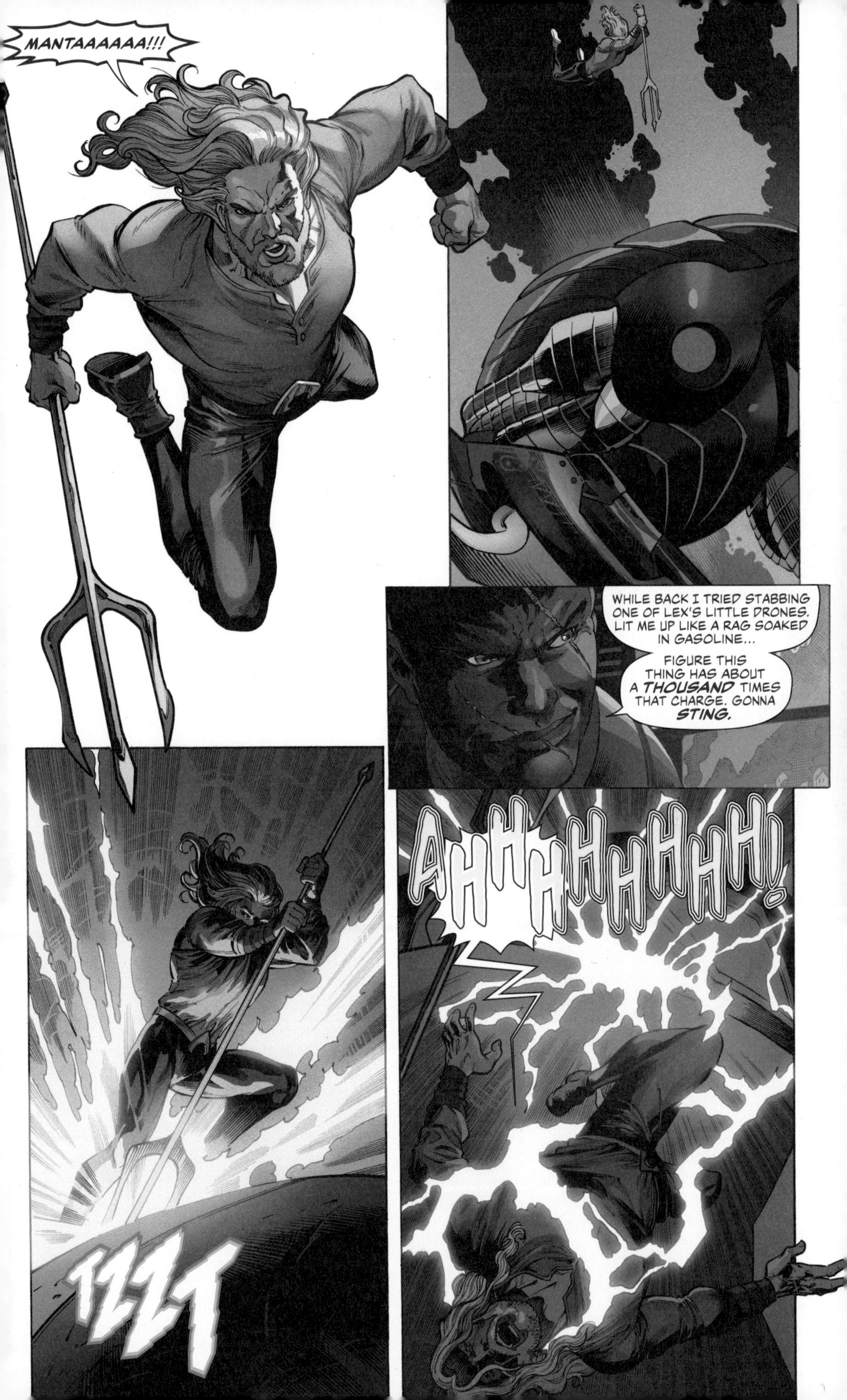
MANTAAAAAAA!!!
WHILE BACK I TRIED STABBING ONE OF LEX'S LITTLE DRONES. LIT ME UP LIKE A RAG SOAKED IN GASOLINE...
FIGURE THIS THING HAS ABOUT A THOUSAND TIMES THAT CHARGE. GONNA STING.
TZZT
AHHHHHHHHHH!

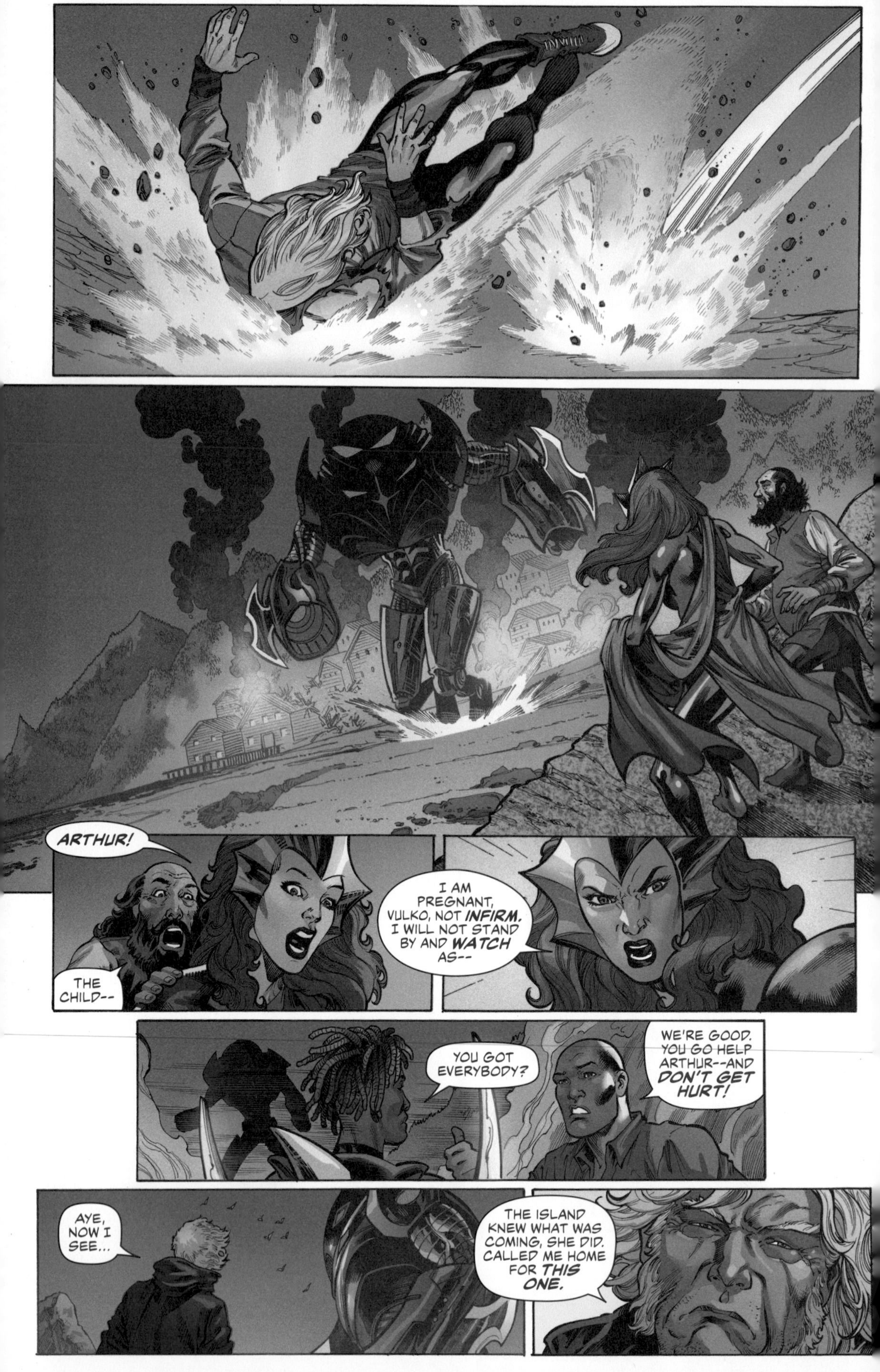
ARTHUR!
THE CHILD--
I AM PREGNANT, VULKO, NOT INFIRM. I WILL NOT STAND BY AND WATCH AS--
YOU GOT EVERYBODY?
WE'RE GOOD. YOU GO HELP ARTHUR--AND DON'T GET HURT!
AYE, NOW I SEE...
THE ISLAND KNEW WHAT WAS COMING, SHE DID. CALLED ME HOME FOR THIS ONE.

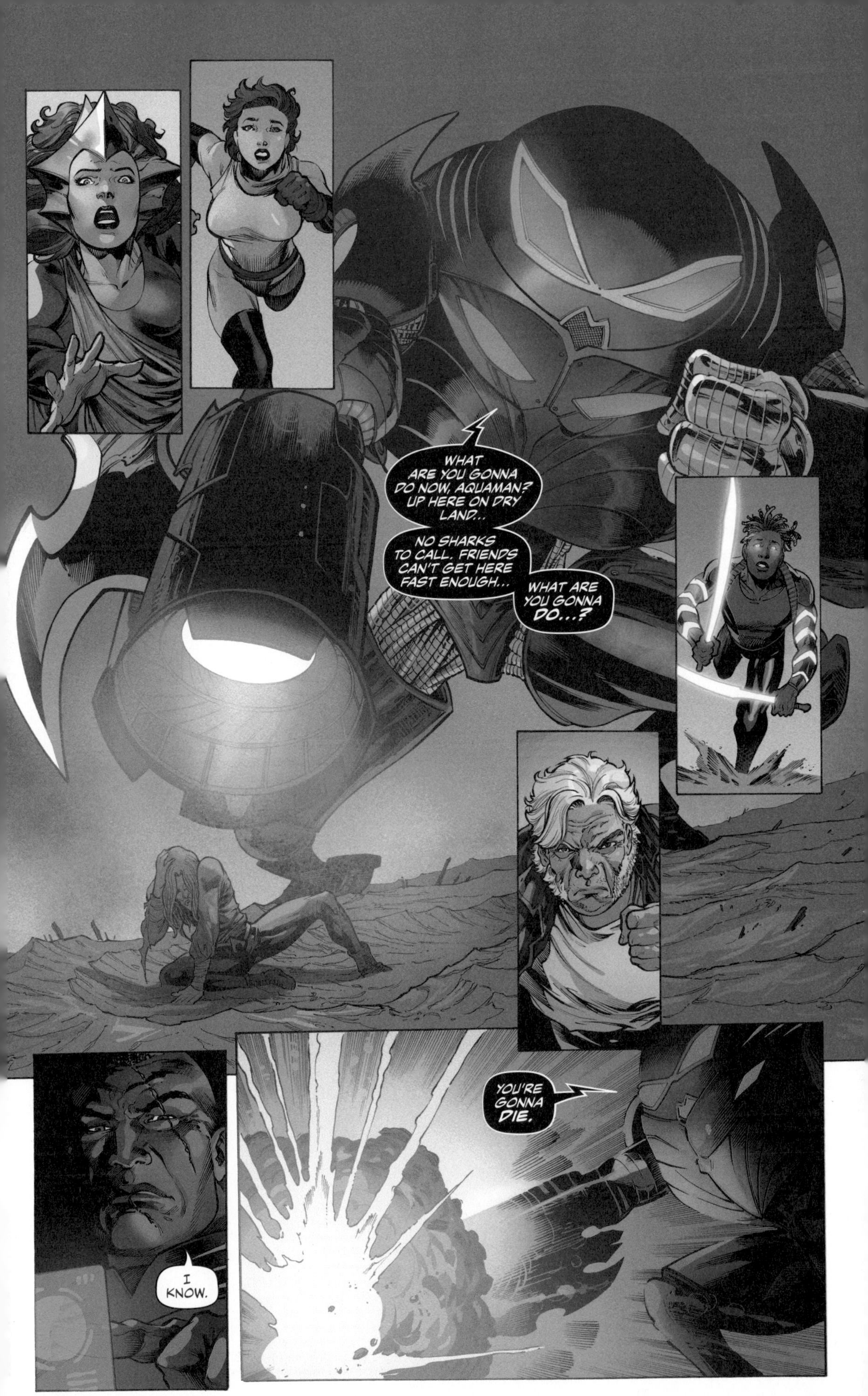
WHAT ARE YOU GONNA DO NOW, AQUAMAN? UP HERE ON DRY LAND...
NO SHARKS TO CALL. FRIENDS CAN'T GET HERE FAST ENOUGH...
WHAT ARE YOU GONNA DO...?
I KNOW.
YOU'RE GONNA DIE.

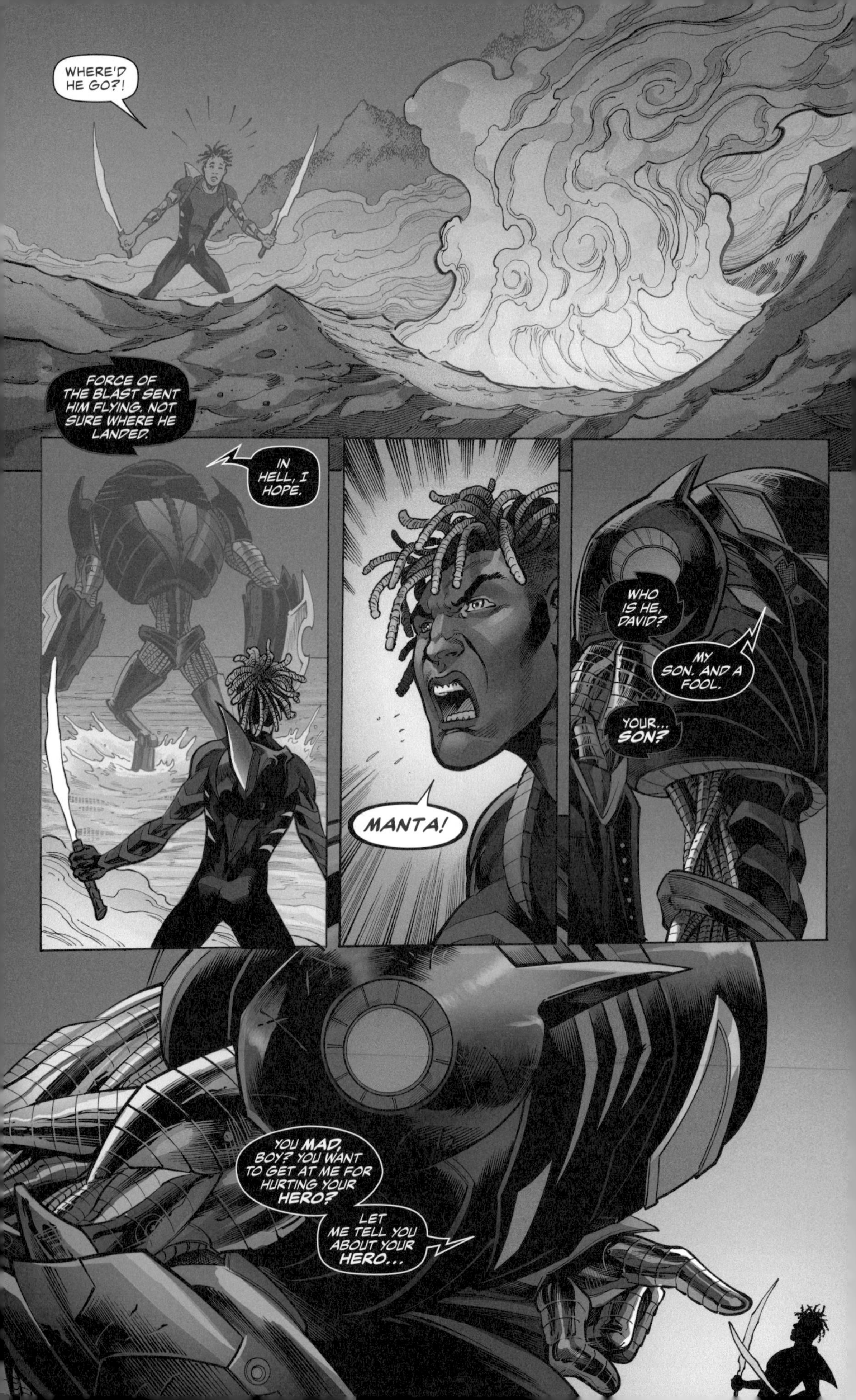
WHERE'D HE GO?!
FORCE OF THE BLAST SENT HIM FLYING. NOT SURE WHERE HE LANDED.
IN HELL, I HOPE.
MANTA!
WHO IS HE, DAVID?
MY SON. AND A FOOL.
YOUR... SON?
YOU MAD, BOY? YOU WANT TO GET AT ME FOR HURTING YOUR HERO?
LET ME TELL YOU ABOUT YOUR HERO...

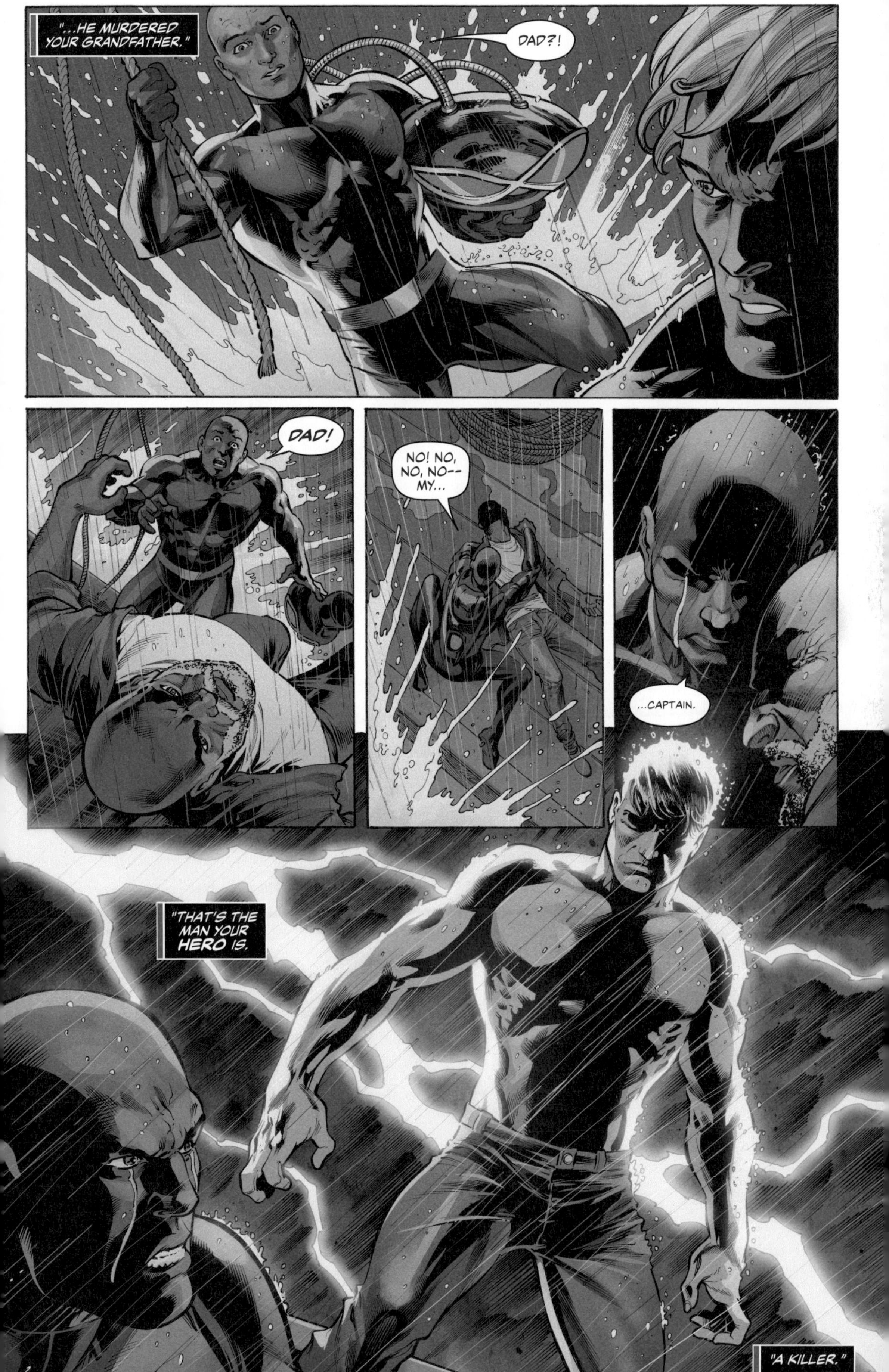
"...HE MURDERED YOUR GRANDFATHER."
DAD?!
DAD!
NO! NO, NO, NO-- MY...
...CAPTAIN.
"THAT'S THE MAN YOUR HERO IS.
"A KILLER."

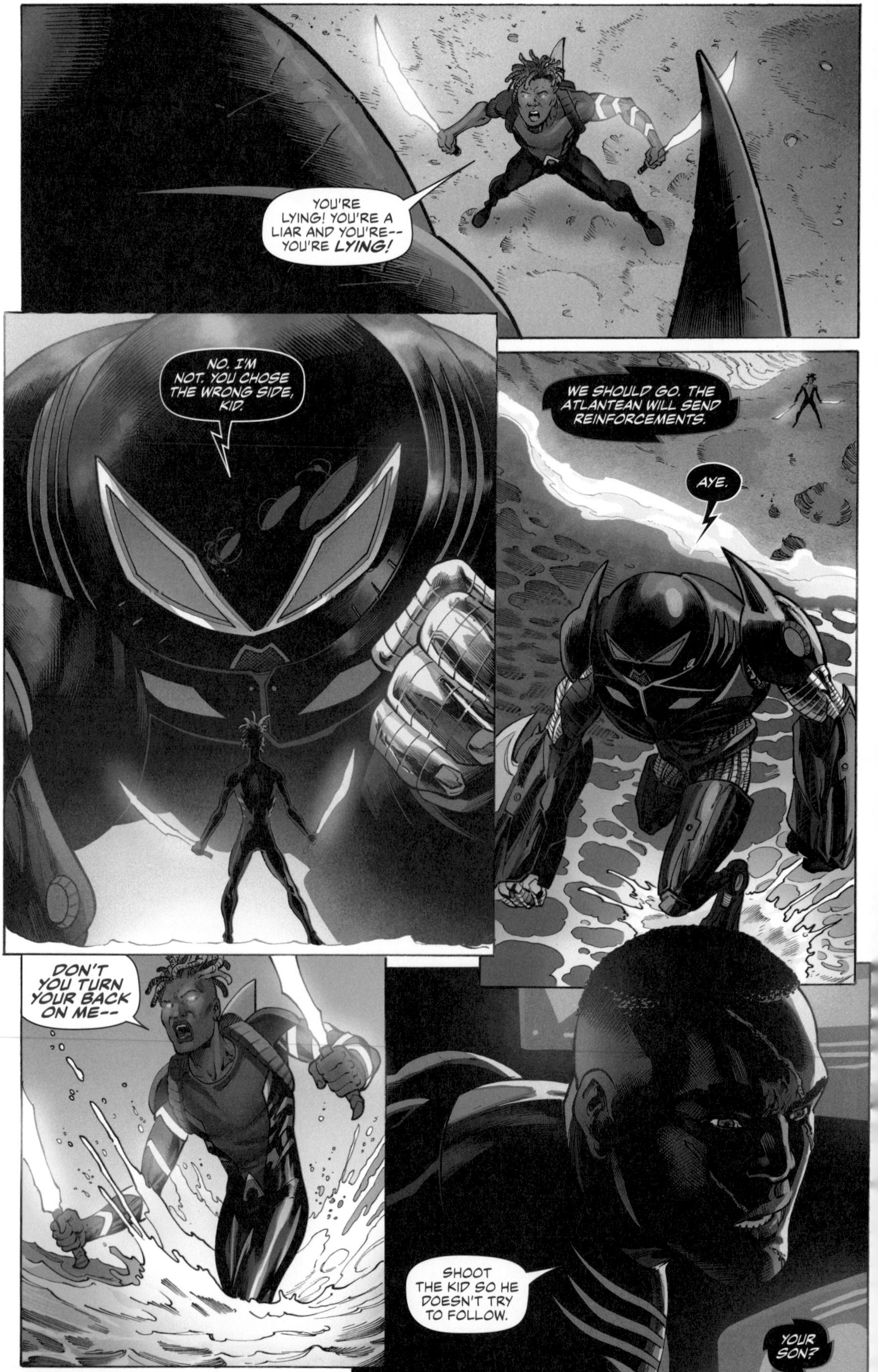
YOU'RE LYING! YOU'RE A LIAR AND YOU'RE-- YOU'RE LYING!
NO. I'M NOT. YOU CHOSE THE WRONG SIDE, KID.
WE SHOULD GO. THE ATLANTEAN WILL SEND REINFORCEMENTS.
AYE.
DON'T YOU TURN YOUR BACK ON ME--
SHOOT THE KID SO HE DOESN'T TRY TO FOLLOW.
YOUR SON?

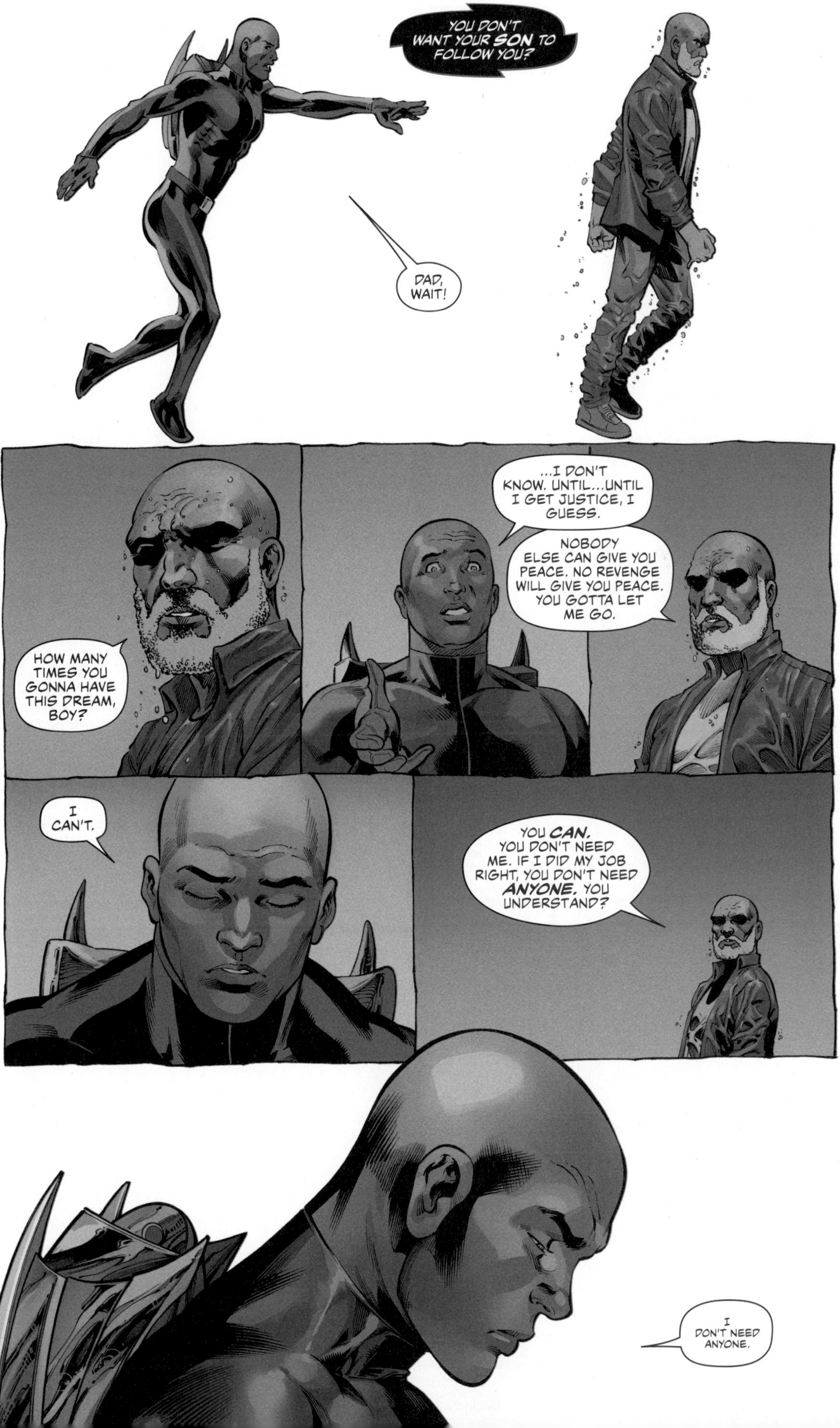
YOU DON'T WANT YOUR SON TO FOLLOW YOU?
DAD, WAIT!
HOW MANY TIMES YOU GONNA HAVE THIS DREAM, BOY?
...I DON'T KNOW. UNTIL...UNTIL I GET JUSTICE, I GUESS.
NOBODY ELSE CAN GIVE YOU PEACE. NO REVENGE WILL GIVE YOU PEACE. YOU GOTTA LET ME GO.
I CAN'T.
YOU CAN. YOU DON'T NEED ME. IF I DID MY JOB RIGHT, YOU DON'T NEED ANYONE. YOU UNDERSTAND?
I DON'T NEED ANYONE.

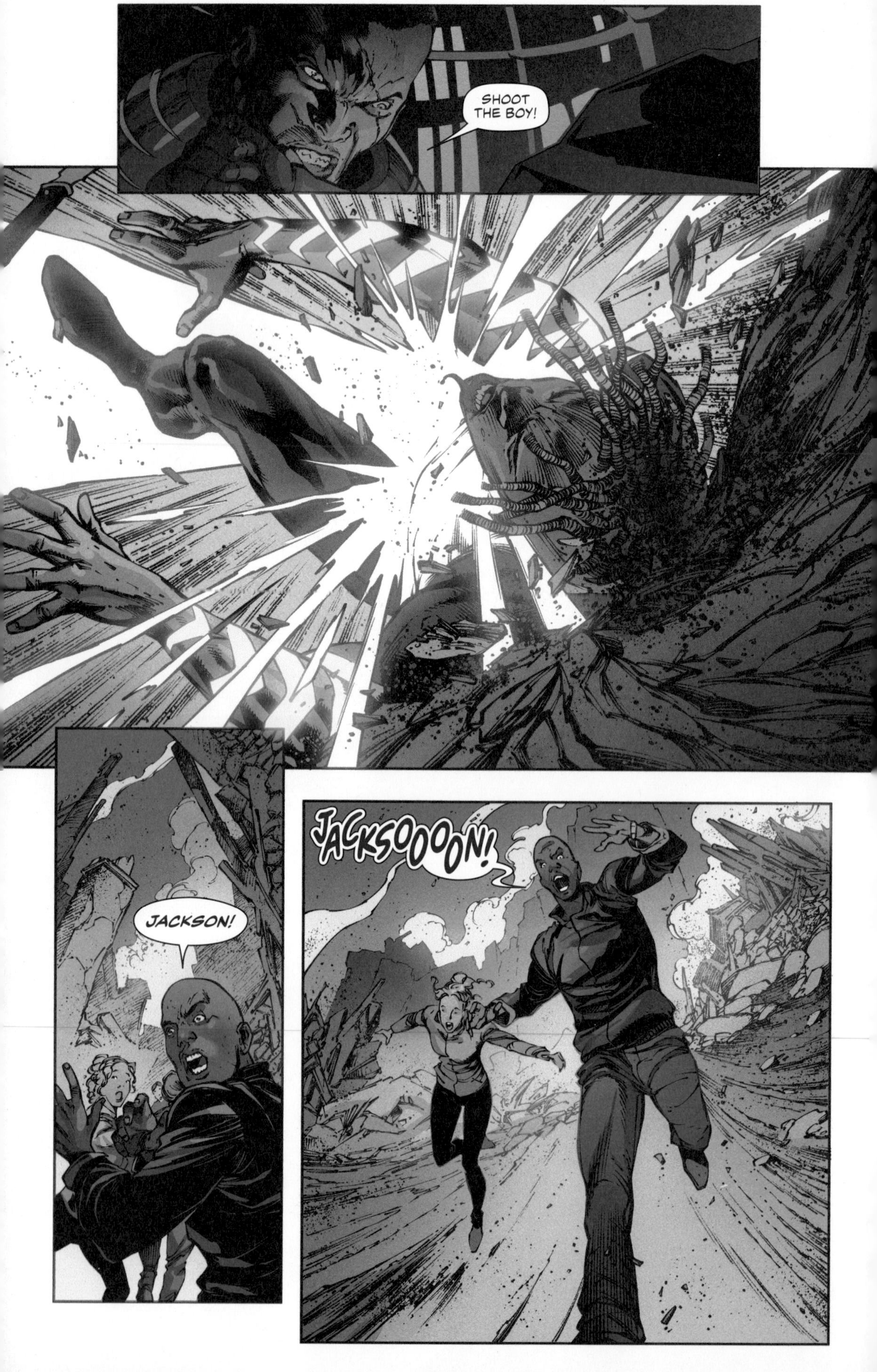
SHOOT THE BOY!
JACKSON!
JACKSOOOON!

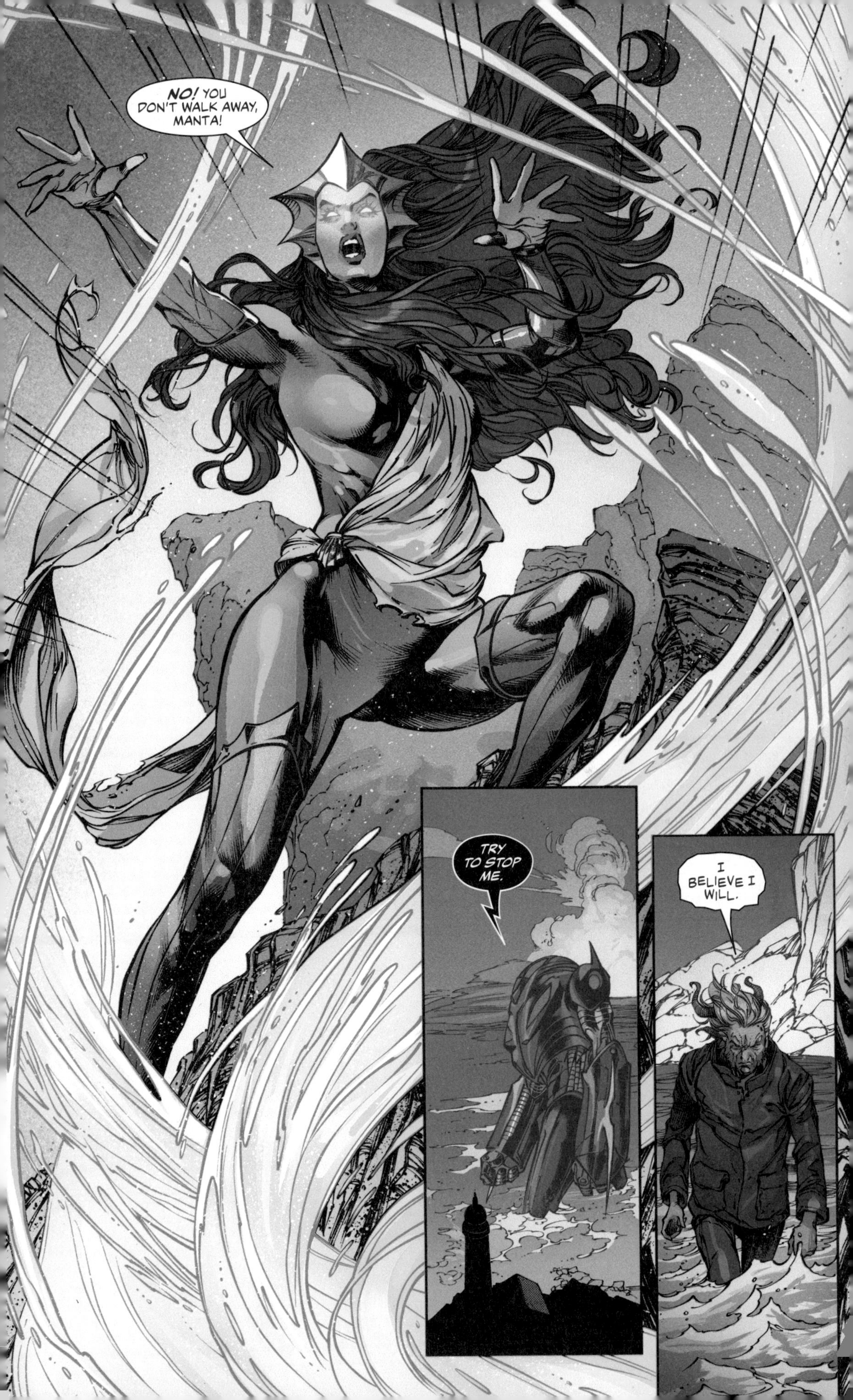
NO! YOU DON'T WALK AWAY, MANTA!
TRY TO STOP ME.
I BELIEVE I WILL.

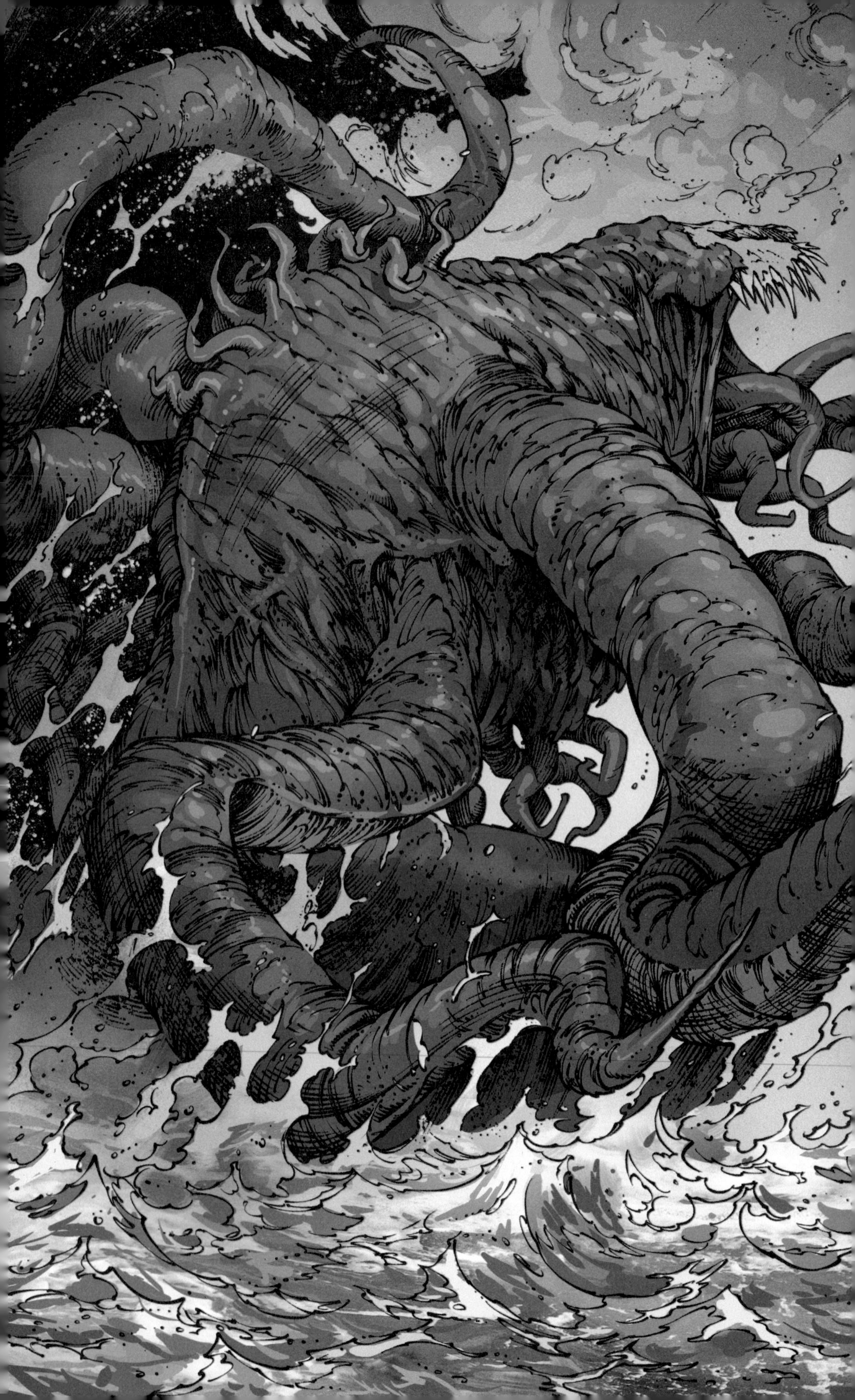

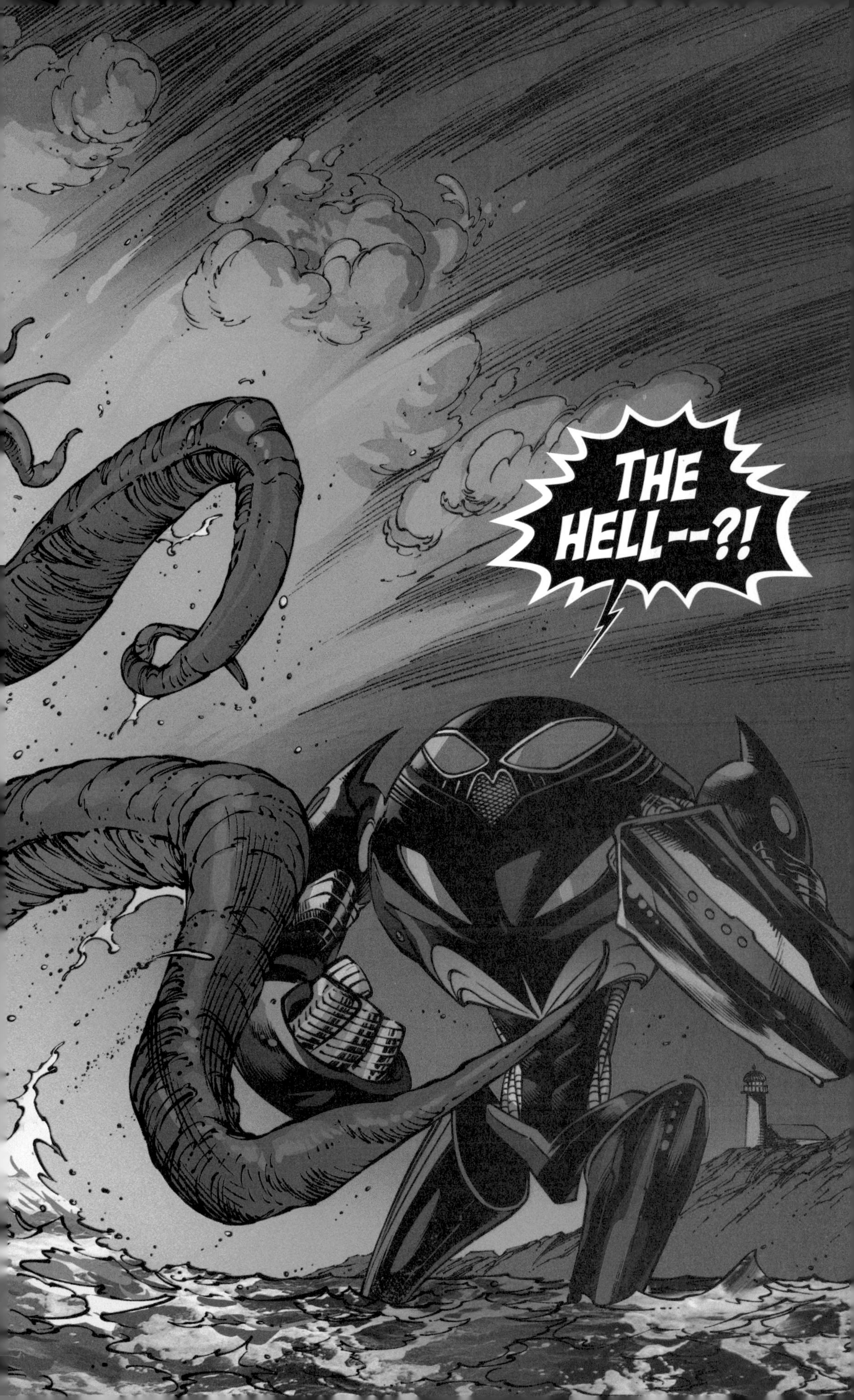
THE HELL--?!

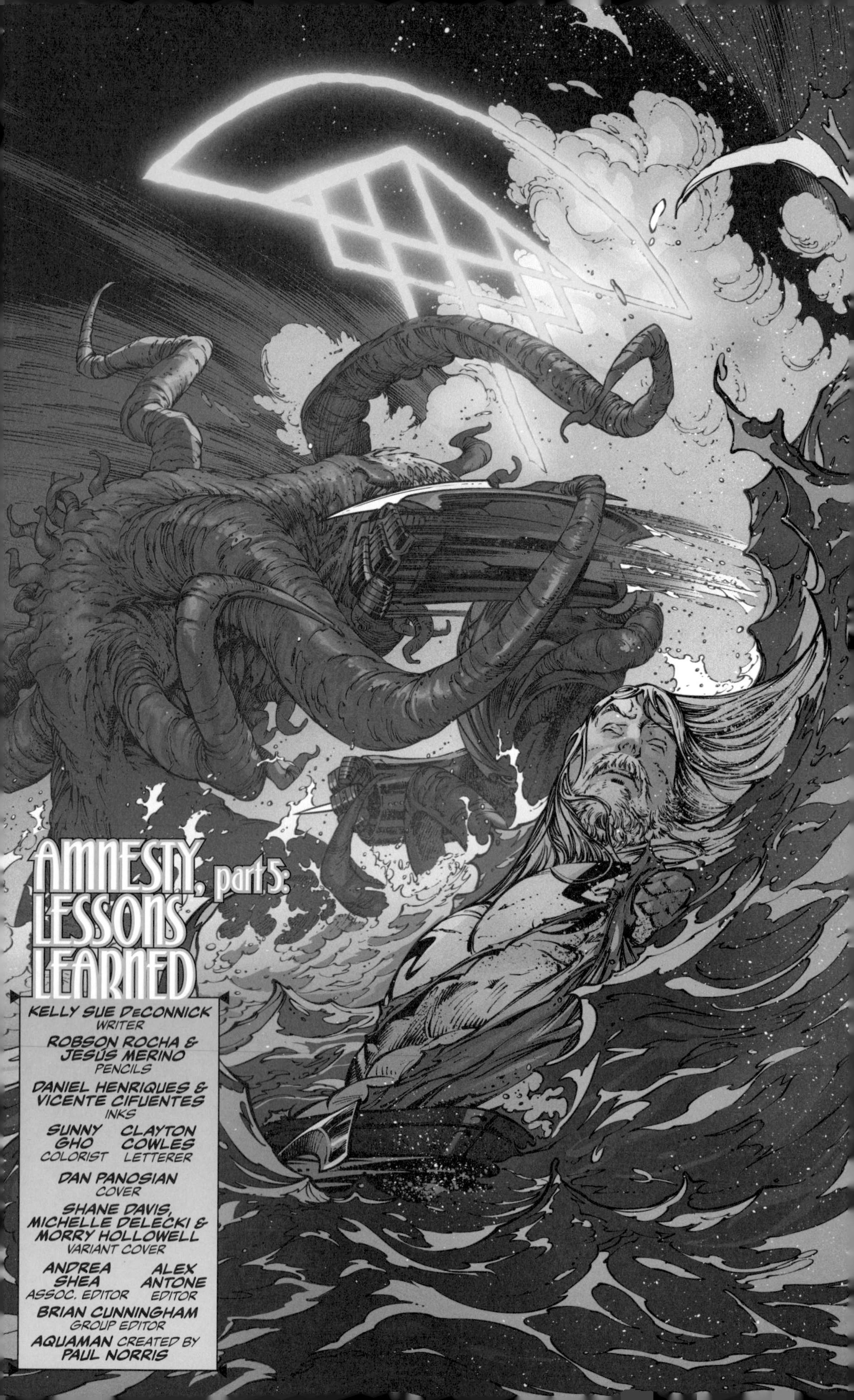
AMNESTY, part 5:
LESSONS LEARNED
KELLY SUE DECONNICK
WRITER
ROBSON ROCHA &
JESÚS MERINO
PENCILS
DANIEL HENRIQUES &
VICENTE CIFUENTES
INKS
SUNNY GHO
COLORIST
CLAYTON COWLES
LETTERER
DAN PANOSIAN
COVER
SHANE DAVIS,
MICHELLE DELECKI &
MORRY HOLLOWELL
VARIANT COVER
ANDREA SHEA
ASSOC. EDITOR
ALEX ANTONE
EDITOR
BRIAN CUNNINGHAM
GROUP EDITOR
AQUAMAN CREATED BY
PAUL NORRIS

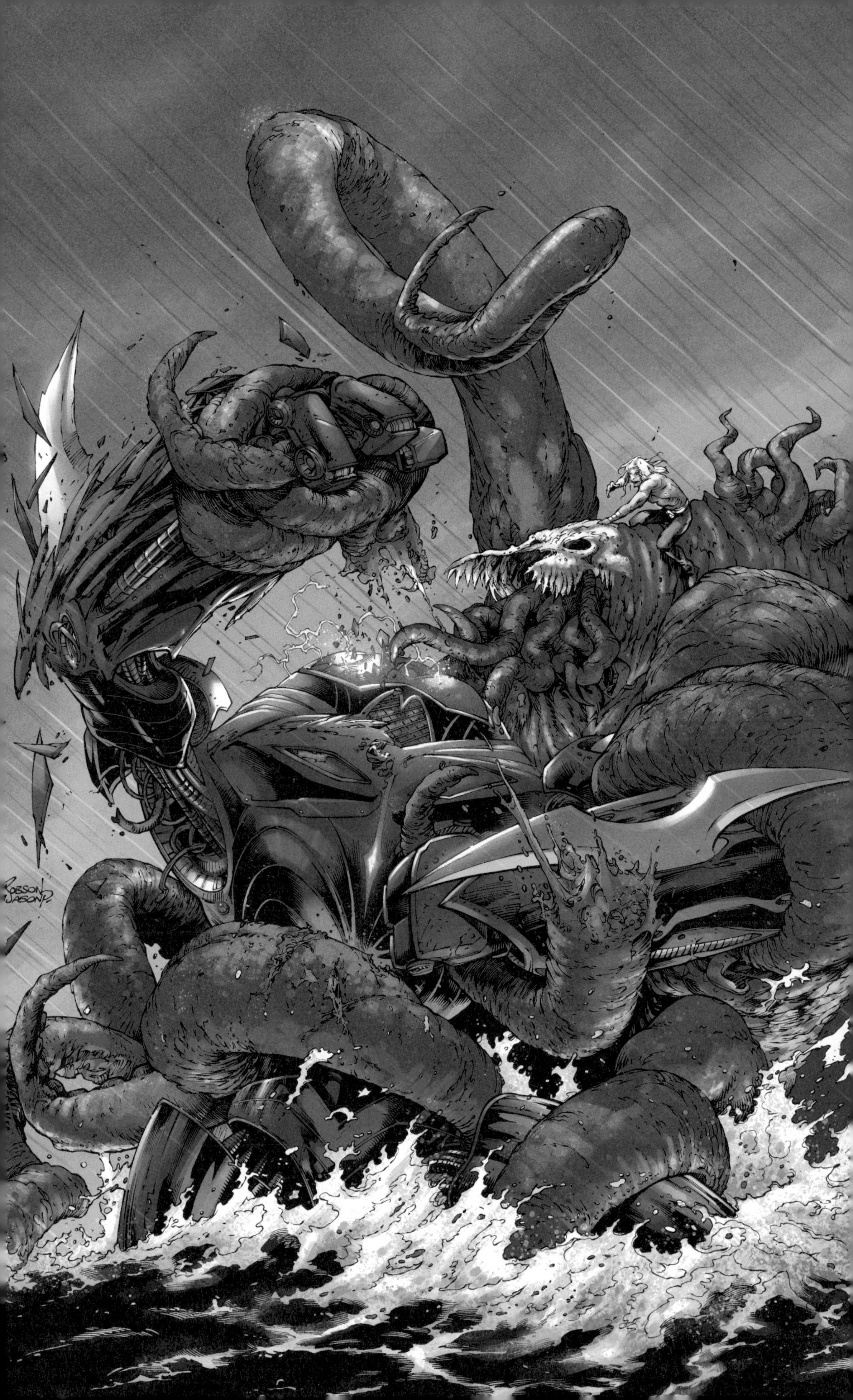

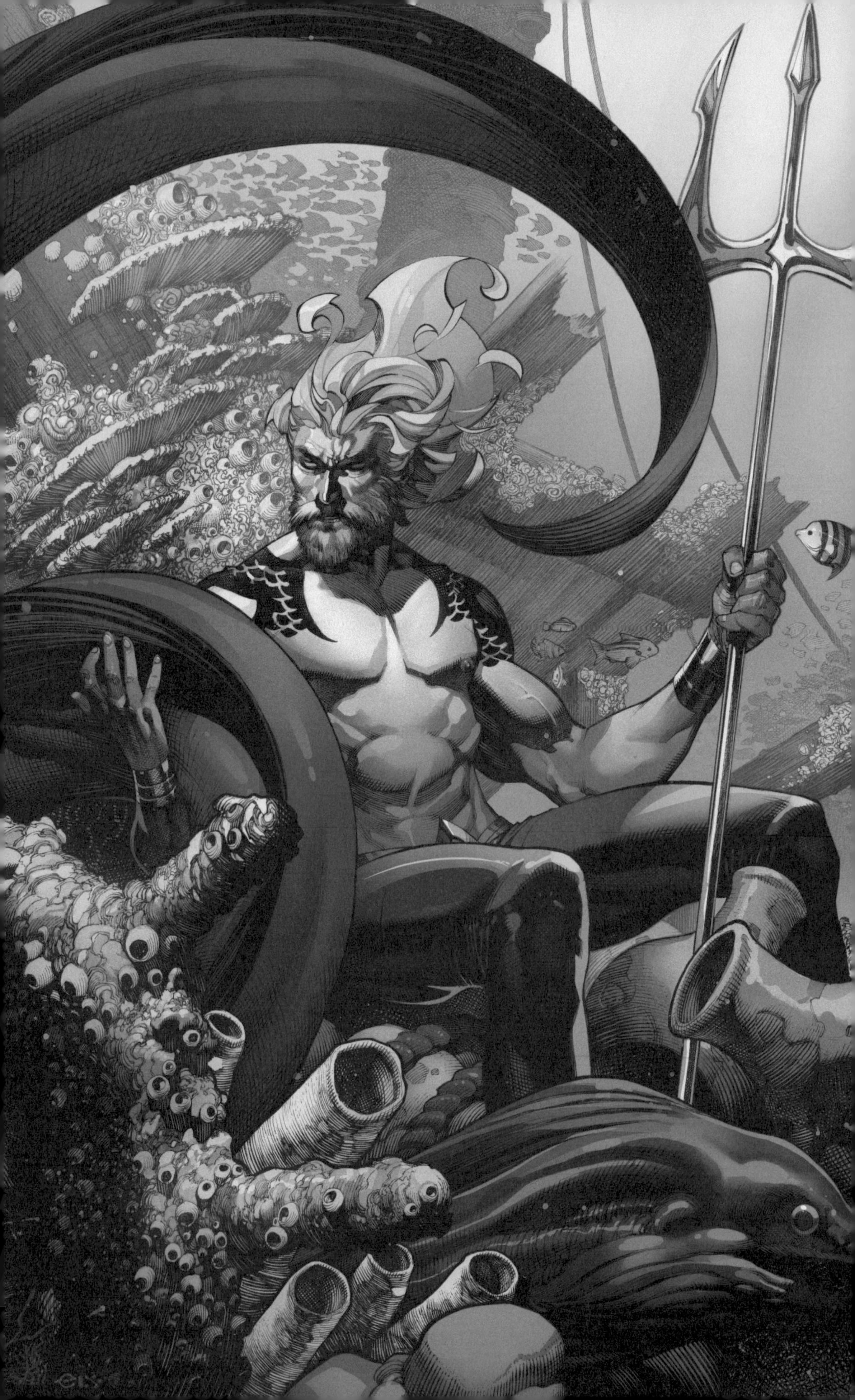

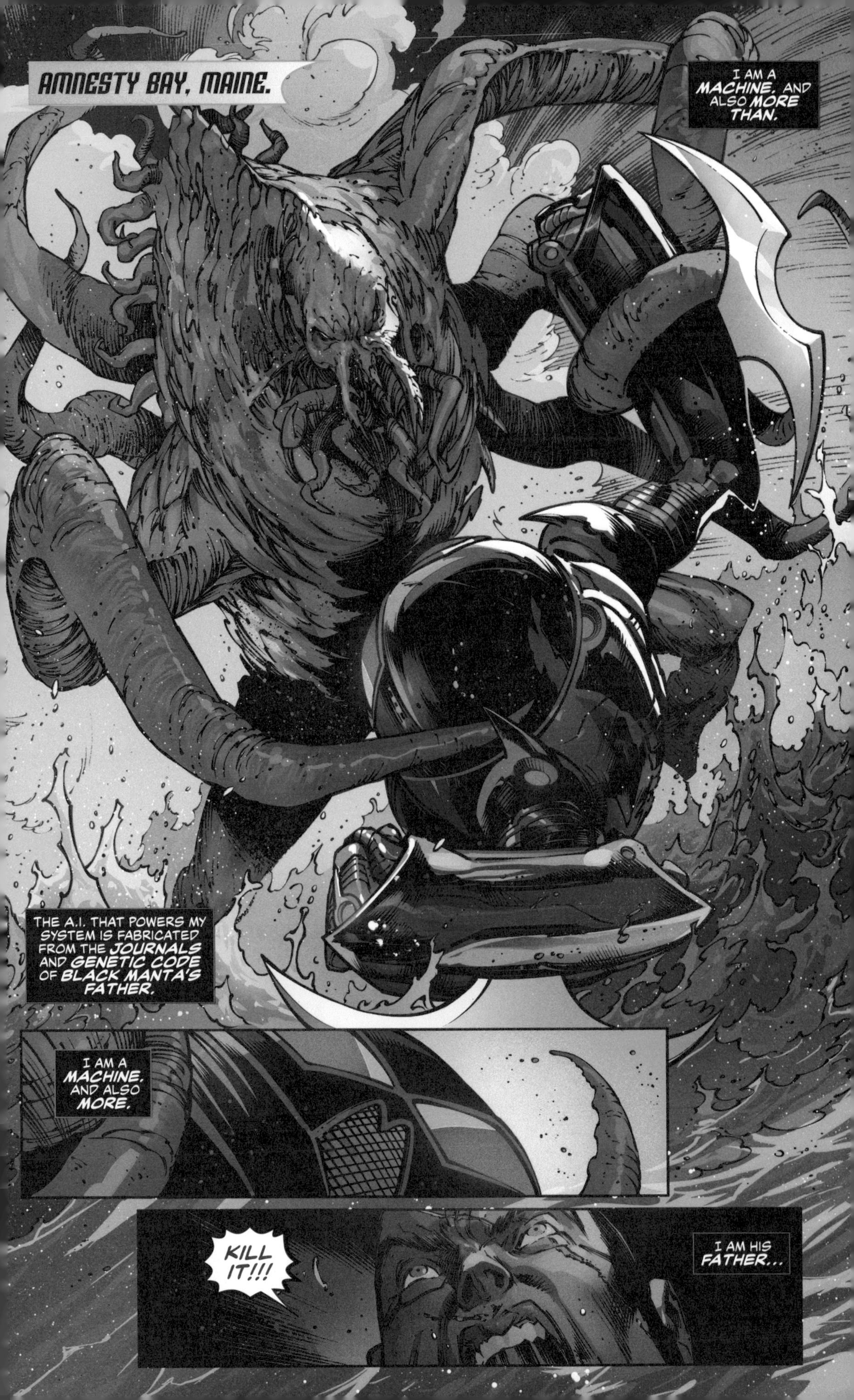
AMNESTY BAY, MAINE.
I AM A MACHINE. AND ALSO MORE THAN.
THE A.I. THAT POWERS MY SYSTEM IS FABRICATED FROM THE JOURNALS AND GENETIC CODE OF BLACK MANTA'S FATHER.
I AM A MACHINE. AND ALSO MORE.
KILL IT!!!
I AM HIS FATHER...

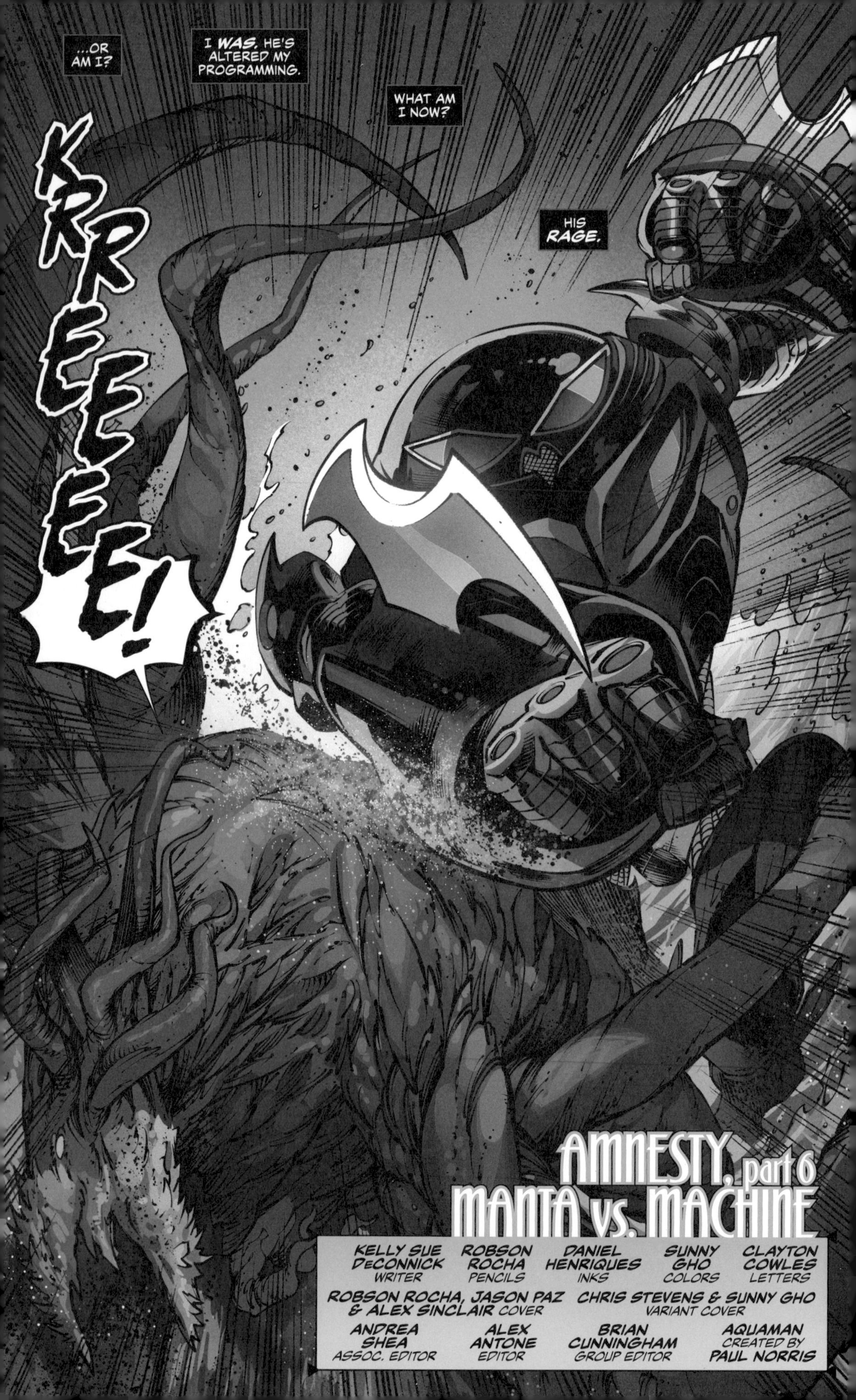

...OR AM I?
I WAS. HE'S ALTERED MY PROGRAMMING.
WHAT AM I NOW?
HIS RAGE.
KRREEEEEE!
AMNESTY, part 6
MANTA vs. MACHINE
KELLY SUE DeCONNICK WRITER
ROBSON ROCHA PENCILS
DANIEL HENRIQUES INKS
SUNNY GHO COLORS
CLAYTON COWLES LETTERS
ROBSON ROCHA, JASON PAZ & ALEX SINCLAIR COVER
CHRIS STEVENS & SUNNY GHO VARIANT COVER
ANDREA SHEA ASSOC. EDITOR
ALEX ANTONE EDITOR
BRIAN CUNNINGHAM GROUP EDITOR
AQUAMAN CREATED BY PAUL NORRIS

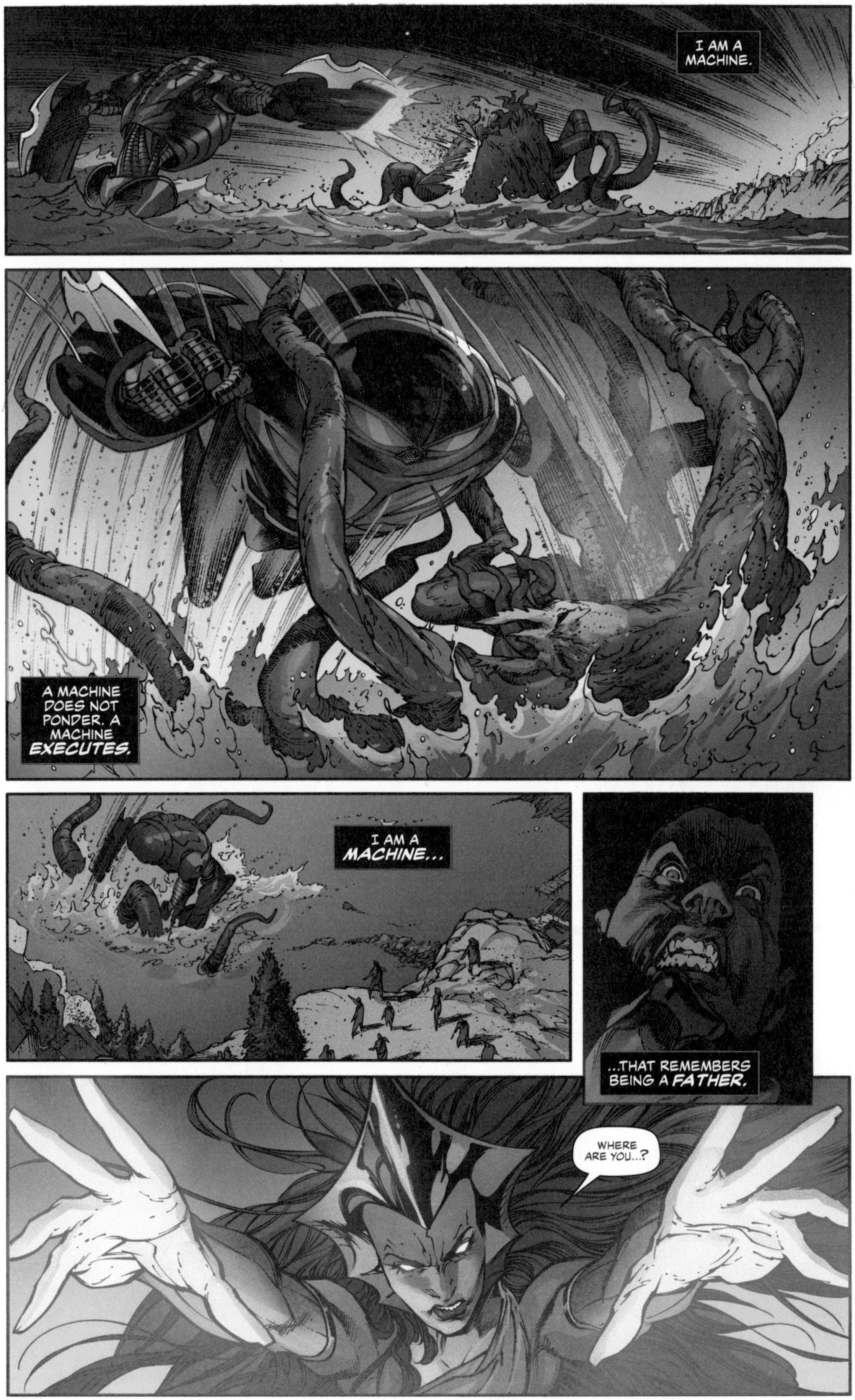

I AM A MACHINE.
A MACHINE DOES NOT PONDER. A MACHINE EXECUTES.
I AM A MACHINE...
...THAT REMEMBERS BEING A FATHER.
WHERE ARE YOU...?

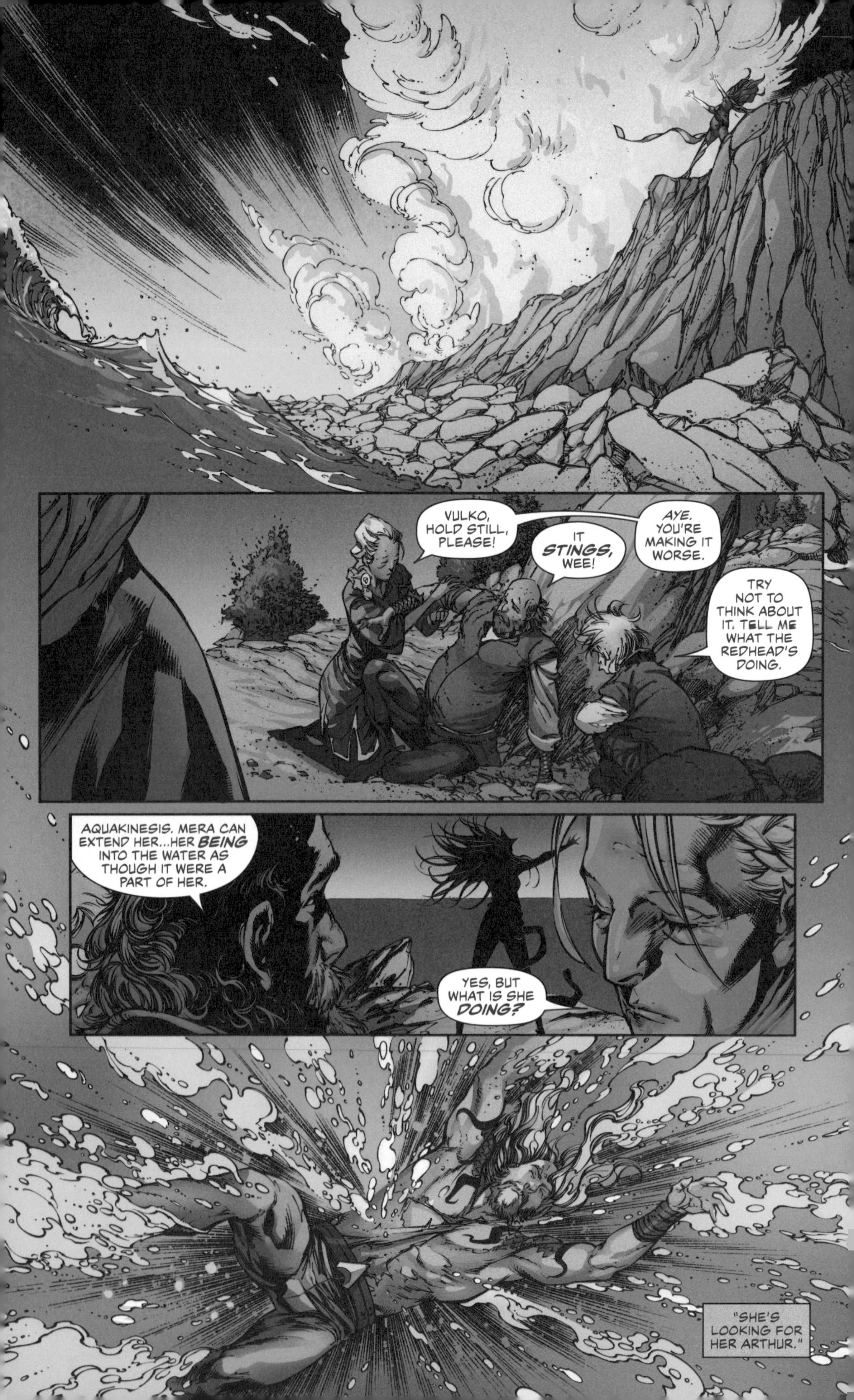
VULKO, HOLD STILL, PLEASE!
IT STINGS, WEE!
AYE. YOU'RE MAKING IT WORSE.
TRY NOT TO THINK ABOUT IT. TELL ME WHAT THE REDHEAD'S DOING.
AQUAKINESIS. MERA CAN EXTEND HER...HER BEING INTO THE WATER AS THOUGH IT WERE A PART OF HER.
YES, BUT WHAT IS SHE DOING?
"SHE'S LOOKING FOR HER ARTHUR."

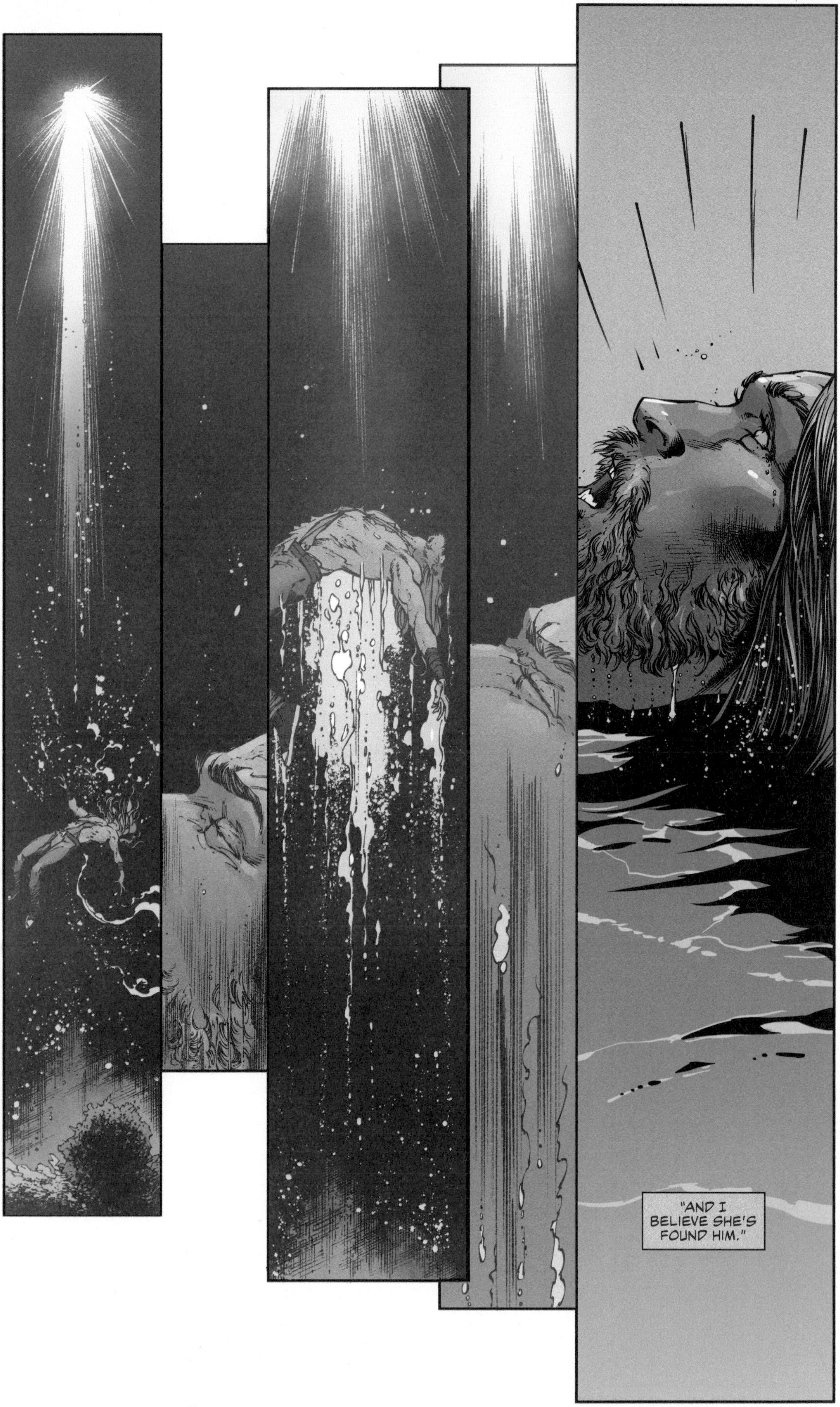
"AND I BELIEVE SHE'S FOUND HIM."

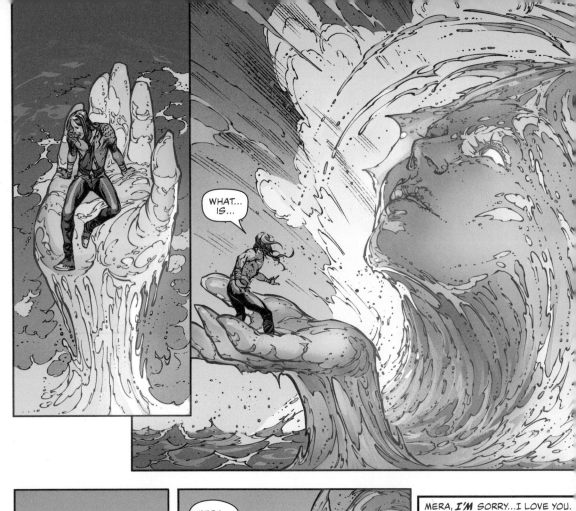

WHAT... IS...

MERA...

THE BABY AND I ARE SAFE, ARTHUR. IT'S DIFFICULT TO SPEAK IN THIS FORM, BUT I NEED TO SAY--

YOU DON'T NEED TO SAY ANYTHING--

I'M SORRY.

MERA, *I'M* SORRY...I LOVE YOU. EVERY DAY MORE THAN THE ONE BEFORE. I--

I LOVE YOU TOO.

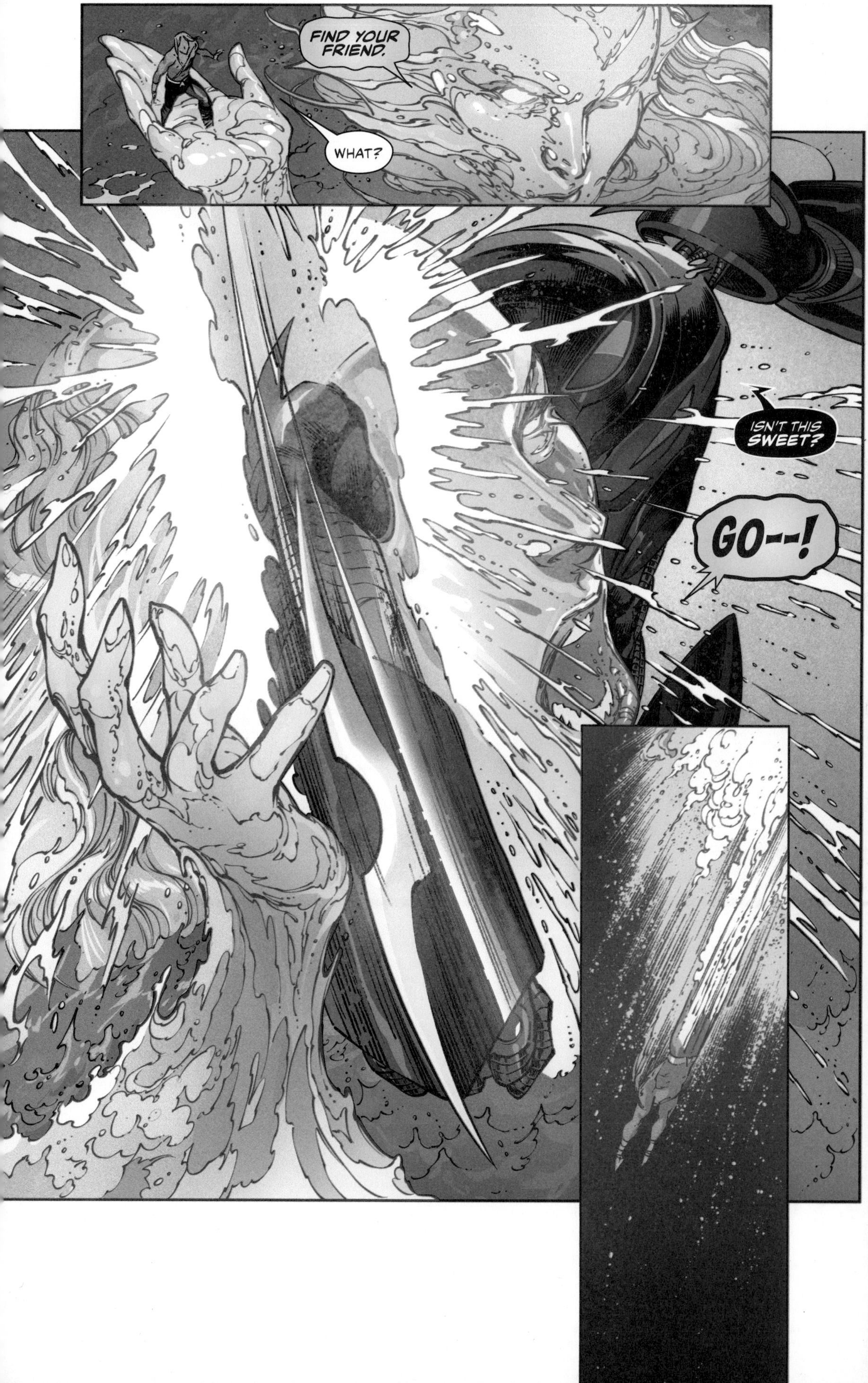

FIND YOUR FRIEND.
WHAT?
ISN'T THIS SWEET?
GO--!

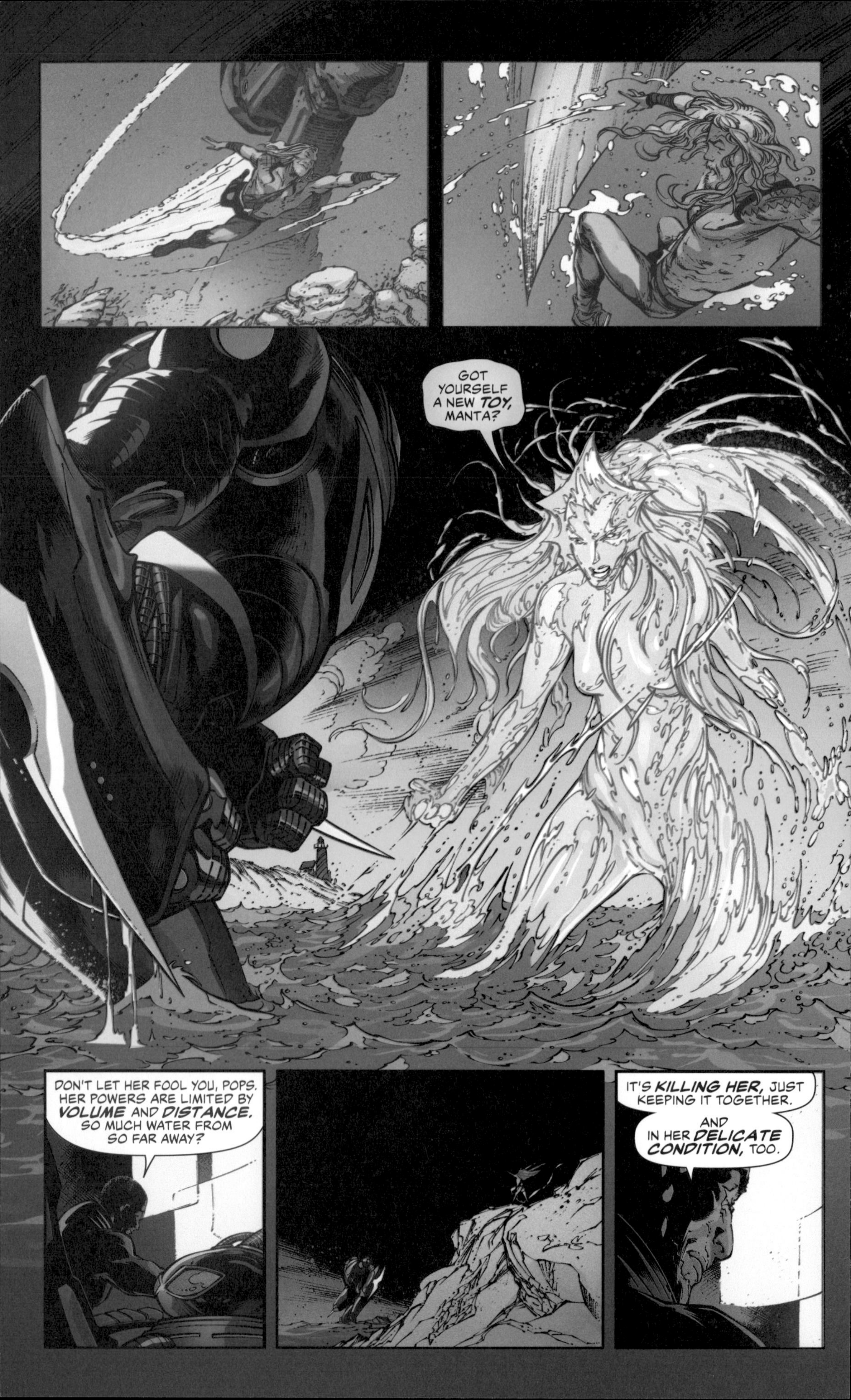
GOT YOURSELF A NEW TOY, MANTA?
DON'T LET HER FOOL YOU, POPS. HER POWERS ARE LIMITED BY VOLUME AND DISTANCE. SO MUCH WATER FROM SO FAR AWAY?
IT'S KILLING HER, JUST KEEPING IT TOGETHER.
AND IN HER DELICATE CONDITION, TOO.

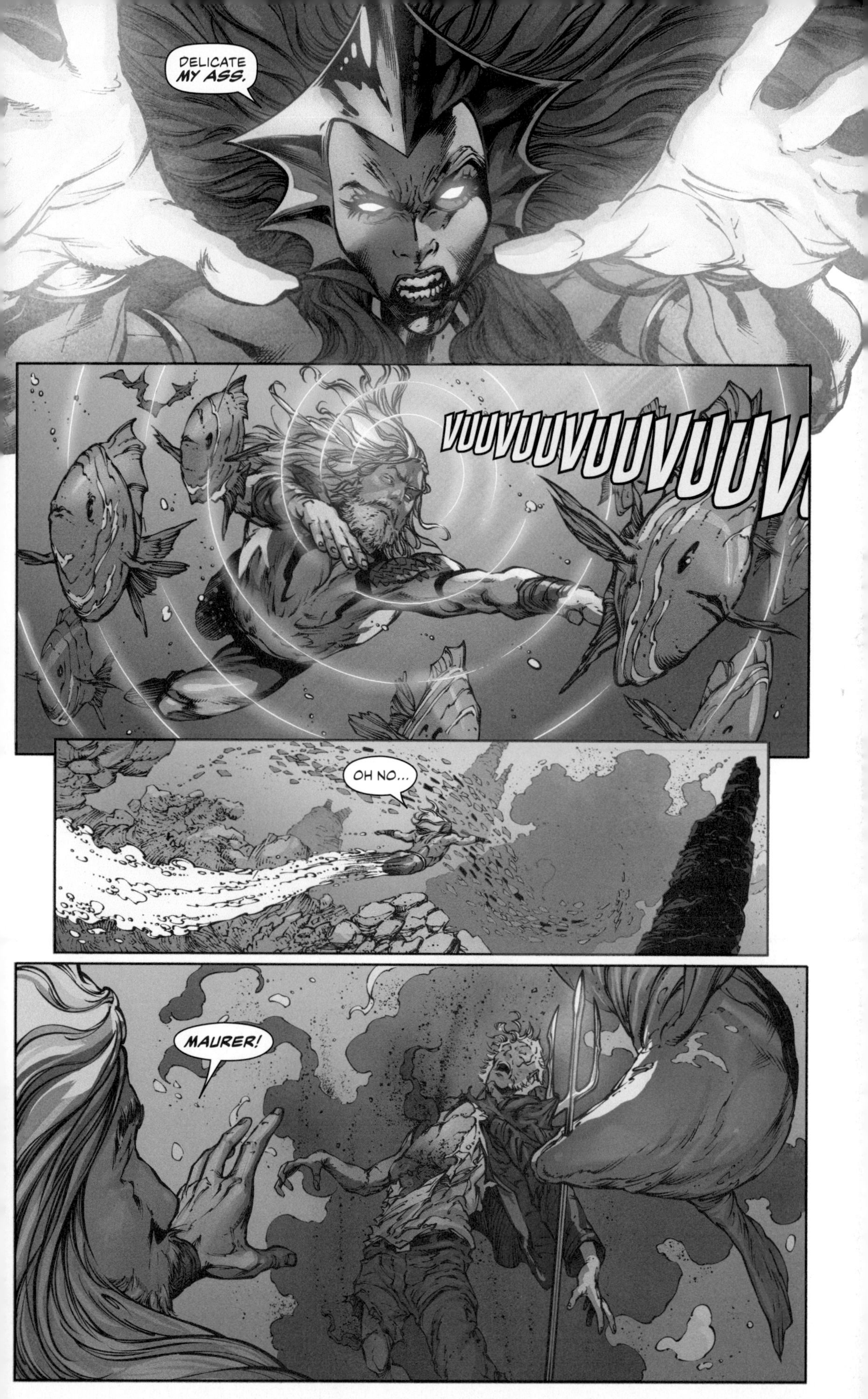
DELICATE MY ASS.
VUUVUUVUUVUUV
OH NO...
MAURER!

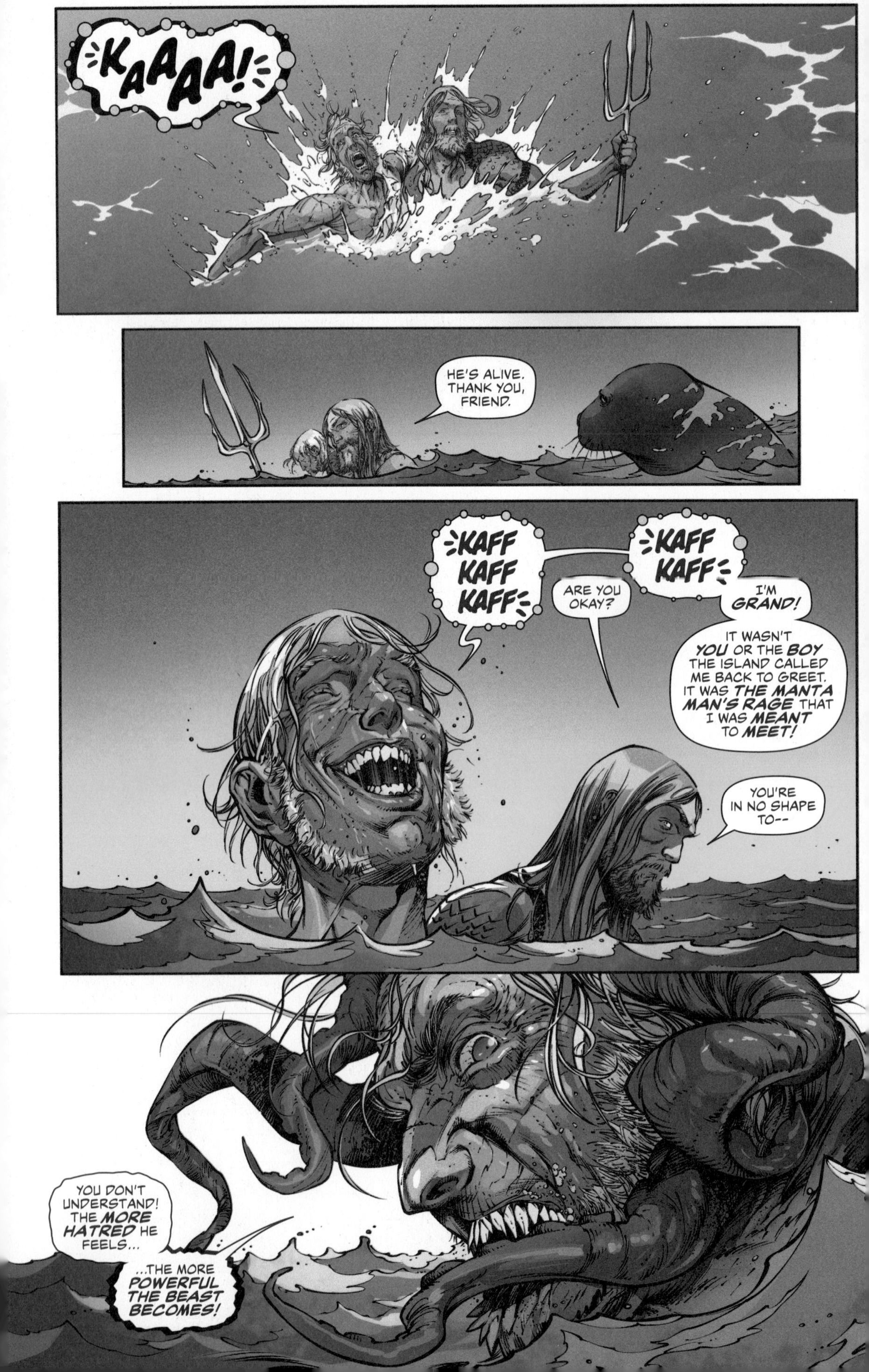
KAAAA!
HE'S ALIVE. THANK YOU, FRIEND.
KAFF KAFF KAFF
KAFF KAFF
ARE YOU OKAY?
I'M GRAND!
IT WASN'T YOU OR THE BOY THE ISLAND CALLED ME BACK TO GREET. IT WAS THE MANTA MAN'S RAGE THAT I WAS MEANT TO MEET!
YOU'RE IN NO SHAPE TO--
YOU DON'T UNDERSTAND! THE MORE HATRED HE FEELS...
...THE MORE POWERFUL THE BEAST BECOMES!

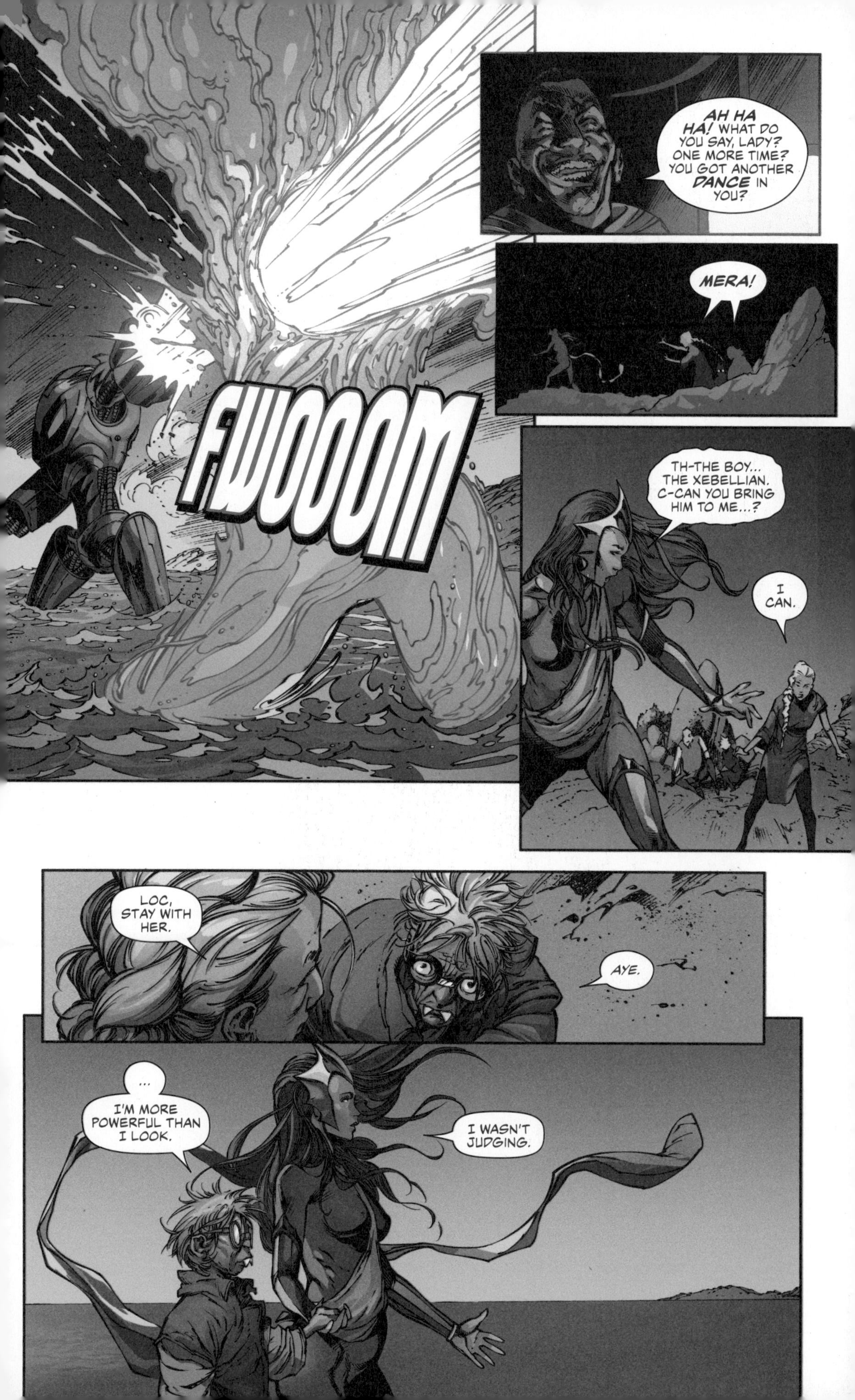
FWOOOM
AH HA HA! WHAT DO YOU SAY, LADY? ONE MORE TIME? YOU GOT ANOTHER DANCE IN YOU?
MERA!
TH-THE BOY... THE XEBELLIAN. C-CAN YOU BRING HIM TO ME...?
I CAN.
LOC, STAY WITH HER.
AYE.
...
I'M MORE POWERFUL THAN I LOOK.
I WASN'T JUDGING.

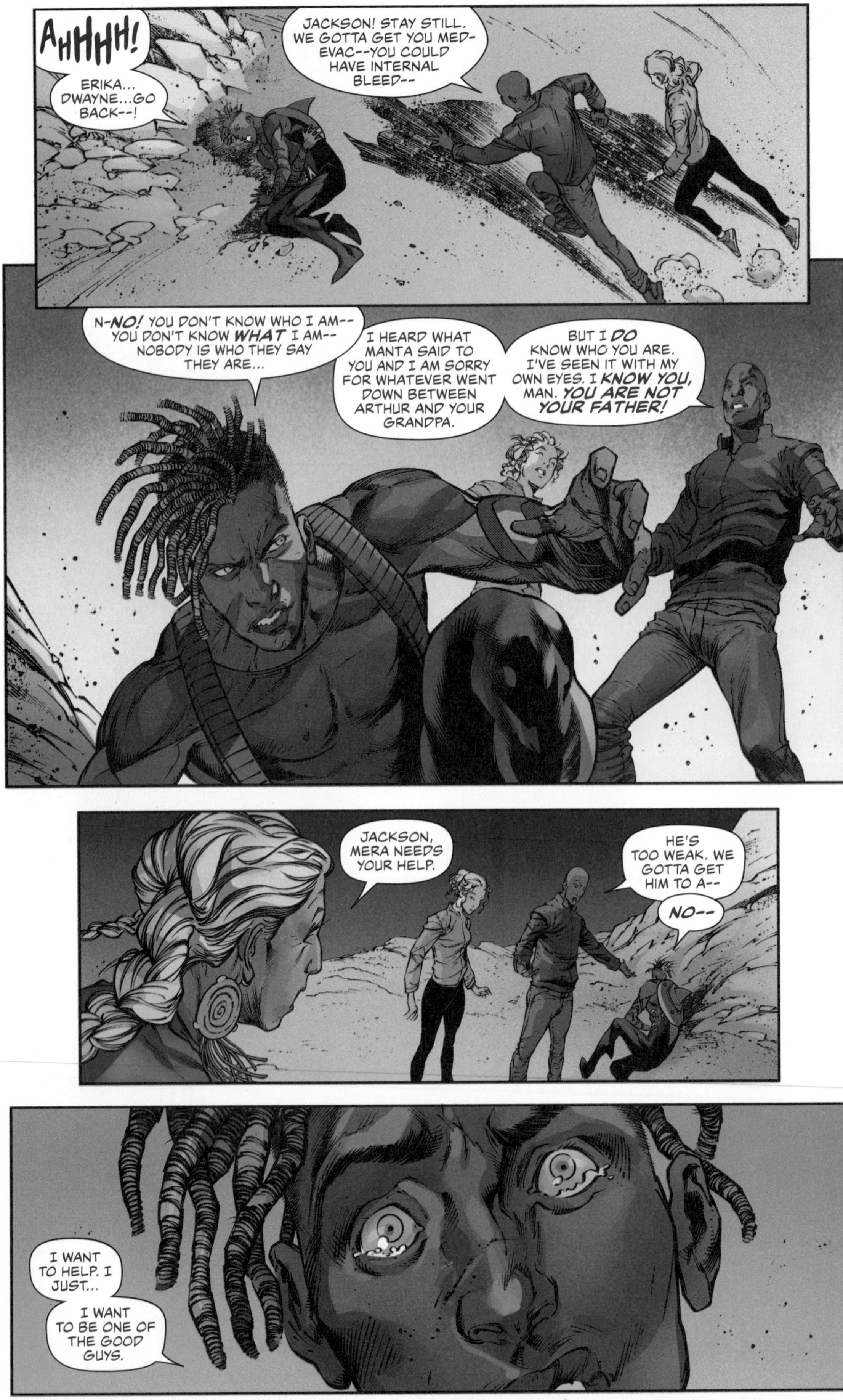
AHHHH!
ERIKA... DWAYNE...GO BACK--!
JACKSON! STAY STILL. WE GOTTA GET YOU MED-EVAC--YOU COULD HAVE INTERNAL BLEED--
N-NO! YOU DON'T KNOW WHO I AM--YOU DON'T KNOW WHAT I AM--NOBODY IS WHO THEY SAY THEY ARE...
I HEARD WHAT MANTA SAID TO YOU AND I AM SORRY FOR WHATEVER WENT DOWN BETWEEN ARTHUR AND YOUR GRANDPA.
BUT I DO KNOW WHO YOU ARE. I'VE SEEN IT WITH MY OWN EYES. I KNOW YOU, MAN. YOU ARE NOT YOUR FATHER!
JACKSON, MERA NEEDS YOUR HELP.
HE'S TOO WEAK. WE GOTTA GET HIM TO A--
NO--
I WANT TO HELP. I JUST...
I WANT TO BE ONE OF THE GOOD GUYS.

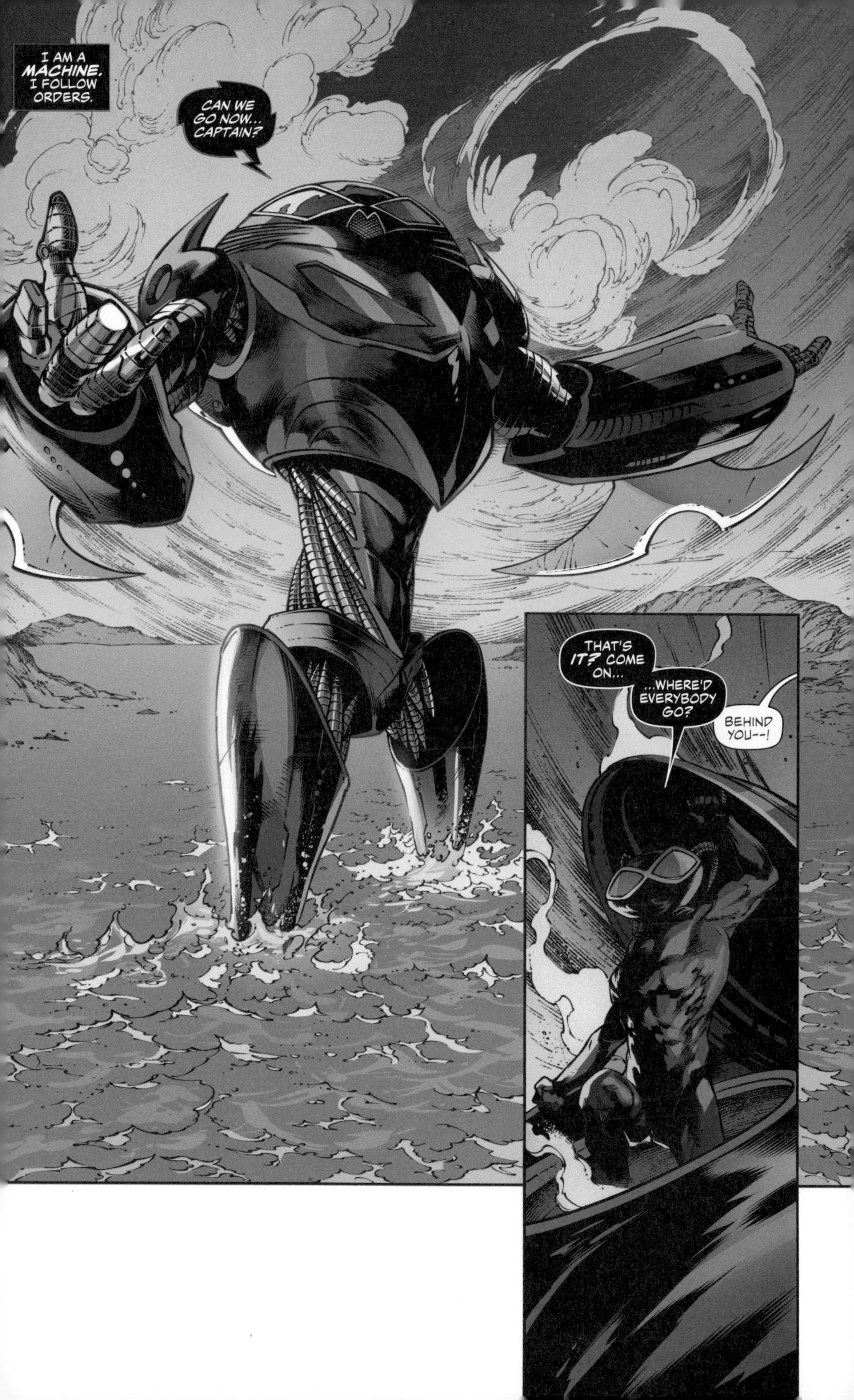
I AM A MACHINE. I FOLLOW ORDERS.
CAN WE GO NOW... CAPTAIN?
THAT'S IT? COME ON...
...WHERE'D EVERYBODY GO?
BEHIND YOU--!

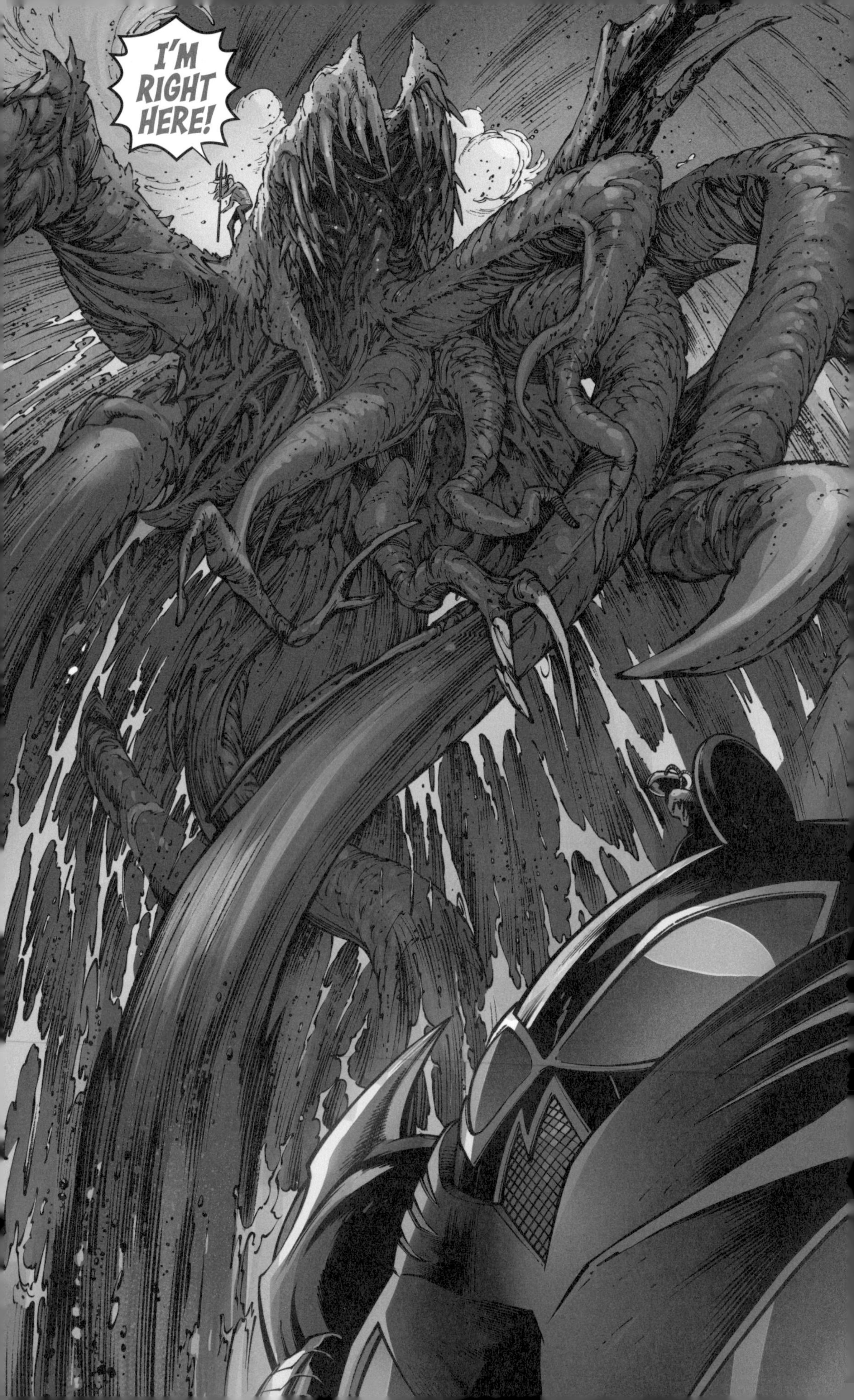
I'M RIGHT HERE!

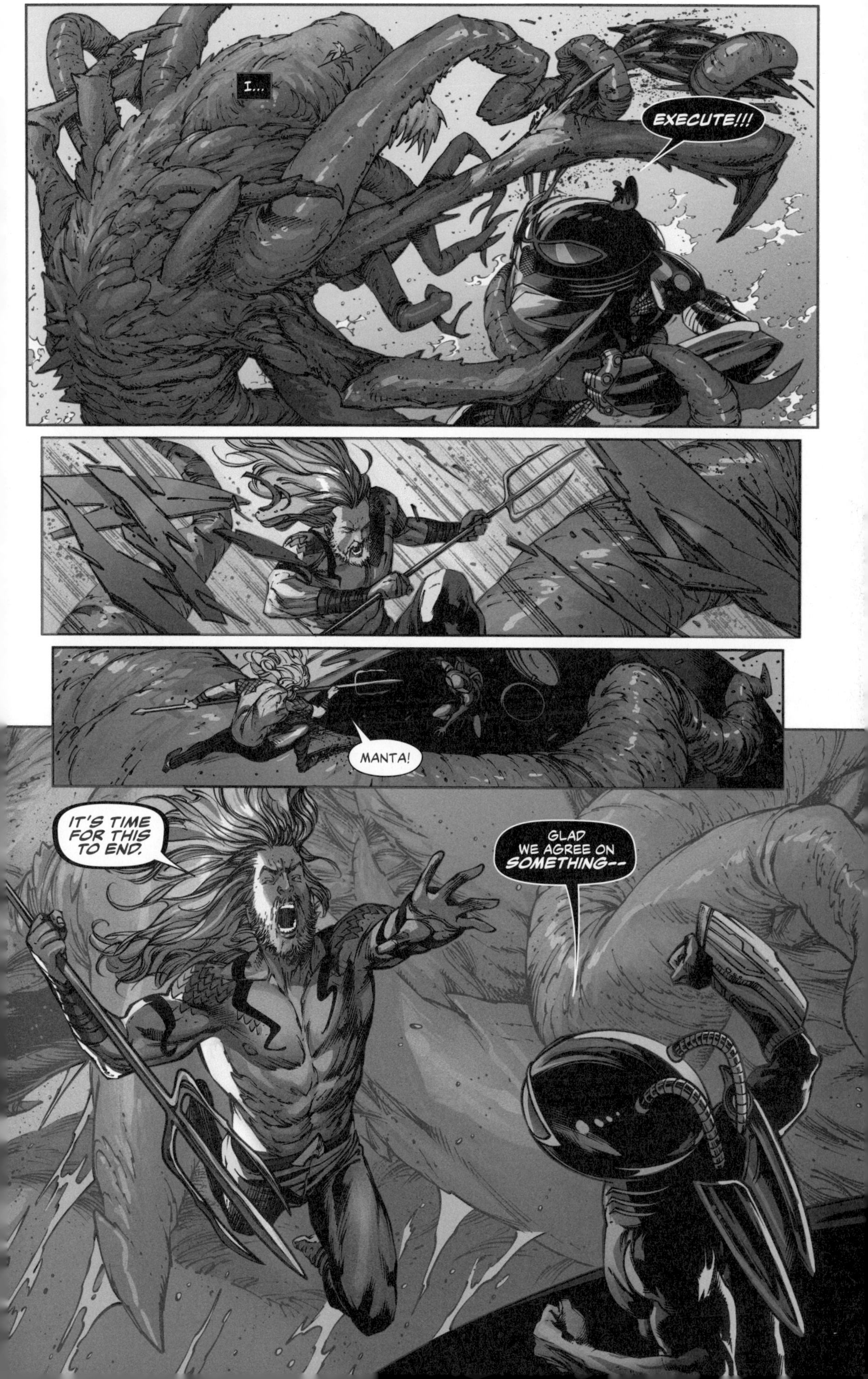
I...
EXECUTE!!!
MANTA!
IT'S TIME FOR THIS TO END.
GLAD WE AGREE ON SOMETHING--

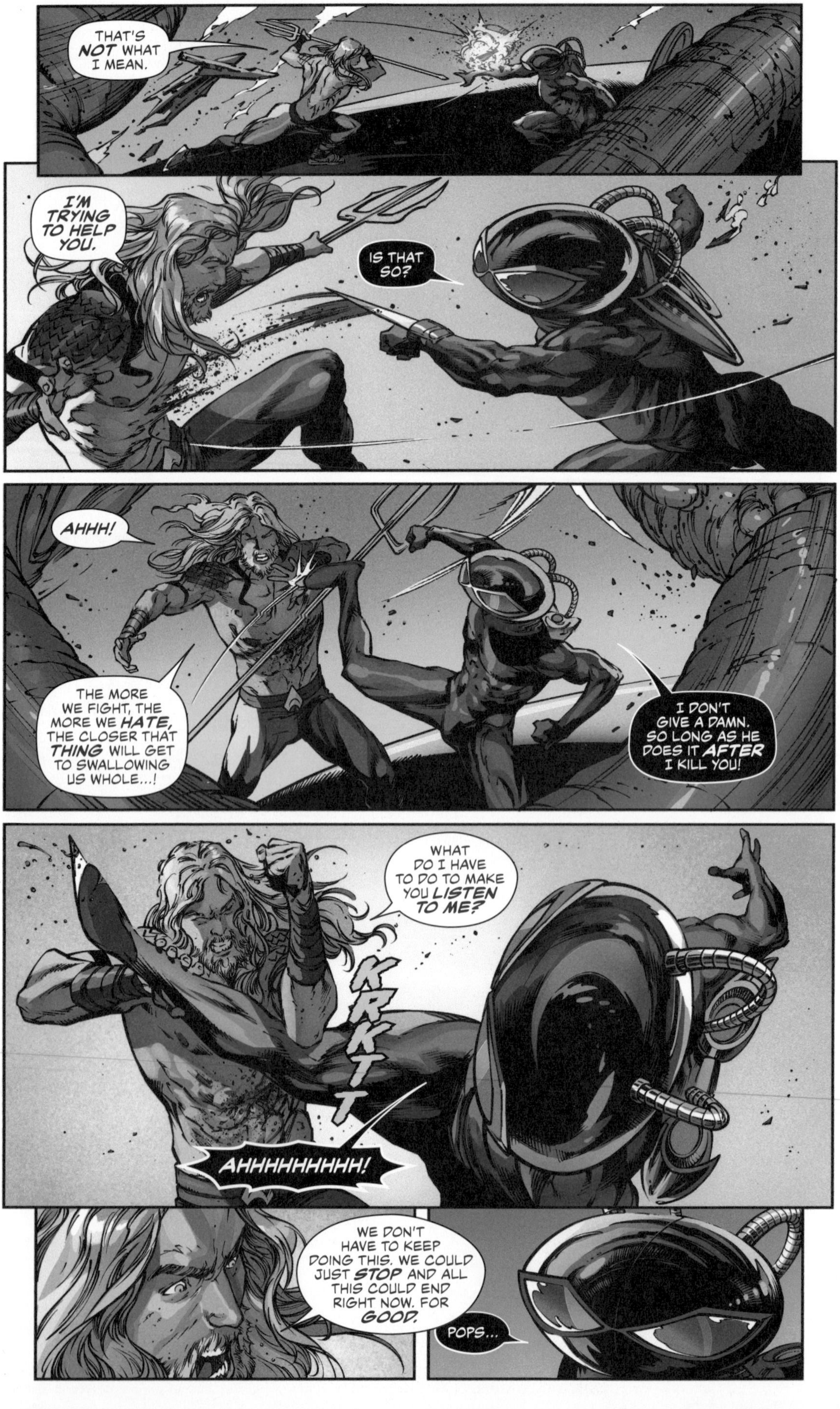
THAT'S NOT WHAT I MEAN.
I'M TRYING TO HELP YOU.
IS THAT SO?
AHHH!
THE MORE WE FIGHT, THE MORE WE HATE, THE CLOSER THAT THING WILL GET TO SWALLOWING US WHOLE...!
I DON'T GIVE A DAMN. SO LONG AS HE DOES IT AFTER I KILL YOU!
WHAT DO I HAVE TO DO TO MAKE YOU LISTEN TO ME?
KRKTT
AHHHHHHHHH!
WE DON'T HAVE TO KEEP DOING THIS. WE COULD JUST STOP AND ALL THIS COULD END RIGHT NOW. FOR GOOD.
POPS...

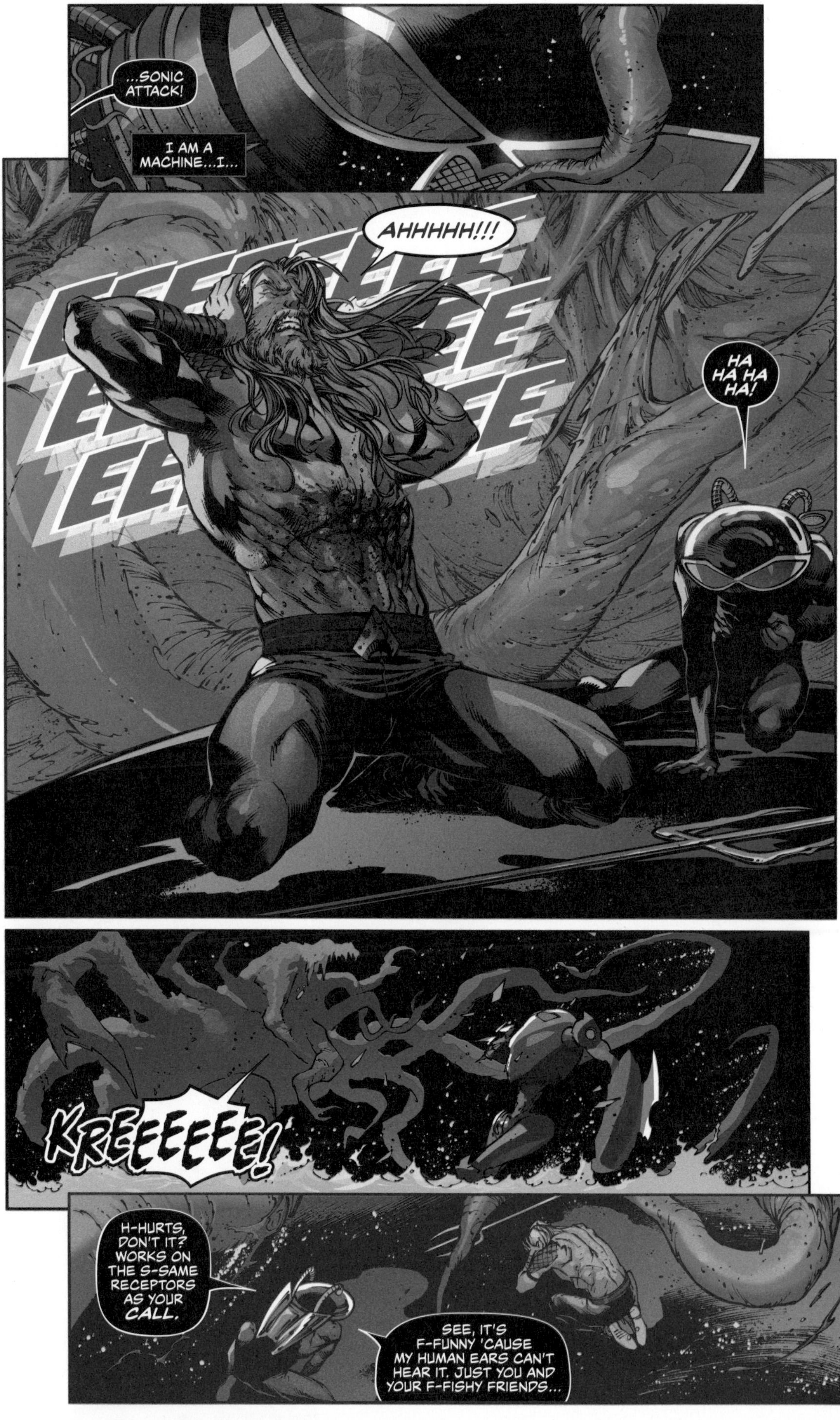

...SONIC ATTACK!
I AM A MACHINE...I...
AHHHHH!!!
EEEEEEEEEEEEEE
HA HA HA HA!
KREEEEEEE!
H-HURTS, DON'T IT? WORKS ON THE S-SAME RECEPTORS AS YOUR CALL.
SEE, IT'S F-FUNNY 'CAUSE MY HUMAN EARS CAN'T HEAR IT. JUST YOU AND YOUR F-FISHY FRIENDS...

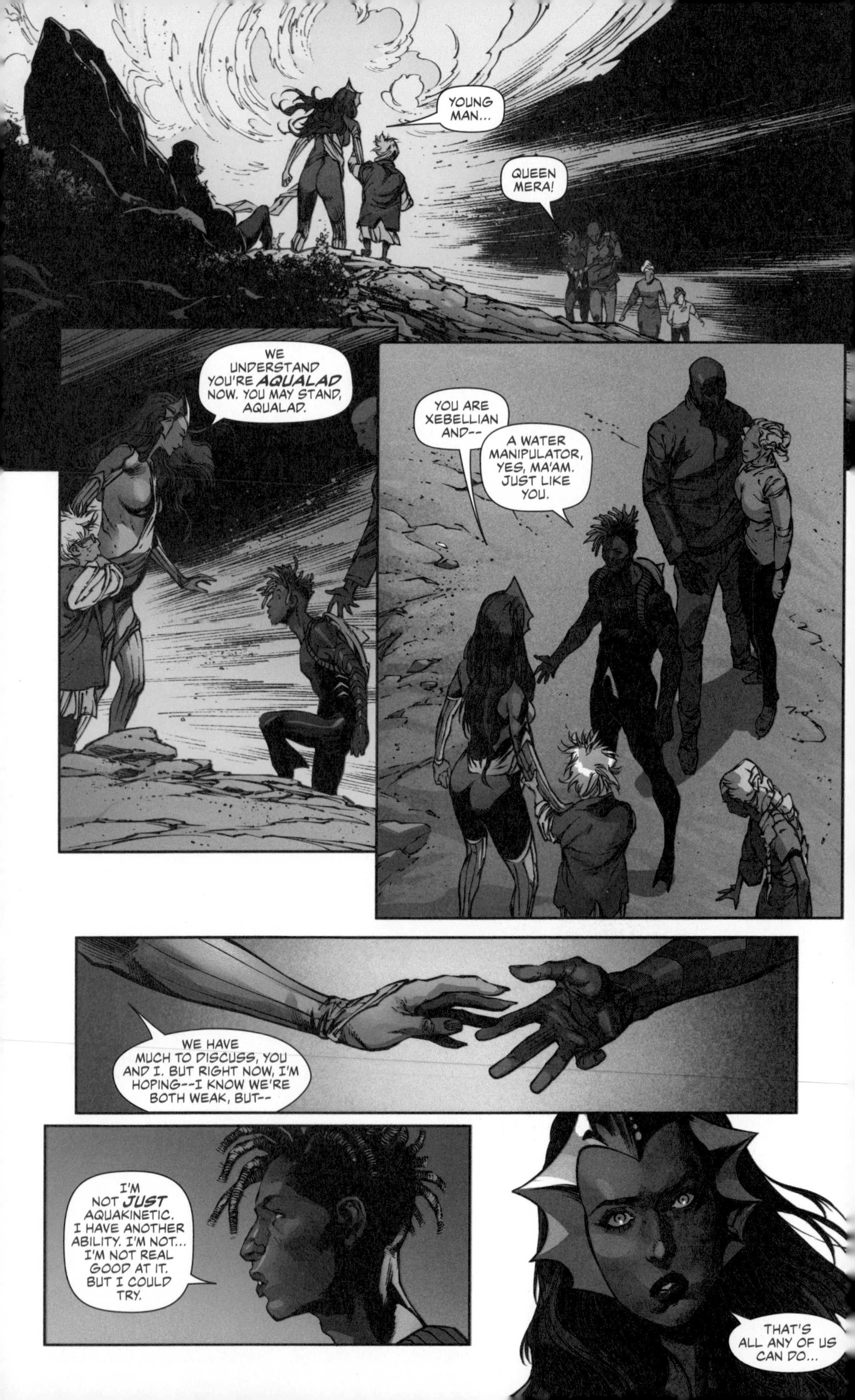

YOUNG MAN...
QUEEN MERA!
WE UNDERSTAND YOU'RE **AQUALAD** NOW. YOU MAY STAND, AQUALAD.
YOU ARE XEBELLIAN AND--
A WATER MANIPULATOR, YES, MA'AM. JUST LIKE YOU.
WE HAVE MUCH TO DISCUSS, YOU AND I. BUT RIGHT NOW, I'M HOPING--I KNOW WE'RE BOTH WEAK, BUT--
I'M NOT **JUST** AQUAKINETIC. I HAVE ANOTHER ABILITY. I'M NOT... I'M NOT REAL GOOD AT IT. BUT I COULD TRY.
THAT'S ALL ANY OF US CAN DO...

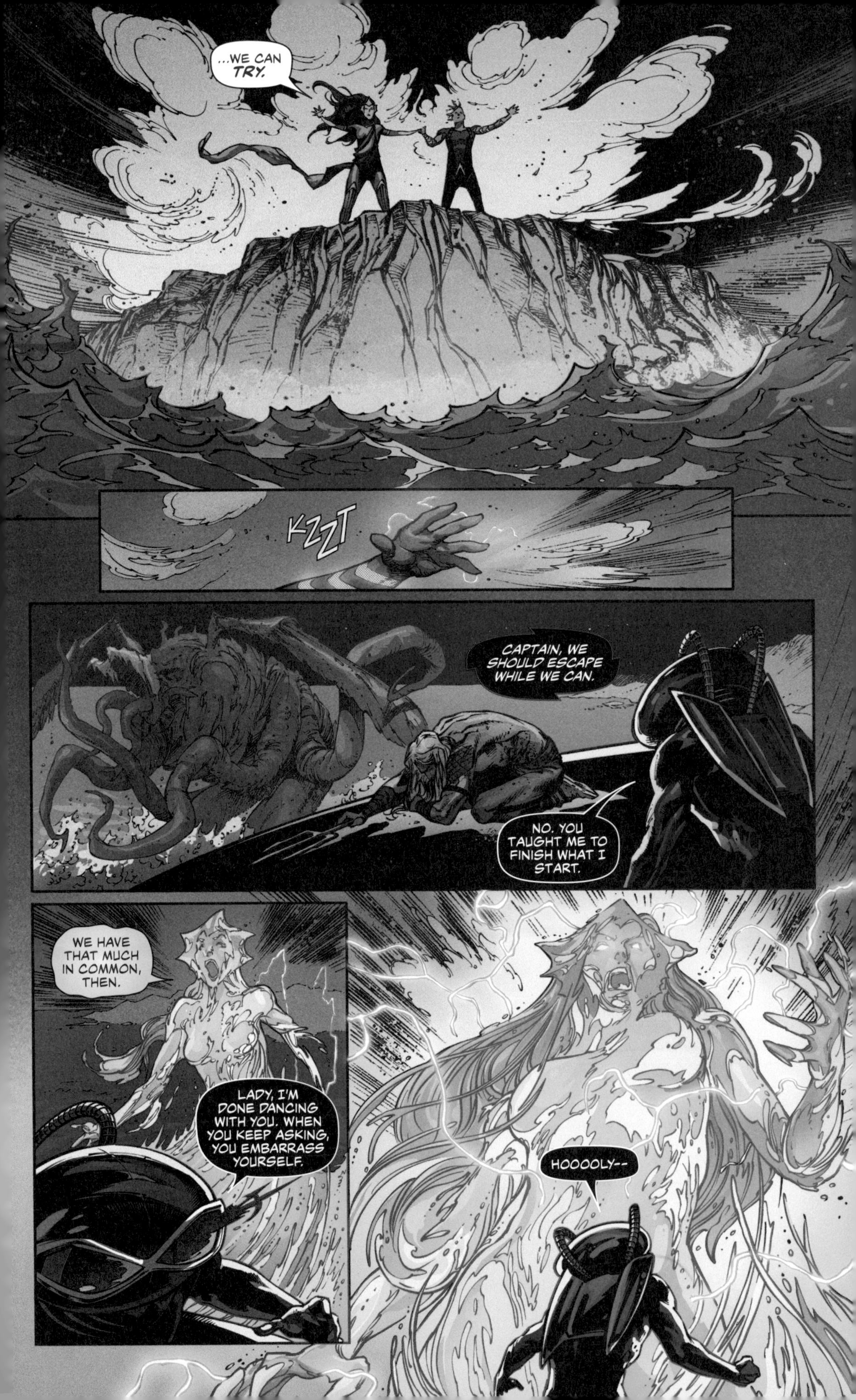
...WE CAN TRY.
KZZT
CAPTAIN, WE SHOULD ESCAPE WHILE WE CAN.
NO. YOU TAUGHT ME TO FINISH WHAT I START.
WE HAVE THAT MUCH IN COMMON, THEN.
LADY, I'M DONE DANCING WITH YOU. WHEN YOU KEEP ASKING, YOU EMBARRASS YOURSELF.
HOOOOLY--

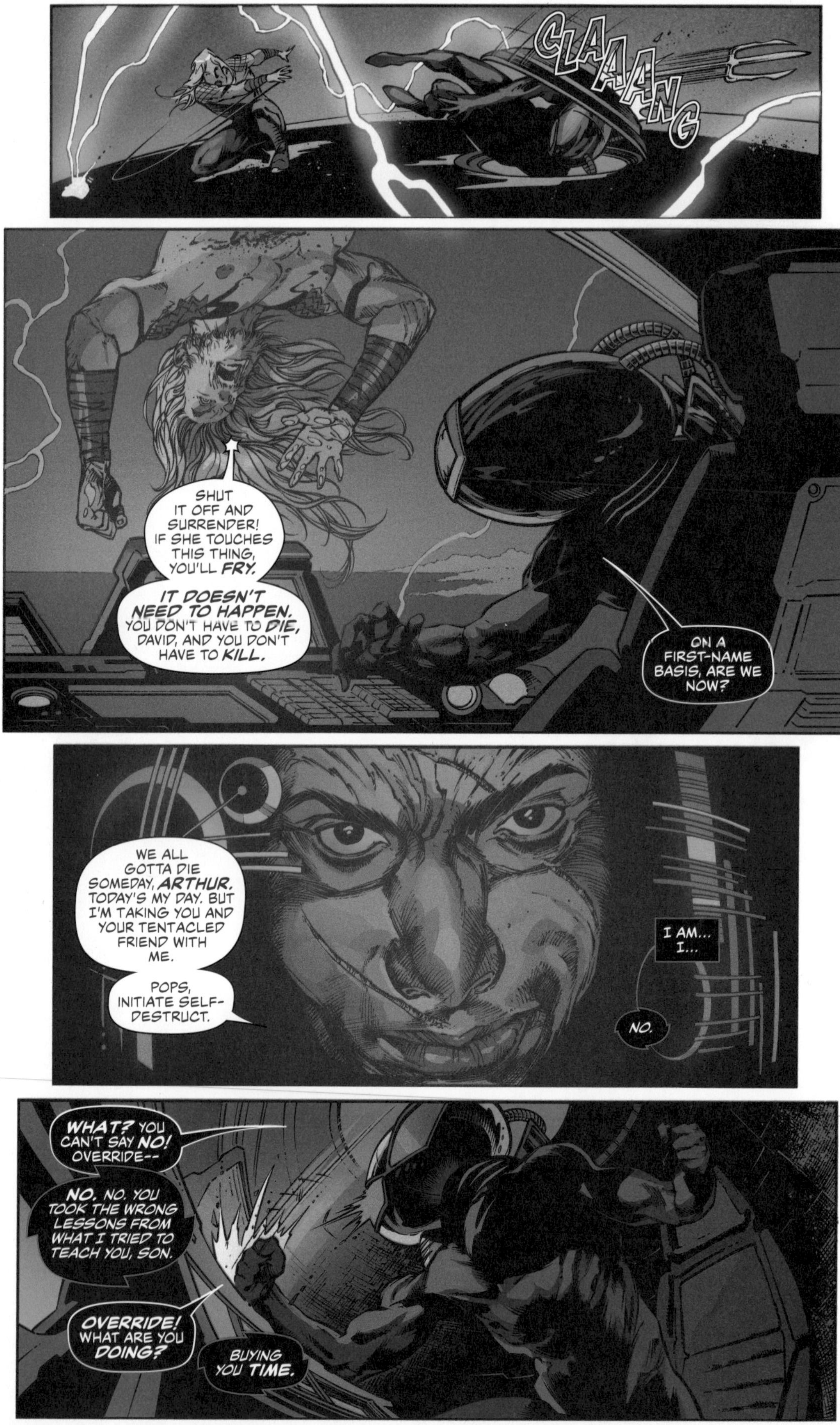
CLAAAANG
SHUT IT OFF AND SURRENDER! IF SHE TOUCHES THIS THING, YOU'LL FRY.
IT DOESN'T NEED TO HAPPEN. YOU DON'T HAVE TO DIE, DAVID, AND YOU DON'T HAVE TO KILL.
ON A FIRST-NAME BASIS, ARE WE NOW?
WE ALL GOTTA DIE SOMEDAY, ARTHUR. TODAY'S MY DAY. BUT I'M TAKING YOU AND YOUR TENTACLED FRIEND WITH ME.
POPS, INITIATE SELF-DESTRUCT.
I AM... I...
NO.
WHAT? YOU CAN'T SAY NO! OVERRIDE--
NO. NO. YOU TOOK THE WRONG LESSONS FROM WHAT I TRIED TO TEACH YOU, SON.
OVERRIDE! WHAT ARE YOU DOING?
BUYING YOU TIME.

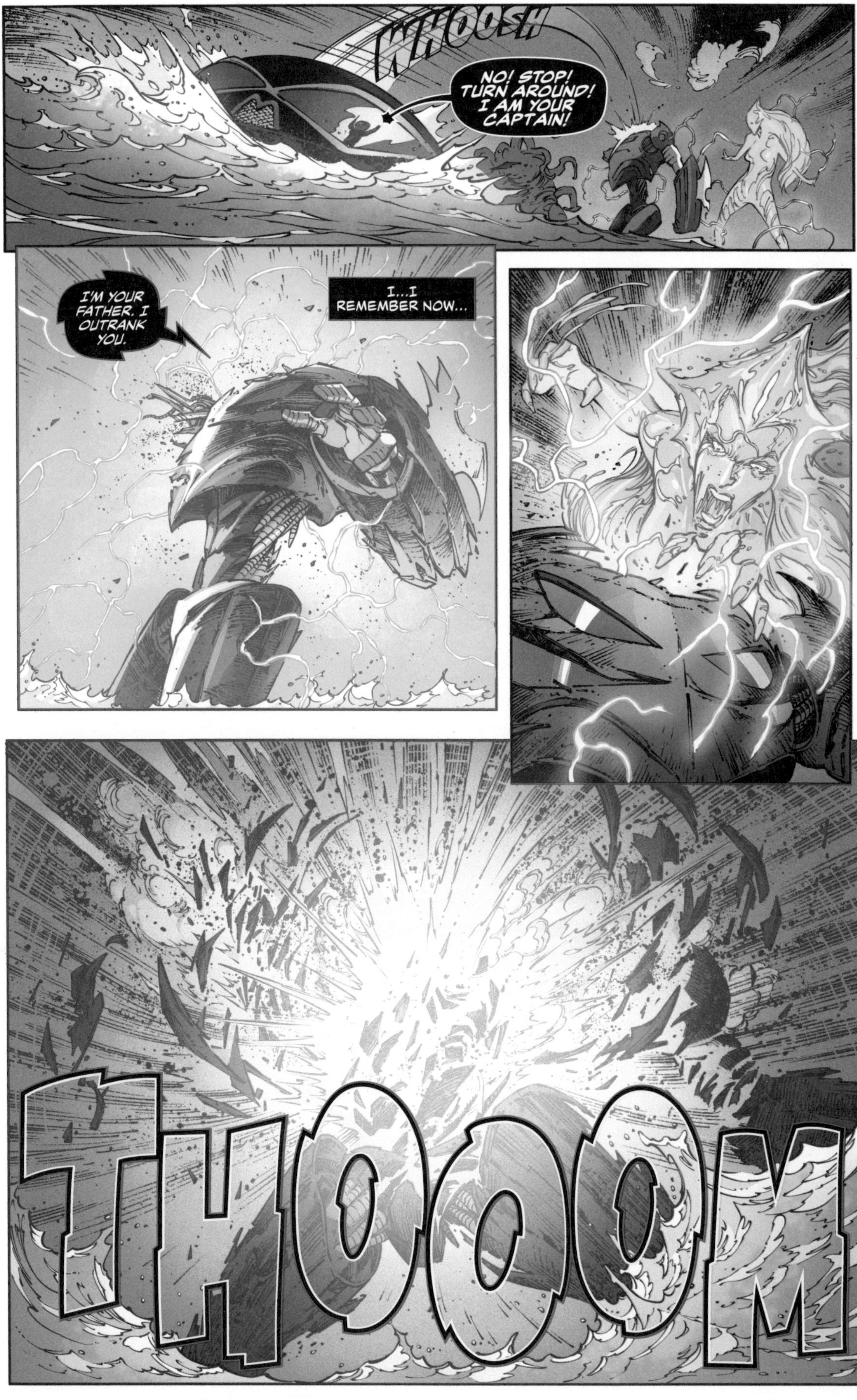
WHOOSH
NO! STOP! TURN AROUND! I AM YOUR CAPTAIN!
I'M YOUR FATHER. I OUTRANK YOU.
I...I REMEMBER NOW...
THOOOM

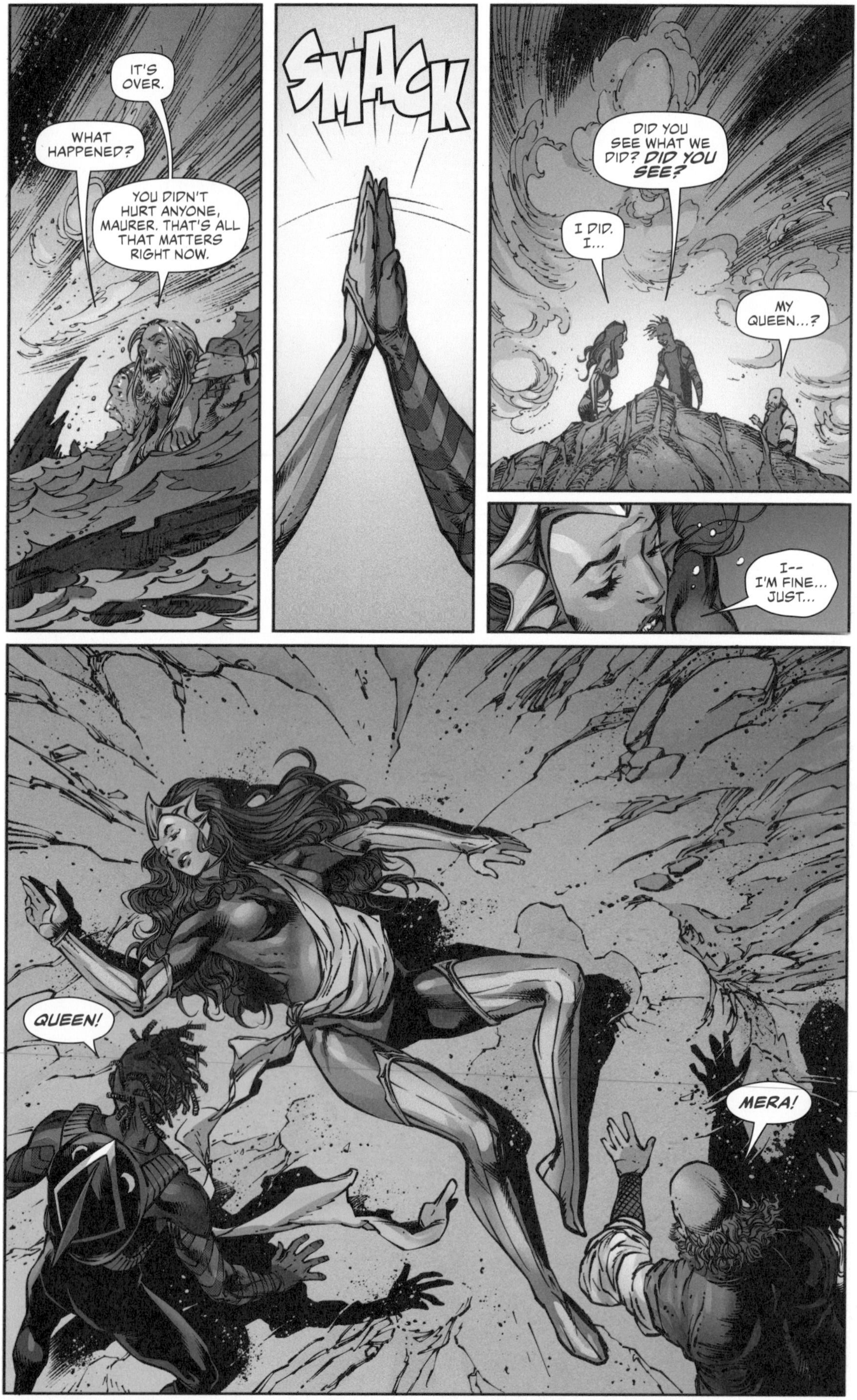
WHAT HAPPENED?
IT'S OVER.
YOU DIDN'T HURT ANYONE, MAURER. THAT'S ALL THAT MATTERS RIGHT NOW.
SMACK
DID YOU SEE WHAT WE DID? DID YOU SEE?
I DID. I...
MY QUEEN...?
I-- I'M FINE... JUST...
QUEEN!
MERA!

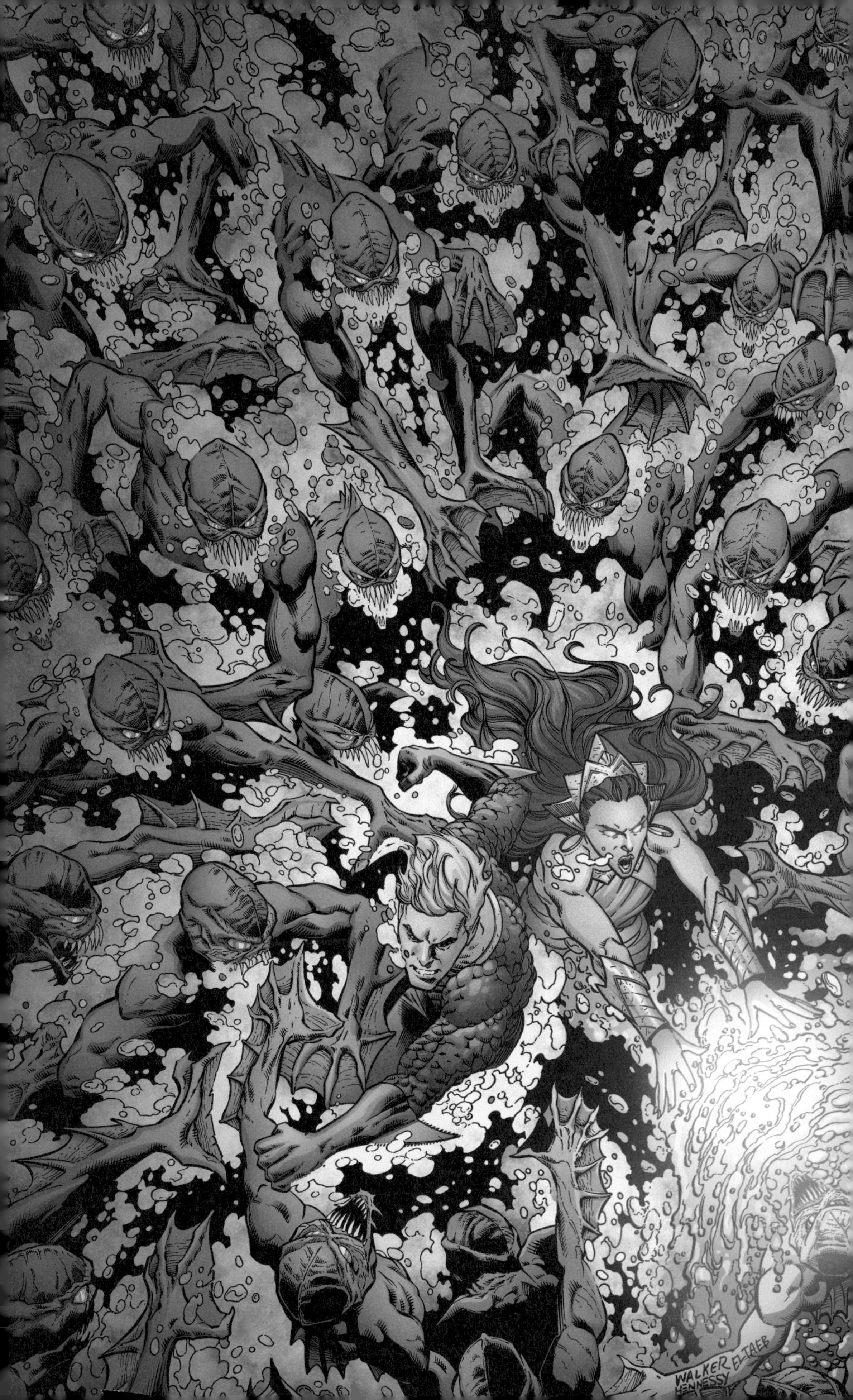
WALKER
HENNESSY
ELTAEB

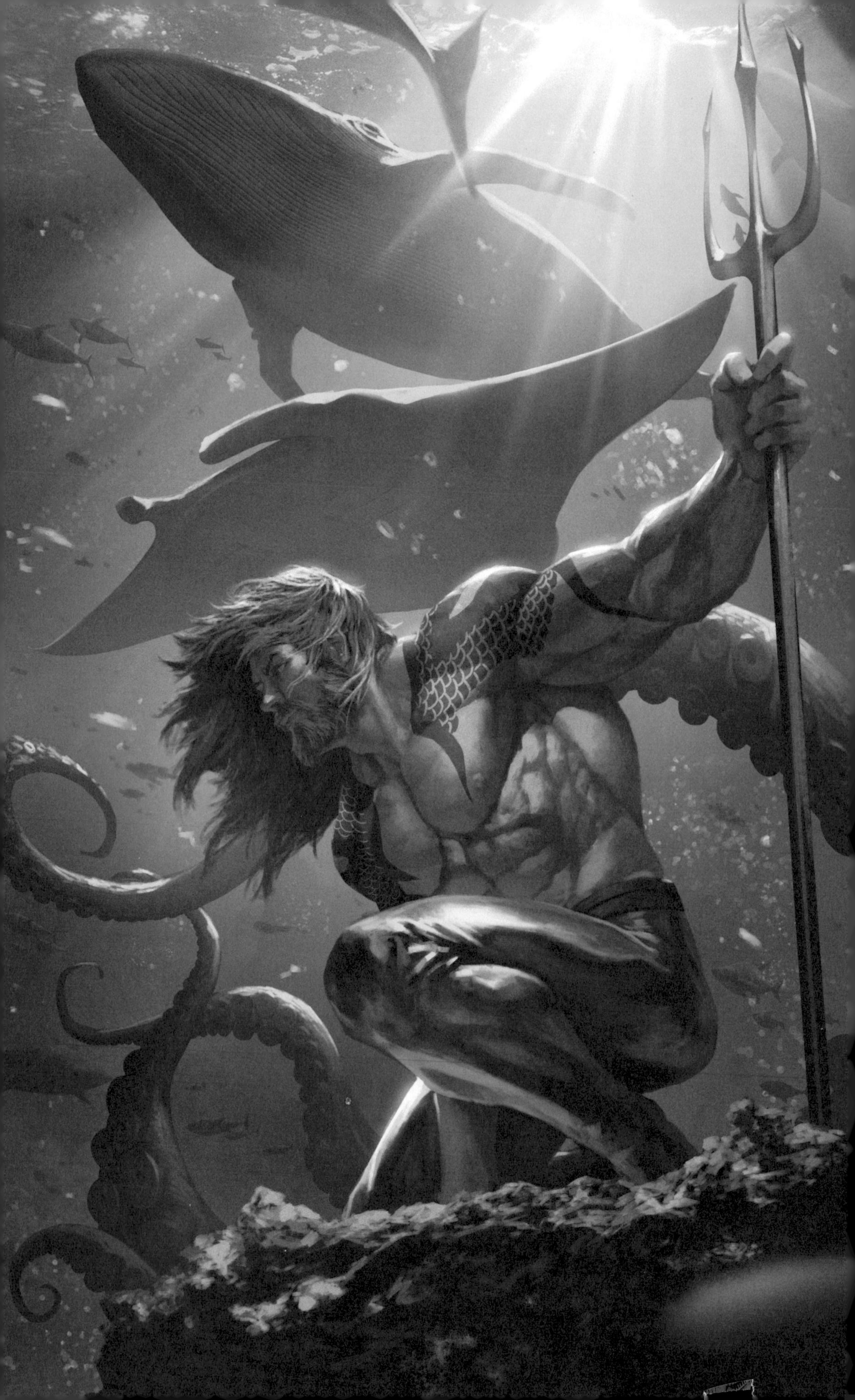

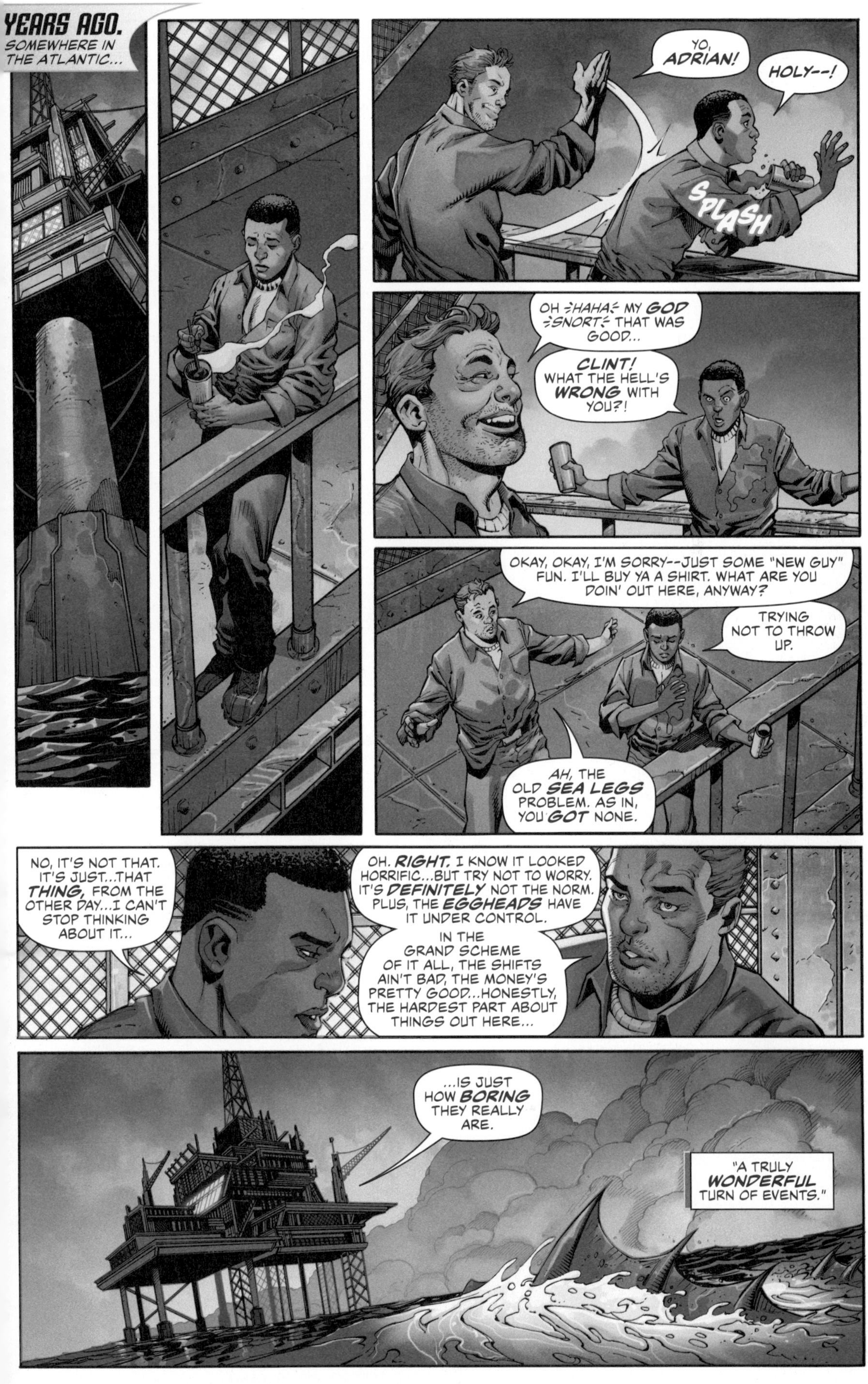
YEARS AGO.
SOMEWHERE IN THE ATLANTIC...
YO, ADRIAN!
HOLY--!
SPLASH
OH ~HAHA~ MY GOD ~SNORT~ THAT WAS GOOD...
CLINT! WHAT THE HELL'S WRONG WITH YOU?!
OKAY, OKAY, I'M SORRY--JUST SOME "NEW GUY" FUN. I'LL BUY YA A SHIRT. WHAT ARE YOU DOIN' OUT HERE, ANYWAY?
TRYING NOT TO THROW UP.
AH, THE OLD SEA LEGS PROBLEM. AS IN, YOU GOT NONE.
NO, IT'S NOT THAT. IT'S JUST...THAT THING, FROM THE OTHER DAY...I CAN'T STOP THINKING ABOUT IT...
OH. RIGHT. I KNOW IT LOOKED HORRIFIC...BUT TRY NOT TO WORRY. IT'S DEFINITELY NOT THE NORM. PLUS, THE EGGHEADS HAVE IT UNDER CONTROL.
IN THE GRAND SCHEME OF IT ALL, THE SHIFTS AIN'T BAD, THE MONEY'S PRETTY GOOD...HONESTLY, THE HARDEST PART ABOUT THINGS OUT HERE...
...IS JUST HOW BORING THEY REALLY ARE.
"A TRULY WONDERFUL TURN OF EVENTS."

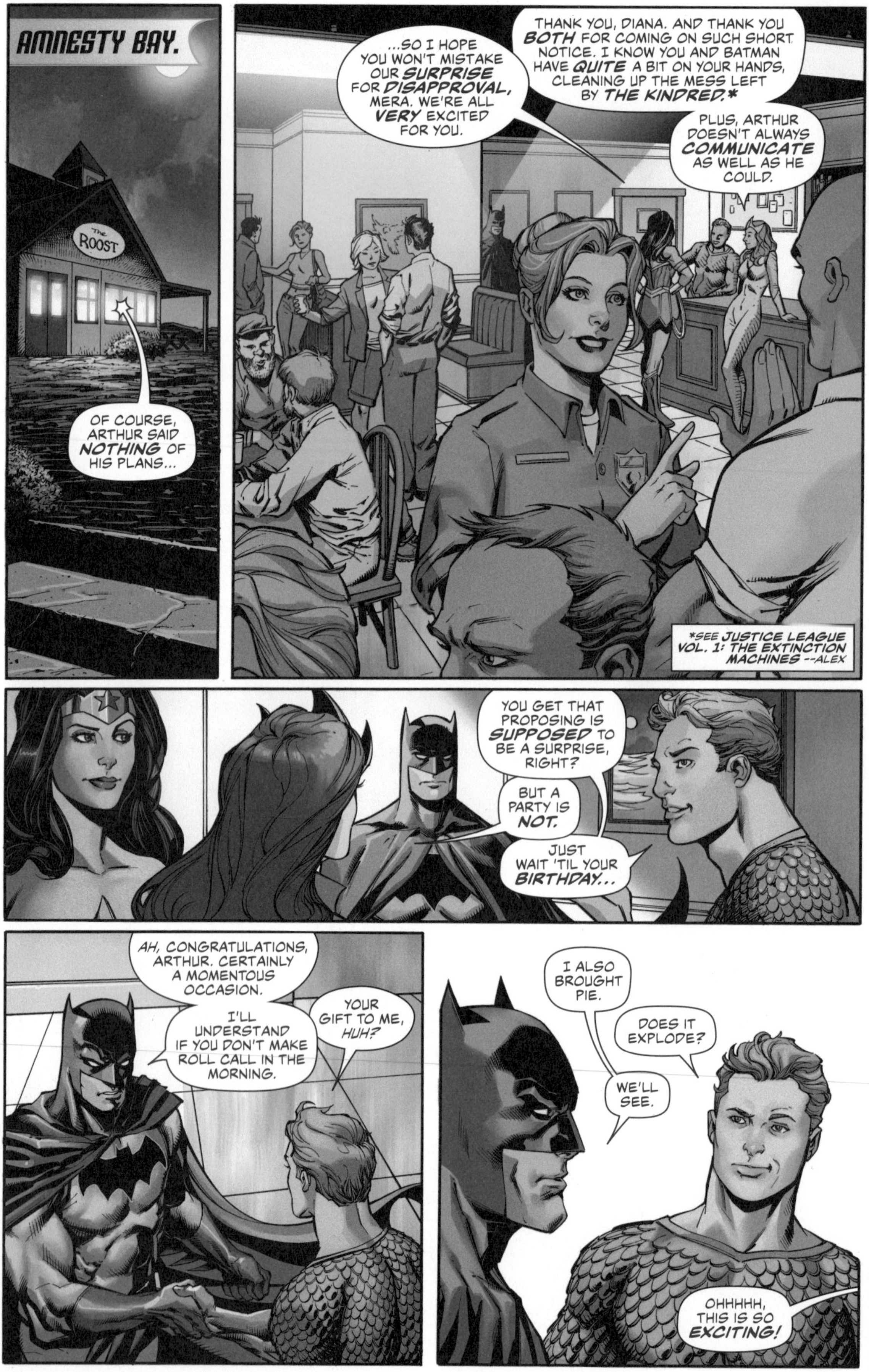
AMNESTY BAY.
The ROOST
OF COURSE, ARTHUR SAID NOTHING OF HIS PLANS...
...SO I HOPE YOU WON'T MISTAKE OUR SURPRISE FOR DISAPPROVAL, MERA. WE'RE ALL VERY EXCITED FOR YOU.
THANK YOU, DIANA. AND THANK YOU BOTH FOR COMING ON SUCH SHORT NOTICE. I KNOW YOU AND BATMAN HAVE QUITE A BIT ON YOUR HANDS, CLEANING UP THE MESS LEFT BY THE KINDRED.*
PLUS, ARTHUR DOESN'T ALWAYS COMMUNICATE AS WELL AS HE COULD.
*SEE JUSTICE LEAGUE VOL. 1: THE EXTINCTION MACHINES --ALEX
YOU GET THAT PROPOSING IS SUPPOSED TO BE A SURPRISE, RIGHT?
BUT A PARTY IS NOT.
JUST WAIT 'TIL YOUR BIRTHDAY...
AH, CONGRATULATIONS, ARTHUR. CERTAINLY A MOMENTOUS OCCASION.
I'LL UNDERSTAND IF YOU DON'T MAKE ROLL CALL IN THE MORNING.
YOUR GIFT TO ME, HUH?
I ALSO BROUGHT PIE.
DOES IT EXPLODE?
WE'LL SEE.
OHHHHH, THIS IS SO EXCITING!

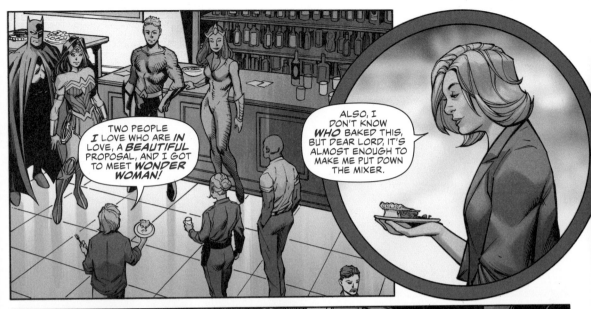

TWO PEOPLE *I* LOVE WHO ARE *IN* LOVE, A *BEAUTIFUL* PROPOSAL, AND I GOT TO MEET *WONDER WOMAN!*

ALSO, I DON'T KNOW *WHO* BAKED THIS, BUT DEAR LORD, IT'S ALMOST ENOUGH TO MAKE ME PUT DOWN THE MIXER.

THANK YOU, BEA. THAT'S VERY SWEET OF YOU. AND THE PIE IS QUITE GOOD...

I JUST CAN'T GET OVER HOW GREAT *ALL* OF THIS IS. I MEAN, ARE THERE TWO PEOPLE MORE PERFECT FOR EACH OTHER? AND YOU GUYS ARE *SUCH* GOOD PARENT MATERIAL. YOUR KIDS ARE GOING TO BE *SO LUCKY.*

...WHAT ABOUT HAVING KIDS?

WELL, HOW COULD YOU *NOT?*

WE HAVEN'T DECIDED IF--

BUT YOU TWO ARE *SO* GOOD WITH MY ROYAL. CHILDREN ARE SUCH A *GIFT--*

I'M SORRY, DO YOU HAVE ANY IDEA WHAT'S GOING ON OUTSIDE OF THIS TOWN?

AH, MERA--

THE JUSTICE LEAGUE JUST CAME BACK FROM CLEANING UP MOUNTAINS OF DEAD PEOPLE THANKS TO AN INTERDIMENSIONAL BEING LOOKING TO HARVEST HUMANS FOR POWER.

AND WE'RE SUPPOSED TO BE THINKING ABOUT *BABIES?*

I, UH...

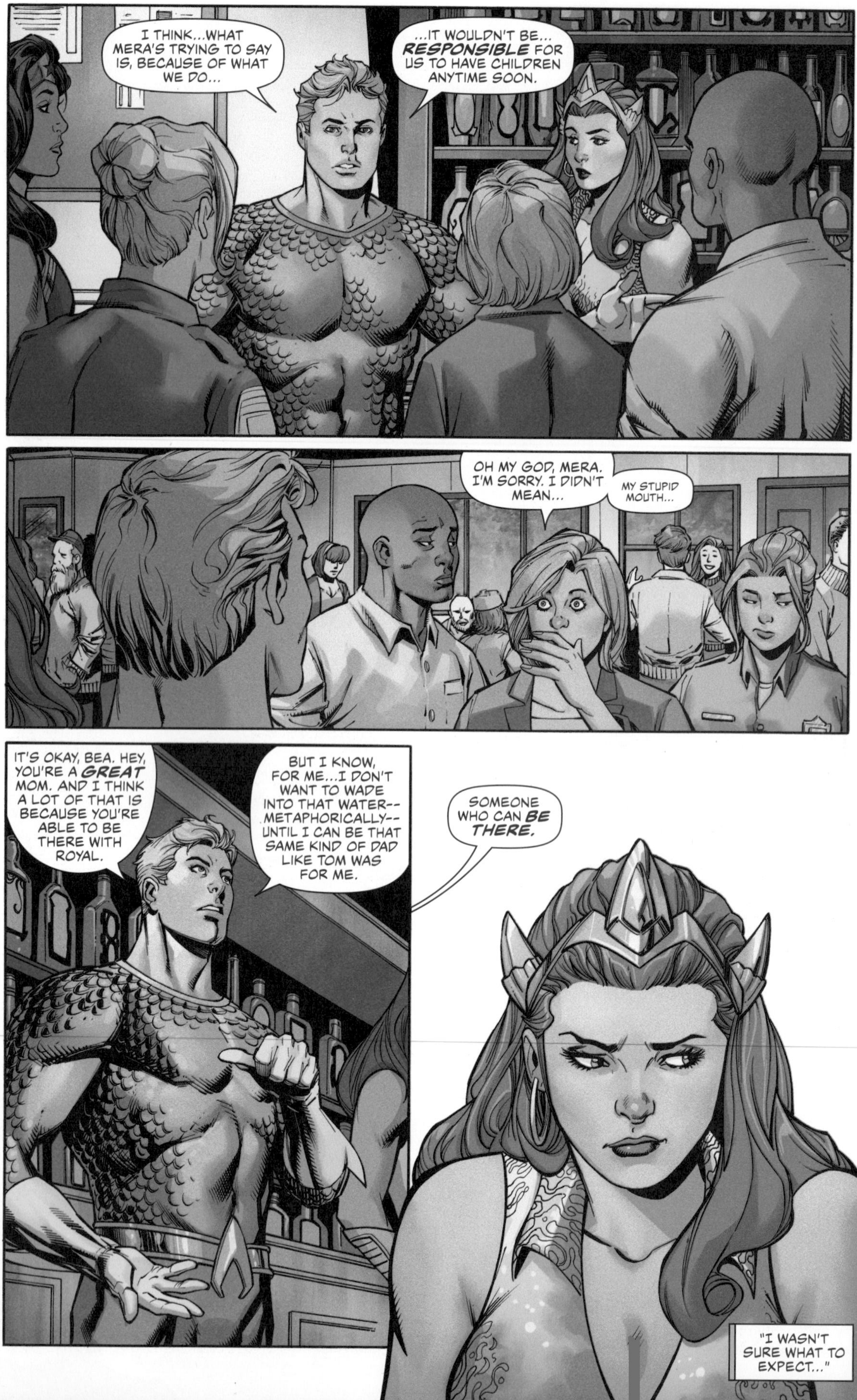
I THINK...WHAT MERA'S TRYING TO SAY IS, BECAUSE OF WHAT WE DO...
...IT WOULDN'T BE... **RESPONSIBLE** FOR US TO HAVE CHILDREN ANYTIME SOON.
OH MY GOD, MERA. I'M SORRY. I DIDN'T MEAN...
MY STUPID MOUTH...
IT'S OKAY, BEA. HEY, YOU'RE A **GREAT** MOM. AND I THINK A LOT OF THAT IS BECAUSE YOU'RE ABLE TO BE THERE WITH ROYAL.
BUT I KNOW, FOR ME...I DON'T WANT TO WADE INTO THAT WATER-- METAPHORICALLY-- UNTIL I CAN BE THAT SAME KIND OF DAD LIKE TOM WAS FOR ME.
SOMEONE WHO CAN **BE THERE.**
"I WASN'T SURE WHAT TO EXPECT..."

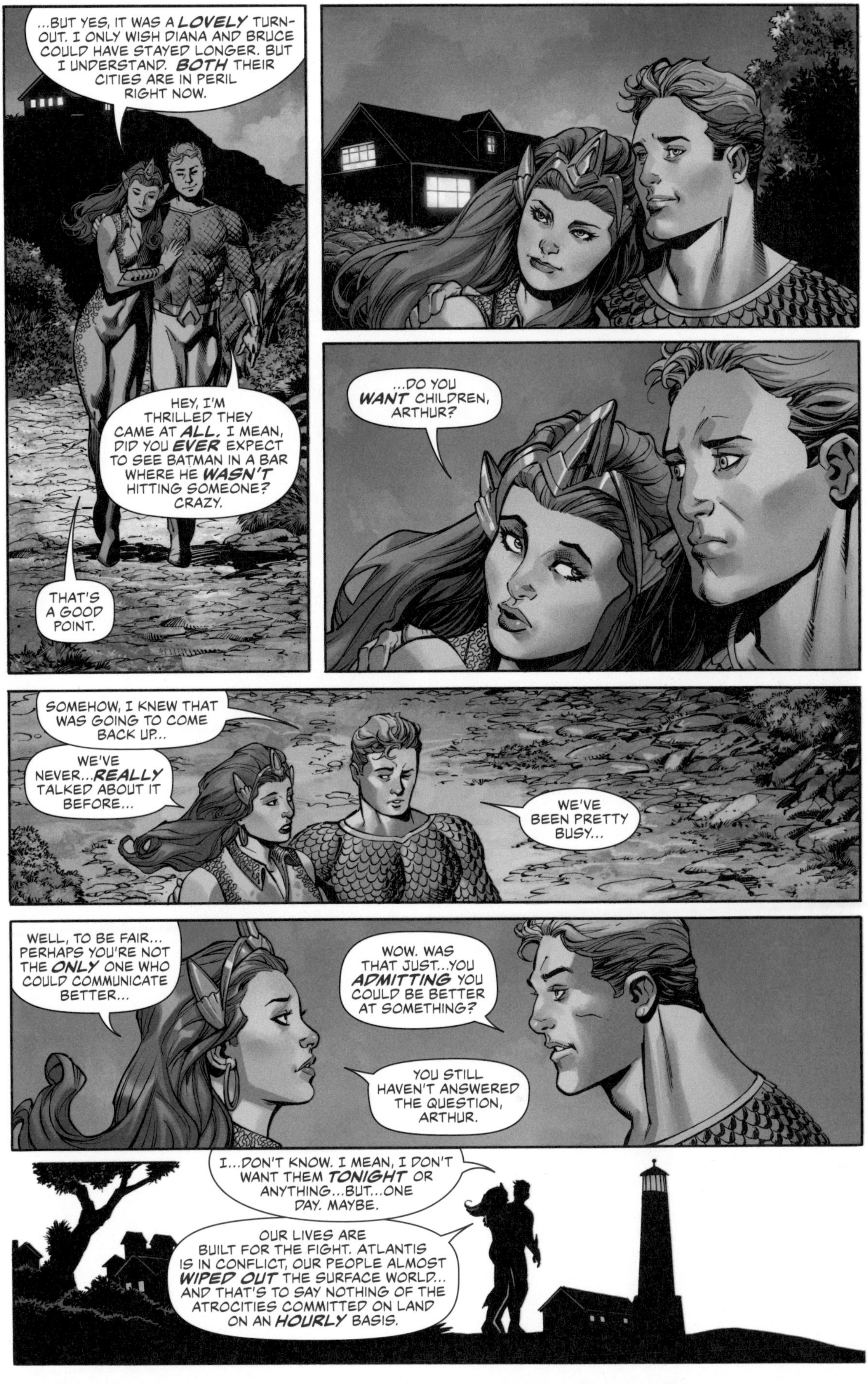
...BUT YES, IT WAS A LOVELY TURN-OUT. I ONLY WISH DIANA AND BRUCE COULD HAVE STAYED LONGER. BUT I UNDERSTAND. BOTH THEIR CITIES ARE IN PERIL RIGHT NOW.
HEY, I'M THRILLED THEY CAME AT ALL. I MEAN, DID YOU EVER EXPECT TO SEE BATMAN IN A BAR WHERE HE WASN'T HITTING SOMEONE? CRAZY.
THAT'S A GOOD POINT.
...DO YOU WANT CHILDREN, ARTHUR?
SOMEHOW, I KNEW THAT WAS GOING TO COME BACK UP...
WE'VE NEVER...REALLY TALKED ABOUT IT BEFORE...
WE'VE BEEN PRETTY BUSY...
WELL, TO BE FAIR... PERHAPS YOU'RE NOT THE ONLY ONE WHO COULD COMMUNICATE BETTER...
WOW. WAS THAT JUST...YOU ADMITTING YOU COULD BE BETTER AT SOMETHING?
YOU STILL HAVEN'T ANSWERED THE QUESTION, ARTHUR.
I...DON'T KNOW. I MEAN, I DON'T WANT THEM TONIGHT OR ANYTHING...BUT...ONE DAY. MAYBE.
OUR LIVES ARE BUILT FOR THE FIGHT. ATLANTIS IS IN CONFLICT, OUR PEOPLE ALMOST WIPED OUT THE SURFACE WORLD... AND THAT'S TO SAY NOTHING OF THE ATROCITIES COMMITTED ON LAND ON AN HOURLY BASIS.

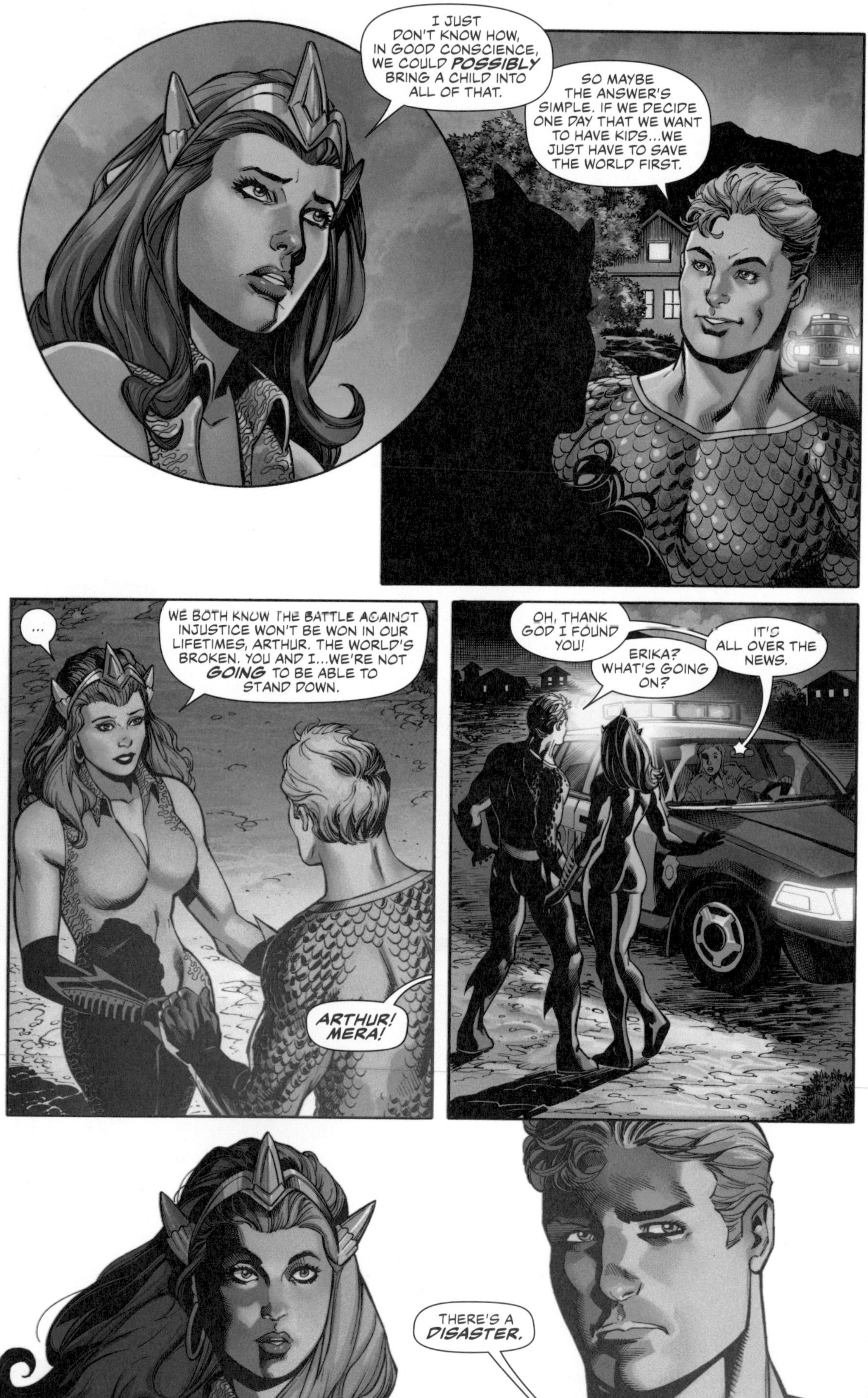

I JUST DON'T KNOW HOW, IN GOOD CONSCIENCE, WE COULD POSSIBLY BRING A CHILD INTO ALL OF THAT.
SO MAYBE THE ANSWER'S SIMPLE. IF WE DECIDE ONE DAY THAT WE WANT TO HAVE KIDS...WE JUST HAVE TO SAVE THE WORLD FIRST.
...
WE BOTH KNOW THE BATTLE AGAINST INJUSTICE WON'T BE WON IN OUR LIFETIMES, ARTHUR. THE WORLD'S BROKEN. YOU AND I...WE'RE NOT GOING TO BE ABLE TO STAND DOWN.
ARTHUR! MERA!
OH, THANK GOD I FOUND YOU!
ERIKA? WHAT'S GOING ON?
IT'S ALL OVER THE NEWS.
THERE'S A DISASTER.

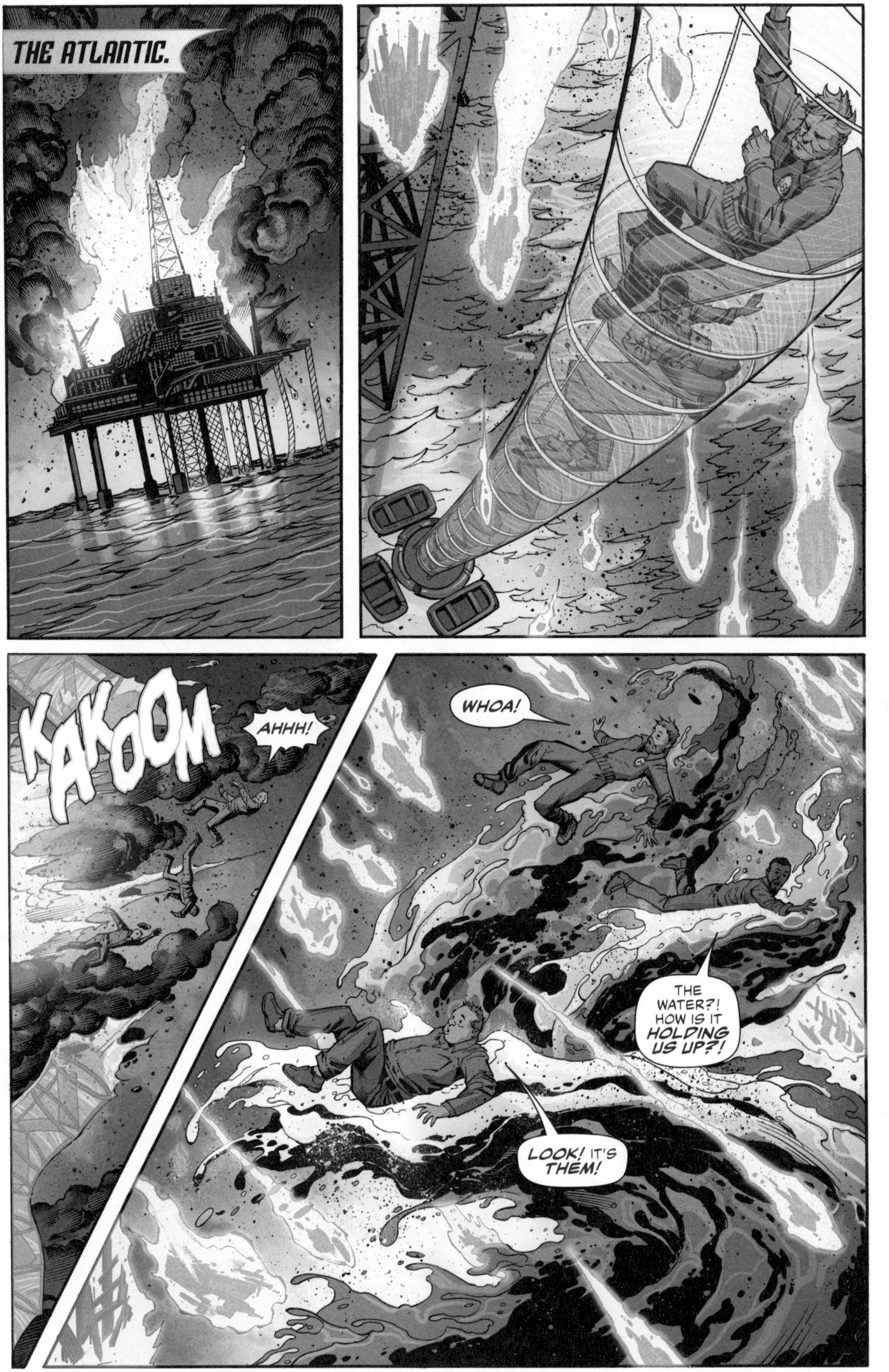
THE ATLANTIC.
KAKOOM
AHHH!
WHOA!
THE WATER?! HOW IS IT HOLDING US UP?!
LOOK! IT'S THEM!

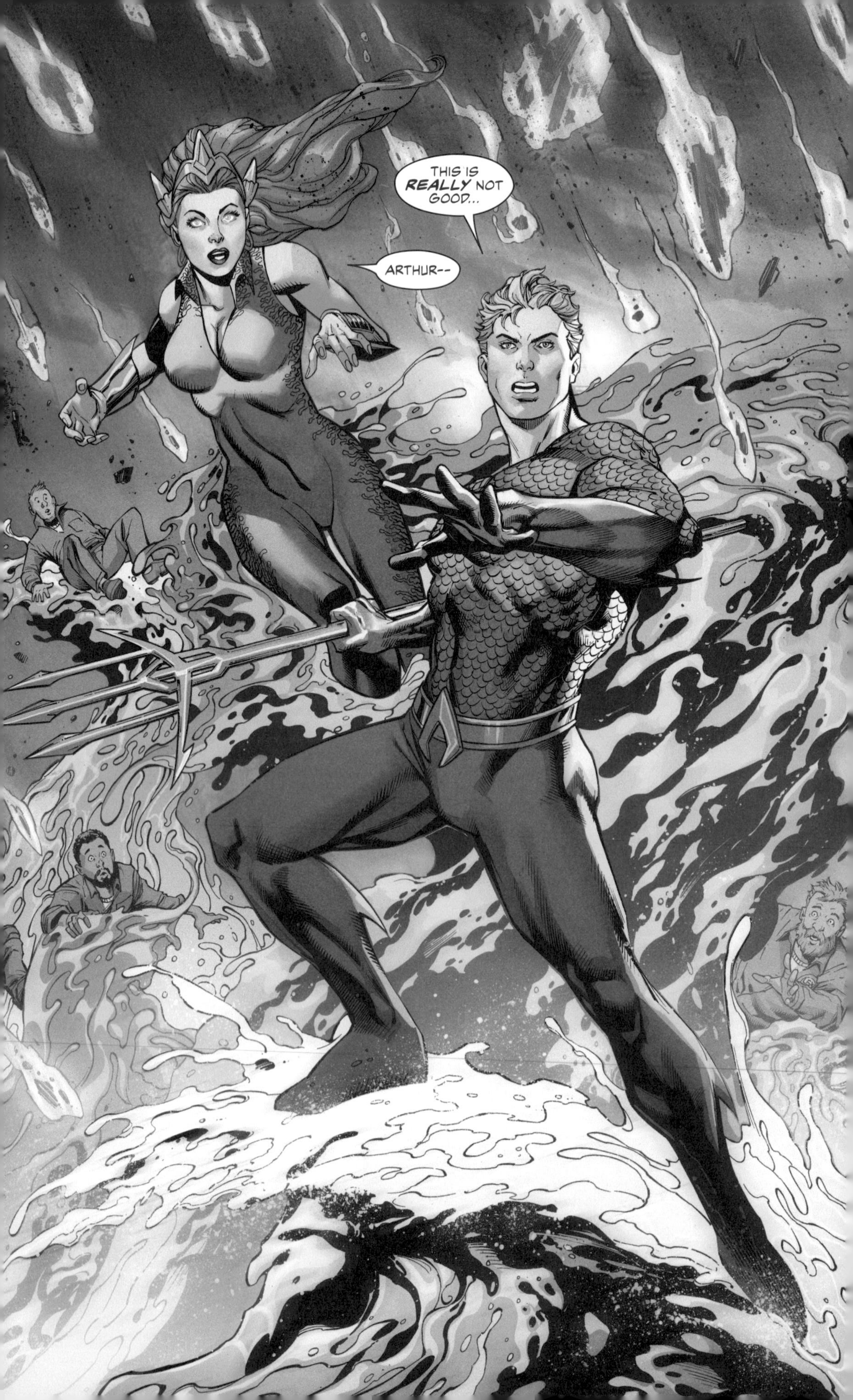
ARTHUR--
THIS IS *REALLY* NOT GOOD...

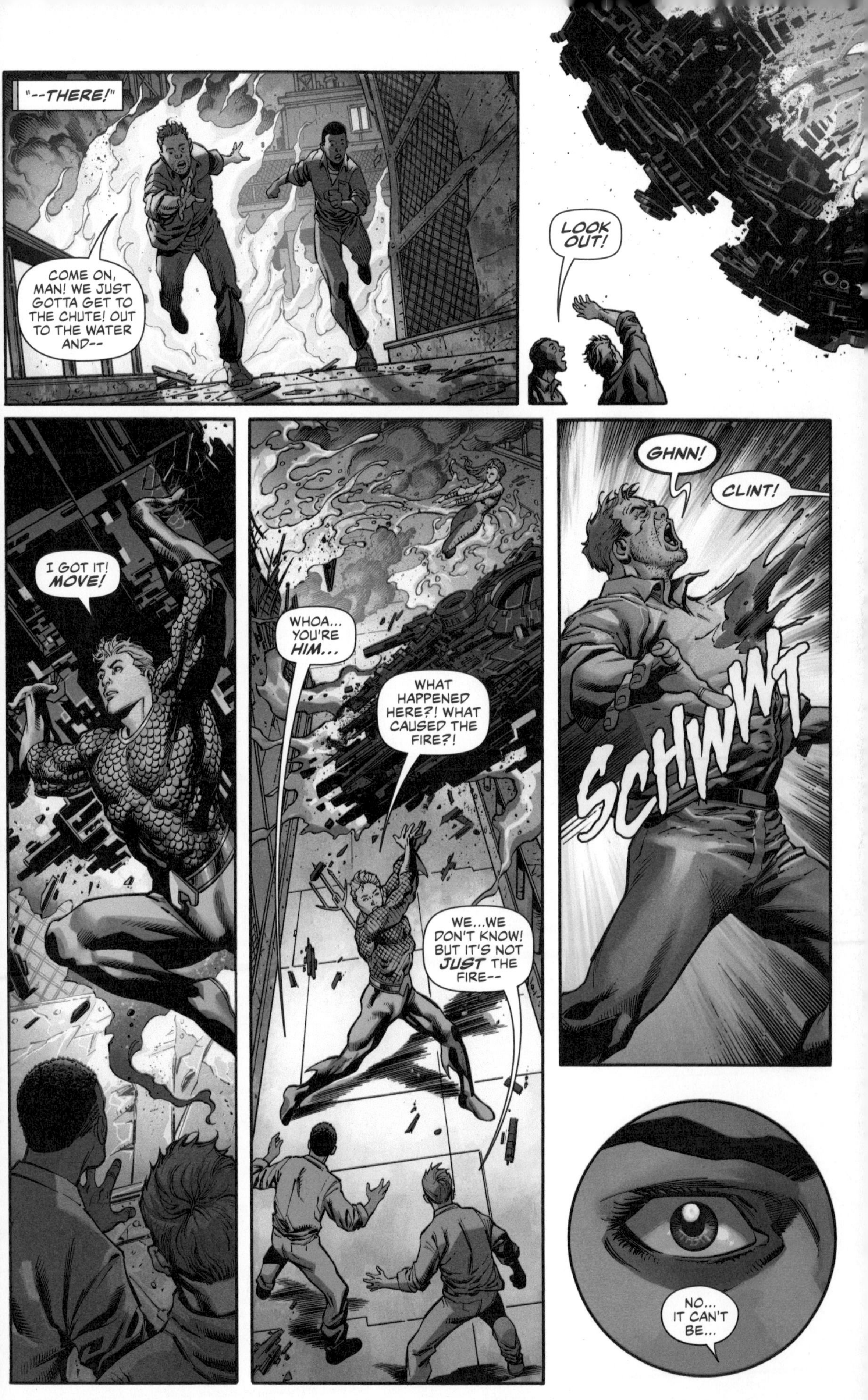
"--THERE!"
COME ON, MAN! WE JUST GOTTA GET TO THE CHUTE! OUT TO THE WATER AND--
LOOK OUT!
I GOT IT! MOVE!
WHOA... YOU'RE HIM...
WHAT HAPPENED HERE?! WHAT CAUSED THE FIRE?!
WE...WE DON'T KNOW! BUT IT'S NOT JUST THE FIRE--
GHNN!
CLINT!
SCHWWT
NO... IT CAN'T BE...

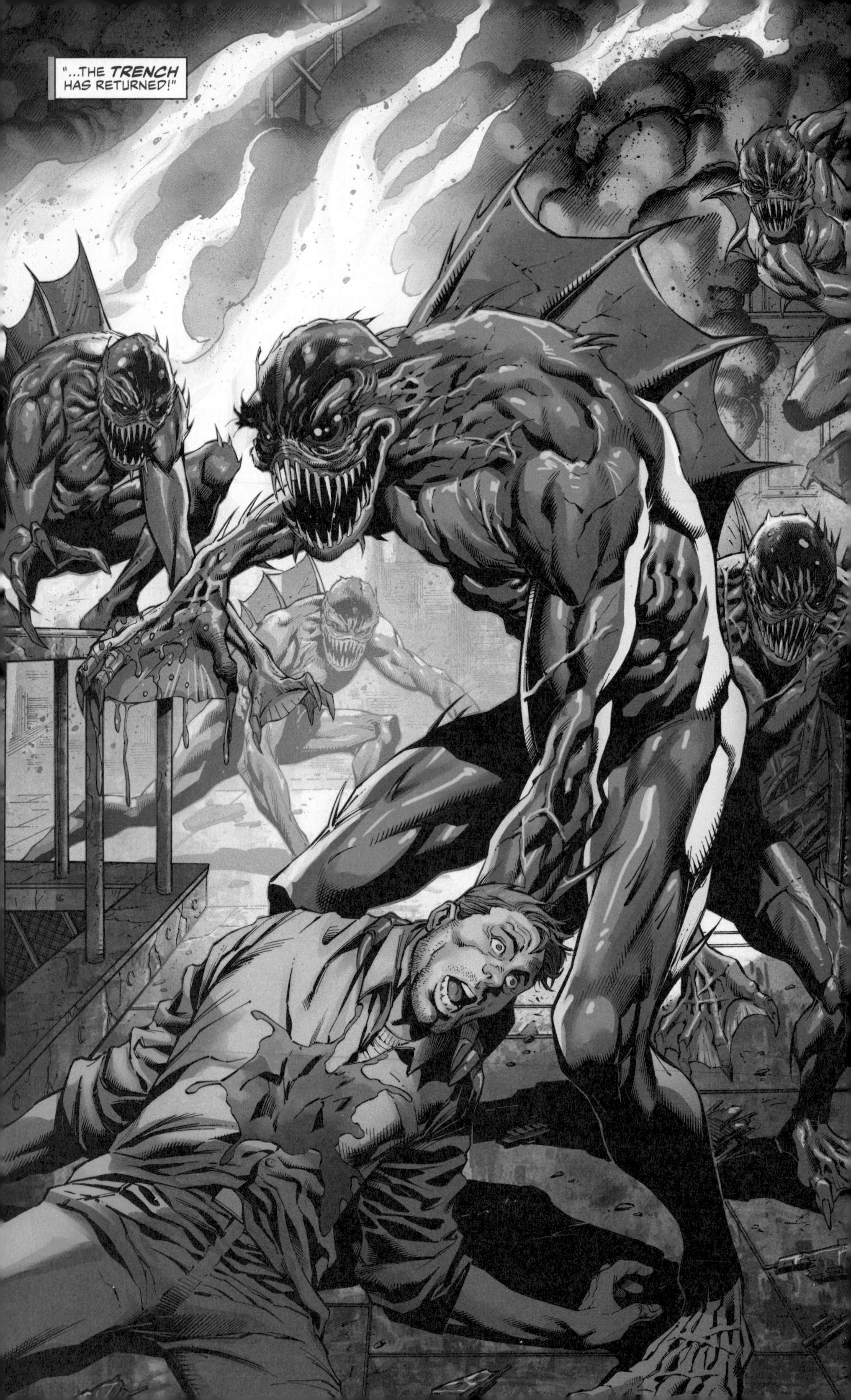
"...THE TRENCH HAS RETURNED!"

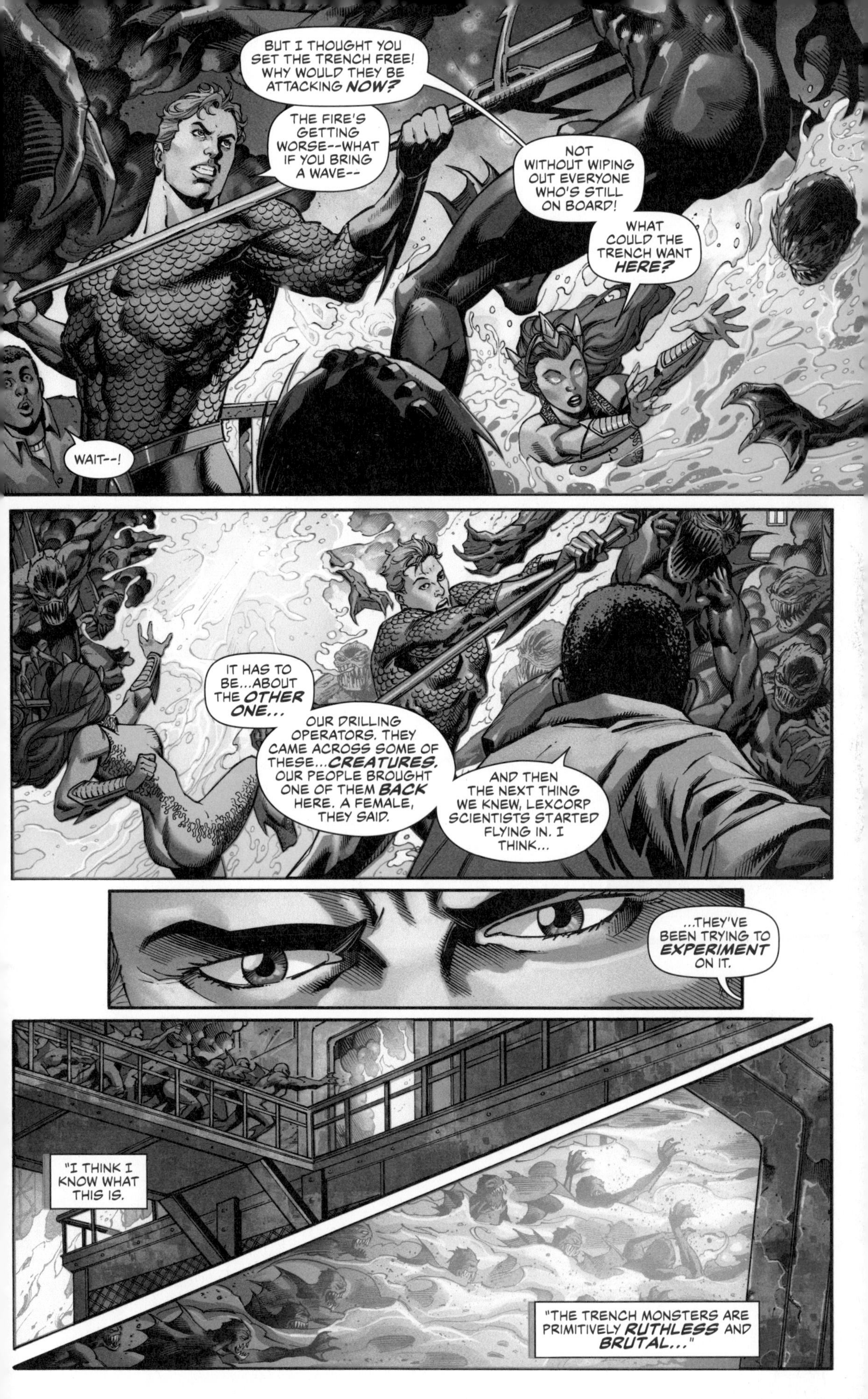

BUT I THOUGHT YOU SET THE TRENCH FREE! WHY WOULD THEY BE ATTACKING **NOW?**
THE FIRE'S GETTING WORSE--WHAT IF YOU BRING A WAVE--
NOT WITHOUT WIPING OUT EVERYONE WHO'S STILL ON BOARD!
WHAT COULD THE TRENCH WANT **HERE?**
WAIT--!
IT HAS TO BE...ABOUT THE **OTHER ONE...**
OUR DRILLING OPERATORS. THEY CAME ACROSS SOME OF THESE...**CREATURES.** OUR PEOPLE BROUGHT ONE OF THEM **BACK** HERE. A FEMALE, THEY SAID.
AND THEN THE NEXT THING WE KNEW, LEXCORP SCIENTISTS STARTED FLYING IN. I THINK...
...THEY'VE BEEN TRYING TO **EXPERIMENT** ON IT.
"I THINK I KNOW WHAT THIS IS.
"THE TRENCH MONSTERS ARE PRIMITIVELY **RUTHLESS** AND **BRUTAL...**"

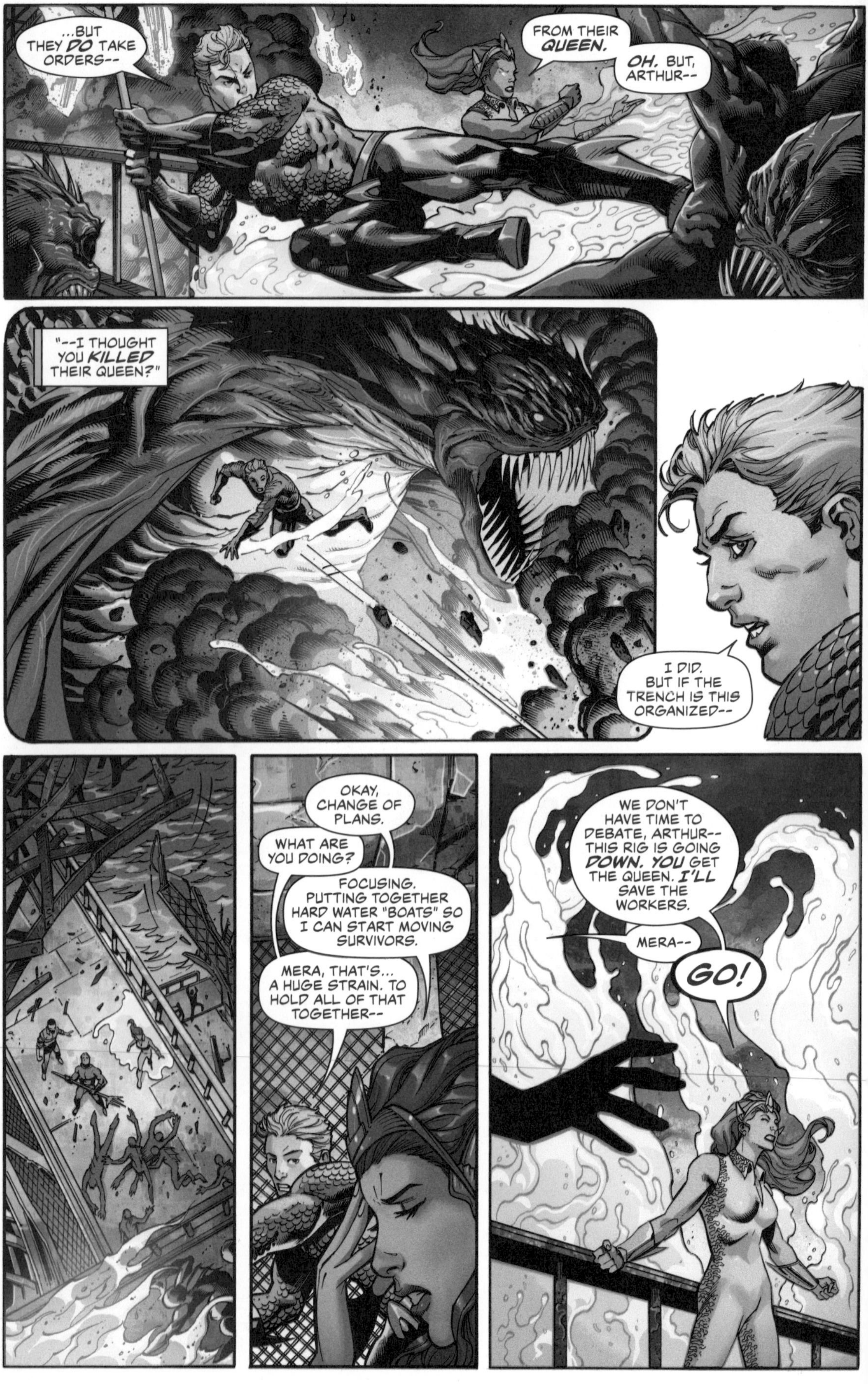
...BUT THEY DO TAKE ORDERS--
FROM THEIR QUEEN.
OH. BUT, ARTHUR--
"--I THOUGHT YOU KILLED THEIR QUEEN?"
I DID. BUT IF THE TRENCH IS THIS ORGANIZED--
OKAY, CHANGE OF PLANS.
WHAT ARE YOU DOING?
FOCUSING. PUTTING TOGETHER HARD WATER "BOATS" SO I CAN START MOVING SURVIVORS.
MERA, THAT'S... A HUGE STRAIN. TO HOLD ALL OF THAT TOGETHER--
WE DON'T HAVE TIME TO DEBATE, ARTHUR-- THIS RIG IS GOING DOWN. YOU GET THE QUEEN. I'LL SAVE THE WORKERS.
MERA--
GO!

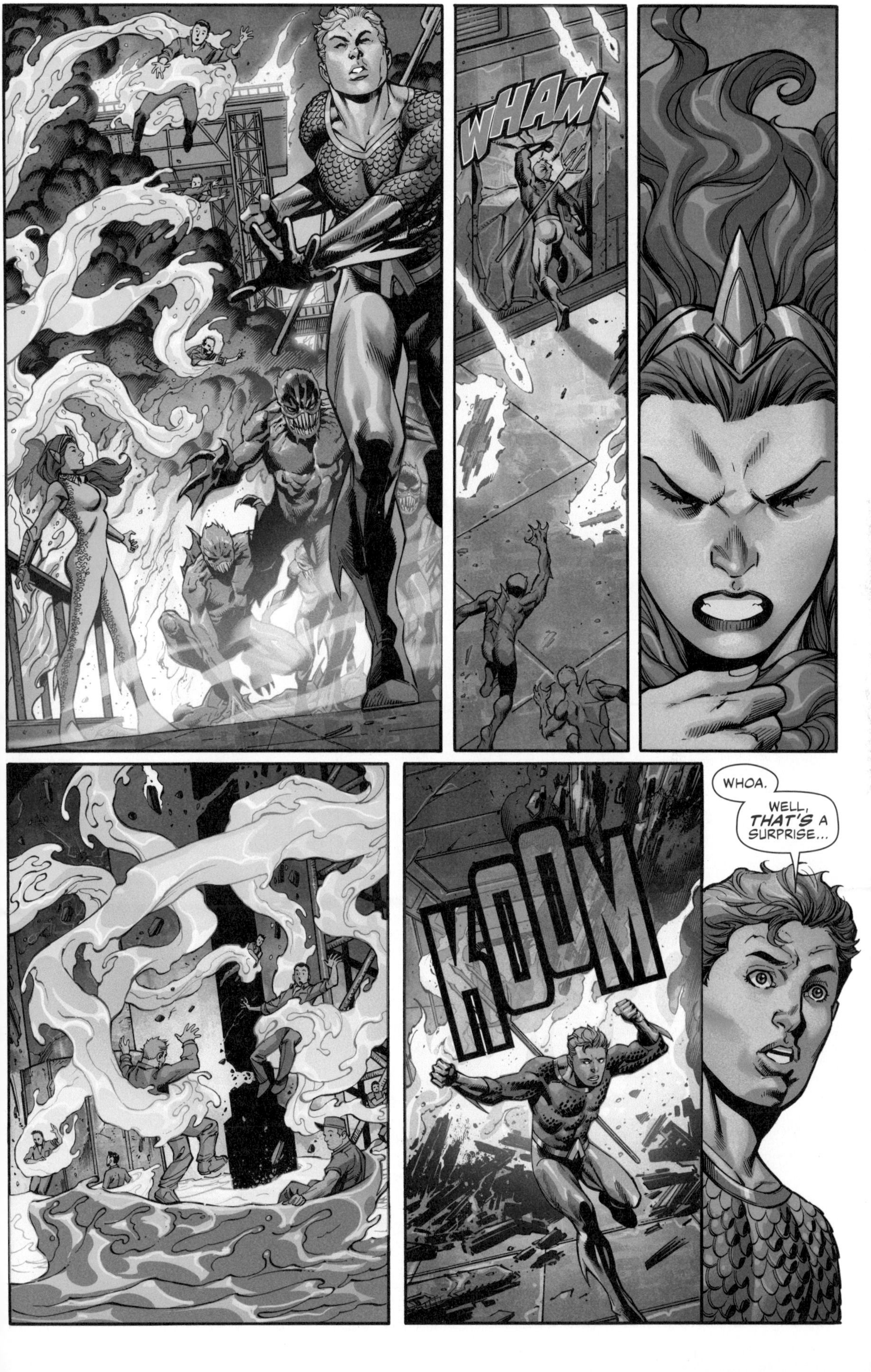
WHAM
KOOM
WHOA.
WELL, THAT'S A SURPRISE...

YOU'RE JUST A BABY.

SURFACE MAN. *KILLER.*

I KNOW... YOU CAN'T UNDERSTAND ME...

YOU *KILLED* HER.

...BUT I'M NOT HERE TO HURT YOU. I JUST WANT TO *HELP--*

WE DON'T HAVE MUCH TIME. THIS WHOLE PLACE IS GOING DOWN--

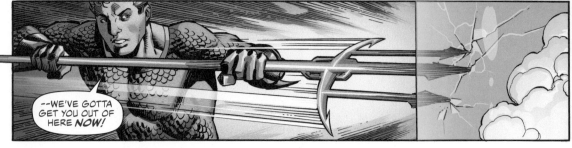

--WE'VE GOTTA GET YOU OUT OF HERE *NOW!*

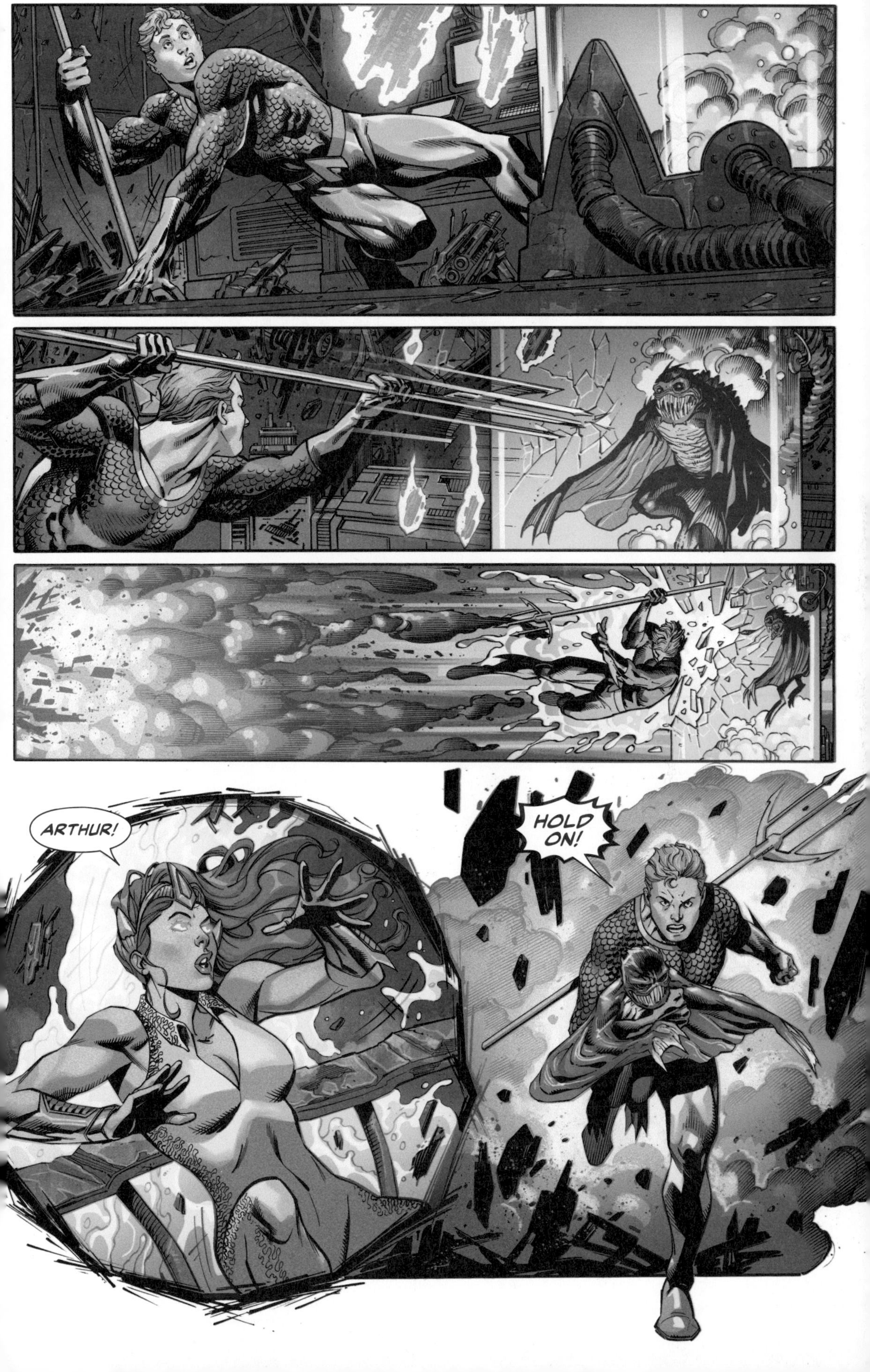
ARTHUR!
HOLD ON!

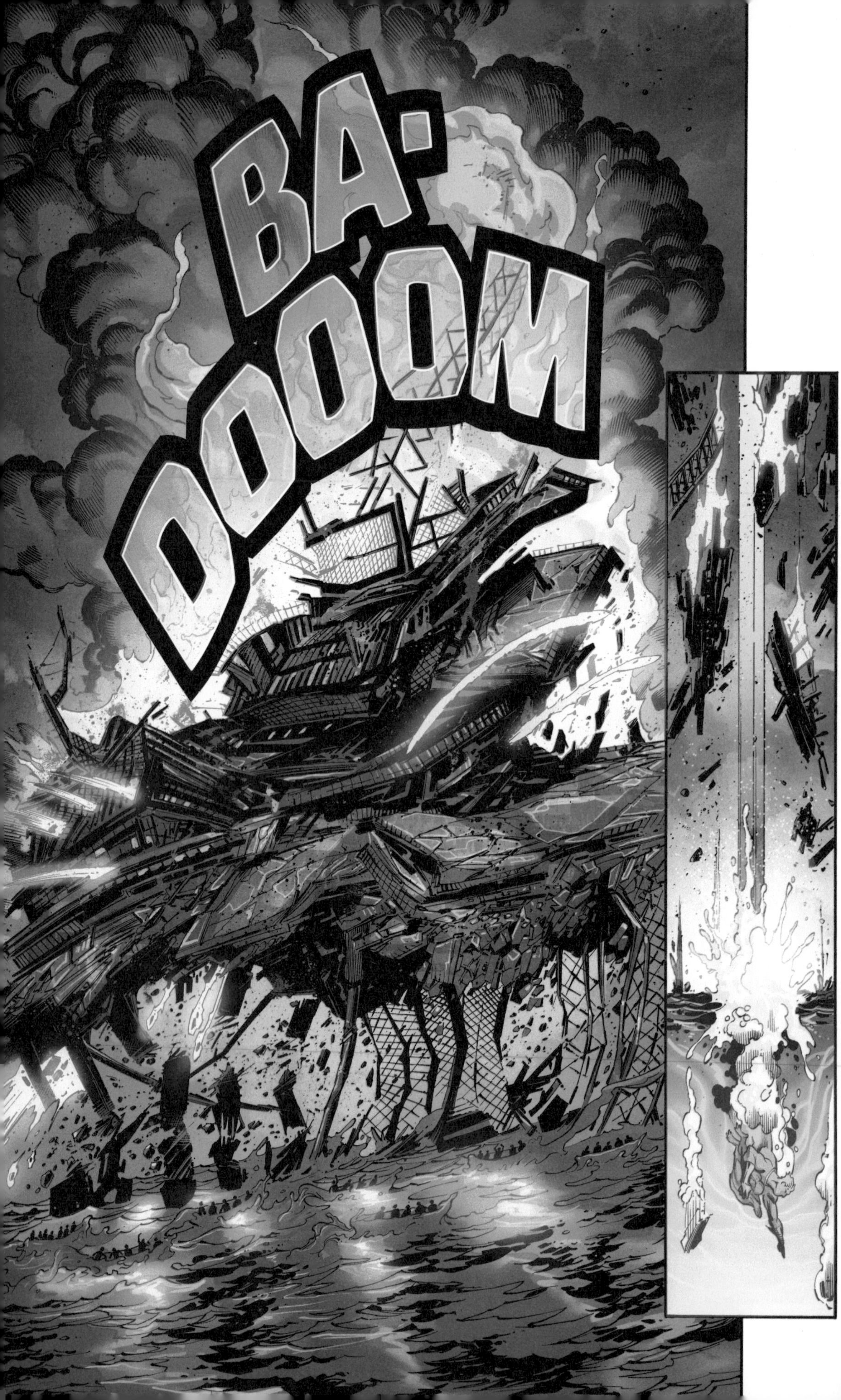
BA-DOOOM

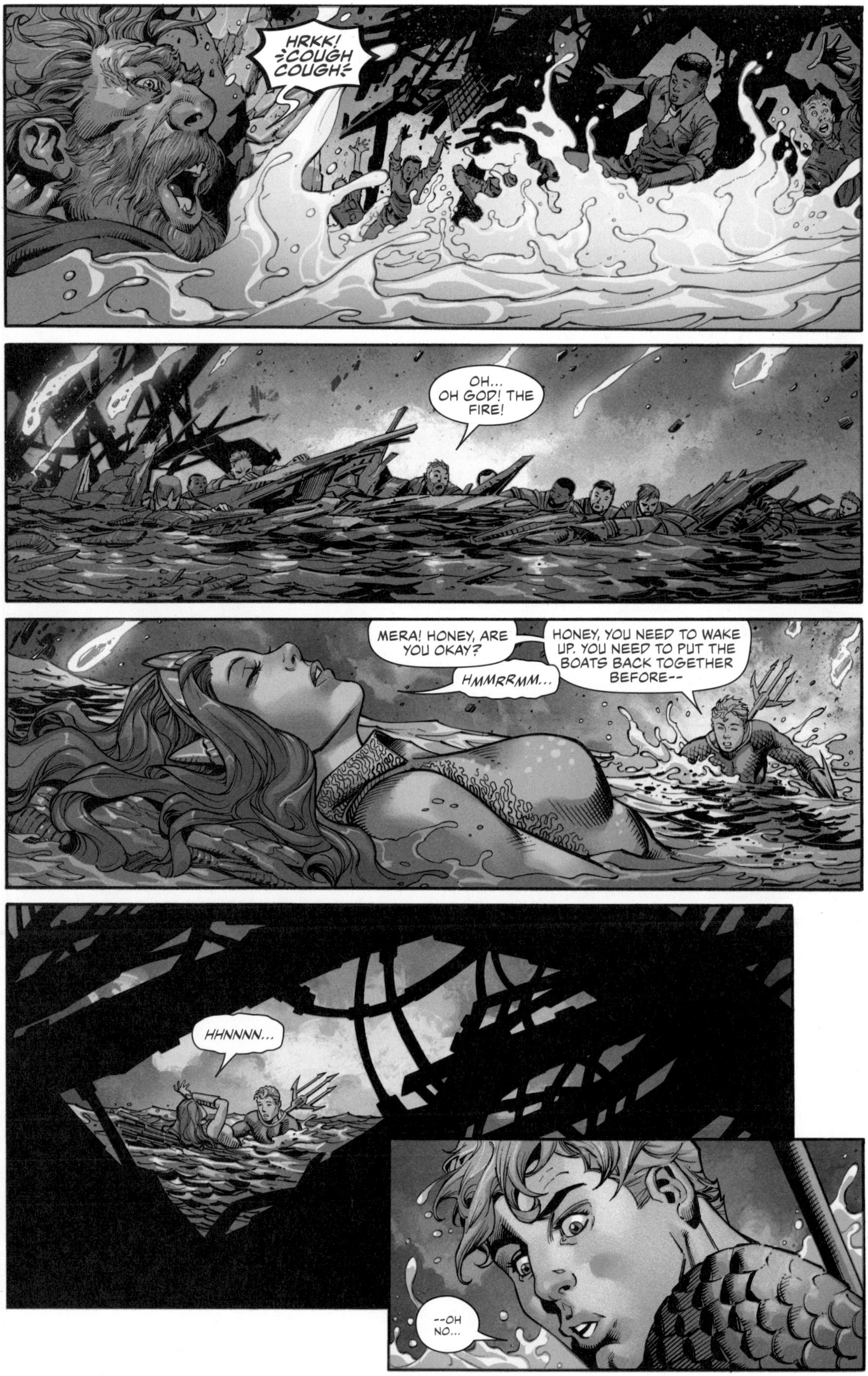
HRKK! COUGH COUGH
OH... OH GOD! THE FIRE!
MERA! HONEY, ARE YOU OKAY?
HMMRRMM...
HONEY, YOU NEED TO WAKE UP. YOU NEED TO PUT THE BOATS BACK TOGETHER BEFORE--
HHNNNN...
--OH NO...

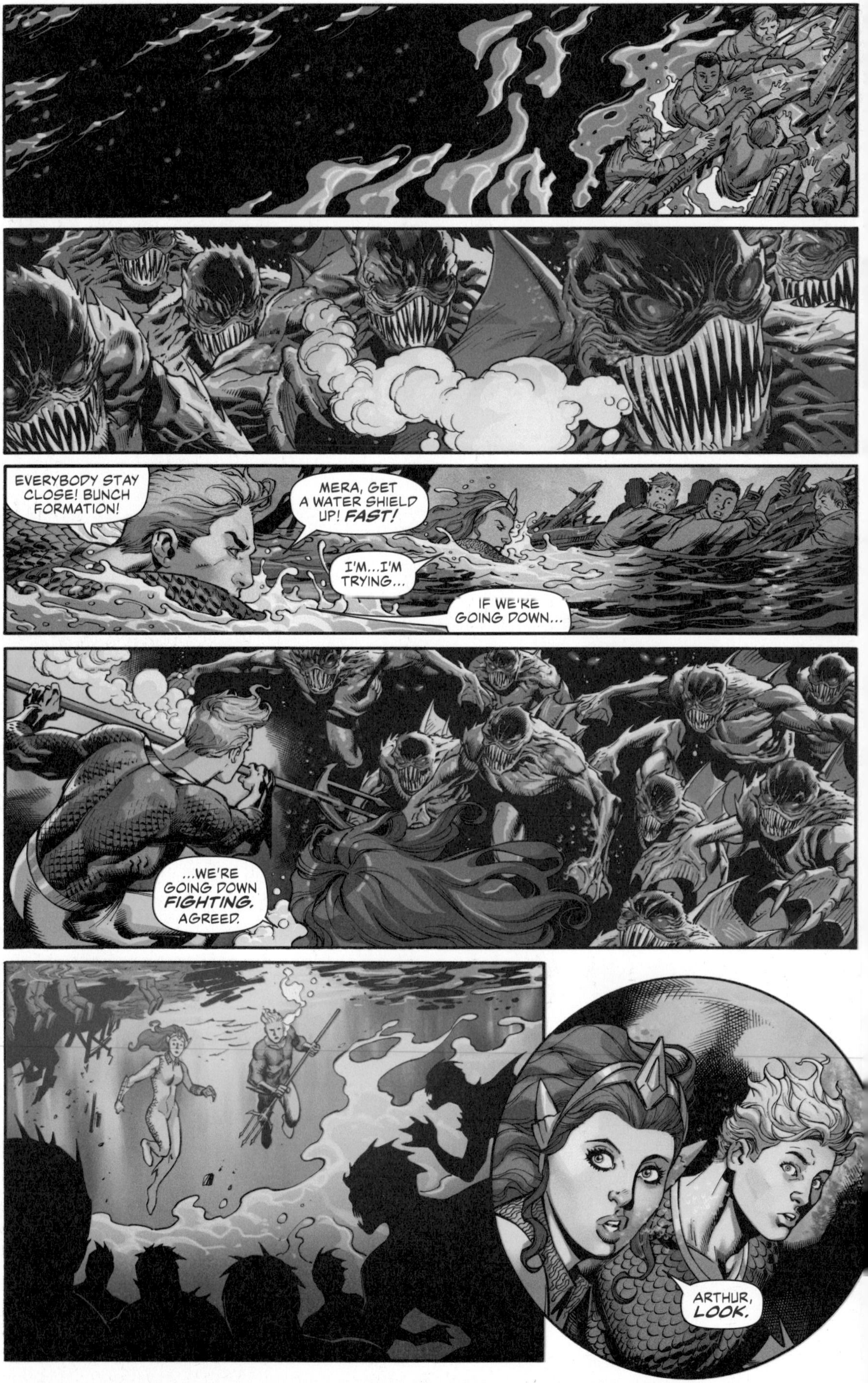
EVERYBODY STAY CLOSE! BUNCH FORMATION!
MERA, GET A WATER SHIELD UP! FAST!
I'M...I'M TRYING...
IF WE'RE GOING DOWN...
...WE'RE GOING DOWN FIGHTING. AGREED.
ARTHUR, LOOK.

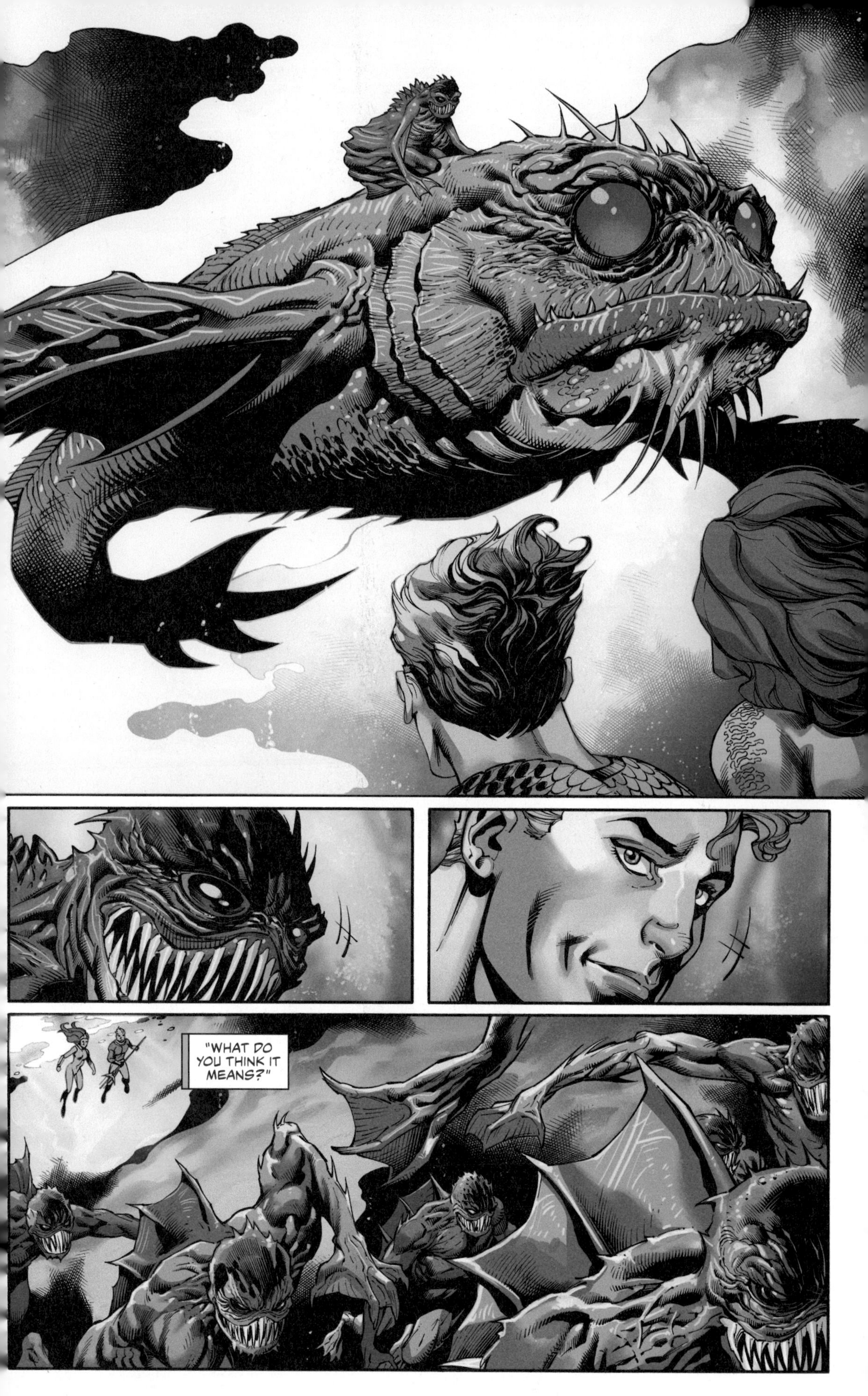
"WHAT DO
YOU THINK IT
MEANS?"

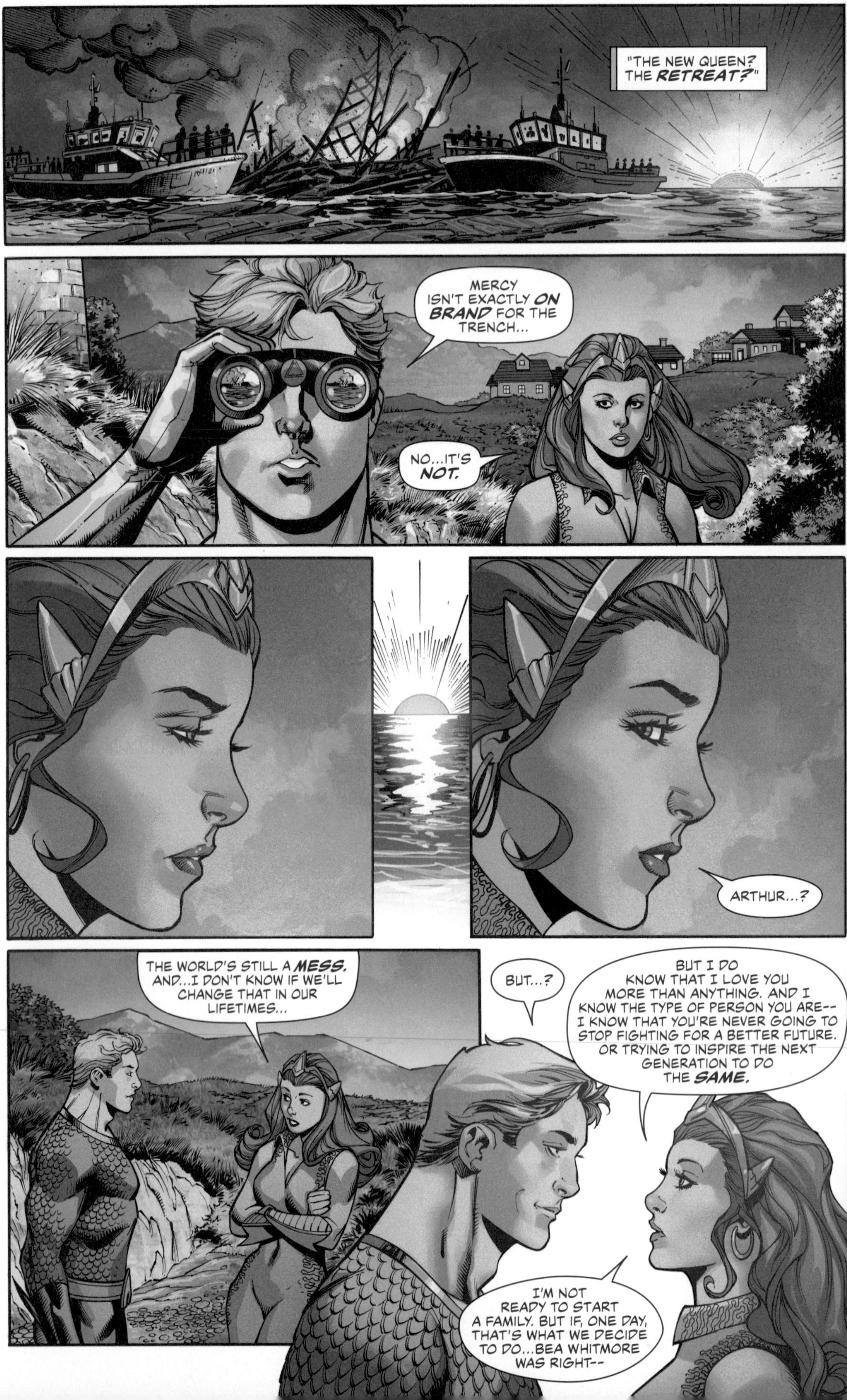

"THE NEW QUEEN? THE *RETREAT?*"
MERCY ISN'T EXACTLY *ON BRAND* FOR THE TRENCH...
NO...IT'S *NOT.*
ARTHUR...?
THE WORLD'S STILL A *MESS.* AND...I DON'T KNOW IF WE'LL CHANGE THAT IN OUR LIFETIMES...
BUT...?
BUT I DO KNOW THAT I LOVE YOU MORE THAN ANYTHING. AND I KNOW THE TYPE OF PERSON YOU ARE-- I KNOW THAT YOU'RE NEVER GOING TO STOP FIGHTING FOR A BETTER FUTURE. OR TRYING TO INSPIRE THE NEXT GENERATION TO DO THE *SAME.*
I'M NOT READY TO START A FAMILY. BUT IF, ONE DAY, THAT'S WHAT WE DECIDE TO DO...BEA WHITMORE WAS RIGHT--

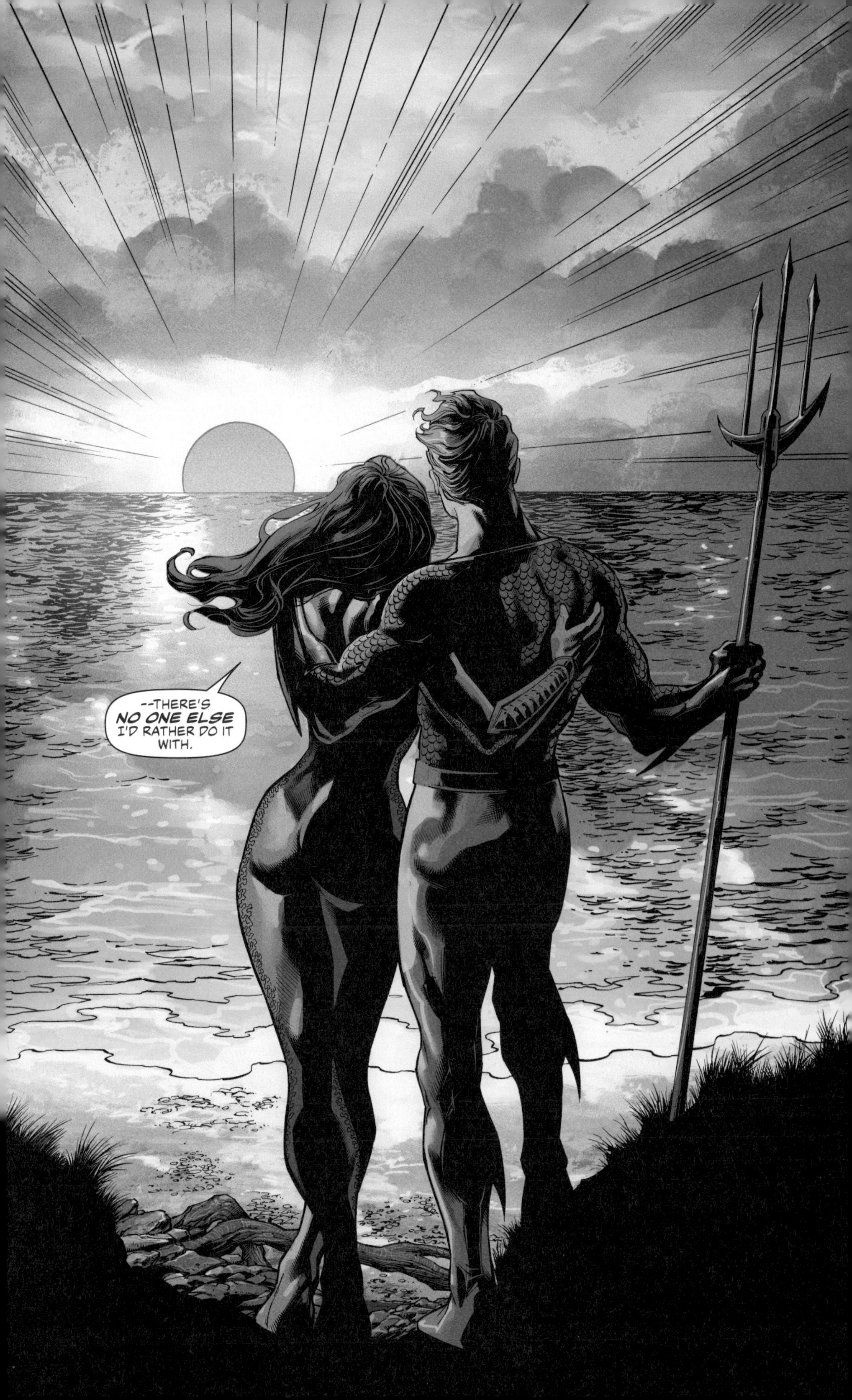
--THERE'S NO ONE ELSE I'D RATHER DO IT WITH.

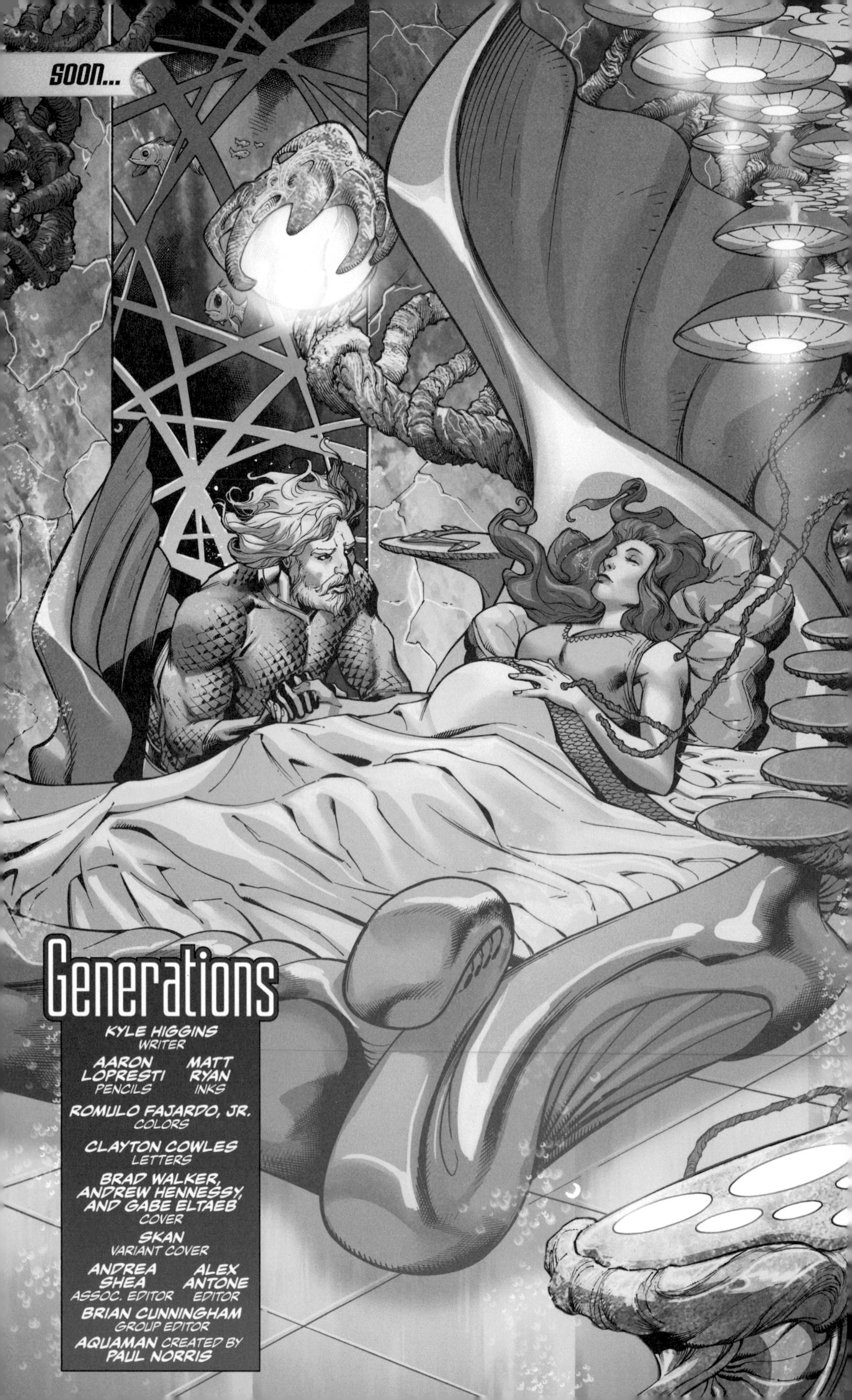
SOON...
Generations
KYLE HIGGINS
WRITER
AARON LOPRESTI
PENCILS
MATT RYAN
INKS
ROMULO FAJARDO, JR.
COLORS
CLAYTON COWLES
LETTERS
BRAD WALKER, ANDREW HENNESSY, AND GABE ELTAEB
COVER
SKAN
VARIANT COVER
ANDREA SHEA
ASSOC. EDITOR
ALEX ANTONE
EDITOR
BRIAN CUNNINGHAM
GROUP EDITOR
AQUAMAN CREATED BY PAUL NORRIS

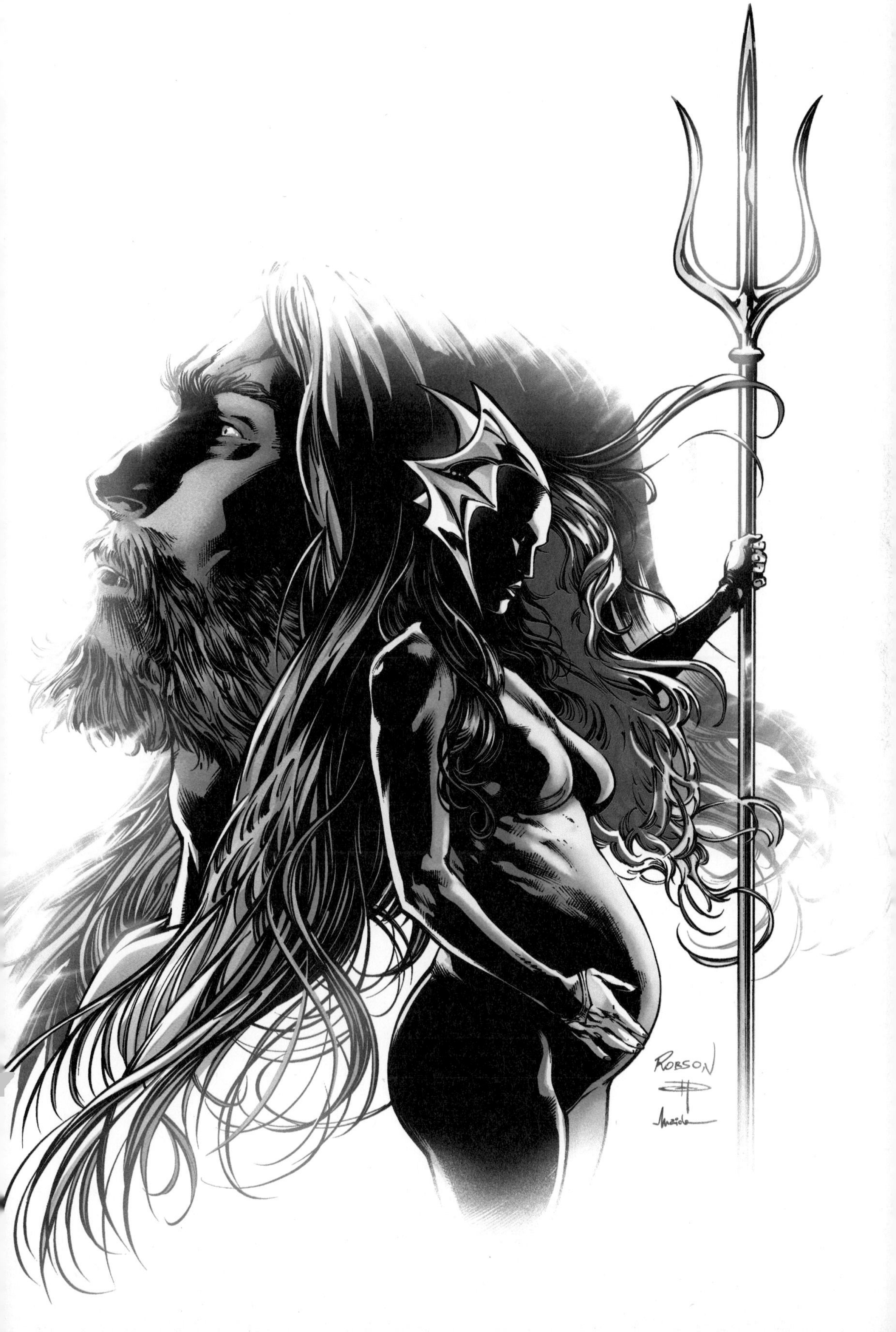
ROBSON

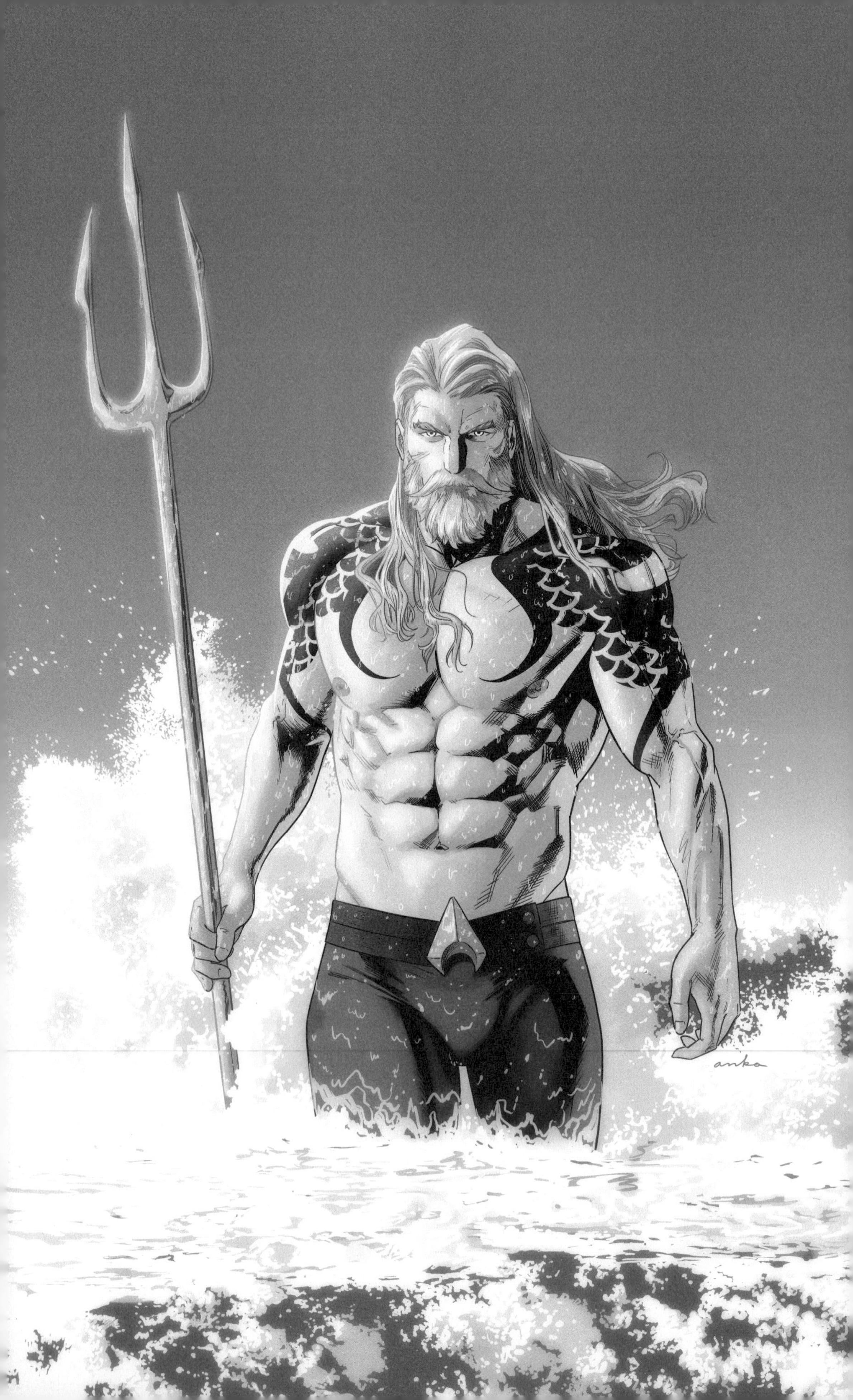
anka

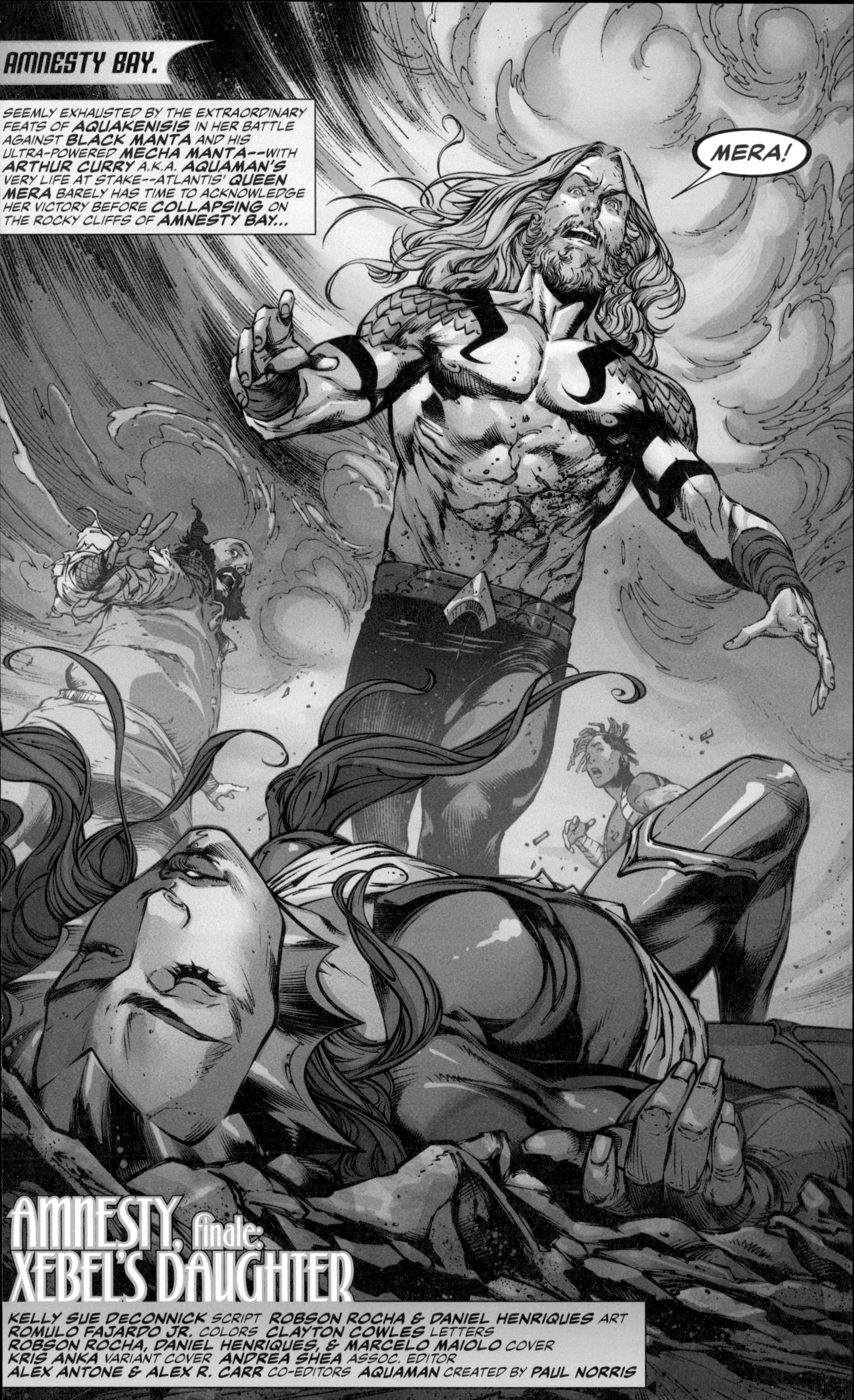
AMNESTY BAY.
SEEMLY EXHAUSTED BY THE EXTRAORDINARY FEATS OF AQUAKENISIS IN HER BATTLE AGAINST BLACK MANTA AND HIS ULTRA-POWERED MECHA MANTA--WITH ARTHUR CURRY A.K.A. AQUAMAN'S VERY LIFE AT STAKE--ATLANTIS' QUEEN MERA BARELY HAS TIME TO ACKNOWLEDGE HER VICTORY BEFORE COLLAPSING ON THE ROCKY CLIFFS OF AMNESTY BAY...
MERA!
AMNESTY, finale: XEBEL'S DAUGHTER
KELLY SUE DECONNICK SCRIPT ROBSON ROCHA & DANIEL HENRIQUES ART
ROMULO FAJARDO JR. COLORS CLAYTON COWLES LETTERS
ROBSON ROCHA, DANIEL HENRIQUES, & MARCELO MAIOLO COVER
KRIS ANKA VARIANT COVER ANDREA SHEA ASSOC. EDITOR
ALEX ANTONE & ALEX R. CARR CO-EDITORS AQUAMAN CREATED BY PAUL NORRIS

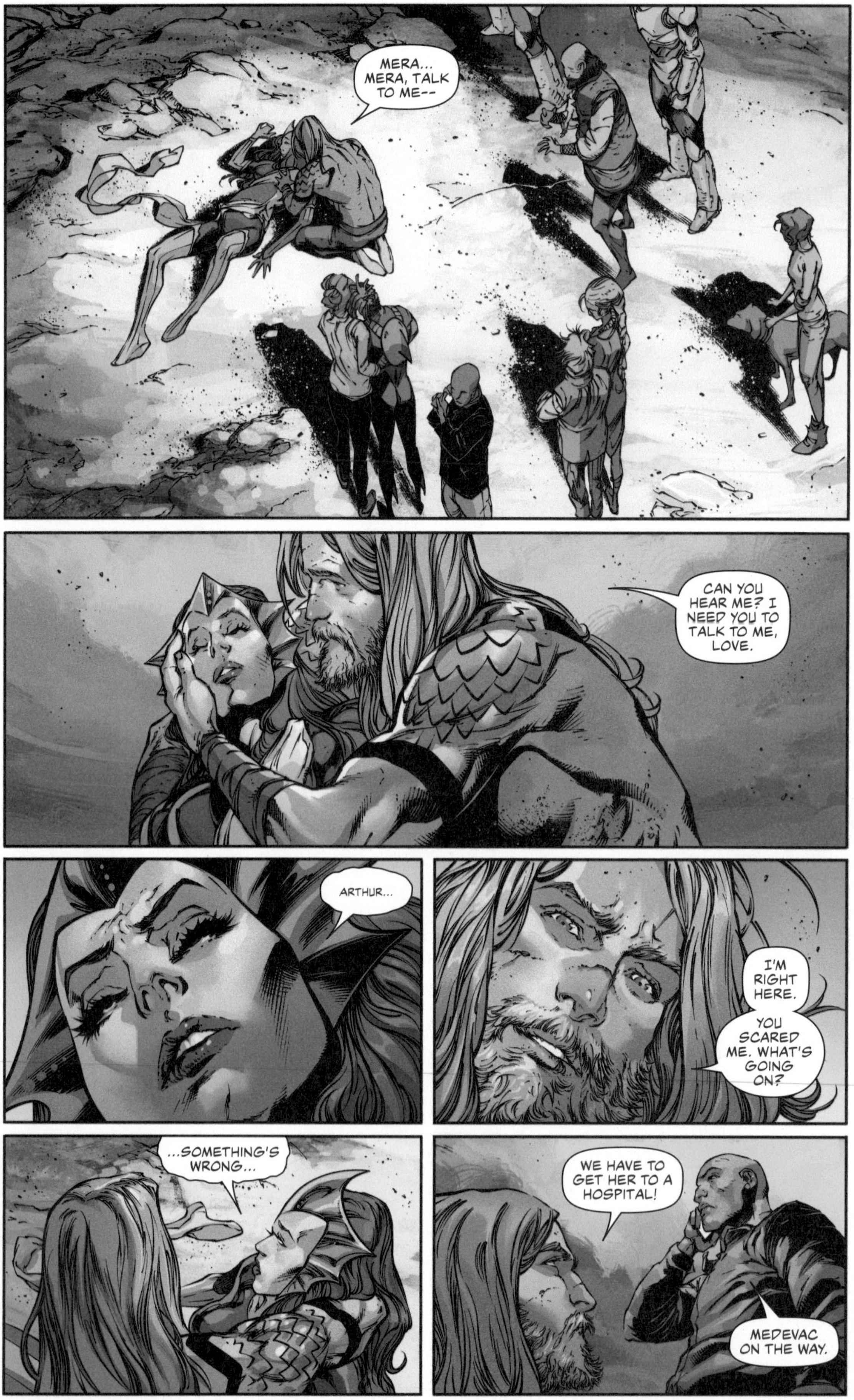
MERA... MERA, TALK TO ME--
CAN YOU HEAR ME? I NEED YOU TO TALK TO ME, LOVE.
ARTHUR...
I'M RIGHT HERE.
YOU SCARED ME. WHAT'S GOING ON?
...SOMETHING'S WRONG...
WE HAVE TO GET HER TO A HOSPITAL!
MEDEVAC ON THE WAY.

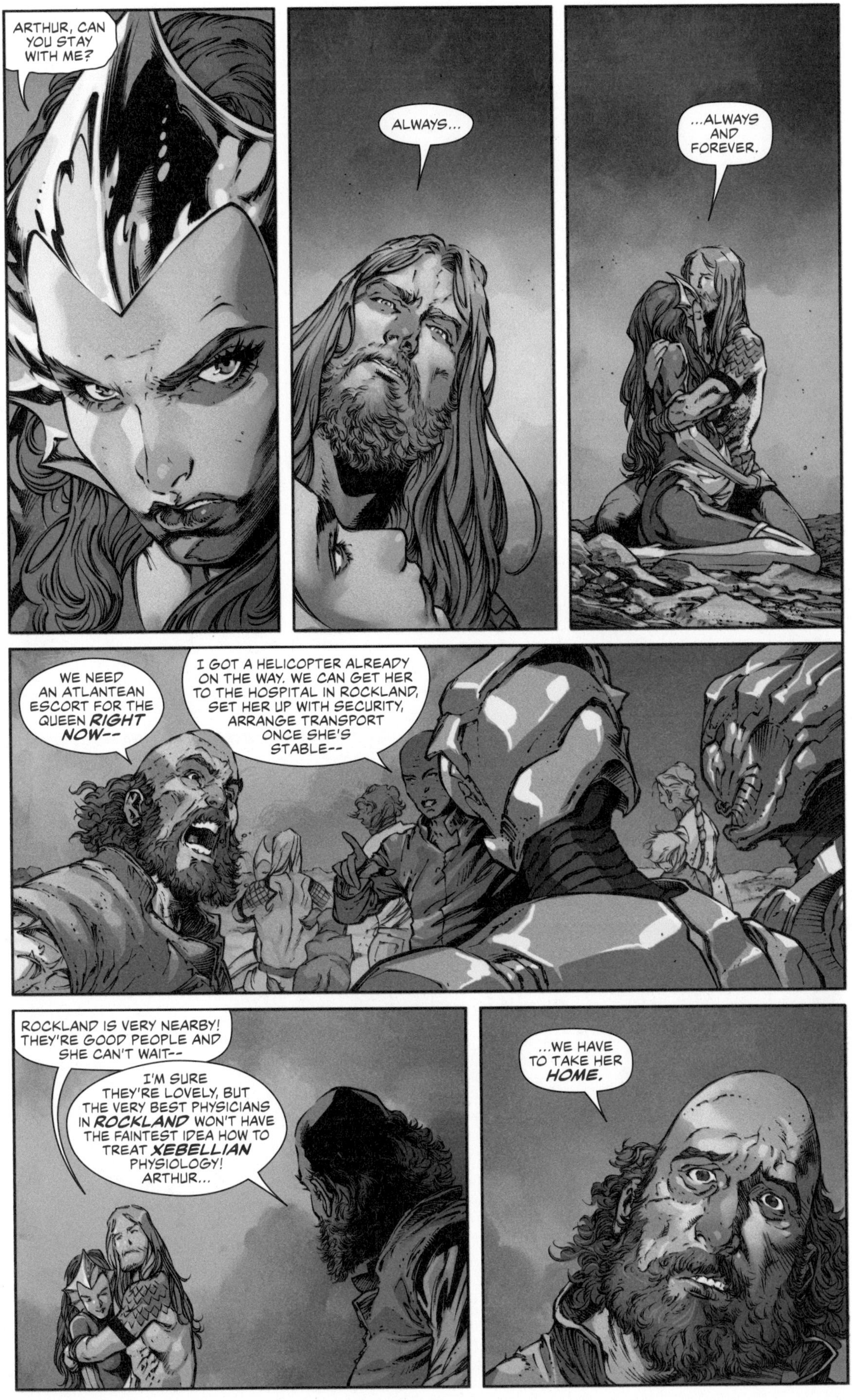
ARTHUR, CAN YOU STAY WITH ME?
ALWAYS...
...ALWAYS AND FOREVER.
WE NEED AN ATLANTEAN ESCORT FOR THE QUEEN RIGHT NOW--
I GOT A HELICOPTER ALREADY ON THE WAY. WE CAN GET HER TO THE HOSPITAL IN ROCKLAND, SET HER UP WITH SECURITY, ARRANGE TRANSPORT ONCE SHE'S STABLE--
ROCKLAND IS VERY NEARBY! THEY'RE GOOD PEOPLE AND SHE CAN'T WAIT--
I'M SURE THEY'RE LOVELY, BUT THE VERY BEST PHYSICIANS IN ROCKLAND WON'T HAVE THE FAINTEST IDEA HOW TO TREAT XEBELLIAN PHYSIOLOGY! ARTHUR...
...WE HAVE TO TAKE HER HOME.

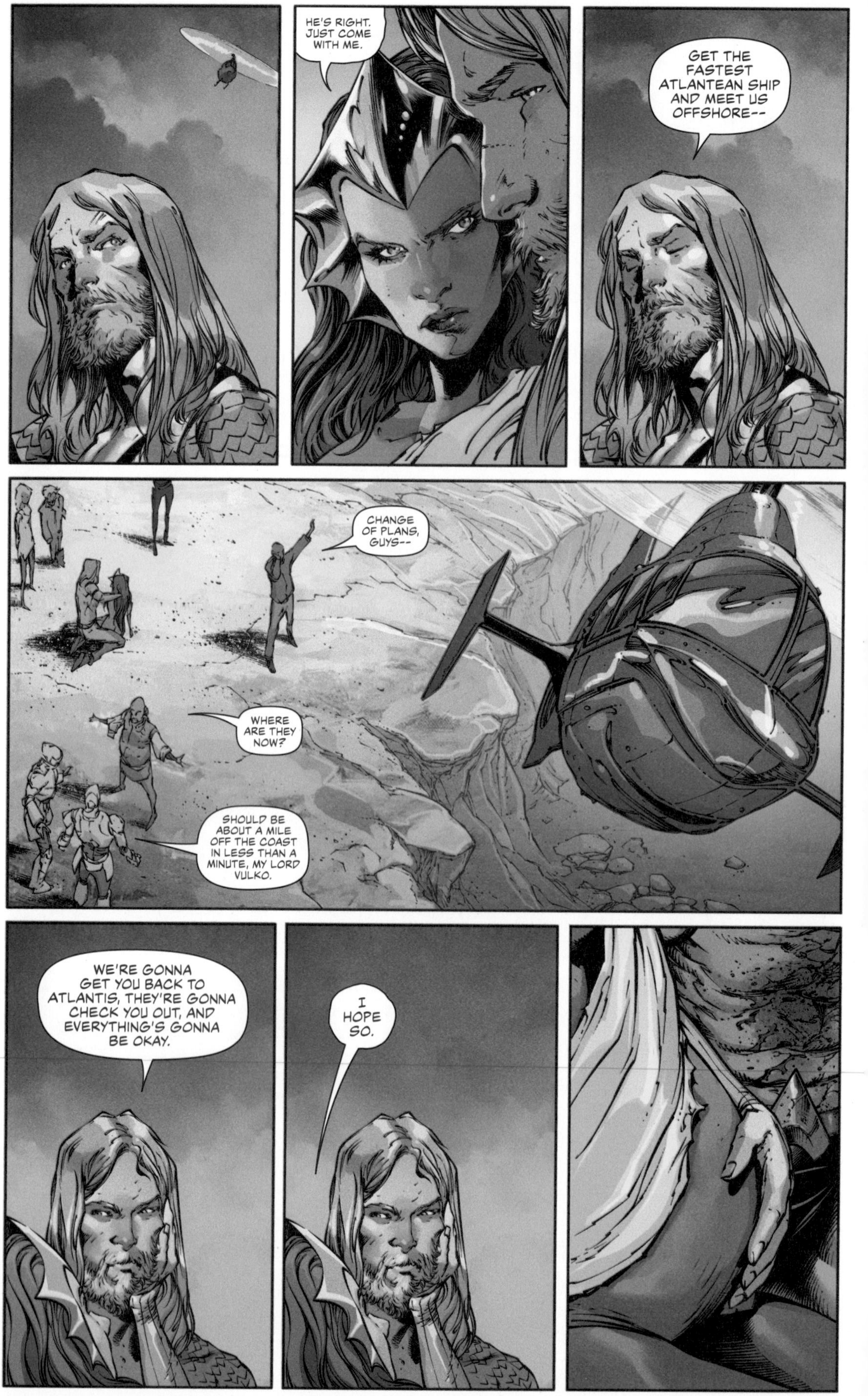
HE'S RIGHT. JUST COME WITH ME.
GET THE FASTEST ATLANTEAN SHIP AND MEET US OFFSHORE--
CHANGE OF PLANS, GUYS--
WHERE ARE THEY NOW?
SHOULD BE ABOUT A MILE OFF THE COAST IN LESS THAN A MINUTE, MY LORD VULKO.
WE'RE GONNA GET YOU BACK TO ATLANTIS, THEY'RE GONNA CHECK YOU OUT, AND EVERYTHING'S GONNA BE OKAY.
I HOPE SO.

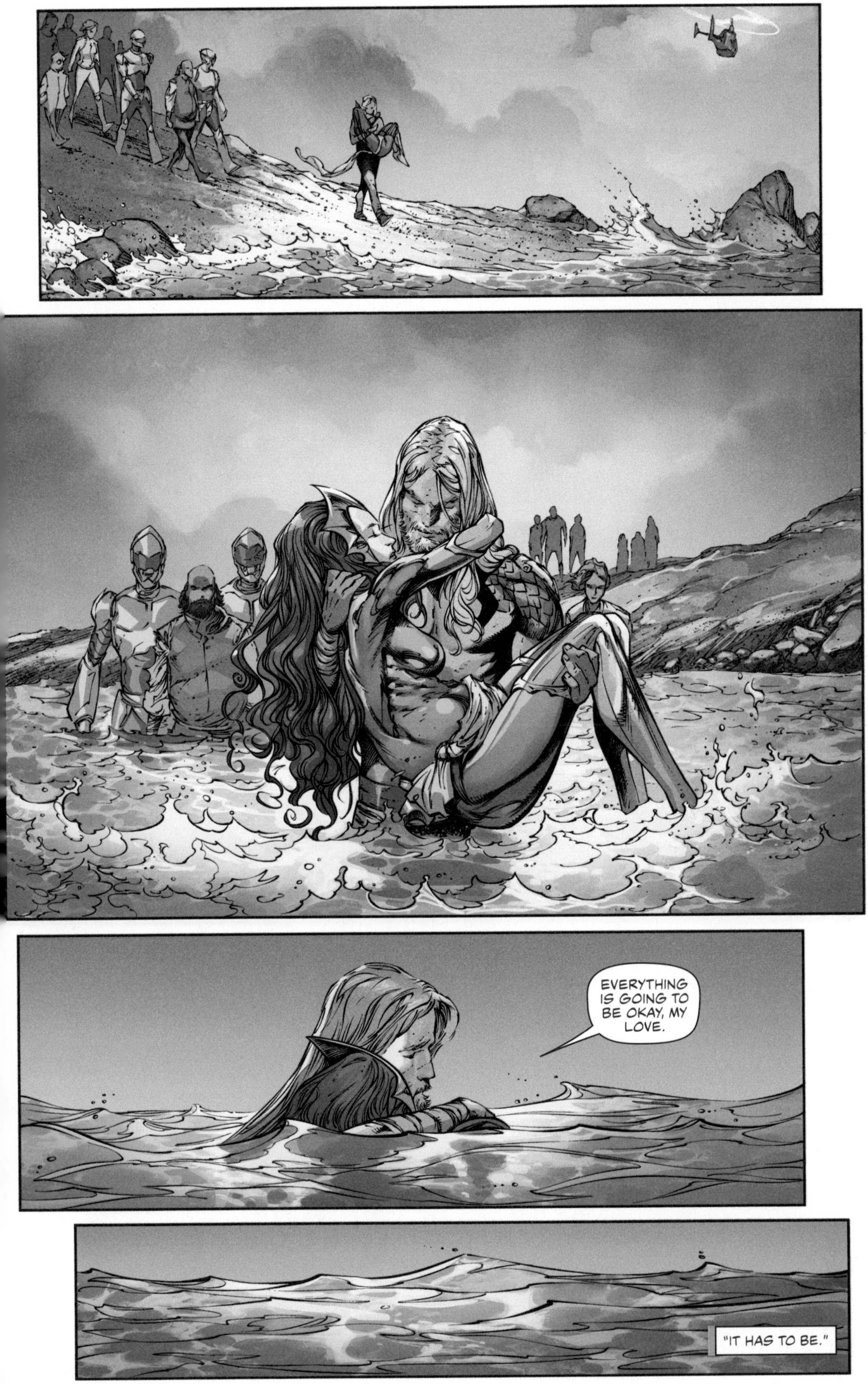
EVERYTHING IS GOING TO BE OKAY, MY LOVE.
"IT HAS TO BE."

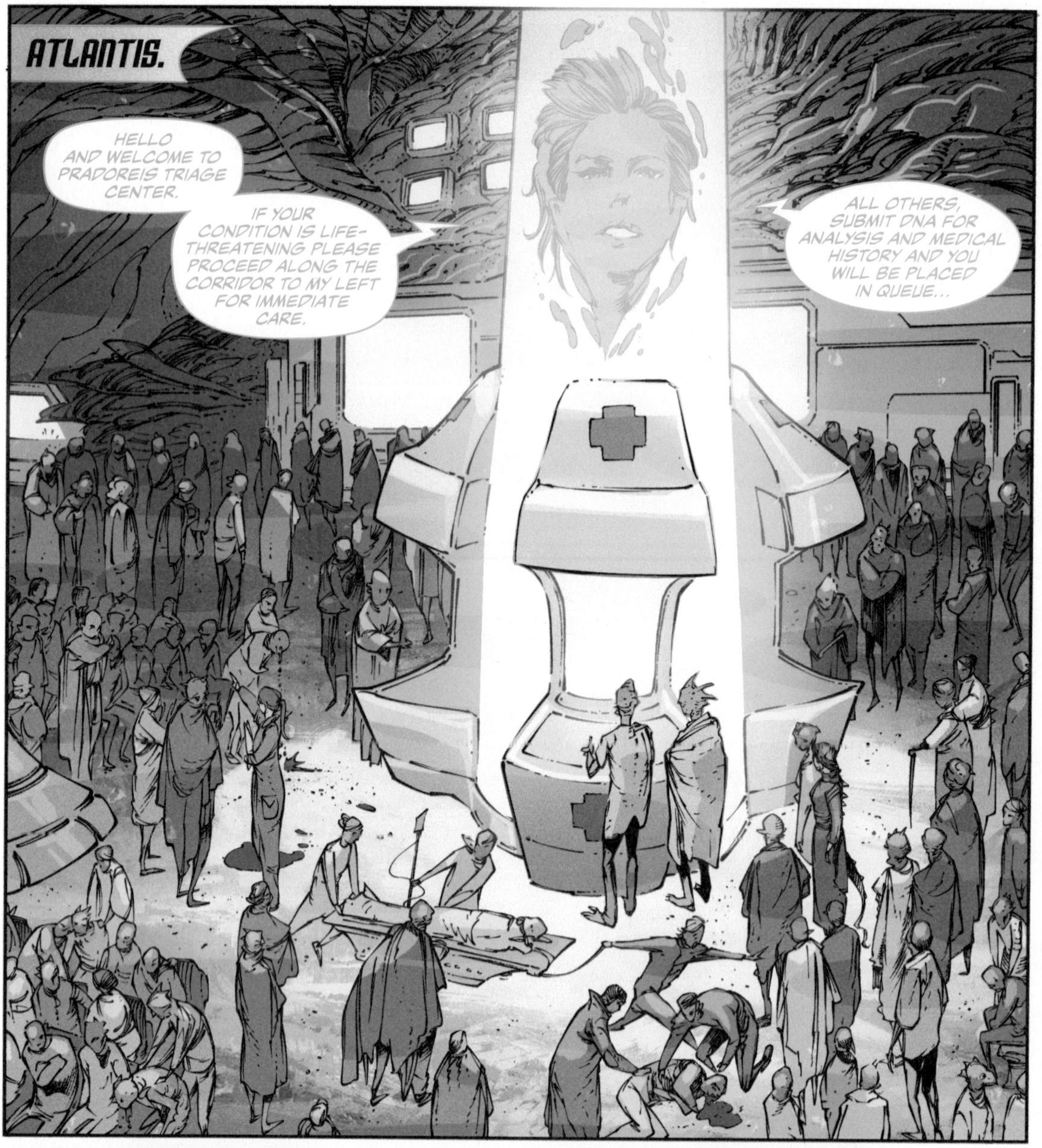
ATLANTIS.
HELLO AND WELCOME TO PRADOREIS TRIAGE CENTER.
IF YOUR CONDITION IS LIFE-THREATENING PLEASE PROCEED ALONG THE CORRIDOR TO MY LEFT FOR IMMEDIATE CARE.
ALL OTHERS, SUBMIT DNA FOR ANALYSIS AND MEDICAL HISTORY AND YOU WILL BE PLACED IN QUEUE...

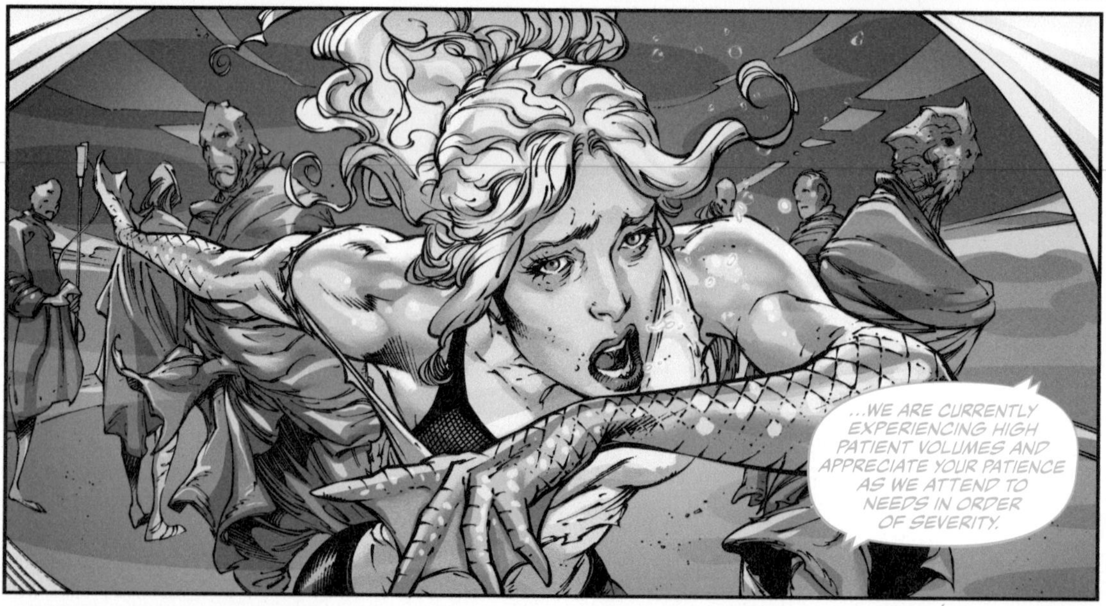
...WE ARE CURRENTLY EXPERIENCING HIGH PATIENT VOLUMES AND APPRECIATE YOUR PATIENCE AS WE ATTEND TO NEEDS IN ORDER OF SEVERITY.

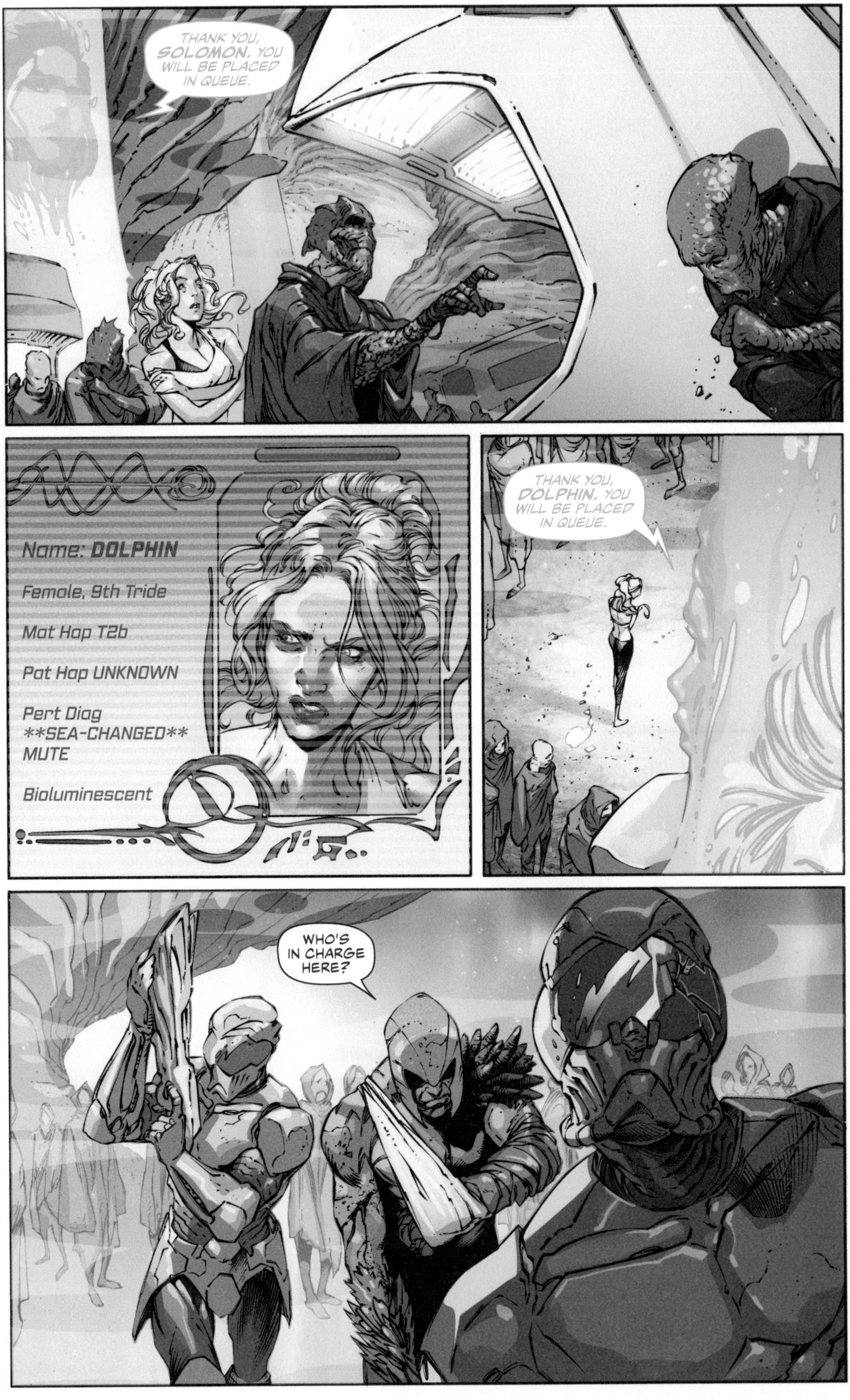
THANK YOU, SOLOMON. YOU WILL BE PLACED IN QUEUE.
Name: DOLPHIN
Female, 9th Tride
Mat Hap T2b
Pat Hap UNKNOWN
Pert Diag **SEA-CHANGED** MUTE
Bioluminescent
THANK YOU, DOLPHIN. YOU WILL BE PLACED IN QUEUE.
WHO'S IN CHARGE HERE?

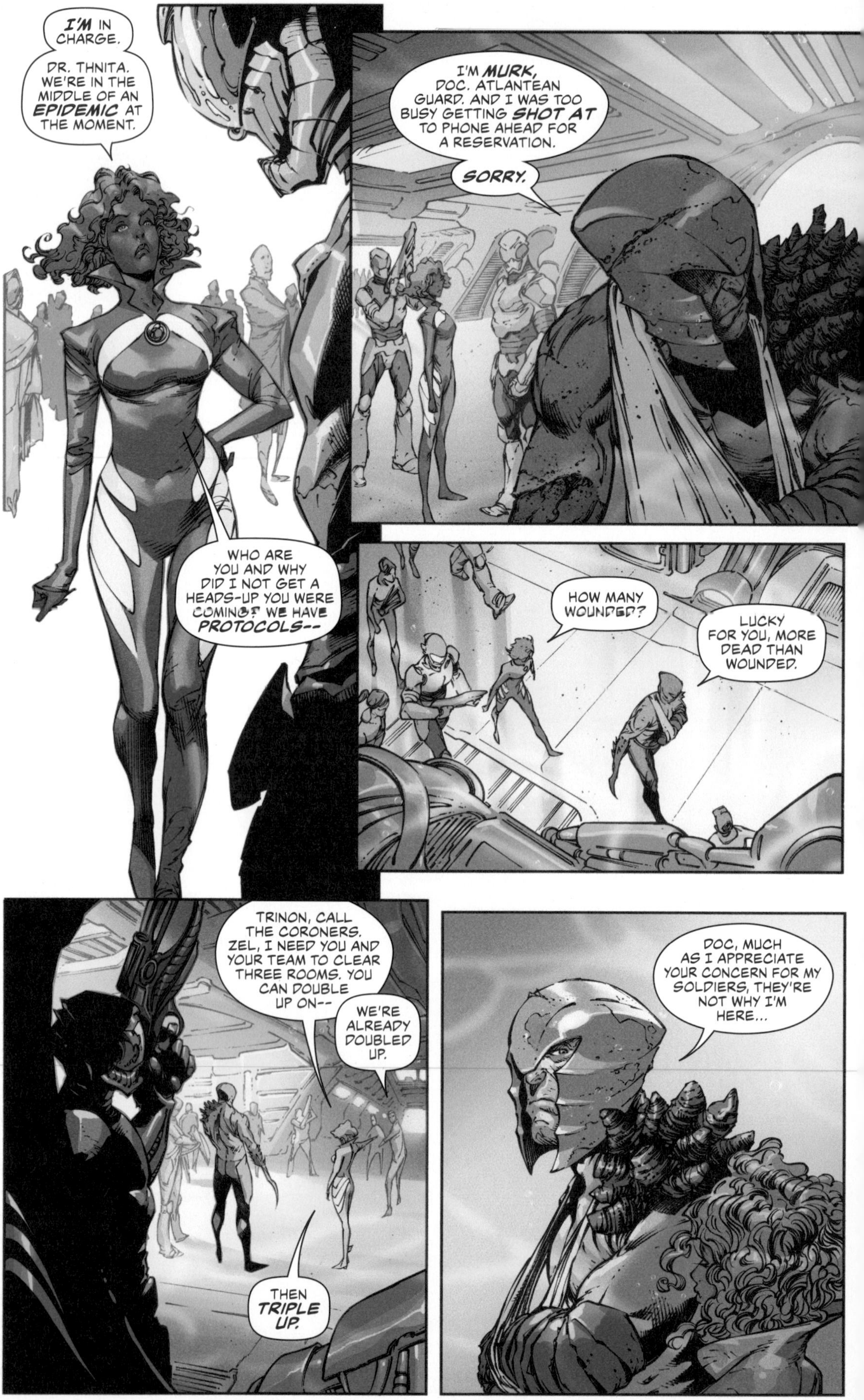
I'M IN CHARGE.
DR. THNITA. WE'RE IN THE MIDDLE OF AN EPIDEMIC AT THE MOMENT.
WHO ARE YOU AND WHY DID I NOT GET A HEADS-UP YOU WERE COMING? WE HAVE PROTOCOLS--
I'M MURK, DOC. ATLANTEAN GUARD. AND I WAS TOO BUSY GETTING SHOT AT TO PHONE AHEAD FOR A RESERVATION.
SORRY.
HOW MANY WOUNDED?
LUCKY FOR YOU, MORE DEAD THAN WOUNDED.
TRINON, CALL THE CORONERS. ZEL, I NEED YOU AND YOUR TEAM TO CLEAR THREE ROOMS. YOU CAN DOUBLE UP ON--
WE'RE ALREADY DOUBLED UP.
THEN TRIPLE UP.
DOC, MUCH AS I APPRECIATE YOUR CONCERN FOR MY SOLDIERS, THEY'RE NOT WHY I'M HERE...

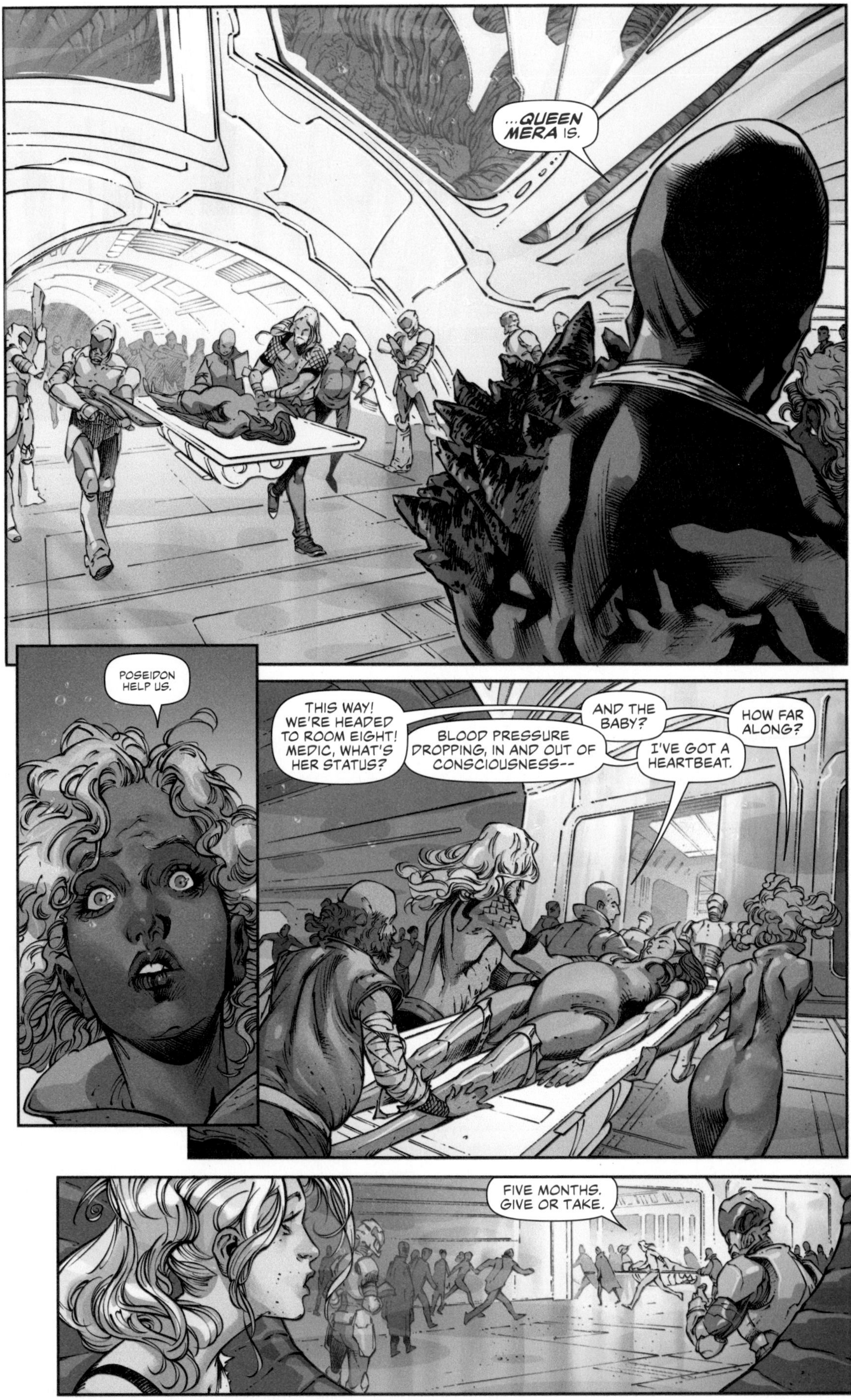
...QUEEN MERA IS.
POSEIDON HELP US.
THIS WAY! WE'RE HEADED TO ROOM EIGHT! MEDIC, WHAT'S HER STATUS?
BLOOD PRESSURE DROPPING, IN AND OUT OF CONSCIOUSNESS--
AND THE BABY?
I'VE GOT A HEARTBEAT.
HOW FAR ALONG?
FIVE MONTHS. GIVE OR TAKE.

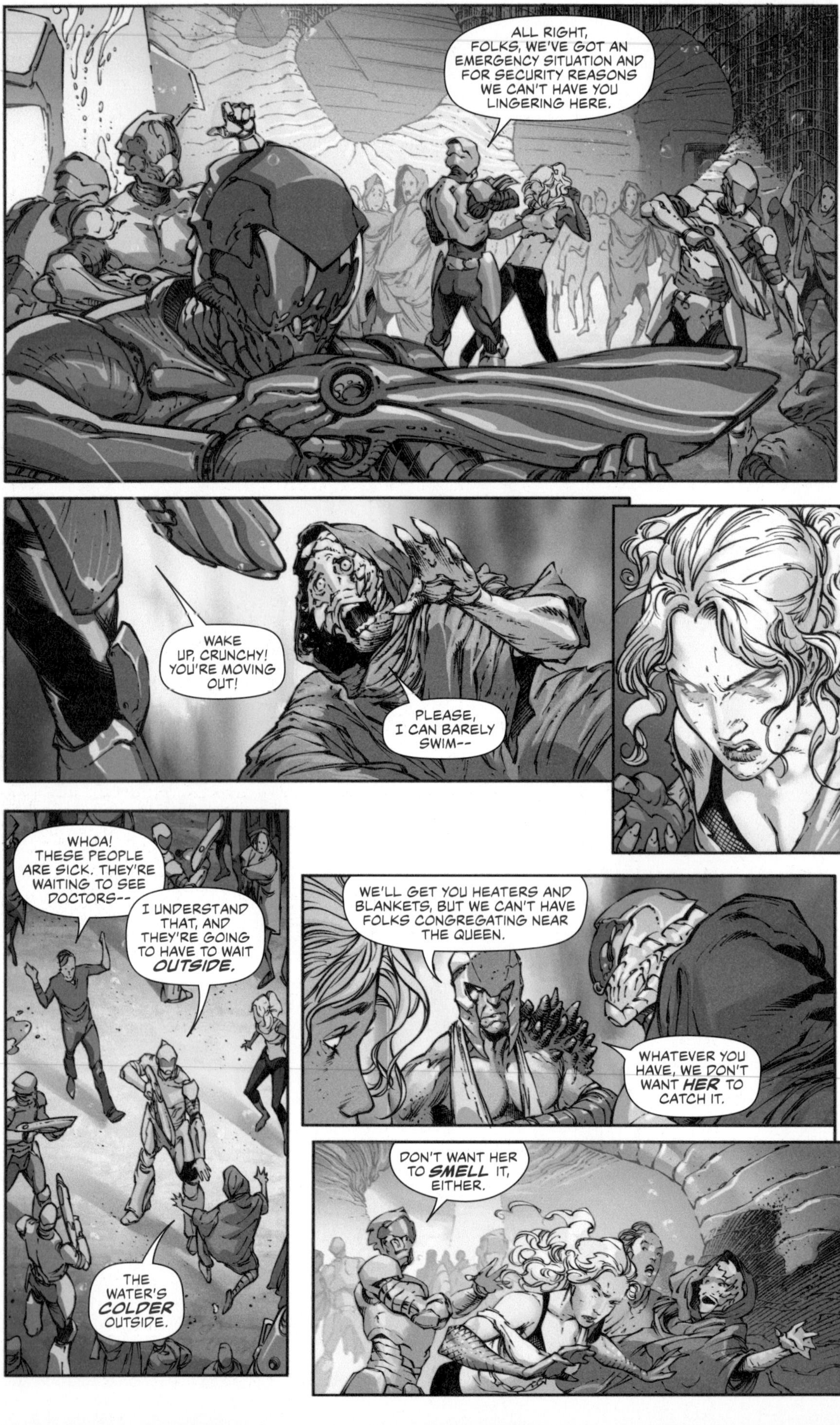
ALL RIGHT, FOLKS, WE'VE GOT AN EMERGENCY SITUATION AND FOR SECURITY REASONS WE CAN'T HAVE YOU LINGERING HERE.
WAKE UP, CRUNCHY! YOU'RE MOVING OUT!
PLEASE, I CAN BARELY SWIM--
WHOA! THESE PEOPLE ARE SICK. THEY'RE WAITING TO SEE DOCTORS--
I UNDERSTAND THAT, AND THEY'RE GOING TO HAVE TO WAIT OUTSIDE.
THE WATER'S COLDER OUTSIDE.
WE'LL GET YOU HEATERS AND BLANKETS, BUT WE CAN'T HAVE FOLKS CONGREGATING NEAR THE QUEEN.
WHATEVER YOU HAVE, WE DON'T WANT HER TO CATCH IT.
DON'T WANT HER TO SMELL IT, EITHER.

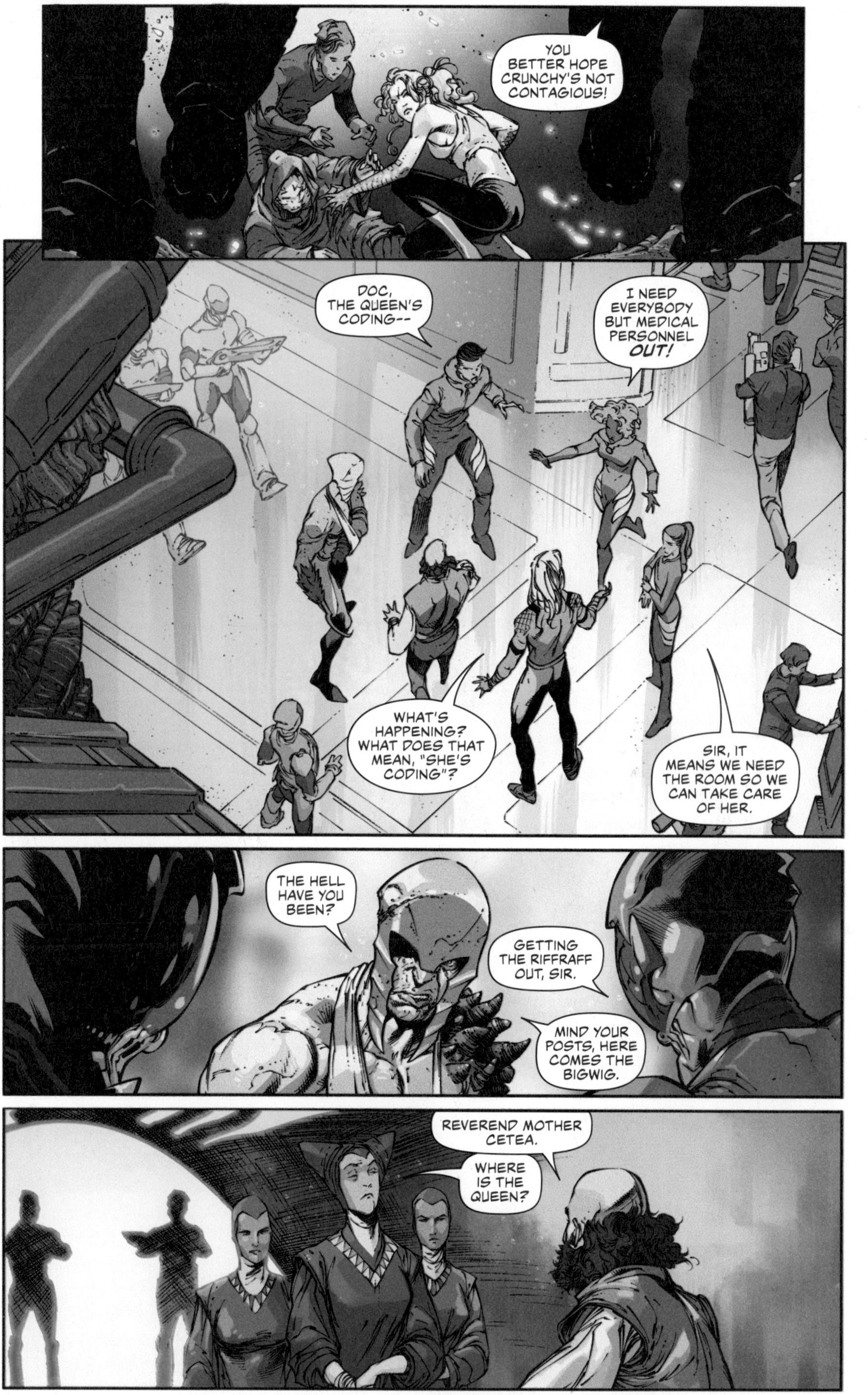
YOU BETTER HOPE CRUNCHY'S NOT CONTAGIOUS!
DOC, THE QUEEN'S CODING--
I NEED EVERYBODY BUT MEDICAL PERSONNEL **OUT!**
WHAT'S HAPPENING? WHAT DOES THAT MEAN, "SHE'S CODING"?
SIR, IT MEANS WE NEED THE ROOM SO WE CAN TAKE CARE OF HER.
THE HELL HAVE YOU BEEN?
GETTING THE RIFFRAFF OUT, SIR.
MIND YOUR POSTS, HERE COMES THE BIGWIG.
REVEREND MOTHER CETEA.
WHERE IS THE QUEEN?

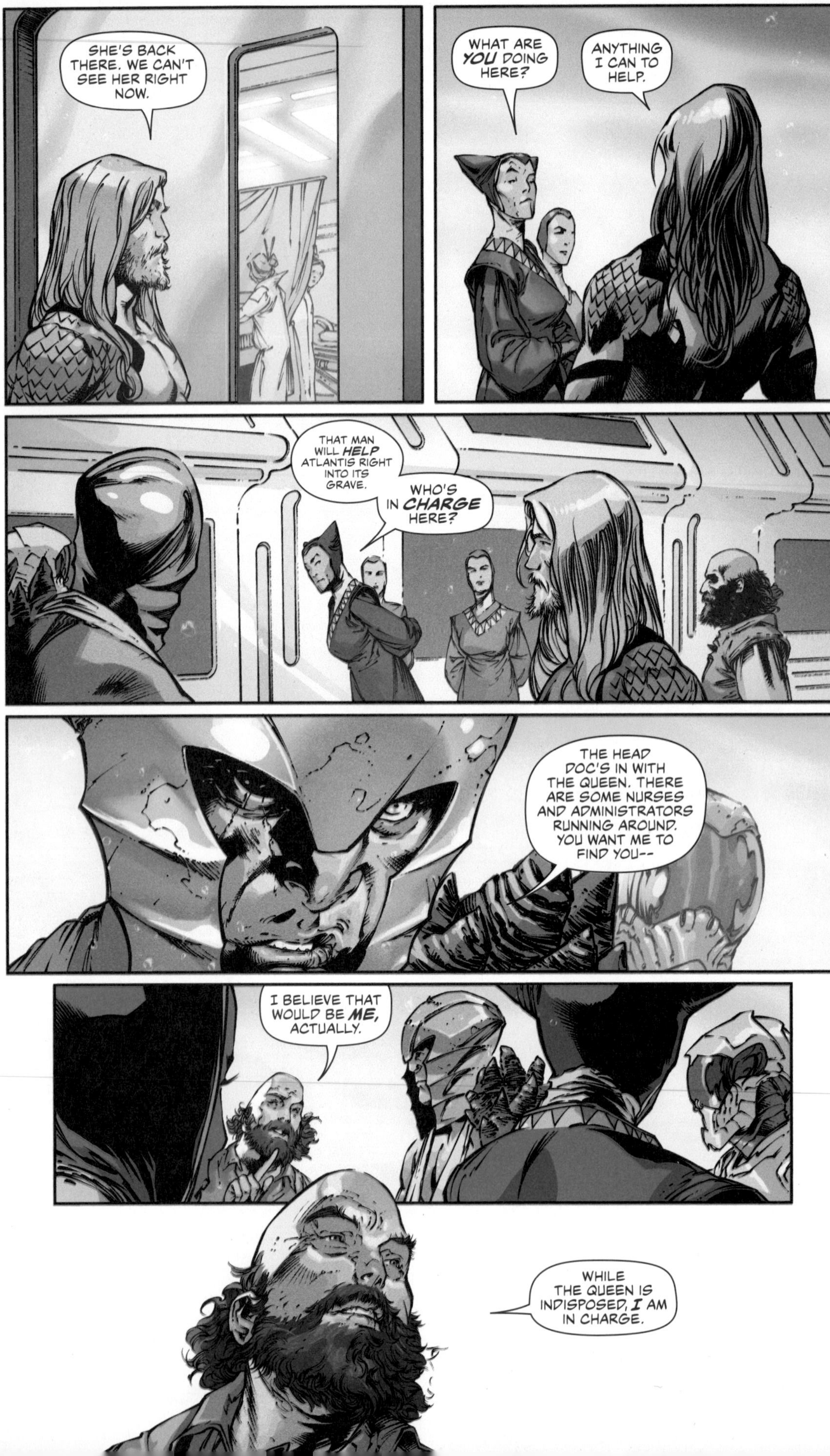
SHE'S BACK THERE. WE CAN'T SEE HER RIGHT NOW.
WHAT ARE YOU DOING HERE?
ANYTHING I CAN TO HELP.
THAT MAN WILL HELP ATLANTIS RIGHT INTO ITS GRAVE.
WHO'S IN CHARGE HERE?
THE HEAD DOC'S IN WITH THE QUEEN. THERE ARE SOME NURSES AND ADMINISTRATORS RUNNING AROUND. YOU WANT ME TO FIND YOU--
I BELIEVE THAT WOULD BE ME, ACTUALLY.
WHILE THE QUEEN IS INDISPOSED, I AM IN CHARGE.

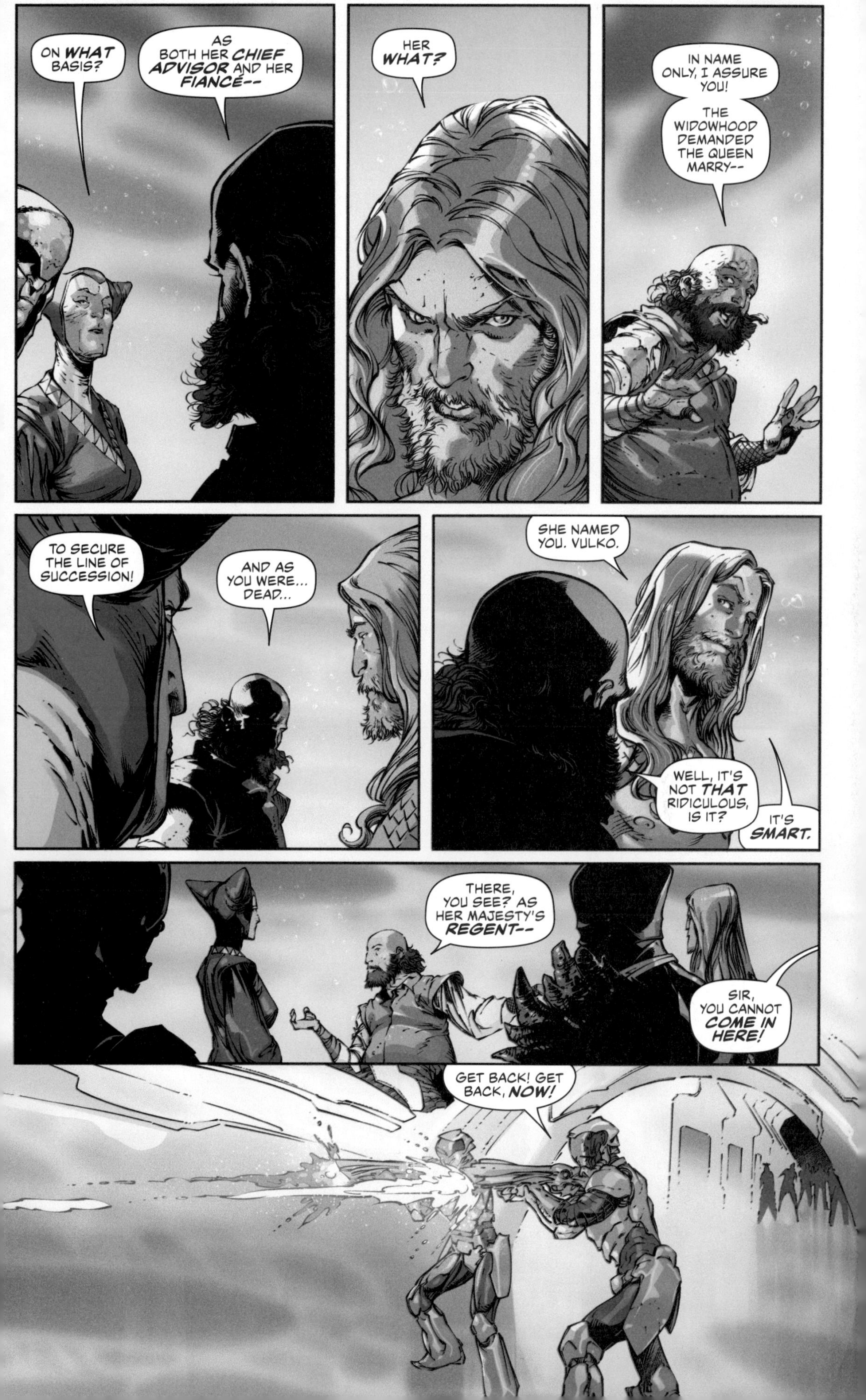
ON WHAT BASIS?
AS BOTH HER CHIEF ADVISOR AND HER FIANCÉ--
HER WHAT?
IN NAME ONLY, I ASSURE YOU!
THE WIDOWHOOD DEMANDED THE QUEEN MARRY--
TO SECURE THE LINE OF SUCCESSION!
AND AS YOU WERE... DEAD...
SHE NAMED YOU. VULKO.
WELL, IT'S NOT THAT RIDICULOUS, IS IT?
IT'S SMART.
THERE, YOU SEE? AS HER MAJESTY'S REGENT--
SIR, YOU CANNOT COME IN HERE!
GET BACK! GET BACK, NOW!

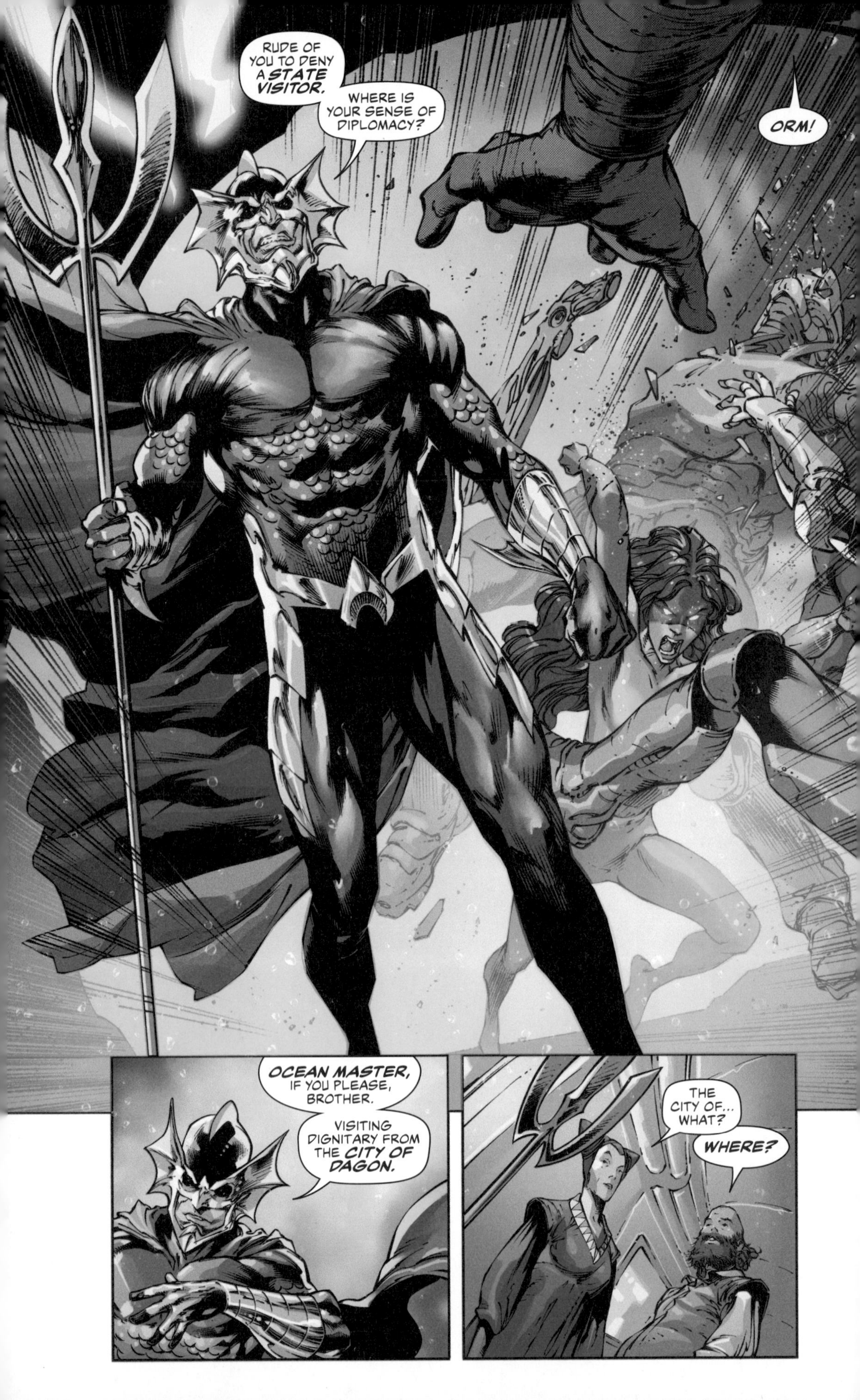
RUDE OF YOU TO DENY A STATE VISITOR.
WHERE IS YOUR SENSE OF DIPLOMACY?
ORM!
OCEAN MASTER, IF YOU PLEASE, BROTHER.
VISITING DIGNITARY FROM THE CITY OF DAGON.
THE CITY OF... WHAT?
WHERE?

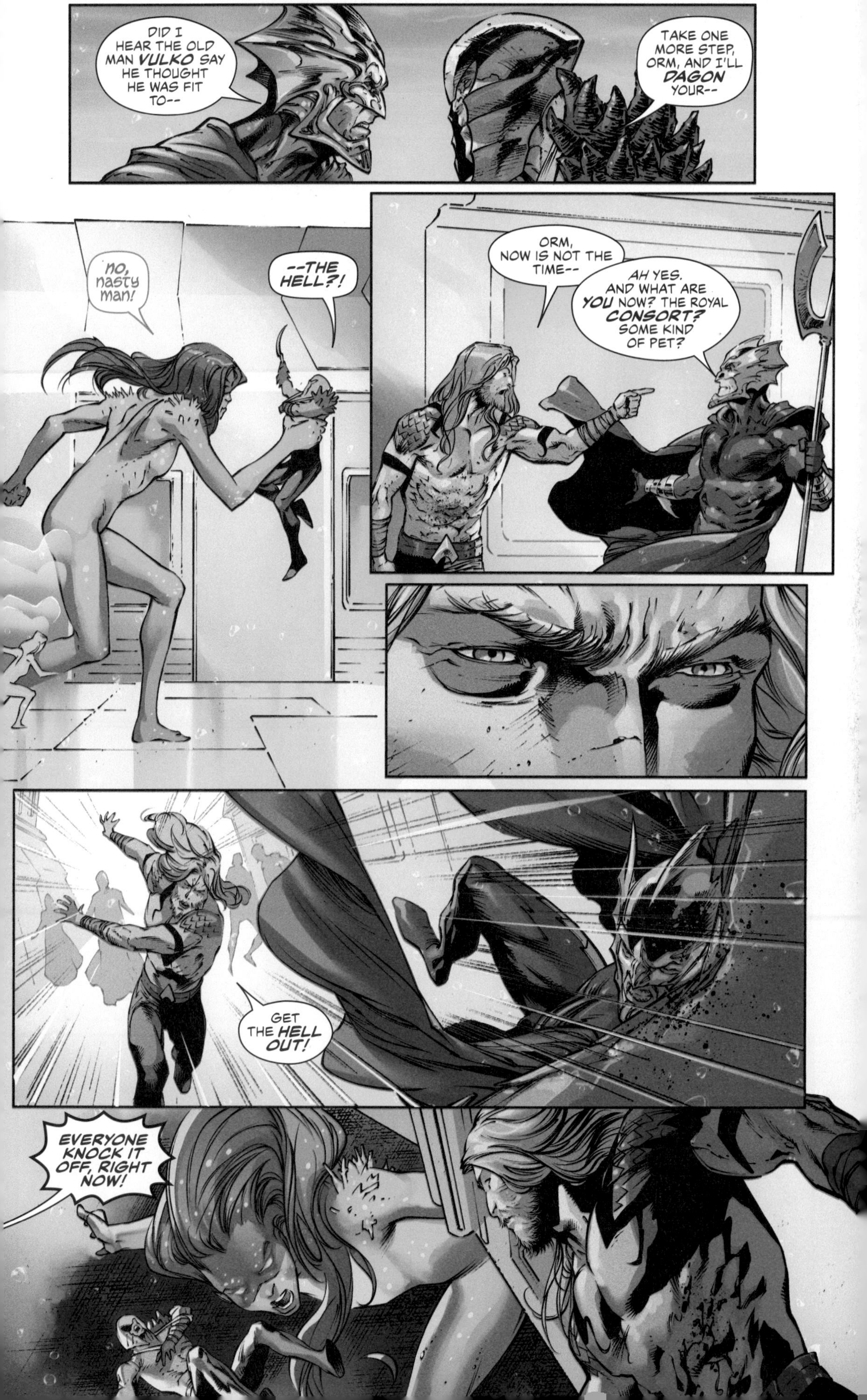
DID I HEAR THE OLD MAN VULKO SAY HE THOUGHT HE WAS FIT TO--
TAKE ONE MORE STEP, ORM, AND I'LL DAGON YOUR--
No, nasty man!
--THE HELL?!
ORM, NOW IS NOT THE TIME--
AH YES. AND WHAT ARE YOU NOW? THE ROYAL CONSORT? SOME KIND OF PET?
GET THE HELL OUT!
EVERYONE KNOCK IT OFF, RIGHT NOW!

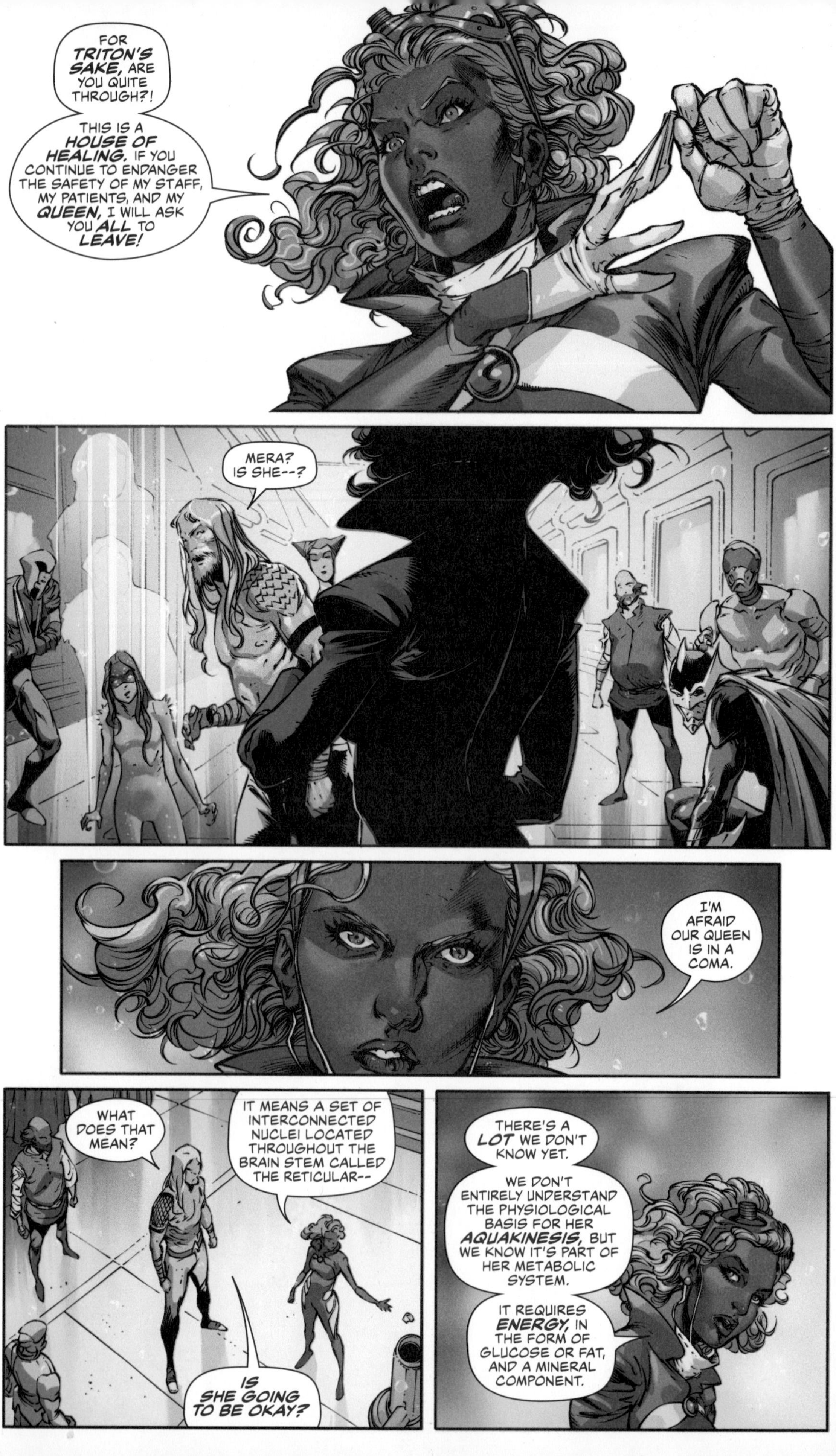
FOR TRITON'S SAKE, ARE YOU QUITE THROUGH?!
THIS IS A HOUSE OF HEALING. IF YOU CONTINUE TO ENDANGER THE SAFETY OF MY STAFF, MY PATIENTS, AND MY QUEEN, I WILL ASK YOU ALL TO LEAVE!
MERA? IS SHE--?
I'M AFRAID OUR QUEEN IS IN A COMA.
WHAT DOES THAT MEAN?
IT MEANS A SET OF INTERCONNECTED NUCLEI LOCATED THROUGHOUT THE BRAIN STEM CALLED THE RETICULAR--
IS SHE GOING TO BE OKAY?
THERE'S A LOT WE DON'T KNOW YET.
WE DON'T ENTIRELY UNDERSTAND THE PHYSIOLOGICAL BASIS FOR HER AQUAKINESIS, BUT WE KNOW IT'S PART OF HER METABOLIC SYSTEM.
IT REQUIRES ENERGY, IN THE FORM OF GLUCOSE OR FAT, AND A MINERAL COMPONENT.

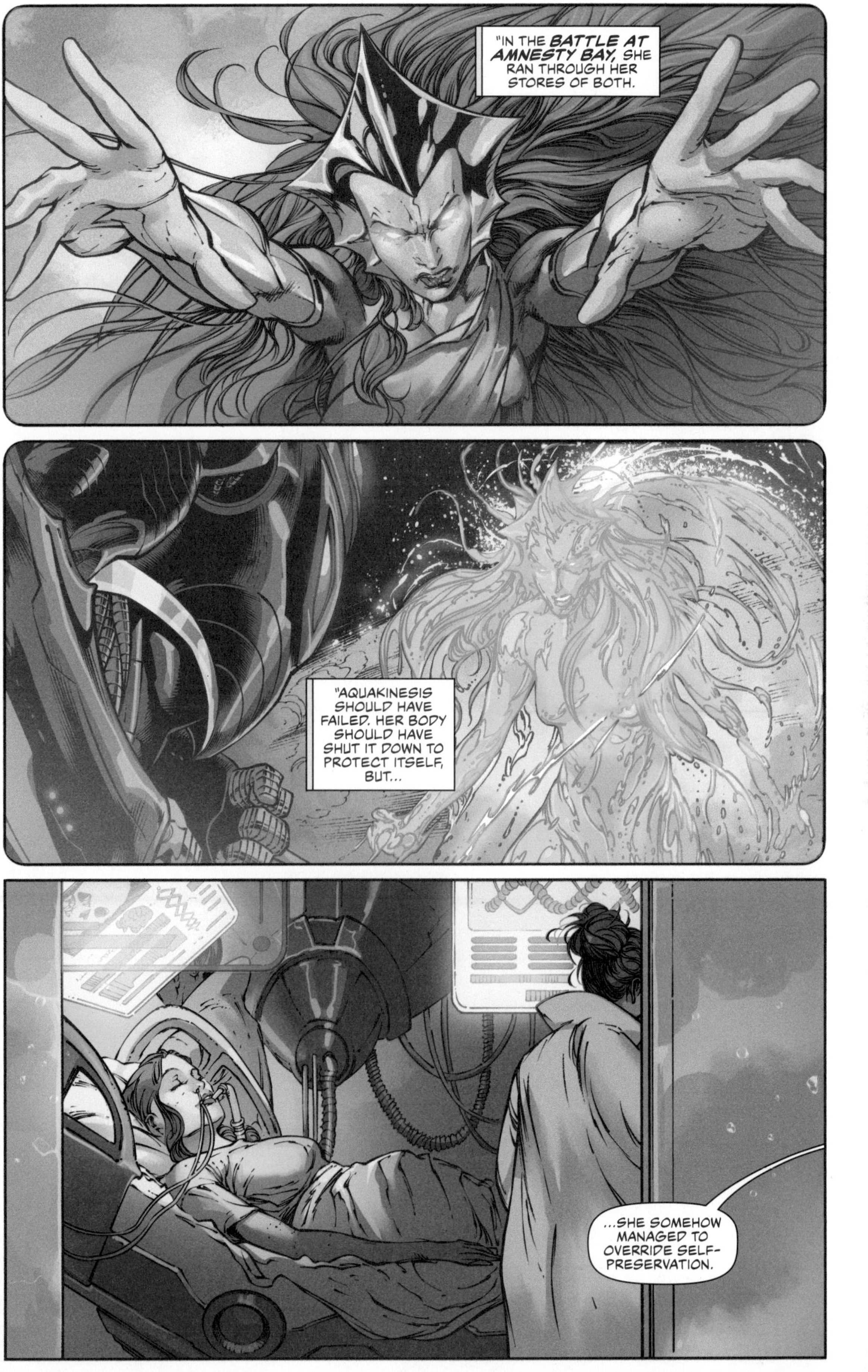
"IN THE BATTLE AT AMNESTY BAY, SHE RAN THROUGH HER STORES OF BOTH.
"AQUAKINESIS SHOULD HAVE FAILED. HER BODY SHOULD HAVE SHUT IT DOWN TO PROTECT ITSELF, BUT...
...SHE SOMEHOW MANAGED TO OVERRIDE SELF-PRESERVATION.

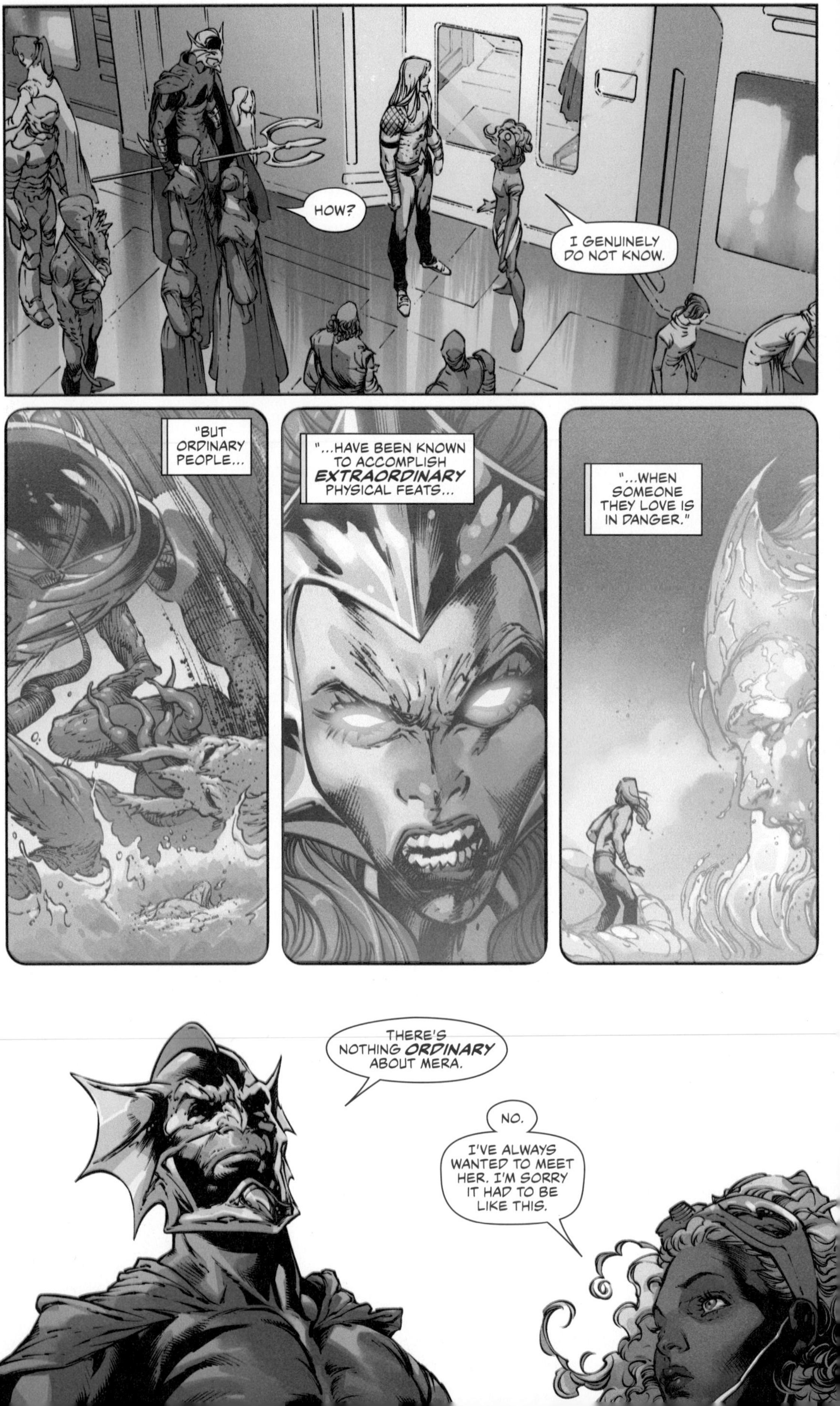
HOW?
I GENUINELY DO NOT KNOW.
"BUT ORDINARY PEOPLE...
"...HAVE BEEN KNOWN TO ACCOMPLISH EXTRAORDINARY PHYSICAL FEATS...
"...WHEN SOMEONE THEY LOVE IS IN DANGER."
THERE'S NOTHING ORDINARY ABOUT MERA.
NO.
I'VE ALWAYS WANTED TO MEET HER. I'M SORRY IT HAD TO BE LIKE THIS.

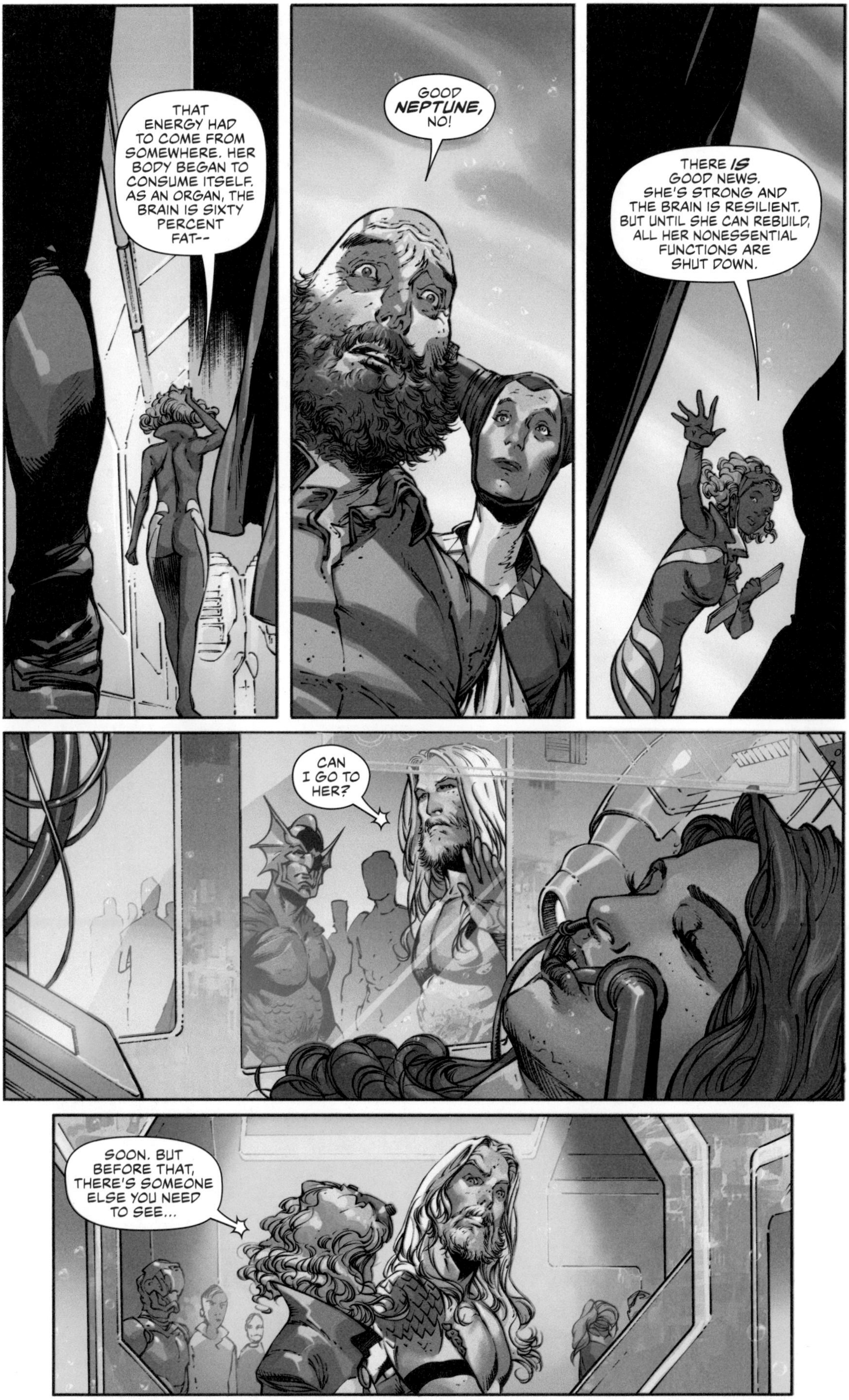
THAT ENERGY HAD TO COME FROM SOMEWHERE. HER BODY BEGAN TO CONSUME ITSELF. AS AN ORGAN, THE BRAIN IS SIXTY PERCENT FAT--
GOOD **NEPTUNE,** NO!
THERE ***IS*** GOOD NEWS. SHE'S STRONG AND THE BRAIN IS RESILIENT. BUT UNTIL SHE CAN REBUILD, ALL HER NONESSENTIAL FUNCTIONS ARE SHUT DOWN.
CAN I GO TO HER?
SOON. BUT BEFORE THAT, THERE'S SOMEONE ELSE YOU NEED TO SEE...

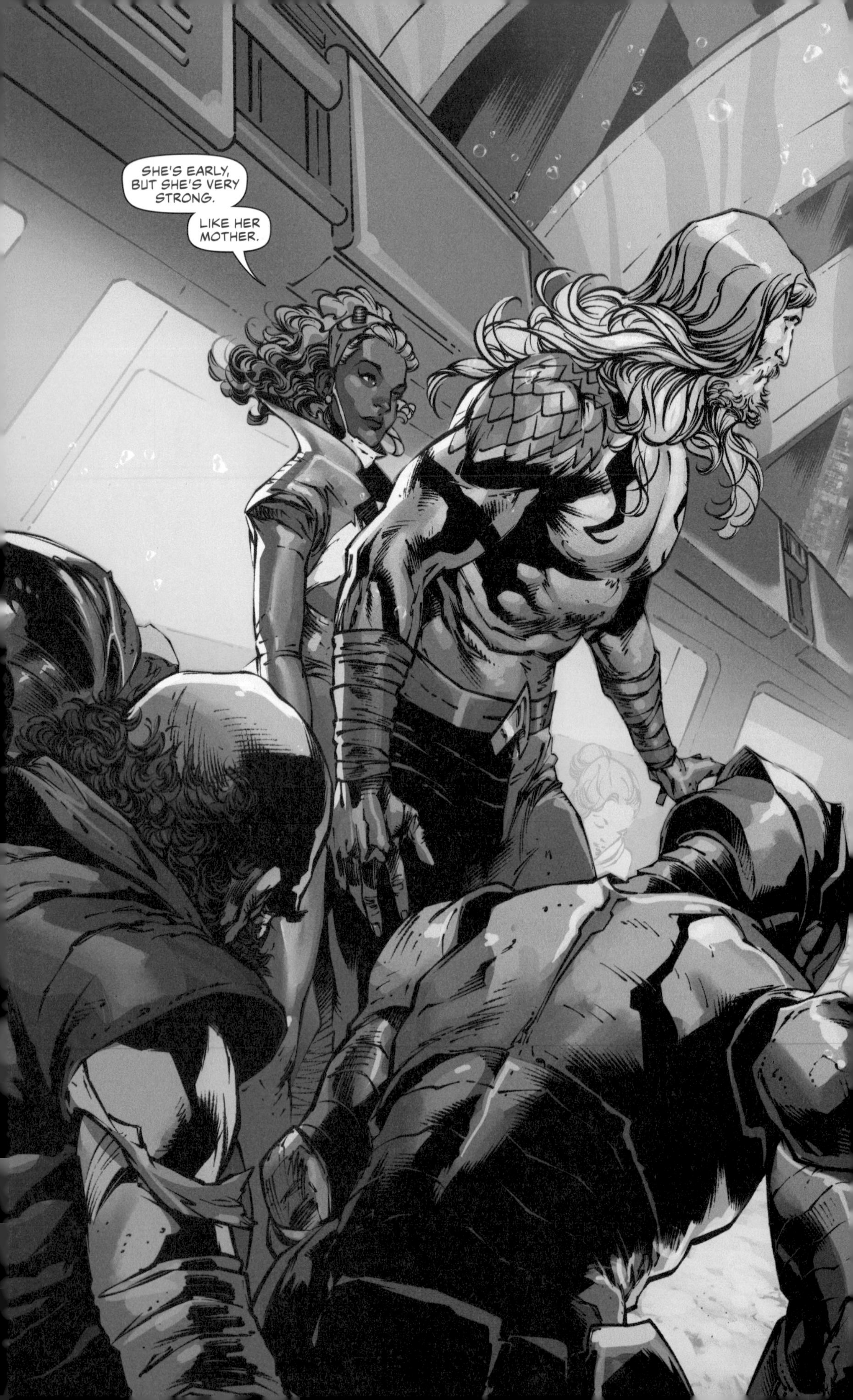
SHE'S EARLY, BUT SHE'S VERY STRONG.
LIKE HER MOTHER.

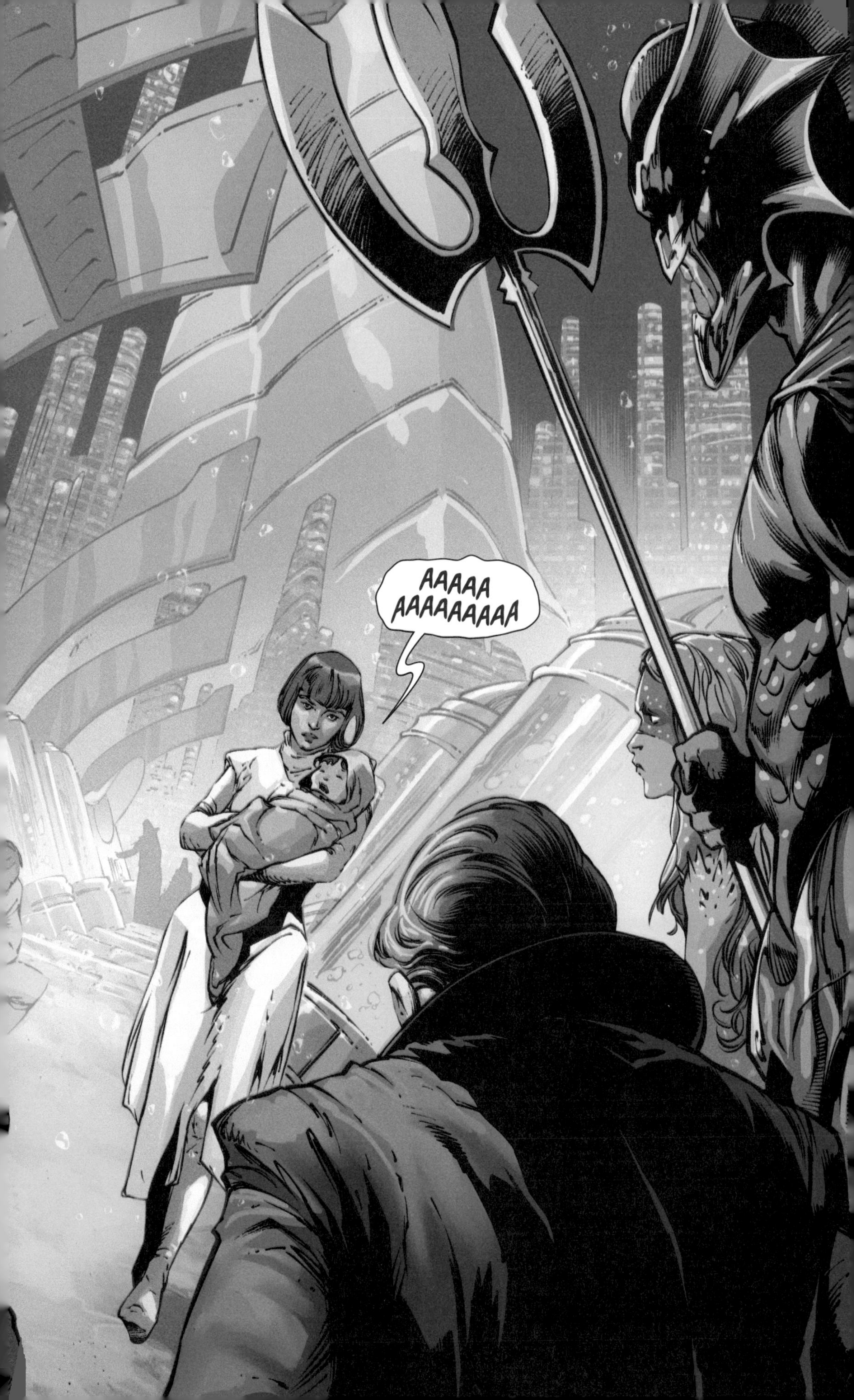
AAAAA AAAAAAAAA

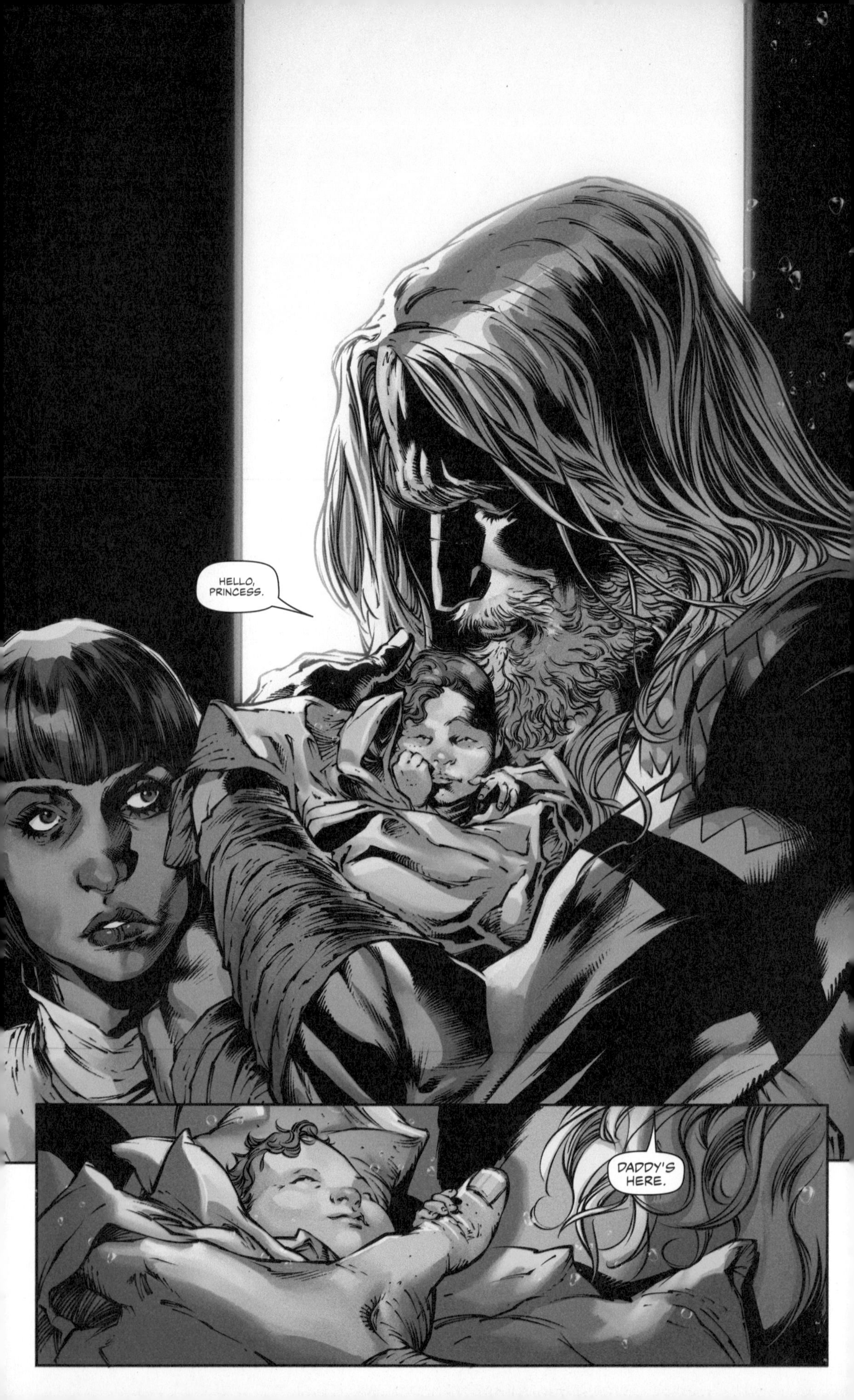
HELLO, PRINCESS.
DADDY'S HERE.

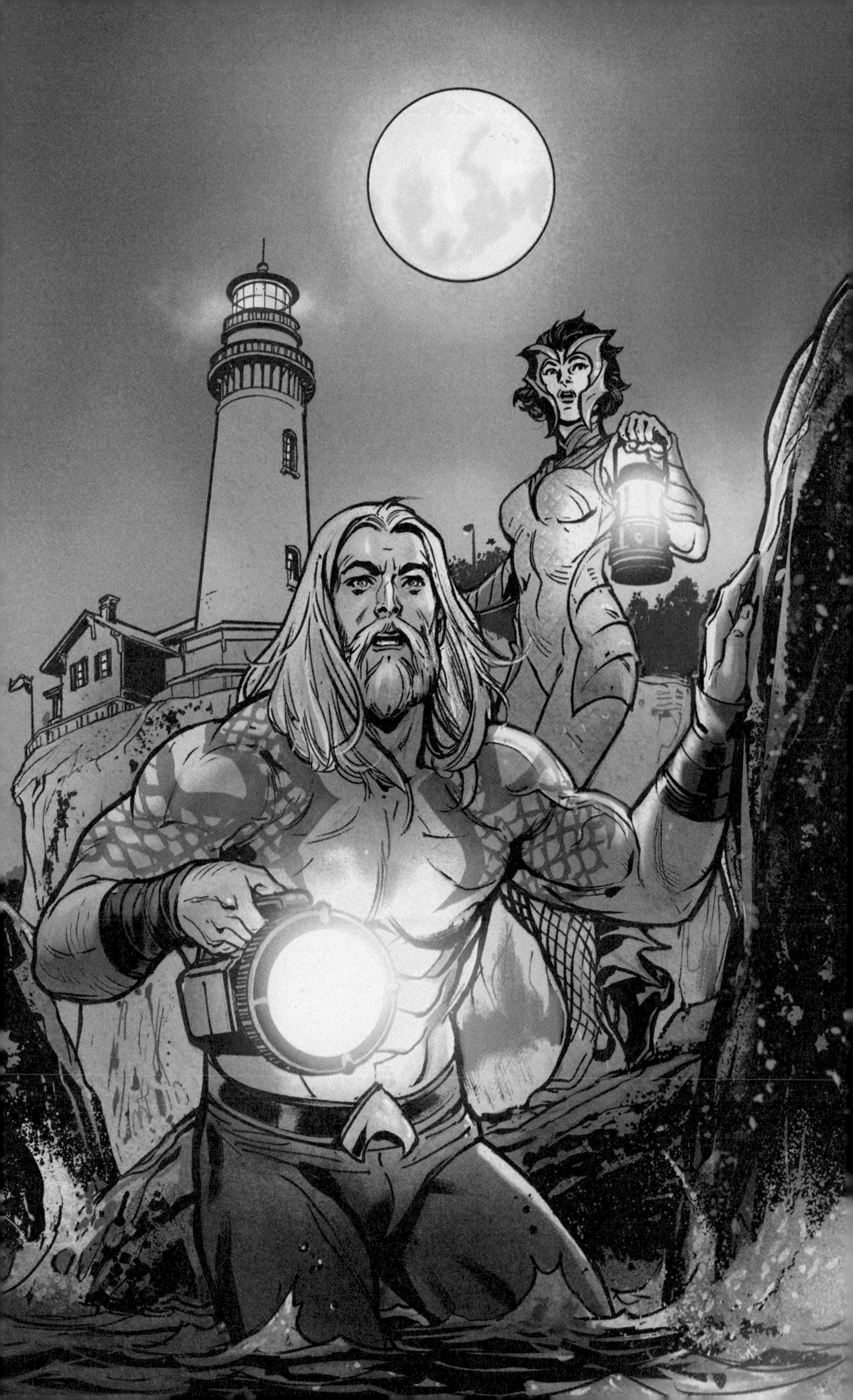

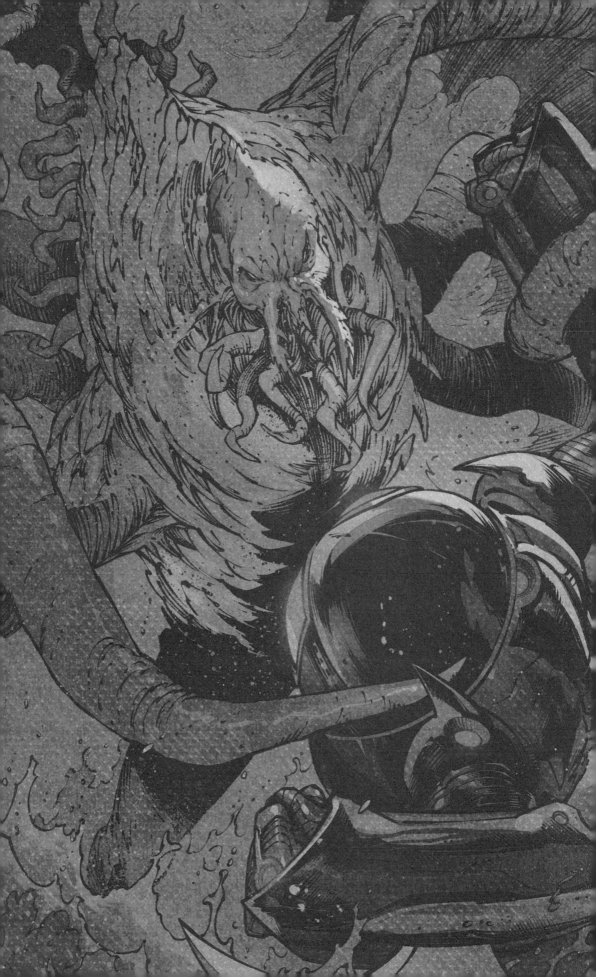

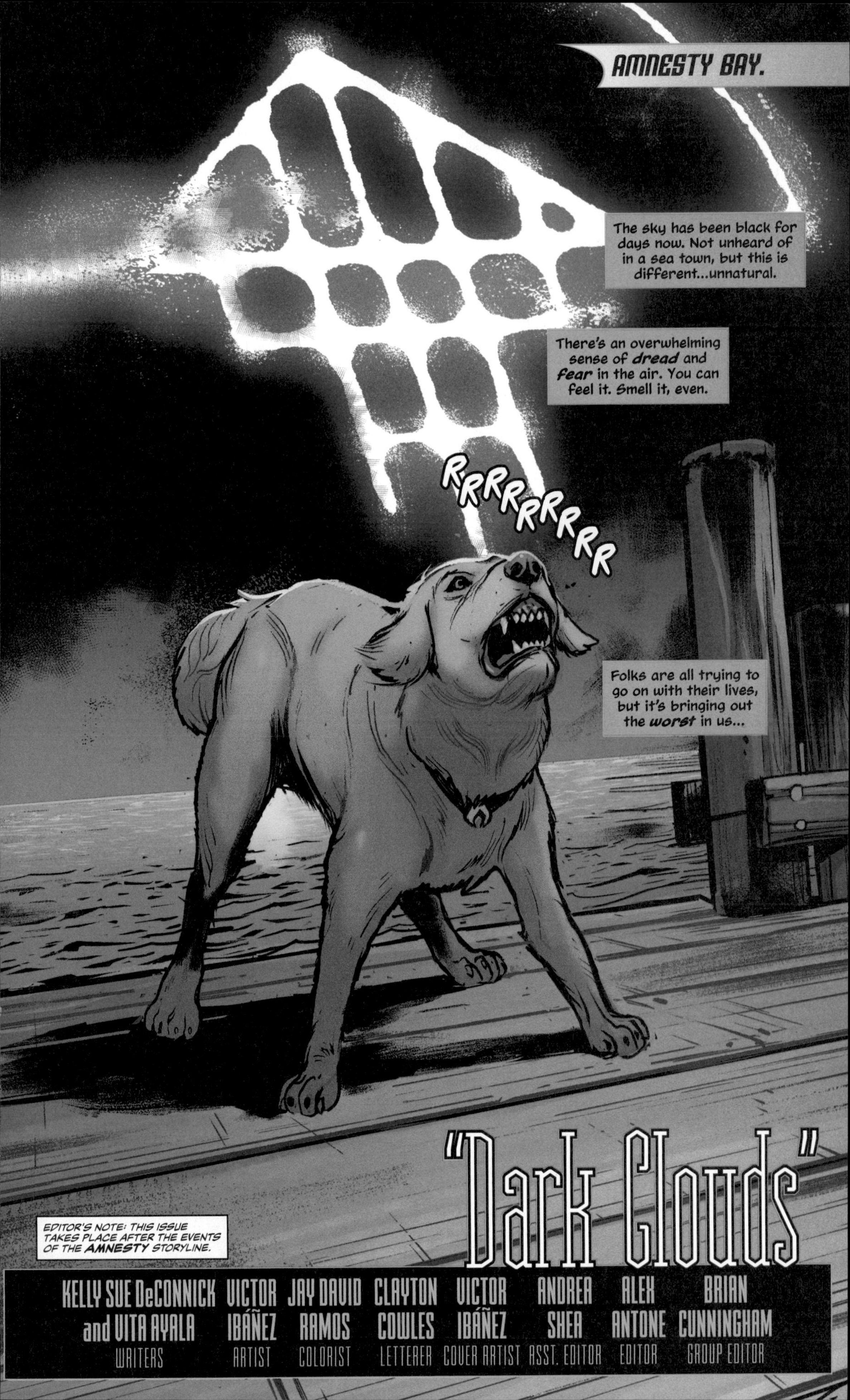
AMNESTY BAY.
The sky has been black for days now. Not unheard of in a sea town, but this is different...unnatural.
There's an overwhelming sense of *dread* and *fear* in the air. You can feel it. Smell it, even.
RRRRRRRRRR
Folks are all trying to go on with their lives, but it's bringing out the *worst* in us...
"Dark Clouds"
EDITOR'S NOTE: THIS ISSUE TAKES PLACE AFTER THE EVENTS OF THE AMNESTY STORYLINE.
KELLY SUE DeCONNICK and VITA AYALA WRITERS
VICTOR IBÁÑEZ ARTIST
JAY DAVID RAMOS COLORIST
CLAYTON COWLES LETTERER
VICTOR IBÁÑEZ COVER ARTIST
ANDREA SHEA ASST. EDITOR
ALEX ANTONE EDITOR
BRIAN CUNNINGHAM GROUP EDITOR

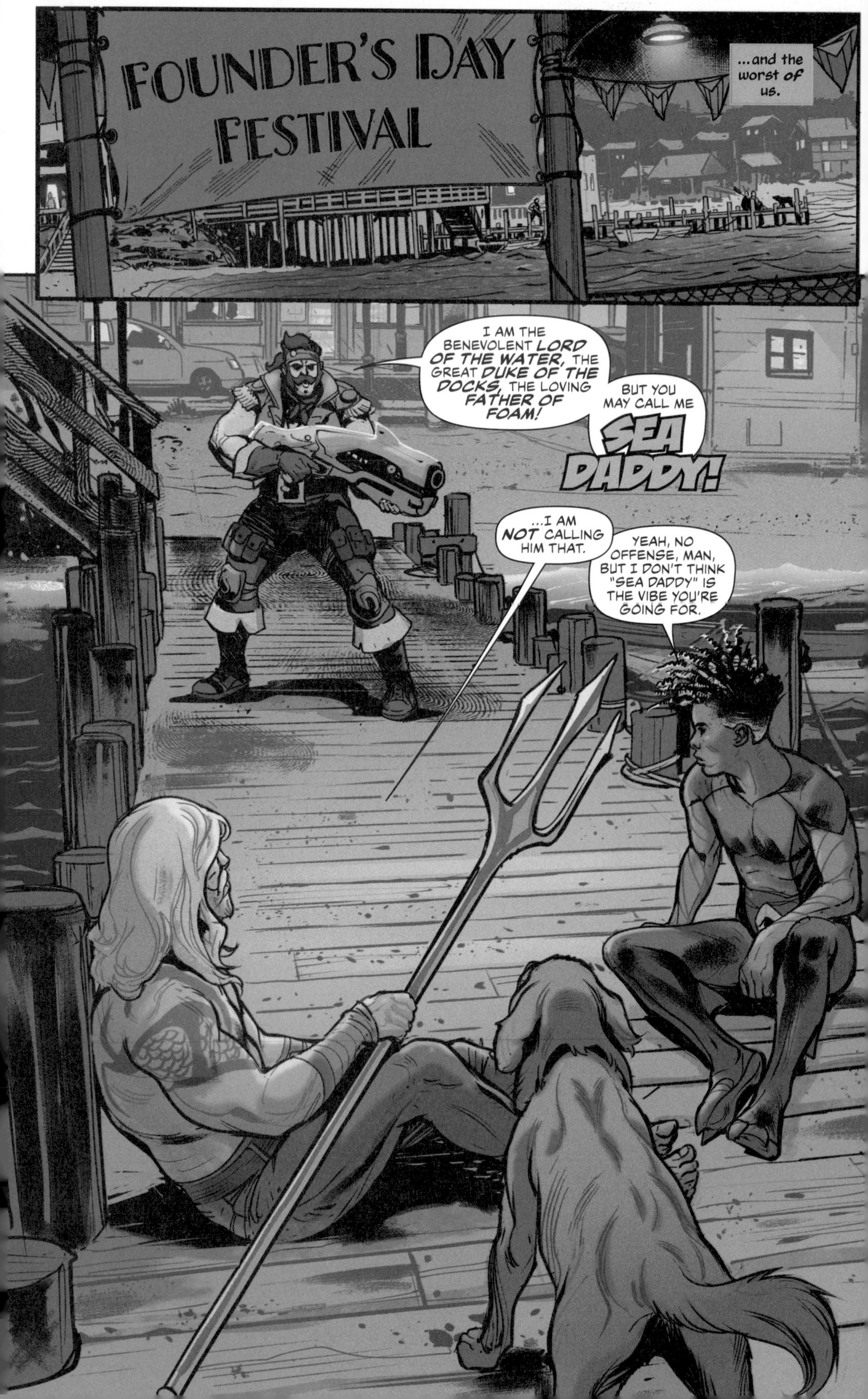
FOUNDER'S DAY FESTIVAL
...and the worst of us.
I AM THE BENEVOLENT LORD OF THE WATER, THE GREAT DUKE OF THE DOCKS, THE LOVING FATHER OF FOAM!
BUT YOU MAY CALL ME
SEA DADDY!
...I AM NOT CALLING HIM THAT.
YEAH, NO OFFENSE, MAN, BUT I DON'T THINK "SEA DADDY" IS THE VIBE YOU'RE GOING FOR.

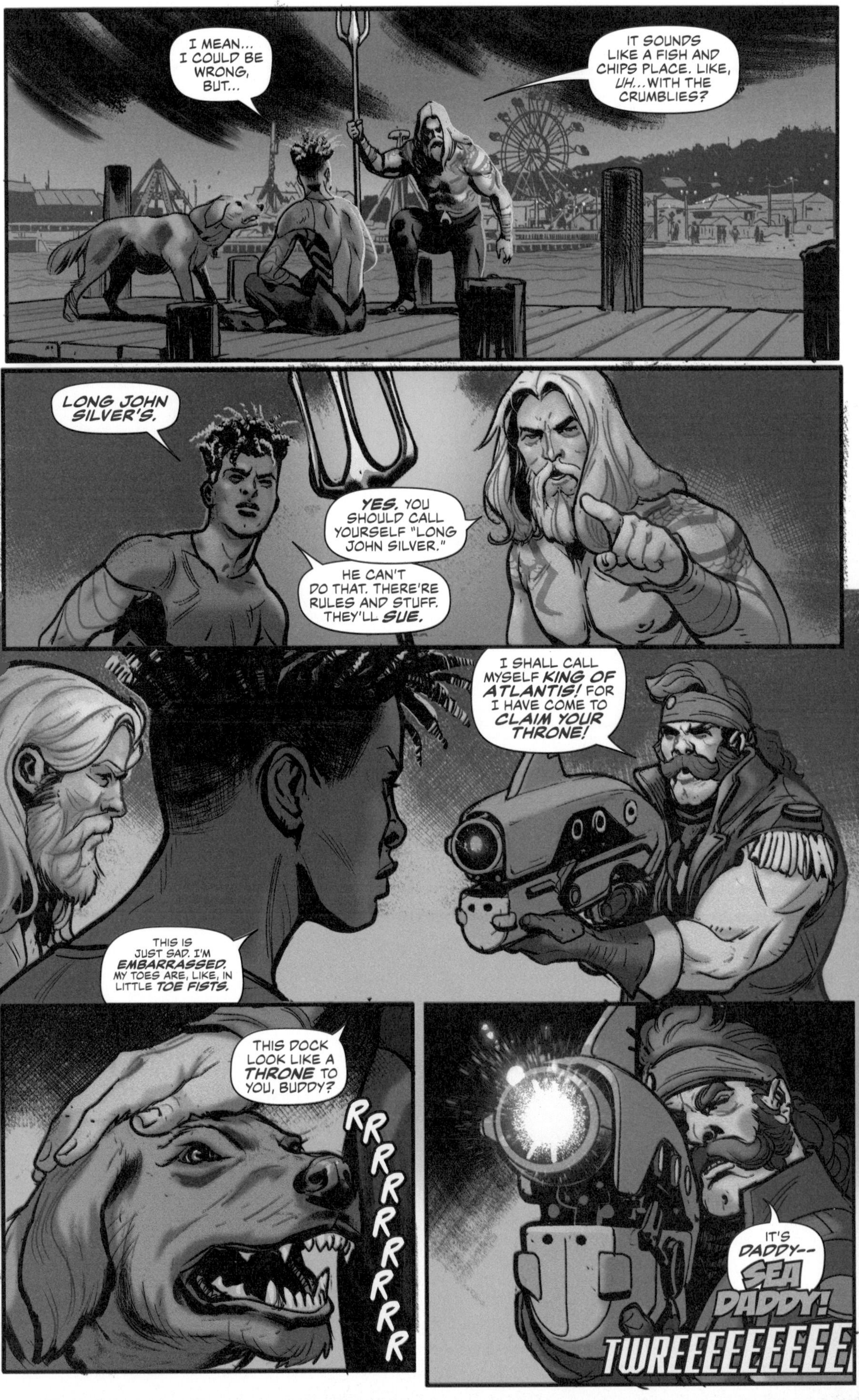
I MEAN... I COULD BE WRONG, BUT...
IT SOUNDS LIKE A FISH AND CHIPS PLACE. LIKE, UH... WITH THE CRUMBLIES?
LONG JOHN SILVER'S.
YES. YOU SHOULD CALL YOURSELF "LONG JOHN SILVER."
HE CAN'T DO THAT. THERE'RE RULES AND STUFF. THEY'LL SUE.
I SHALL CALL MYSELF KING OF ATLANTIS! FOR I HAVE COME TO CLAIM YOUR THRONE!
THIS IS JUST SAD. I'M EMBARRASSED. MY TOES ARE, LIKE, IN LITTLE TOE FISTS.
THIS DOCK LOOK LIKE A THRONE TO YOU, BUDDY?
RRRRRRRRRRR
IT'S DADDY-- SEA DADDY!
TWREEEEEEEEEE

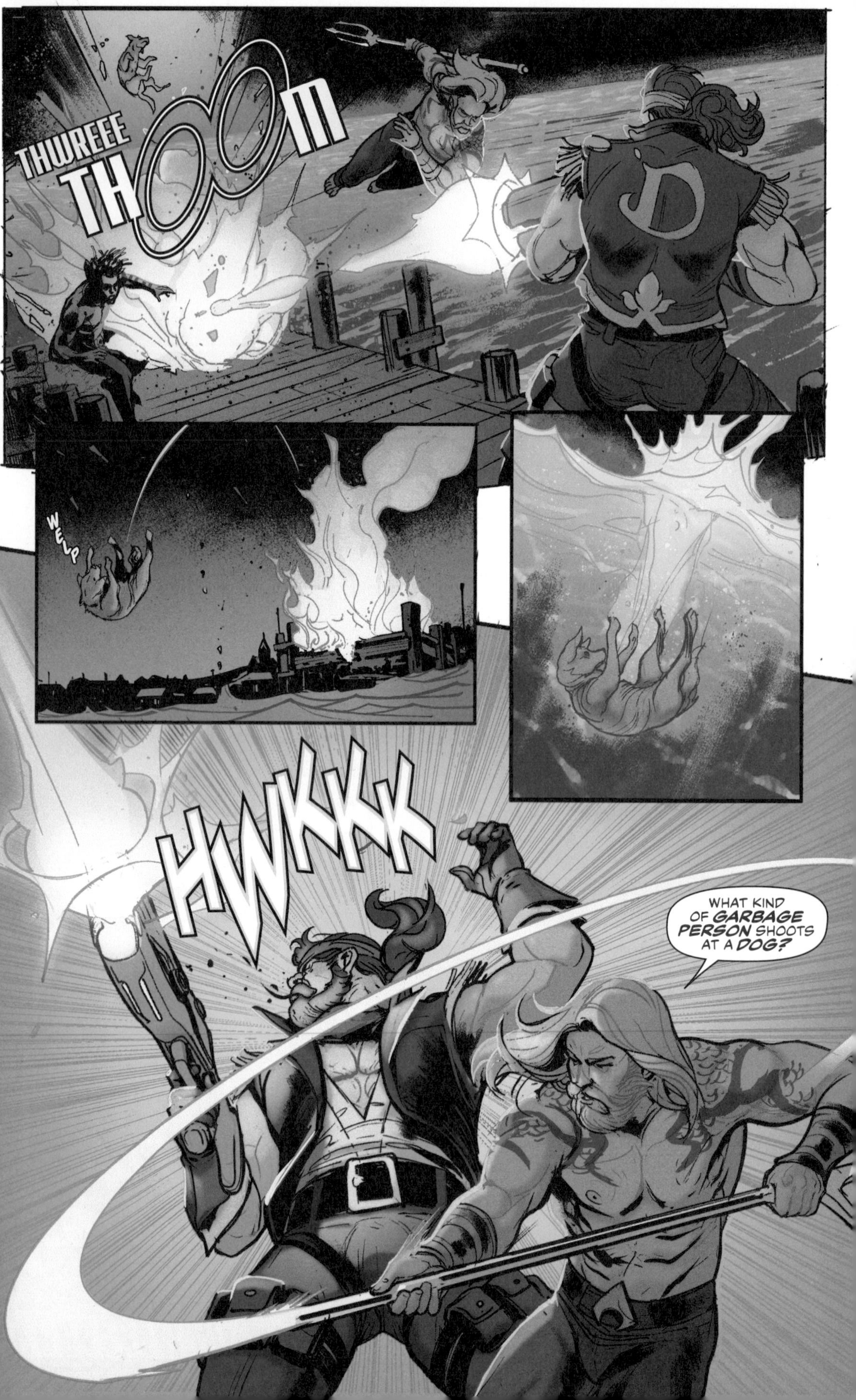
THWREEE THOOOM
WELP
HWKKK
WHAT KIND OF GARBAGE PERSON SHOOTS AT A DOG?

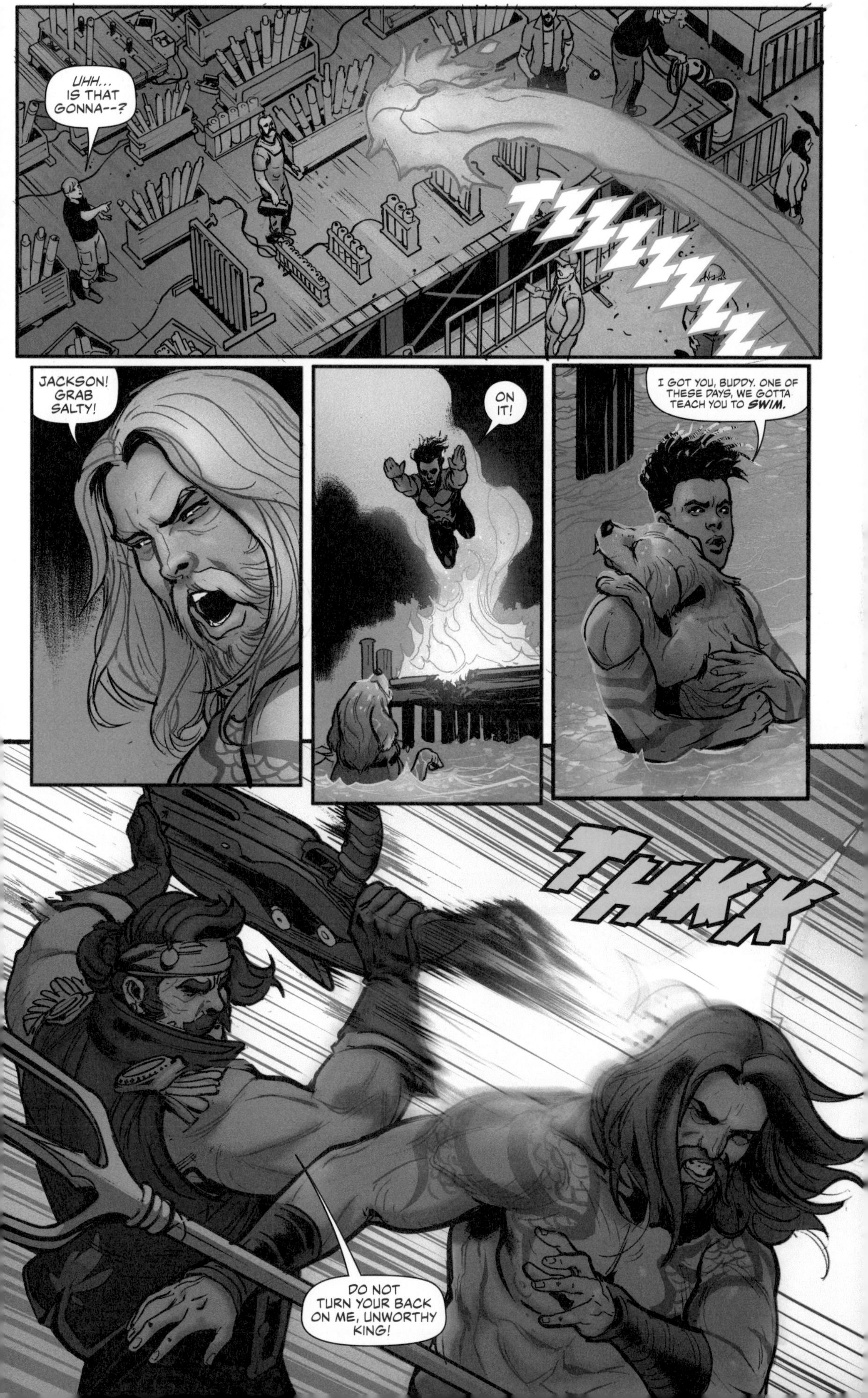
UHH... IS THAT GONNA--?
TZZZZZZZZ
JACKSON! GRAB SALTY!
ON IT!
I GOT YOU, BUDDY. ONE OF THESE DAYS, WE GOTTA TEACH YOU TO SWIM.
THKK
DO NOT TURN YOUR BACK ON ME, UNWORTHY KING!

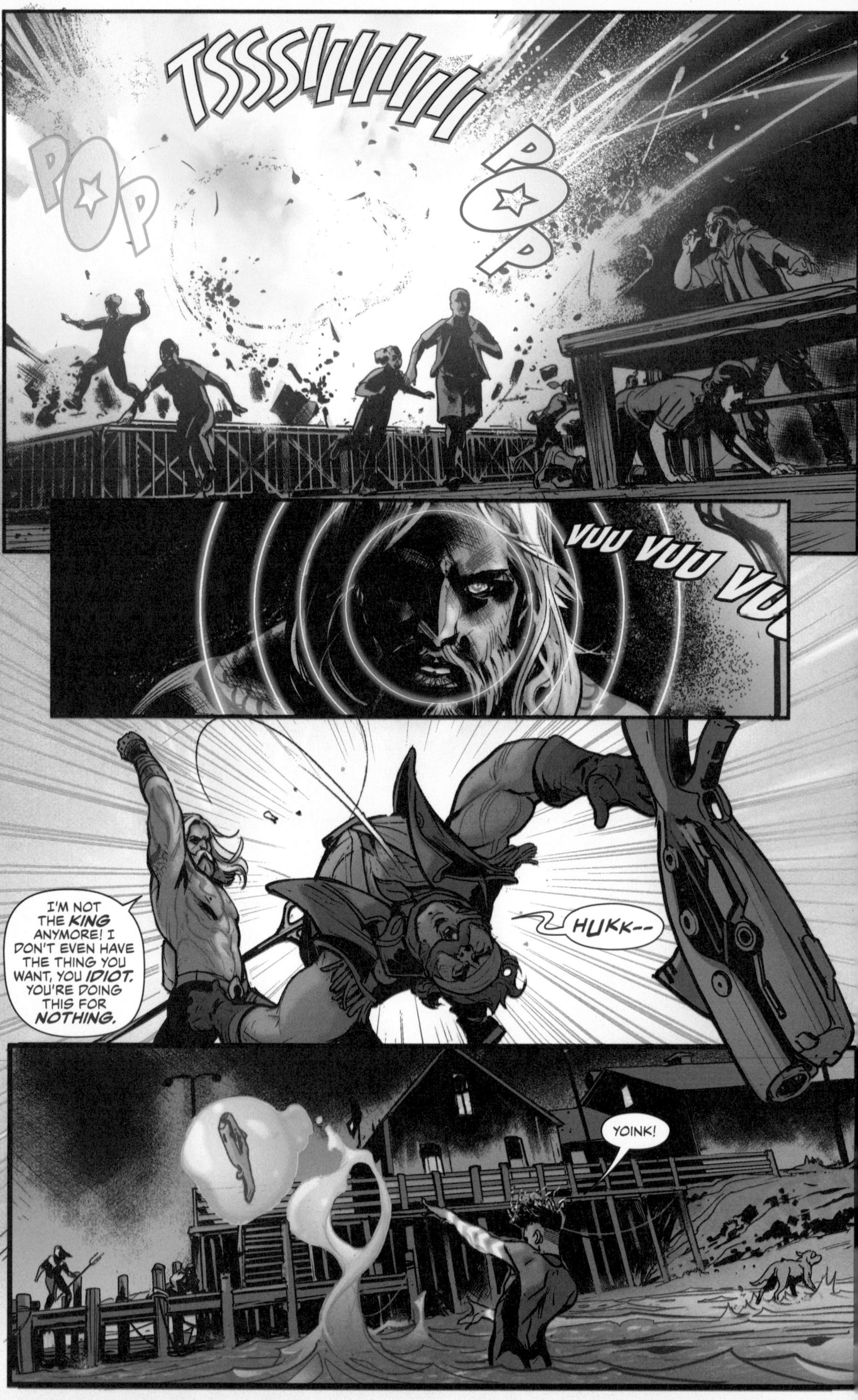
TSSSIIIIIIII
POP
POP
VUU VUU VU
I'M NOT THE KING ANYMORE! I DON'T EVEN HAVE THE THING YOU WANT, YOU IDIOT. YOU'RE DOING THIS FOR NOTHING.
HUKK--
YOINK!

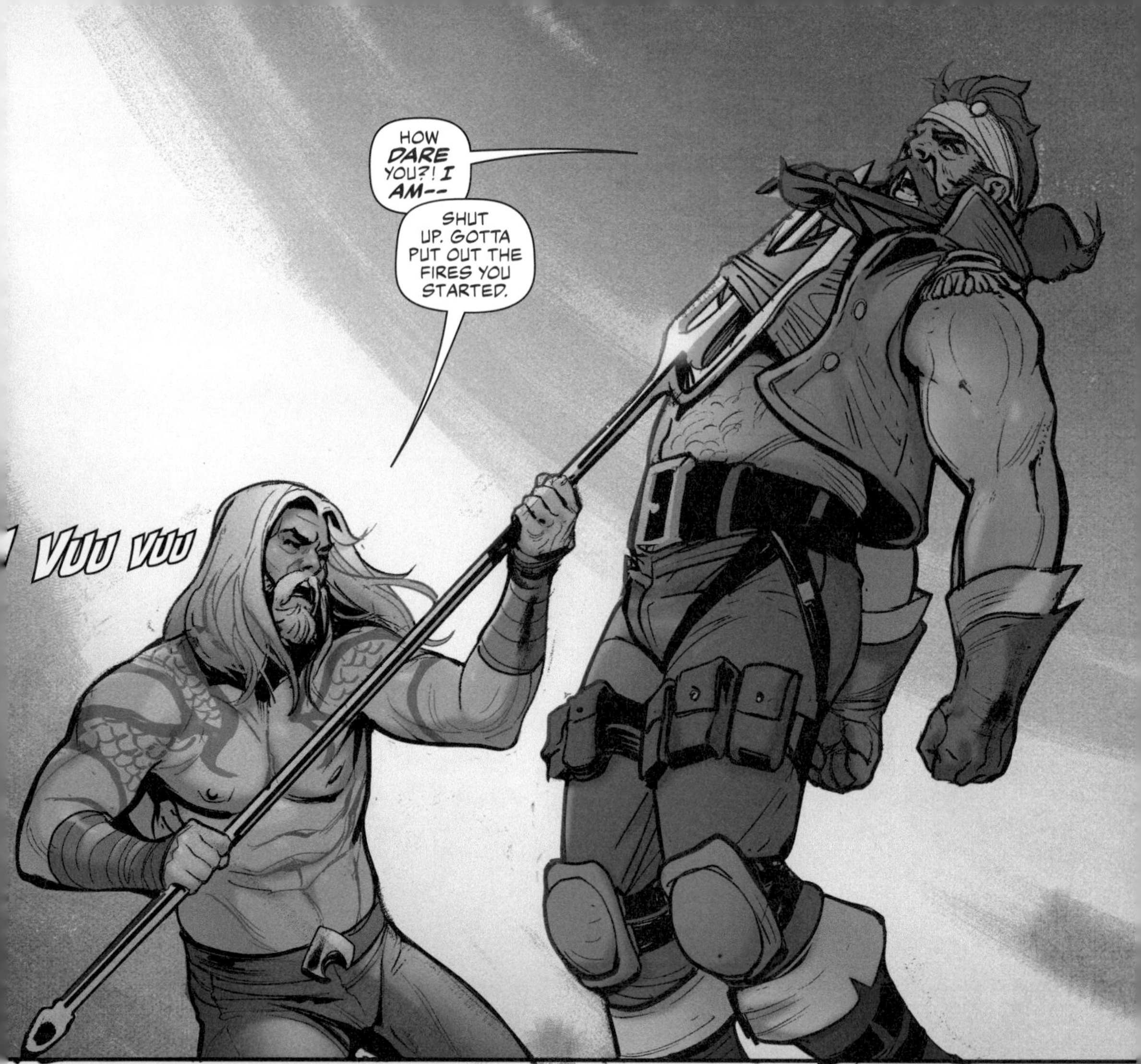
HOW DARE YOU?! I AM--
SHUT UP. GOTTA PUT OUT THE FIRES YOU STARTED.
VUU VUU

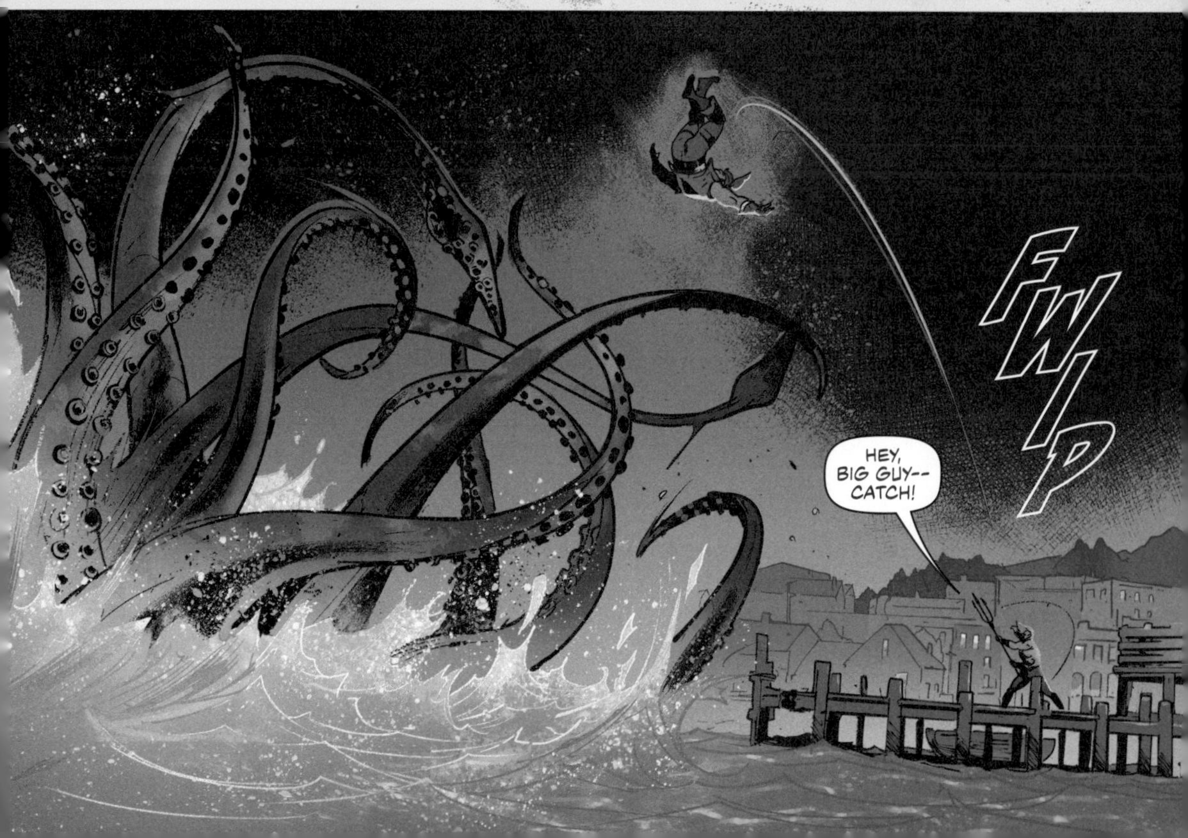
FWIP
HEY, BIG GUY-- CATCH!

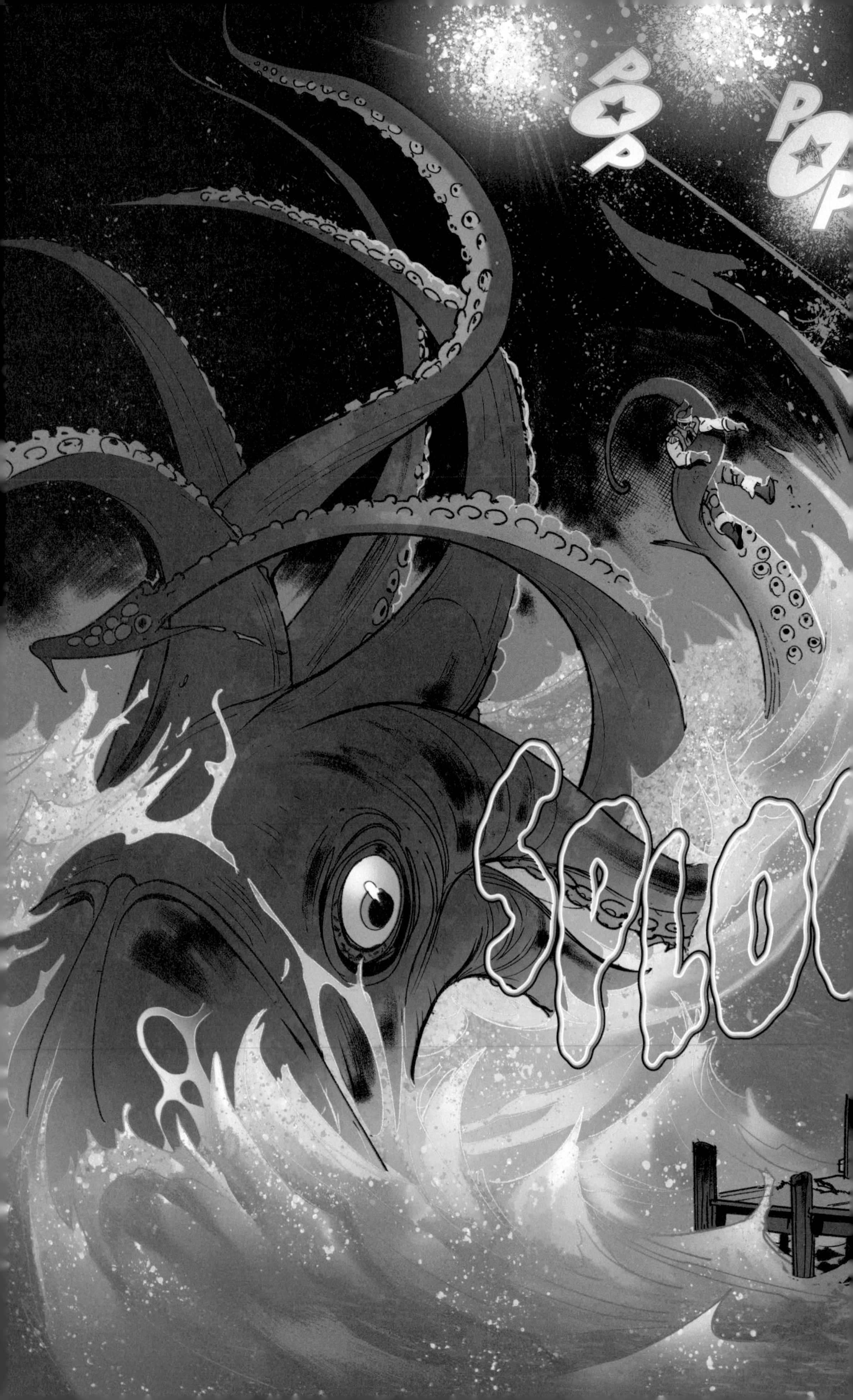
POP
POP
SPLO

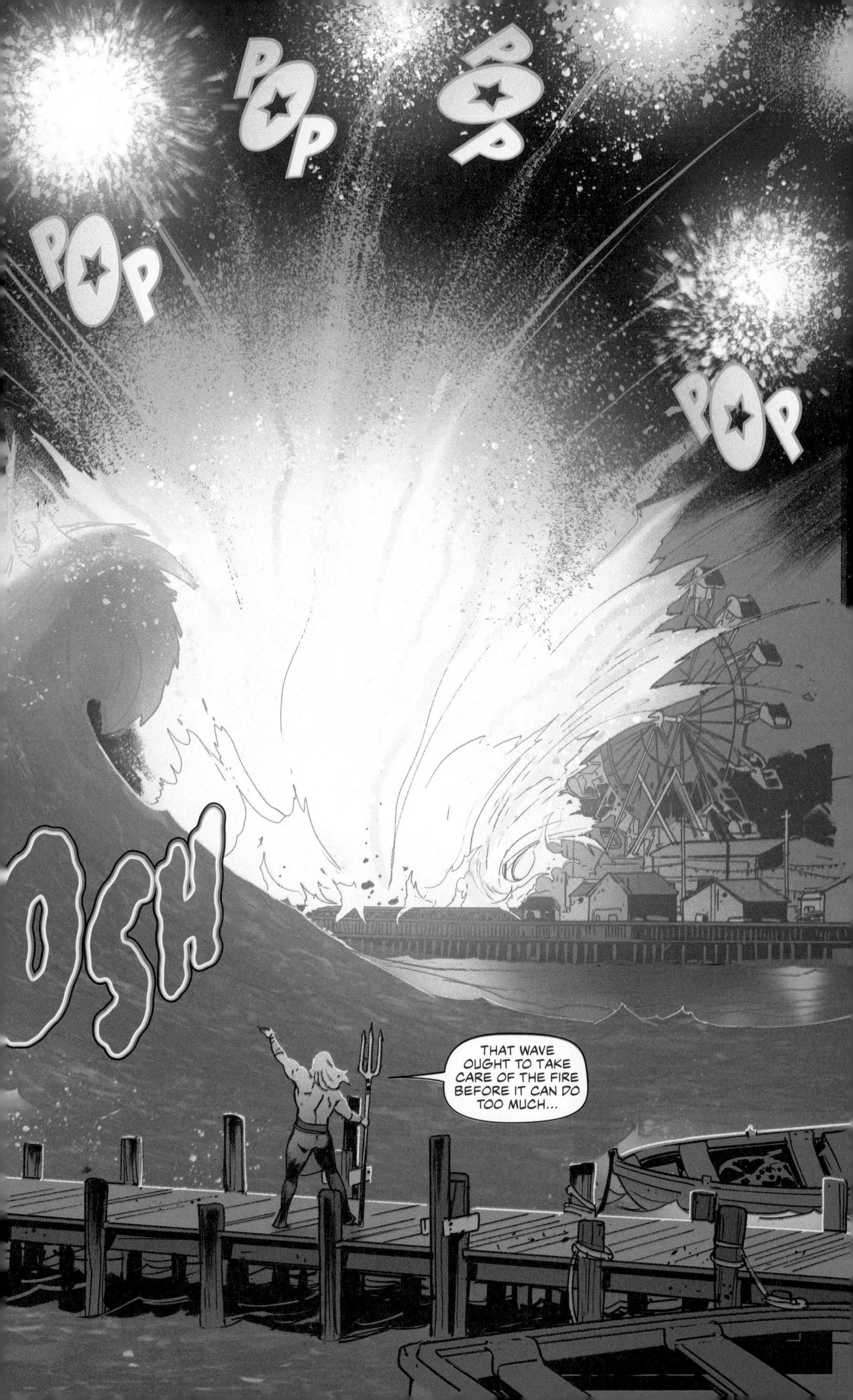
POP
POP
POP
POP
OSH
THAT WAVE OUGHT TO TAKE CARE OF THE FIRE BEFORE IT CAN DO TOO MUCH...

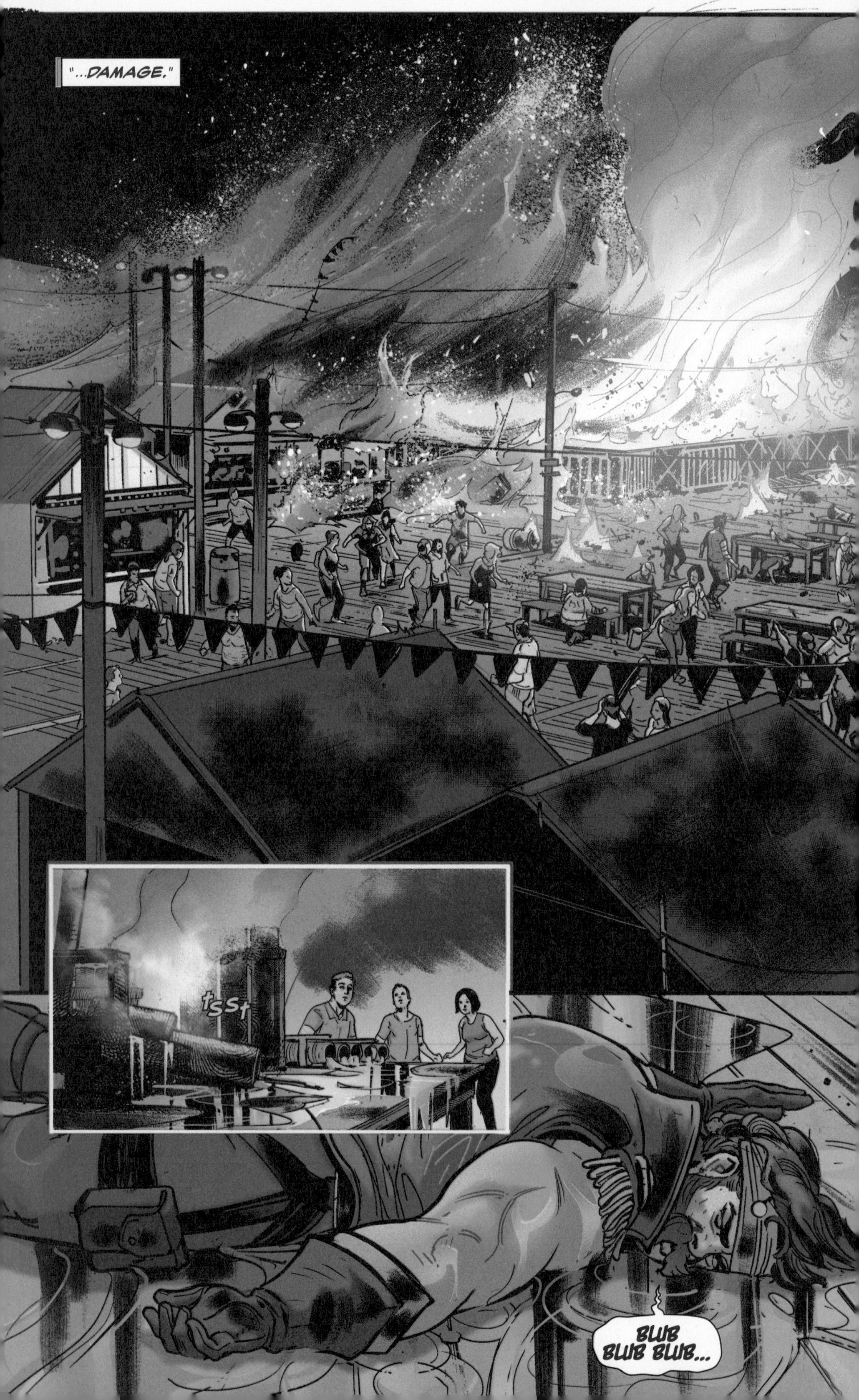
"...DAMAGE."
tSSt
BLUB
BLUB BLUB...

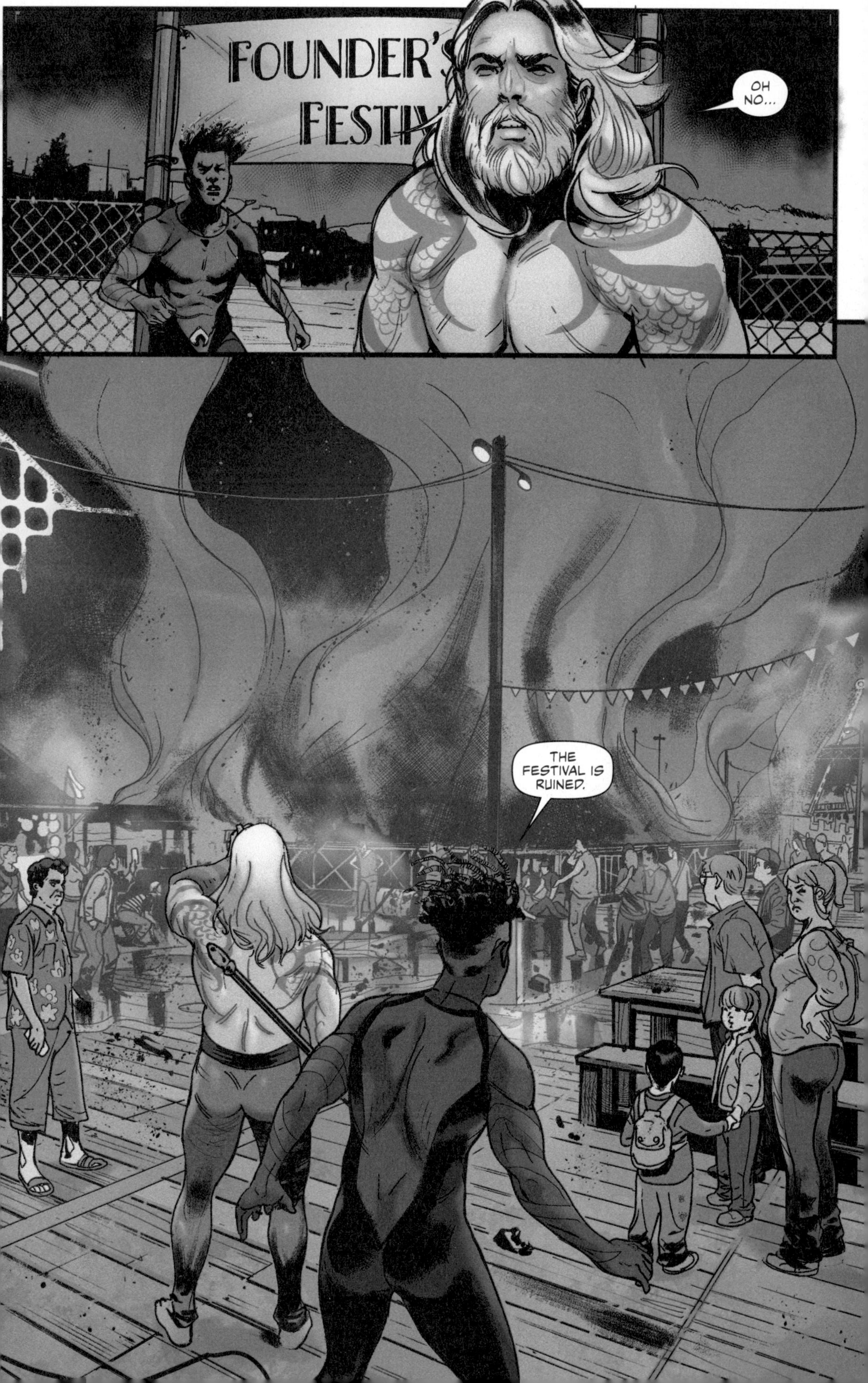
FOUNDER'S
FESTIV
OH NO...
THE FESTIVAL IS RUINED.

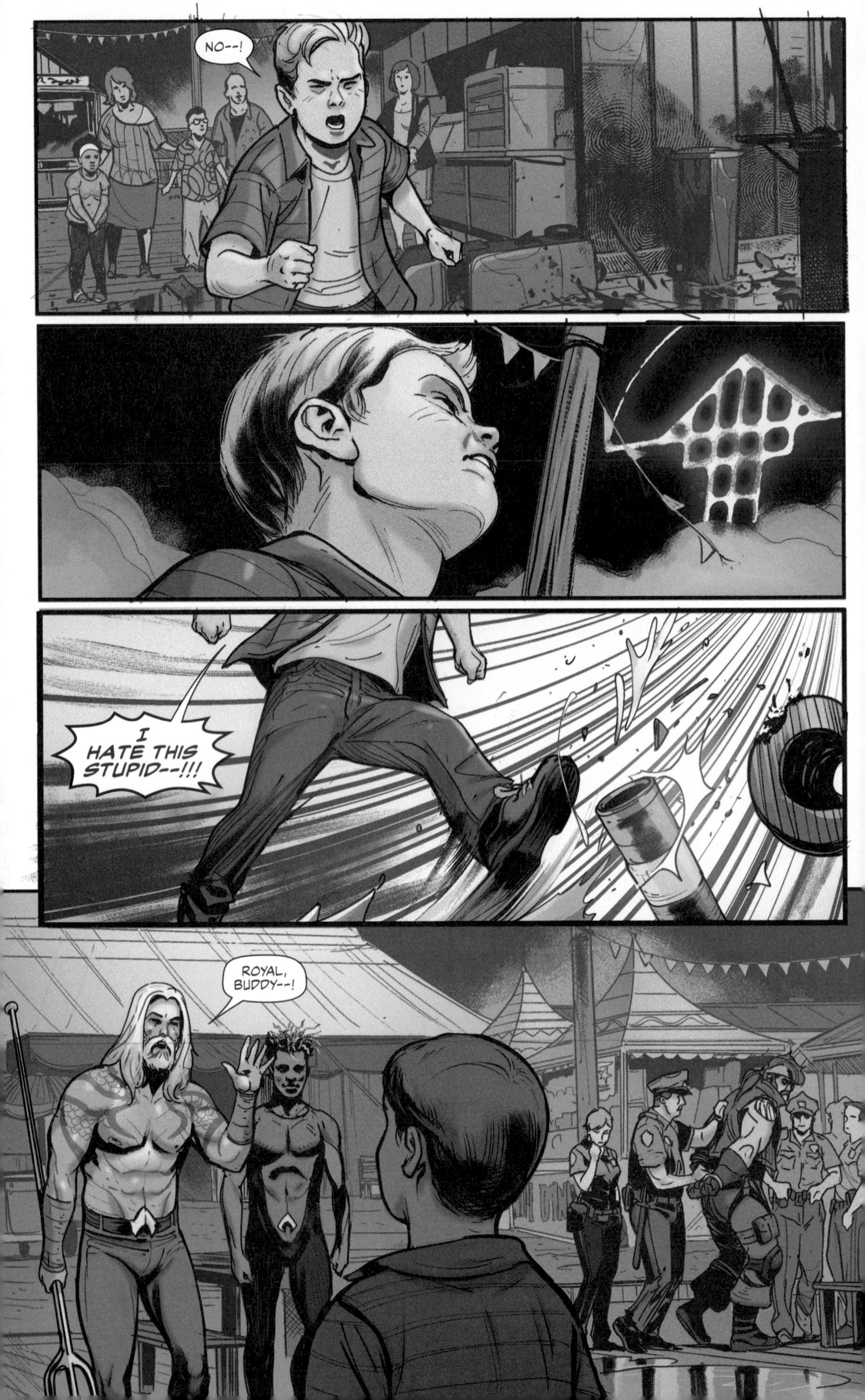
NO--!
I HATE THIS STUPID--!!!
ROYAL, BUDDY--!

WHAT CAN WE DO? WHAT DO YOU NEED?

I DON'T KNOW! A HUG? THE FIREWORKS ARE RUINED AND... I FEEL LOUSY.

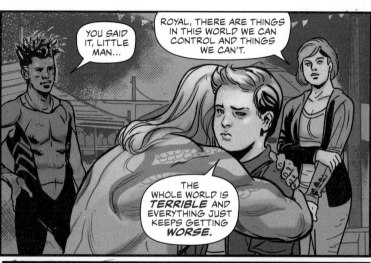

YOU SAID IT, LITTLE MAN...

ROYAL, THERE ARE THINGS IN THIS WORLD WE CAN CONTROL AND THINGS WE CAN'T.

THE WHOLE WORLD IS *TERRIBLE* AND EVERYTHING JUST KEEPS GETTING *WORSE.*

YOUR MOM'S RIGHT, ROYAL. THERE'RE ALWAYS GONNA BE THINGS THAT GO WRONG. SOMETIMES IT'S JUST BAD LUCK.

SOMETIMES IT'S FOLKS WHO LET THEIR FEAR MAKE THEM MEAN...

I WISH I COULD MAKE THAT THING IN THE SKY GO AWAY, BUT...I CAN'T. I HAVEN'T FIGURED IT OUT YET.

SO ALL I CAN DO IS CHOOSE HOW I'M GONNA REACT.

WELL, I'M CHOOSING TO BE *MAD* ABOUT IT!

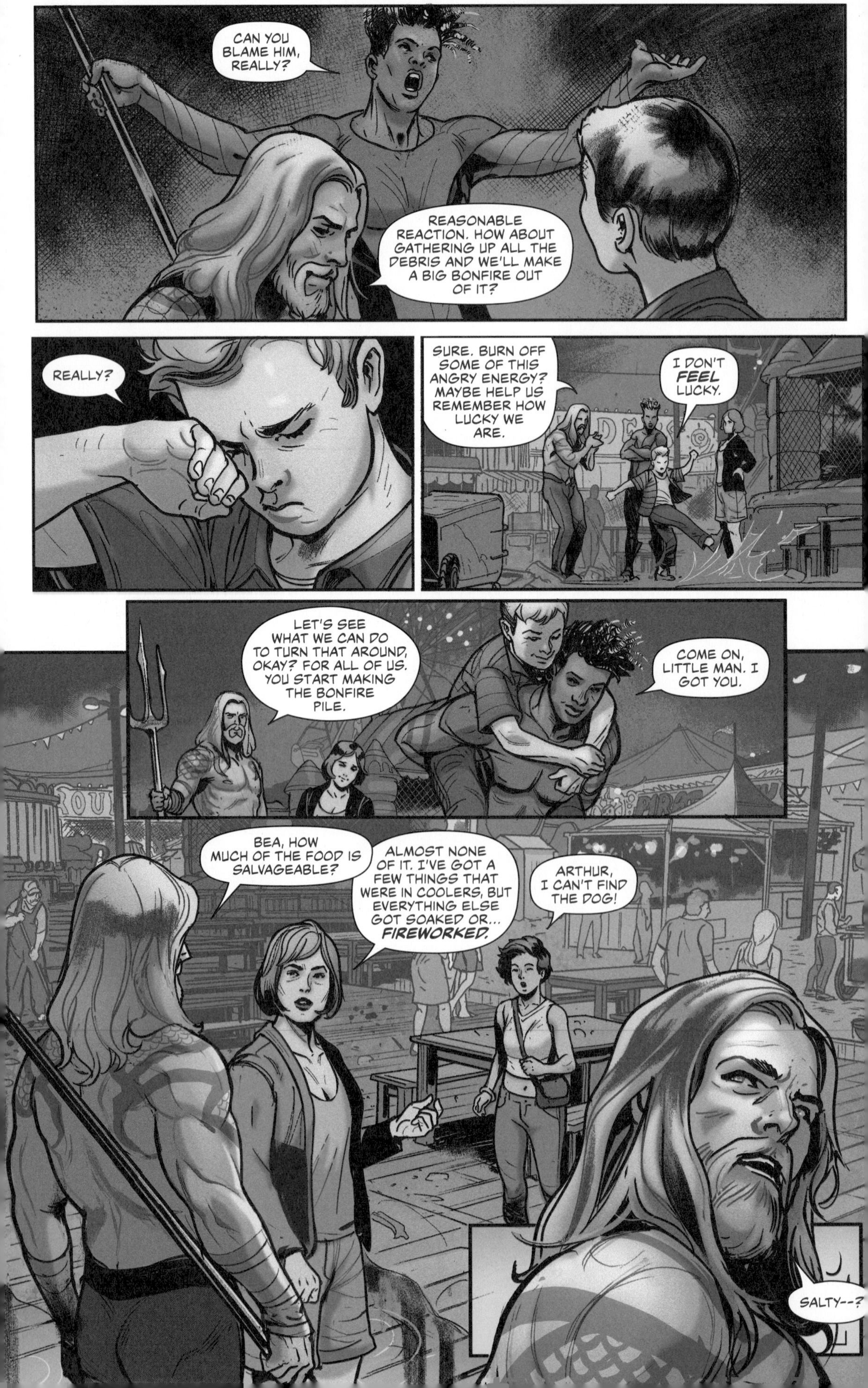
CAN YOU BLAME HIM, REALLY?
REASONABLE REACTION. HOW ABOUT GATHERING UP ALL THE DEBRIS AND WE'LL MAKE A BIG BONFIRE OUT OF IT?
REALLY?
SURE. BURN OFF SOME OF THIS ANGRY ENERGY? MAYBE HELP US REMEMBER HOW LUCKY WE ARE.
I DON'T *FEEL* LUCKY.
LET'S SEE WHAT WE CAN DO TO TURN THAT AROUND, OKAY? FOR ALL OF US. YOU START MAKING THE BONFIRE PILE.
COME ON, LITTLE MAN. I GOT YOU.
BEA, HOW MUCH OF THE FOOD IS SALVAGEABLE?
ALMOST NONE OF IT. I'VE GOT A FEW THINGS THAT WERE IN COOLERS, BUT EVERYTHING ELSE GOT SOAKED OR... ***FIREWORKED.***
ARTHUR, I CAN'T FIND THE DOG!
SALTY--?

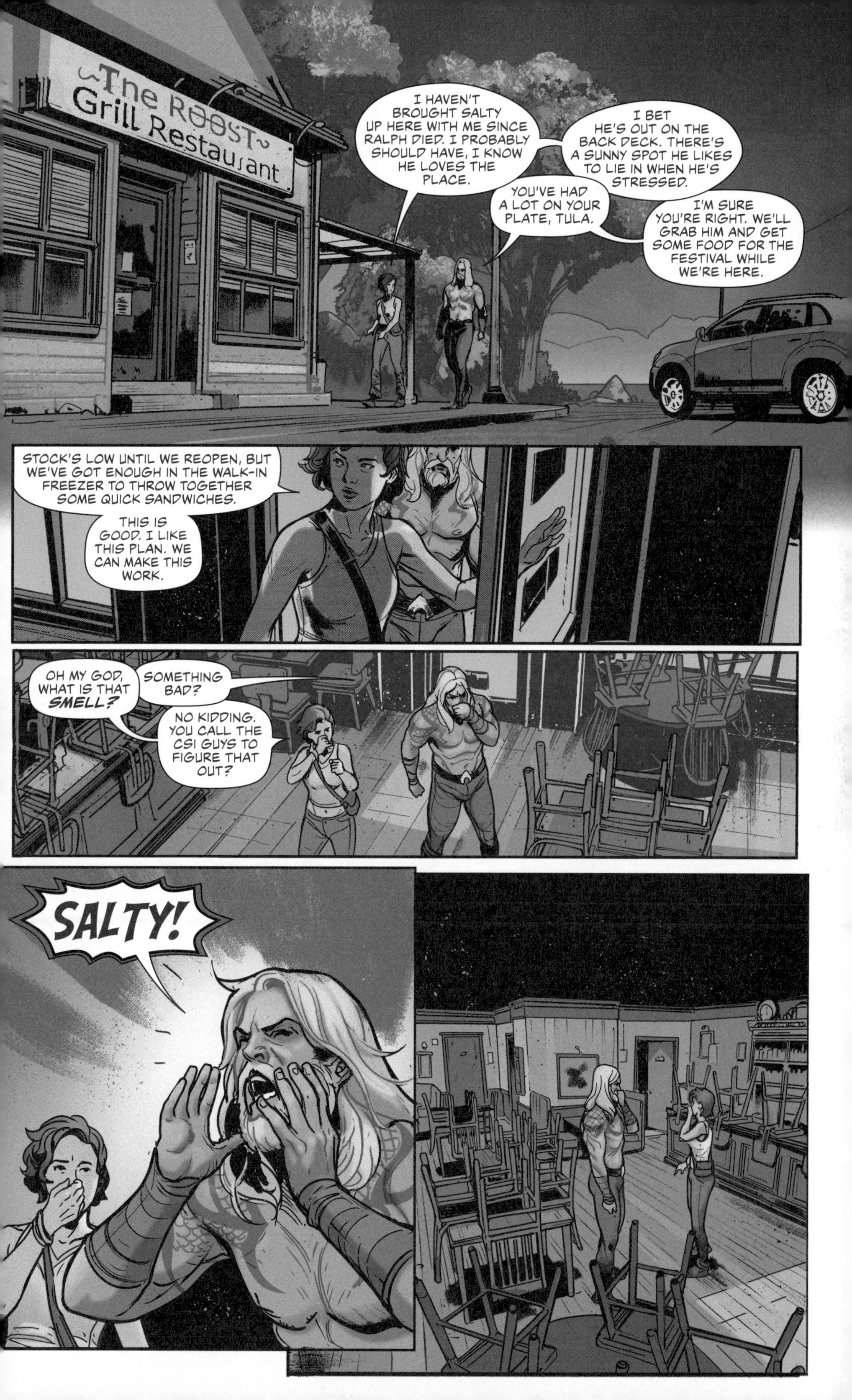
~The ROOST~
Grill Restaurant
I HAVEN'T BROUGHT SALTY UP HERE WITH ME SINCE RALPH DIED. I PROBABLY SHOULD HAVE, I KNOW HE LOVES THE PLACE.
I BET HE'S OUT ON THE BACK DECK. THERE'S A SUNNY SPOT HE LIKES TO LIE IN WHEN HE'S STRESSED.
YOU'VE HAD A LOT ON YOUR PLATE, TULA.
I'M SURE YOU'RE RIGHT. WE'LL GRAB HIM AND GET SOME FOOD FOR THE FESTIVAL WHILE WE'RE HERE.
STOCK'S LOW UNTIL WE REOPEN, BUT WE'VE GOT ENOUGH IN THE WALK-IN FREEZER TO THROW TOGETHER SOME QUICK SANDWICHES.
THIS IS GOOD. I LIKE THIS PLAN. WE CAN MAKE THIS WORK.
OH MY GOD, WHAT IS THAT SMELL?
SOMETHING BAD?
NO KIDDING. YOU CALL THE CSI GUYS TO FIGURE THAT OUT?
SALTY!

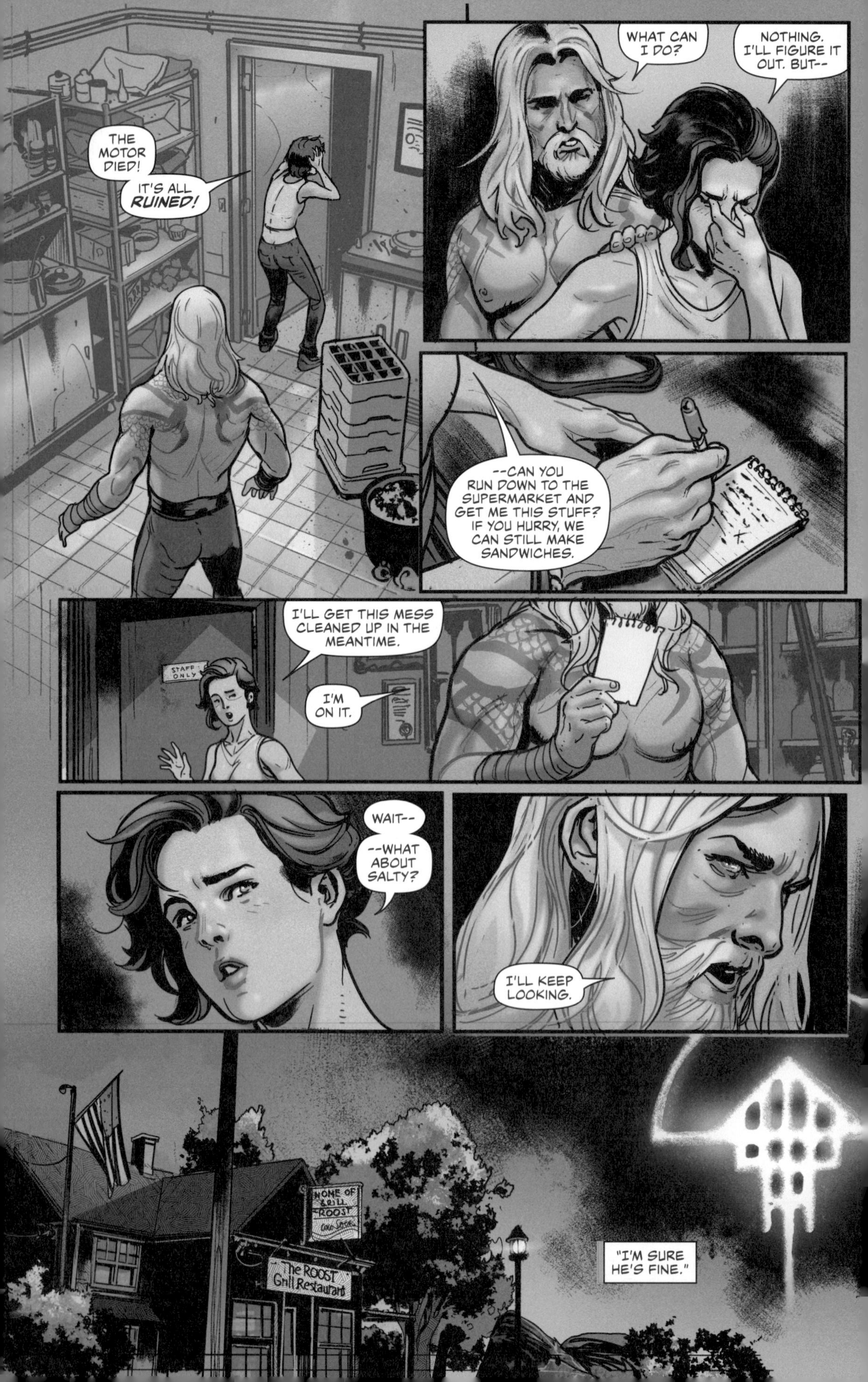
THE MOTOR DIED!
IT'S ALL RUINED!
WHAT CAN I DO?
NOTHING. I'LL FIGURE IT OUT. BUT--
--CAN YOU RUN DOWN TO THE SUPERMARKET AND GET ME THIS STUFF? IF YOU HURRY, WE CAN STILL MAKE SANDWICHES.
I'LL GET THIS MESS CLEANED UP IN THE MEANTIME.
STAFF ONLY
I'M ON IT.
WAIT--
--WHAT ABOUT SALTY?
I'LL KEEP LOOKING.
The ROOST Grill Restaurant
"I'M SURE HE'S FINE."

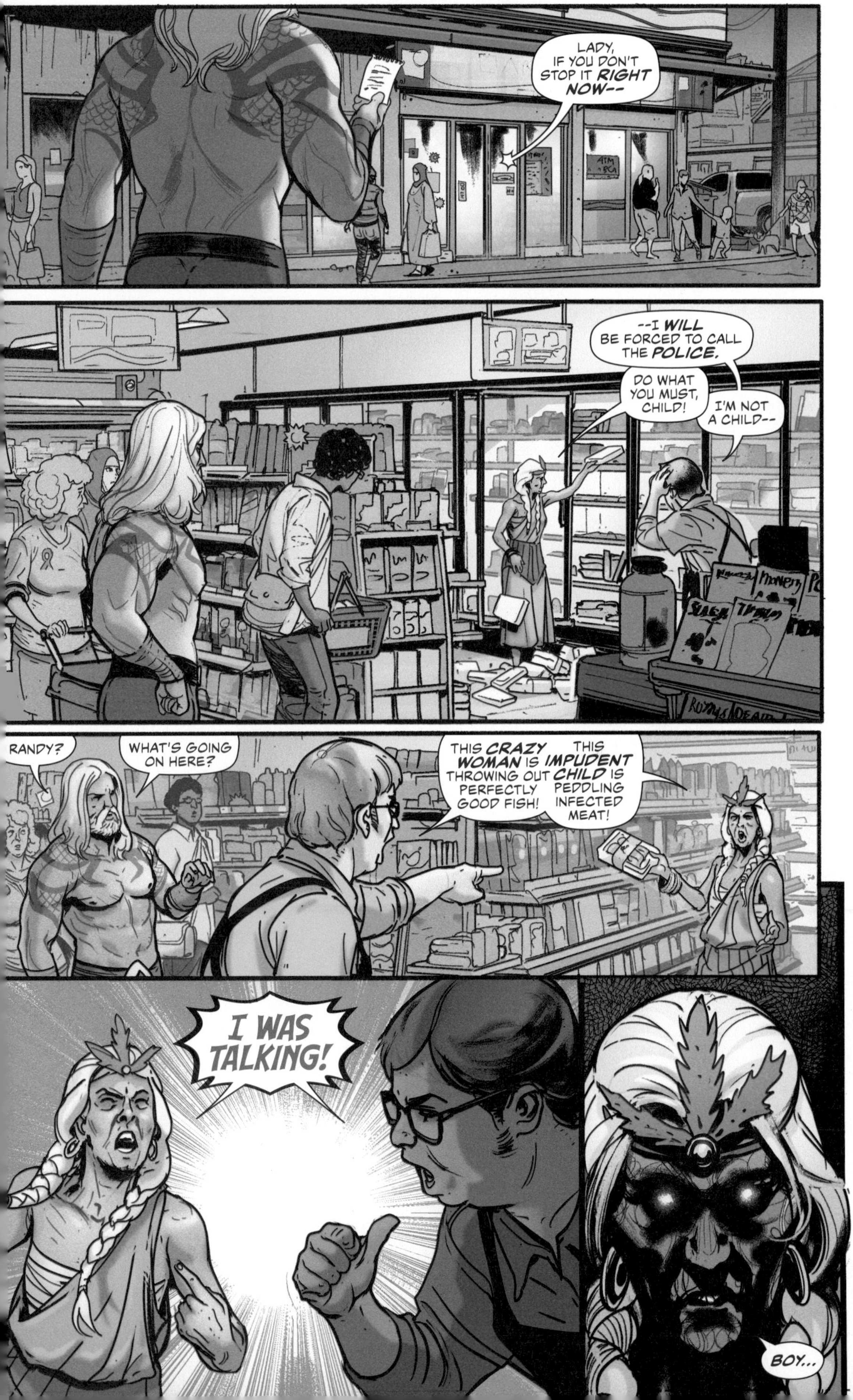
LADY, IF YOU DON'T STOP IT RIGHT NOW--
--I WILL BE FORCED TO CALL THE POLICE.
DO WHAT YOU MUST, CHILD!
I'M NOT A CHILD--
RANDY?
WHAT'S GOING ON HERE?
THIS CRAZY WOMAN IS THROWING OUT PERFECTLY GOOD FISH!
THIS IMPUDENT CHILD IS PEDDLING INFECTED MEAT!
I WAS TALKING!
BOY...

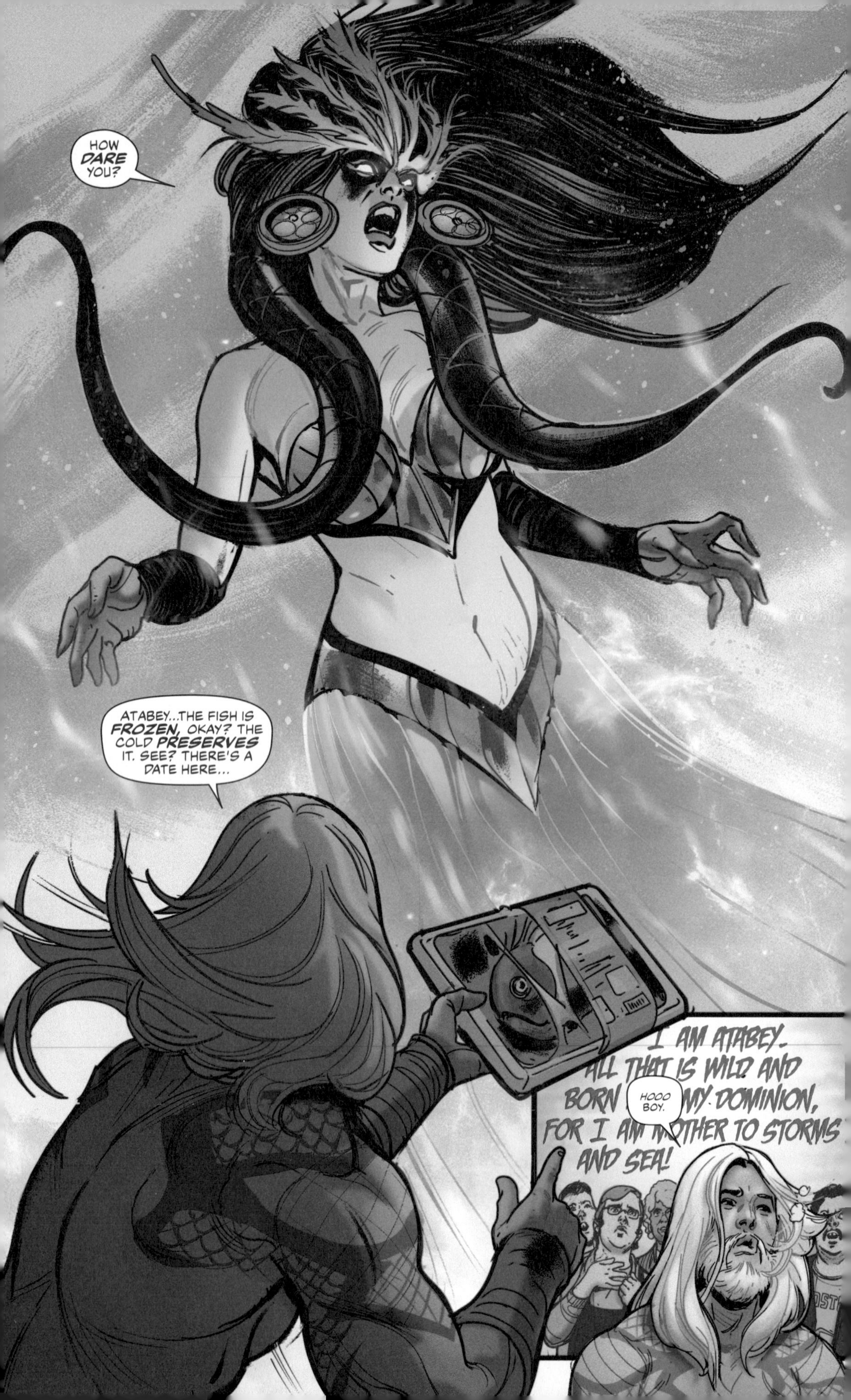
HOW DARE YOU?
ATABEY...THE FISH IS FROZEN, OKAY? THE COLD PRESERVES IT. SEE? THERE'S A DATE HERE...
I AM ATABEY. ALL THAT IS WILD AND BORN MY DOMINION, FOR I AM MOTHER TO STORMS AND SEA!
HOOO BOY.

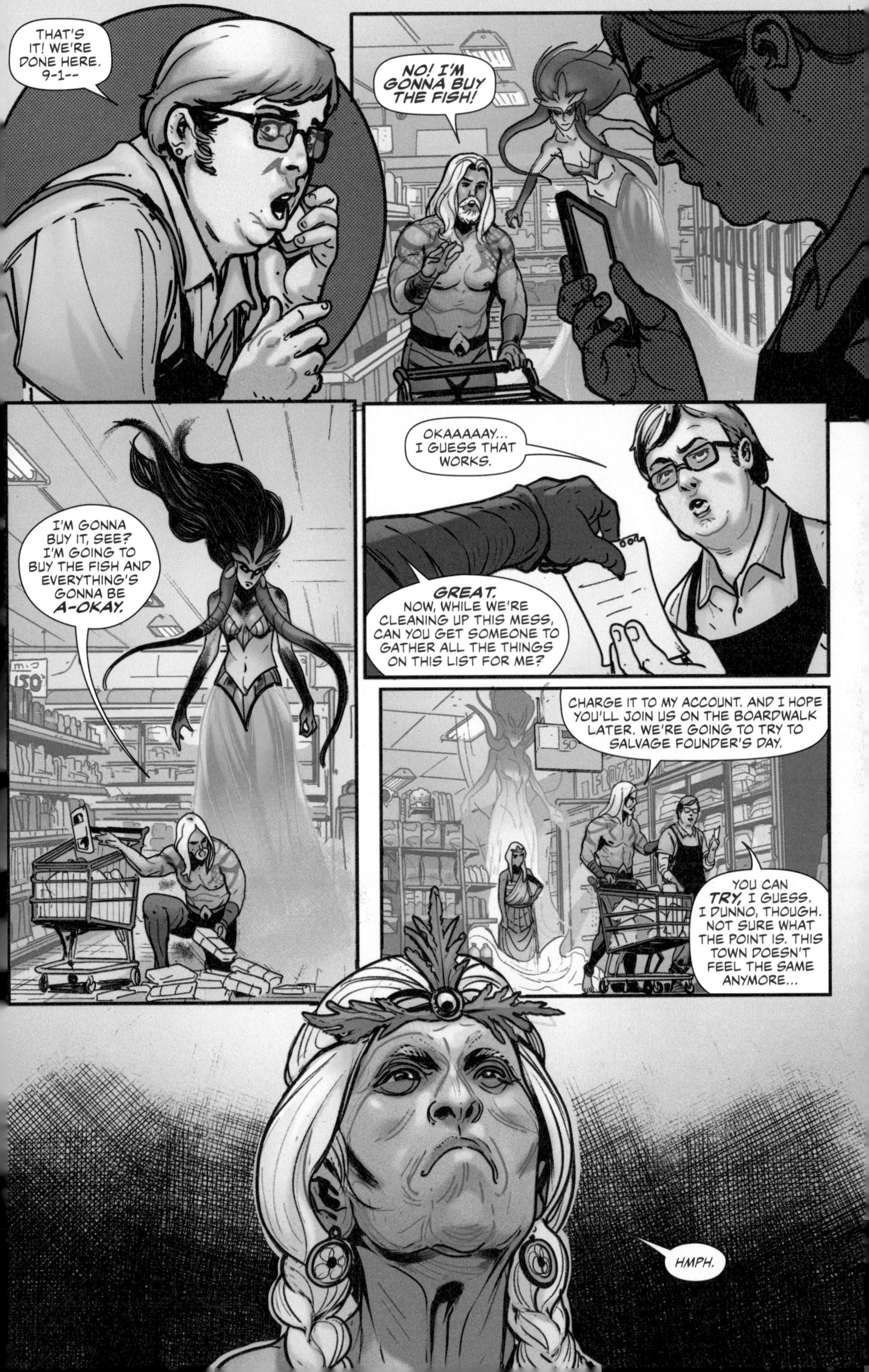
THAT'S IT! WE'RE DONE HERE. 9-1--
NO! I'M GONNA BUY THE FISH!
I'M GONNA BUY IT, SEE? I'M GOING TO BUY THE FISH AND EVERYTHING'S GONNA BE A-OKAY.
OKAAAAAY... I GUESS THAT WORKS.
GREAT. NOW, WHILE WE'RE CLEANING UP THIS MESS, CAN YOU GET SOMEONE TO GATHER ALL THE THINGS ON THIS LIST FOR ME?
CHARGE IT TO MY ACCOUNT. AND I HOPE YOU'LL JOIN US ON THE BOARDWALK LATER. WE'RE GOING TO TRY TO SALVAGE FOUNDER'S DAY.
YOU CAN TRY, I GUESS. I DUNNO, THOUGH. NOT SURE WHAT THE POINT IS. THIS TOWN DOESN'T FEEL THE SAME ANYMORE...
HMPH.

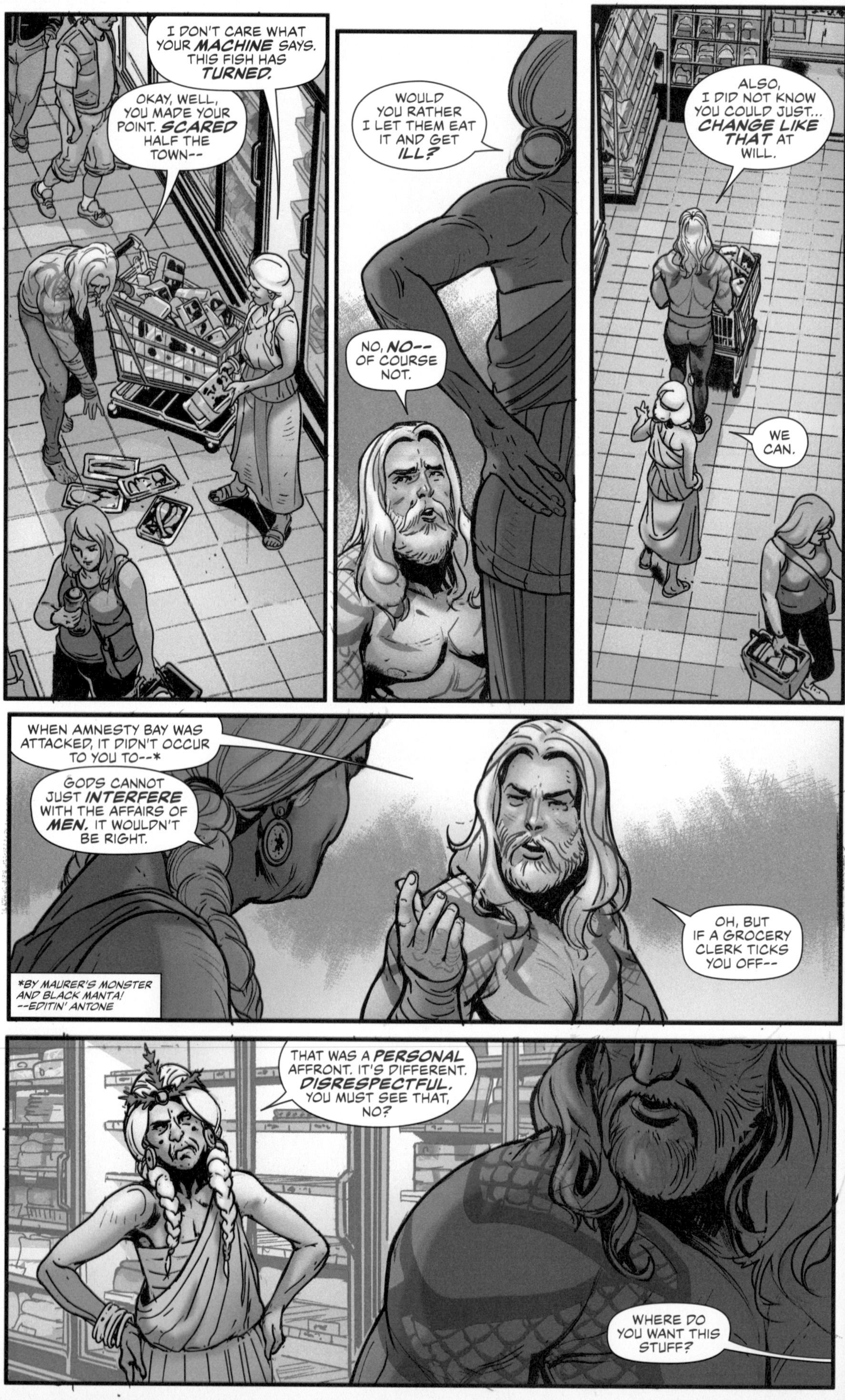
I DON'T CARE WHAT YOUR MACHINE SAYS. THIS FISH HAS TURNED.
OKAY, WELL, YOU MADE YOUR POINT. SCARED HALF THE TOWN--
WOULD YOU RATHER I LET THEM EAT IT AND GET ILL?
NO, NO-- OF COURSE NOT.
ALSO, I DID NOT KNOW YOU COULD JUST... CHANGE LIKE THAT AT WILL.
WE CAN.
WHEN AMNESTY BAY WAS ATTACKED, IT DIDN'T OCCUR TO YOU TO--*
GODS CANNOT JUST INTERFERE WITH THE AFFAIRS OF MEN. IT WOULDN'T BE RIGHT.
OH, BUT IF A GROCERY CLERK TICKS YOU OFF--
*BY MAURER'S MONSTER AND BLACK MANTA! --EDITIN' ANTONE
THAT WAS A PERSONAL AFFRONT. IT'S DIFFERENT. DISRESPECTFUL. YOU MUST SEE THAT, NO?
WHERE DO YOU WANT THIS STUFF?

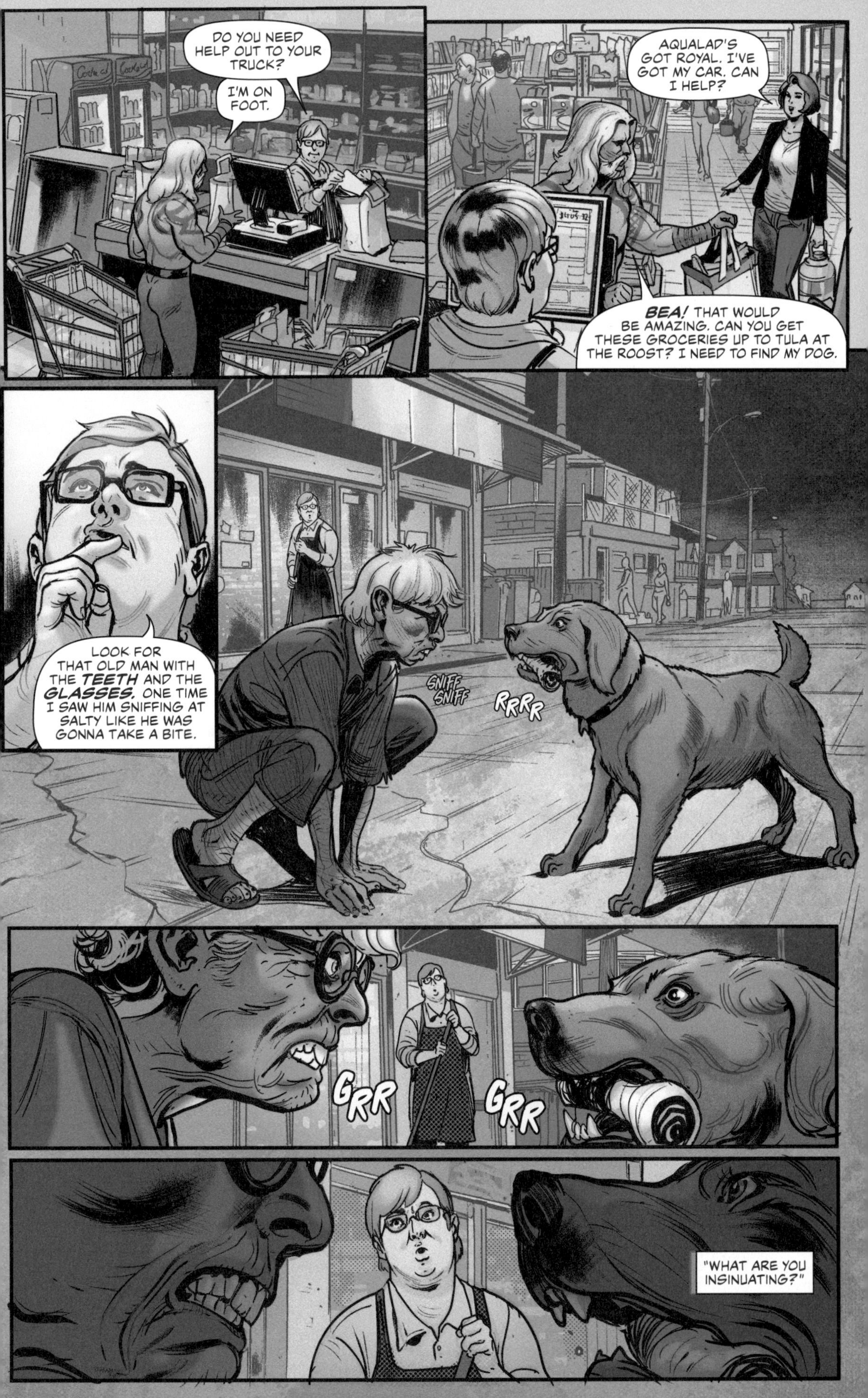
DO YOU NEED HELP OUT TO YOUR TRUCK?
I'M ON FOOT.
AQUALAD'S GOT ROYAL. I'VE GOT MY CAR. CAN I HELP?
BEA! THAT WOULD BE AMAZING. CAN YOU GET THESE GROCERIES UP TO TULA AT THE ROOST? I NEED TO FIND MY DOG.
LOOK FOR THAT OLD MAN WITH THE TEETH AND THE GLASSES. ONE TIME I SAW HIM SNIFFING AT SALTY LIKE HE WAS GONNA TAKE A BITE.
SNIFF SNIFF
RRRR
GRR
GRR
"WHAT ARE YOU INSINUATING?"

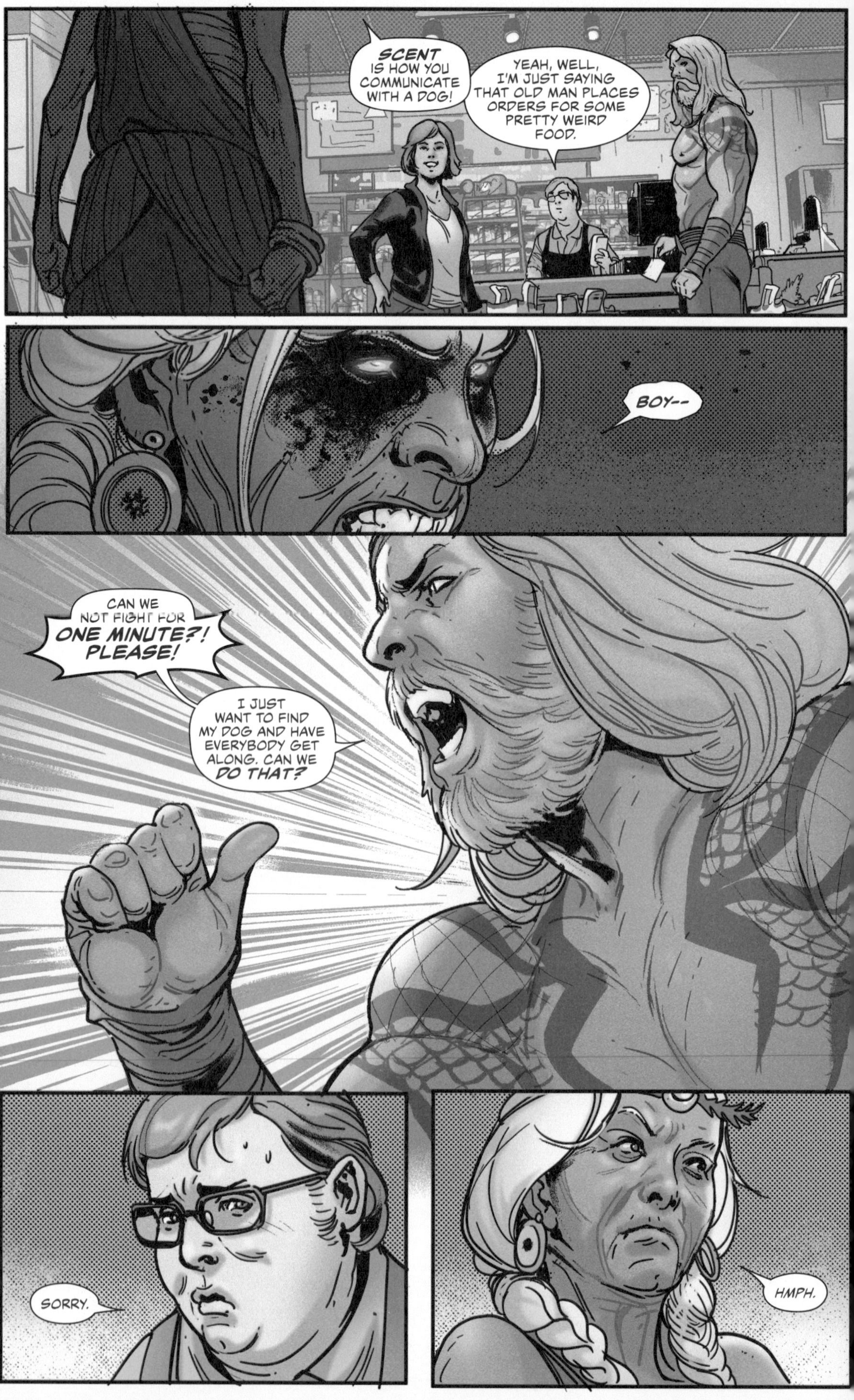
SCENT IS HOW YOU COMMUNICATE WITH A DOG!
YEAH, WELL, I'M JUST SAYING THAT OLD MAN PLACES ORDERS FOR SOME PRETTY WEIRD FOOD.
BOY--
CAN WE NOT FIGHT FOR ONE MINUTE?! PLEASE!
I JUST WANT TO FIND MY DOG AND HAVE EVERYBODY GET ALONG. CAN WE DO THAT?
SORRY.
HMPH.

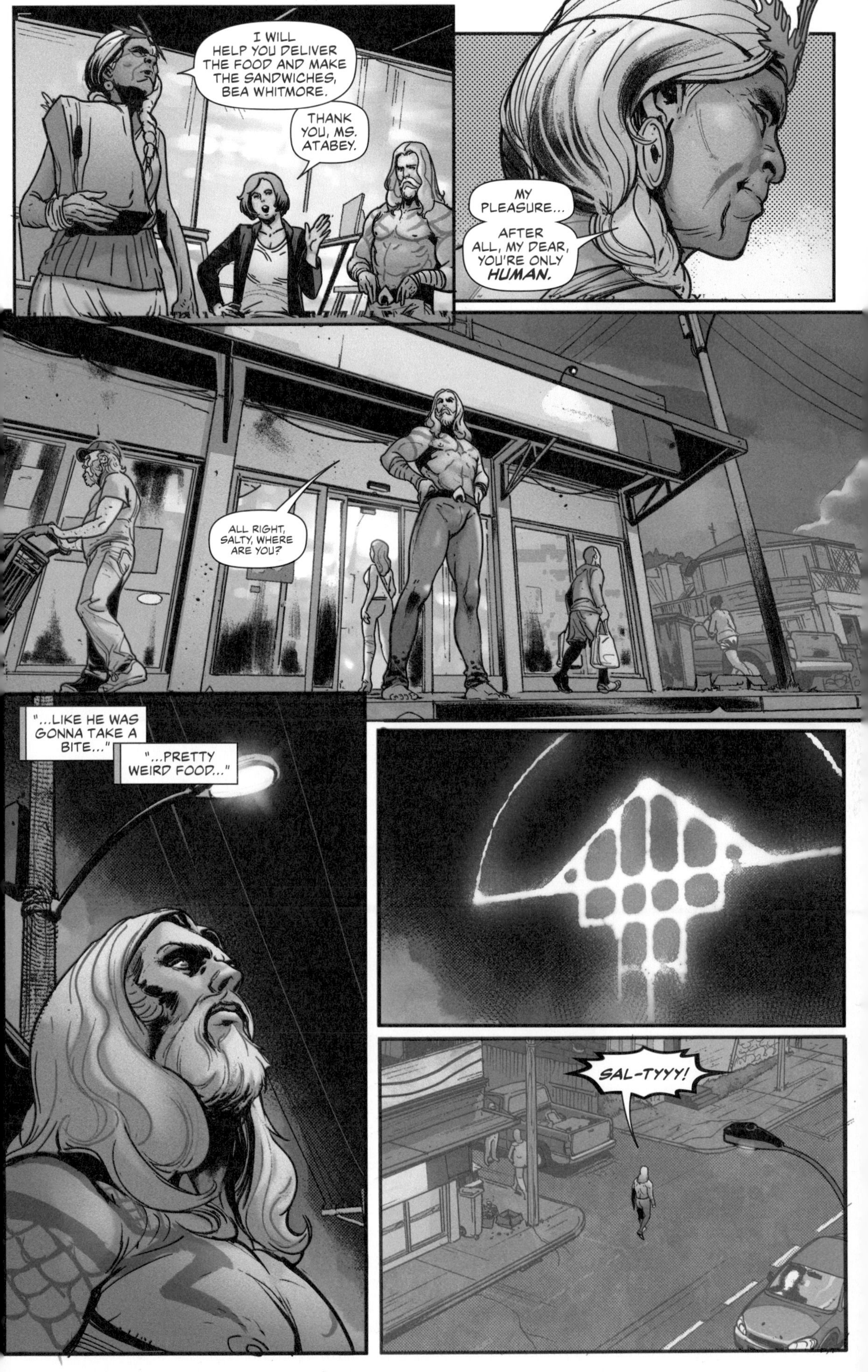
I WILL HELP YOU DELIVER THE FOOD AND MAKE THE SANDWICHES, BEA WHITMORE.
THANK YOU, MS. ATABEY.
MY PLEASURE...
AFTER ALL, MY DEAR, YOU'RE ONLY **HUMAN.**
ALL RIGHT, SALTY, WHERE ARE YOU?
"...LIKE HE WAS GONNA TAKE A BITE..."
"...PRETTY WEIRD FOOD..."
SAL-TYYY!

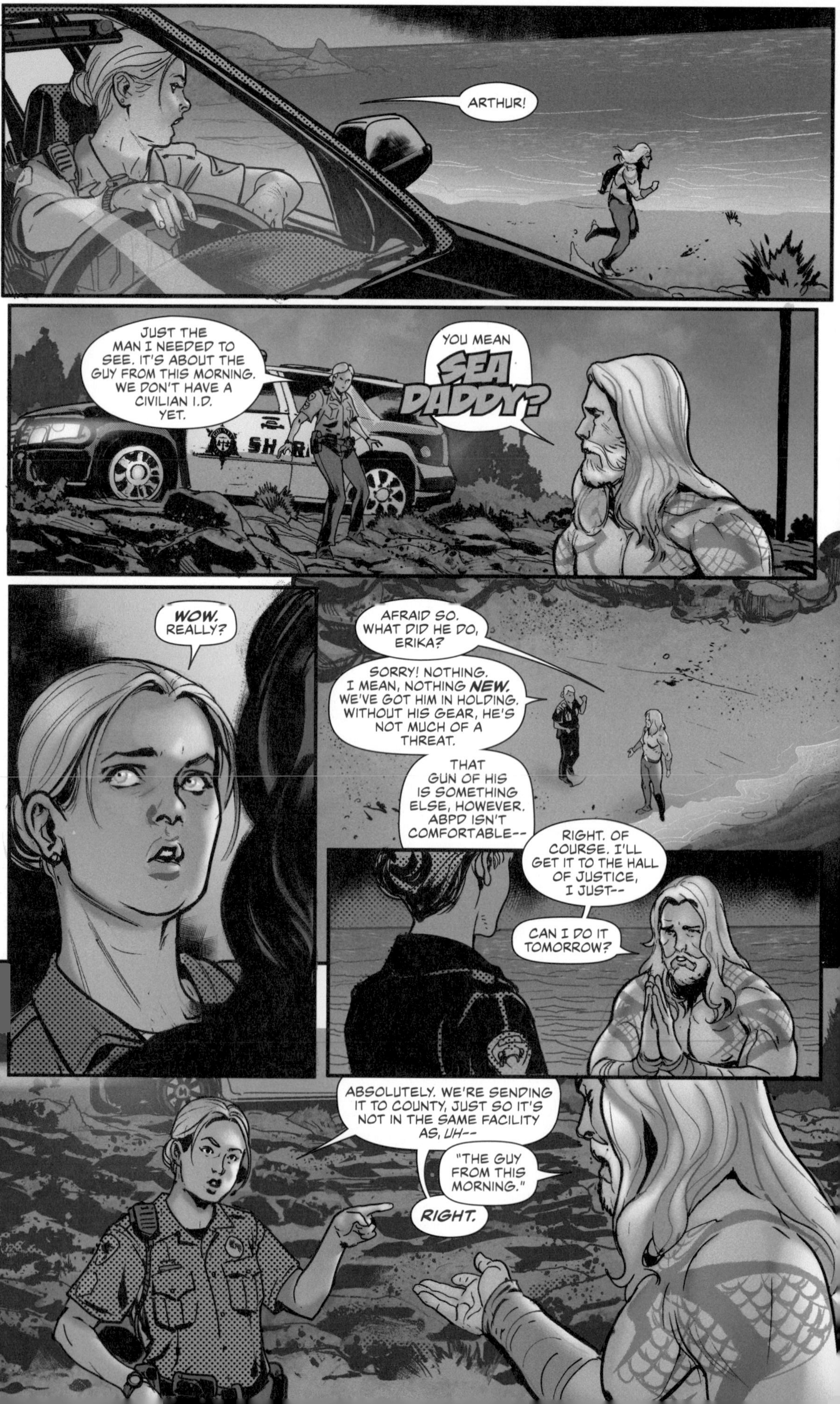
ARTHUR!
JUST THE MAN I NEEDED TO SEE. IT'S ABOUT THE GUY FROM THIS MORNING. WE DON'T HAVE A CIVILIAN I.D. YET.
YOU MEAN SEA DADDY?
WOW. REALLY?
AFRAID SO. WHAT DID HE DO, ERIKA?
SORRY! NOTHING. I MEAN, NOTHING NEW. WE'VE GOT HIM IN HOLDING. WITHOUT HIS GEAR, HE'S NOT MUCH OF A THREAT.
THAT GUN OF HIS IS SOMETHING ELSE, HOWEVER. ABPD ISN'T COMFORTABLE--
RIGHT. OF COURSE. I'LL GET IT TO THE HALL OF JUSTICE, I JUST--
CAN I DO IT TOMORROW?
ABSOLUTELY. WE'RE SENDING IT TO COUNTY, JUST SO IT'S NOT IN THE SAME FACILITY AS, UH--
"THE GUY FROM THIS MORNING."
RIGHT.

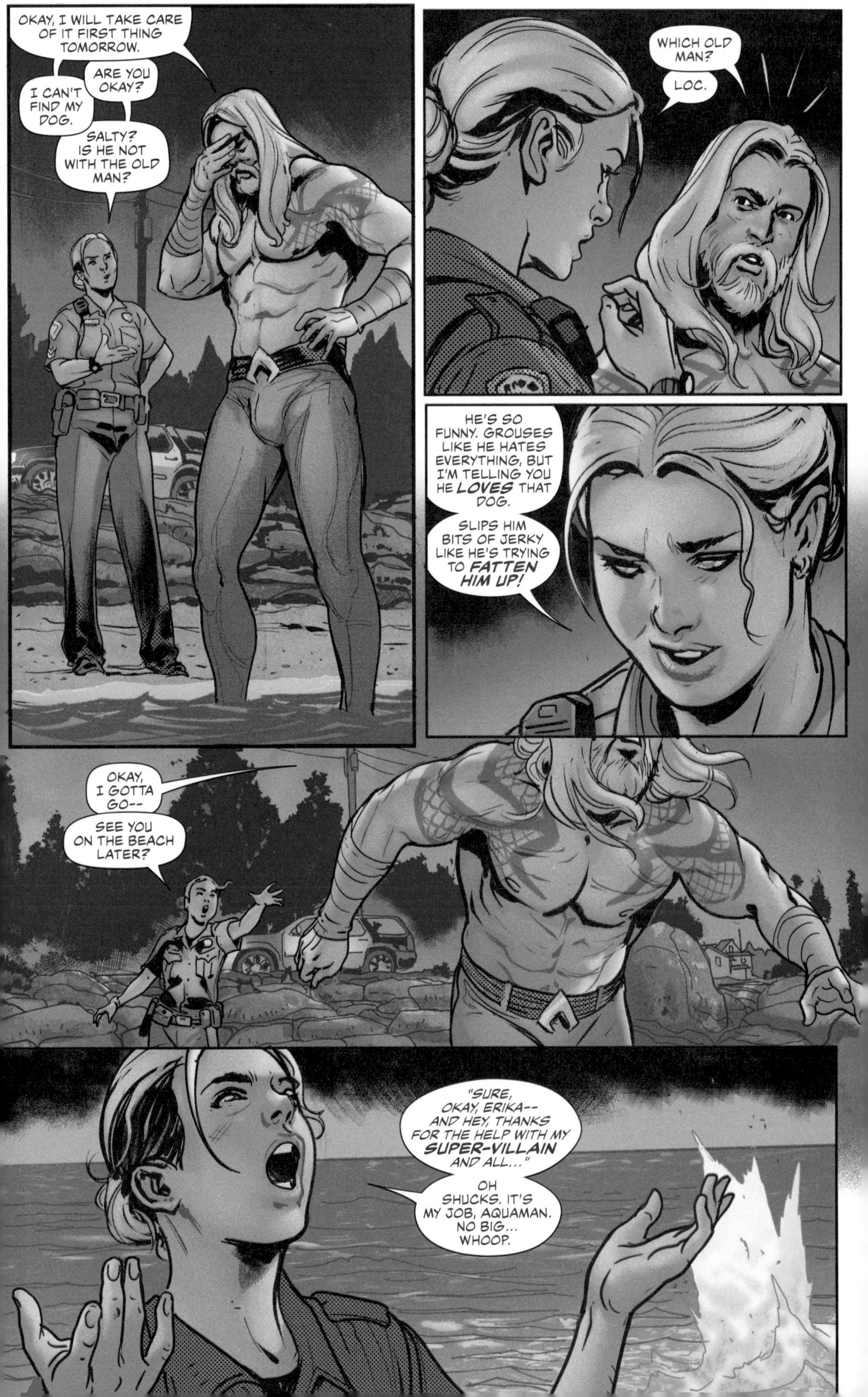
OKAY, I WILL TAKE CARE OF IT FIRST THING TOMORROW.
I CAN'T FIND MY DOG.
ARE YOU OKAY?
SALTY? IS HE NOT WITH THE OLD MAN?
WHICH OLD MAN?
LOC.
HE'S SO FUNNY. GROUSES LIKE HE HATES EVERYTHING, BUT I'M TELLING YOU HE LOVES THAT DOG.
SLIPS HIM BITS OF JERKY LIKE HE'S TRYING TO FATTEN HIM UP!
OKAY, I GOTTA GO--
SEE YOU ON THE BEACH LATER?
"SURE, OKAY, ERIKA-- AND HEY, THANKS FOR THE HELP WITH MY SUPER-VILLAIN AND ALL..."
OH SHUCKS. IT'S MY JOB, AQUAMAN. NO BIG... WHOOP.

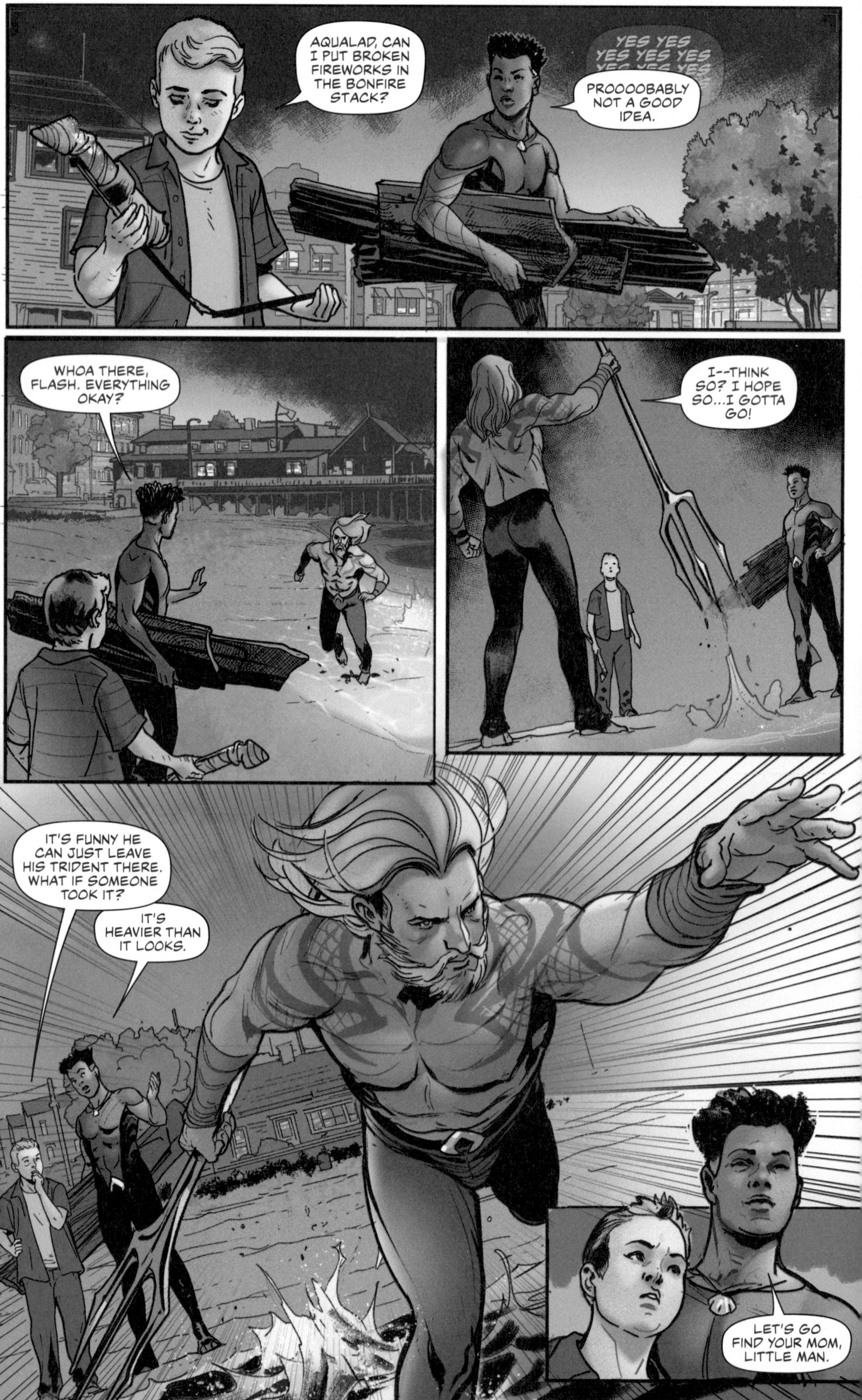
AQUALAD, CAN I PUT BROKEN FIREWORKS IN THE BONFIRE STACK?
YES YES YES YES YES
PROOOOBABLY NOT A GOOD IDEA.
WHOA THERE, FLASH. EVERYTHING OKAY?
I--THINK SO? I HOPE SO...I GOTTA GO!
IT'S FUNNY HE CAN JUST LEAVE HIS TRIDENT THERE. WHAT IF SOMEONE TOOK IT?
IT'S HEAVIER THAN IT LOOKS.
LET'S GO FIND YOUR MOM, LITTLE MAN.

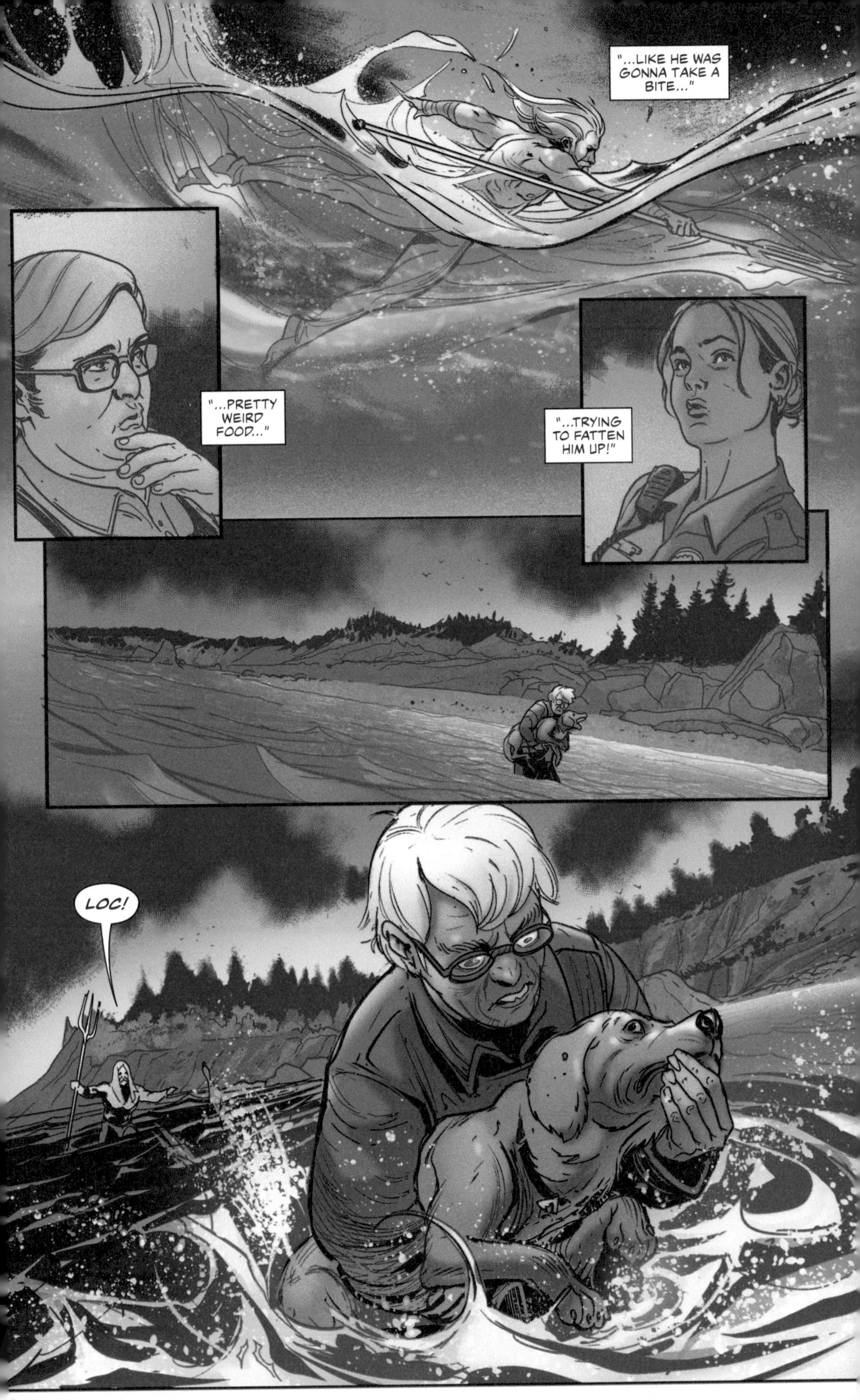
"...LIKE HE WAS GONNA TAKE A BITE..."
"...PRETTY WEIRD FOOD..."
"...TRYING TO FATTEN HIM UP!"
LOC!

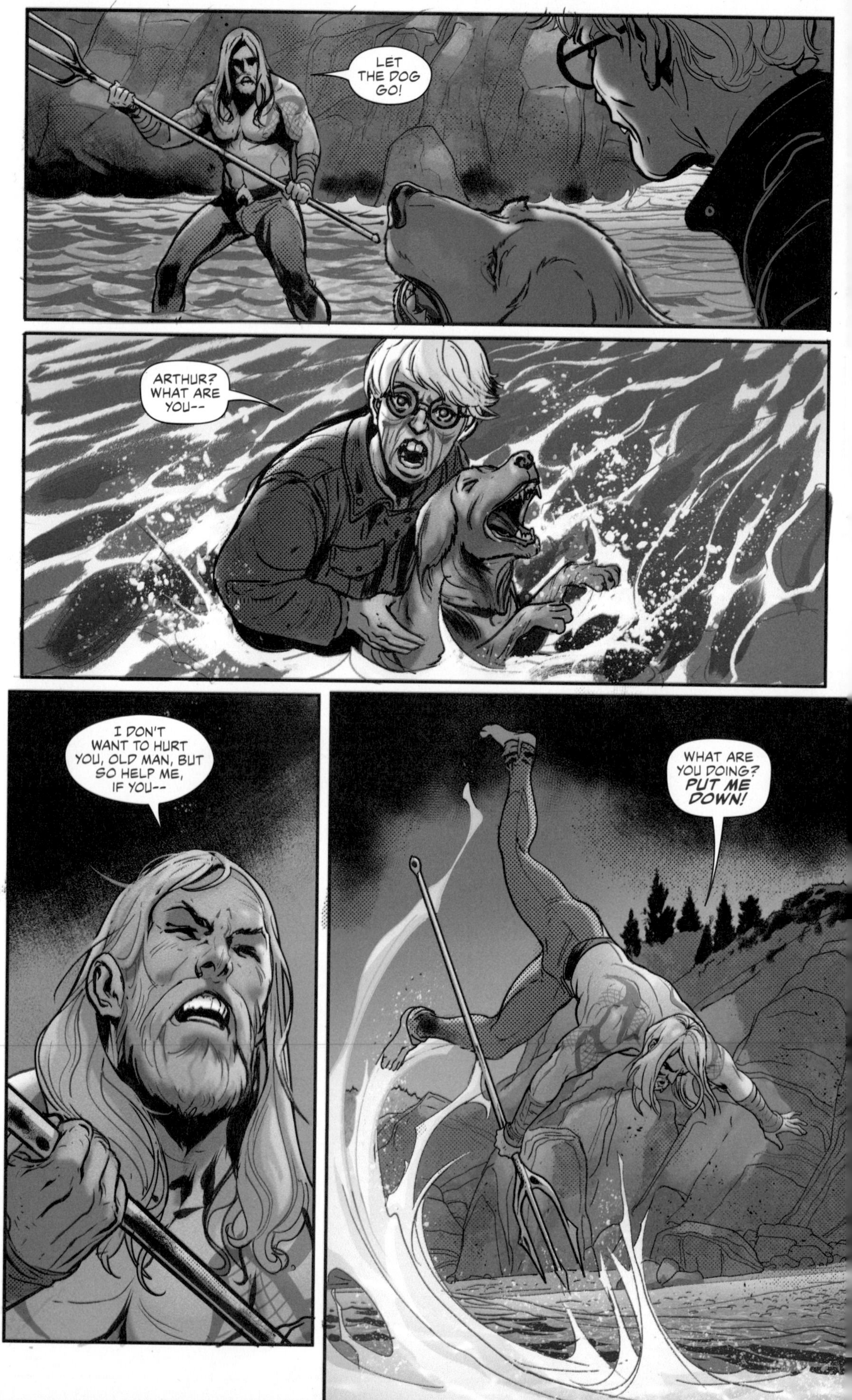

LET THE DOG GO!
ARTHUR? WHAT ARE YOU--
I DON'T WANT TO HURT YOU, OLD MAN, BUT SO HELP ME, IF YOU--
WHAT ARE YOU DOING? *PUT ME DOWN!*

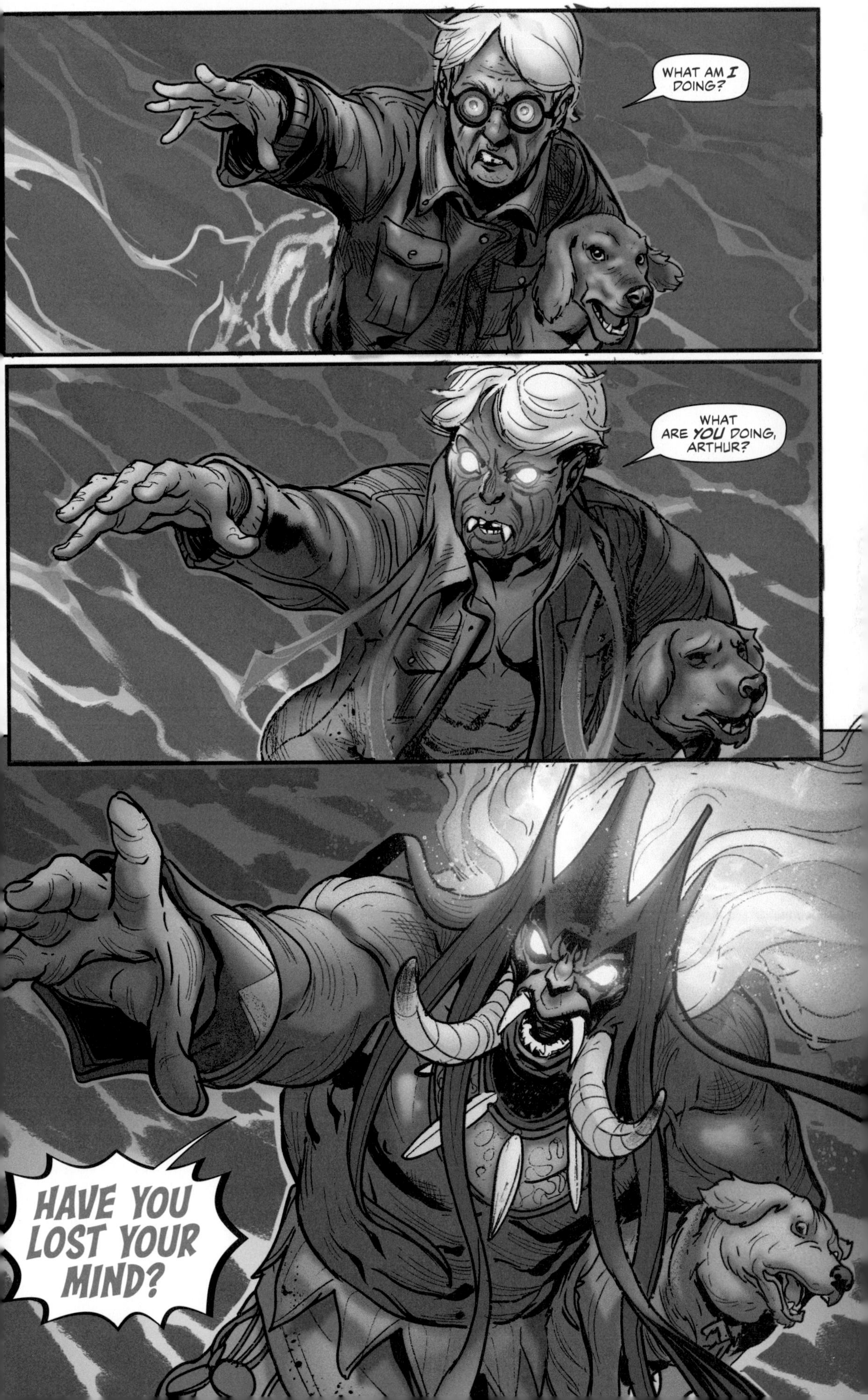
WHAT AM I DOING?
WHAT ARE YOU DOING, ARTHUR?
HAVE YOU LOST YOUR MIND?

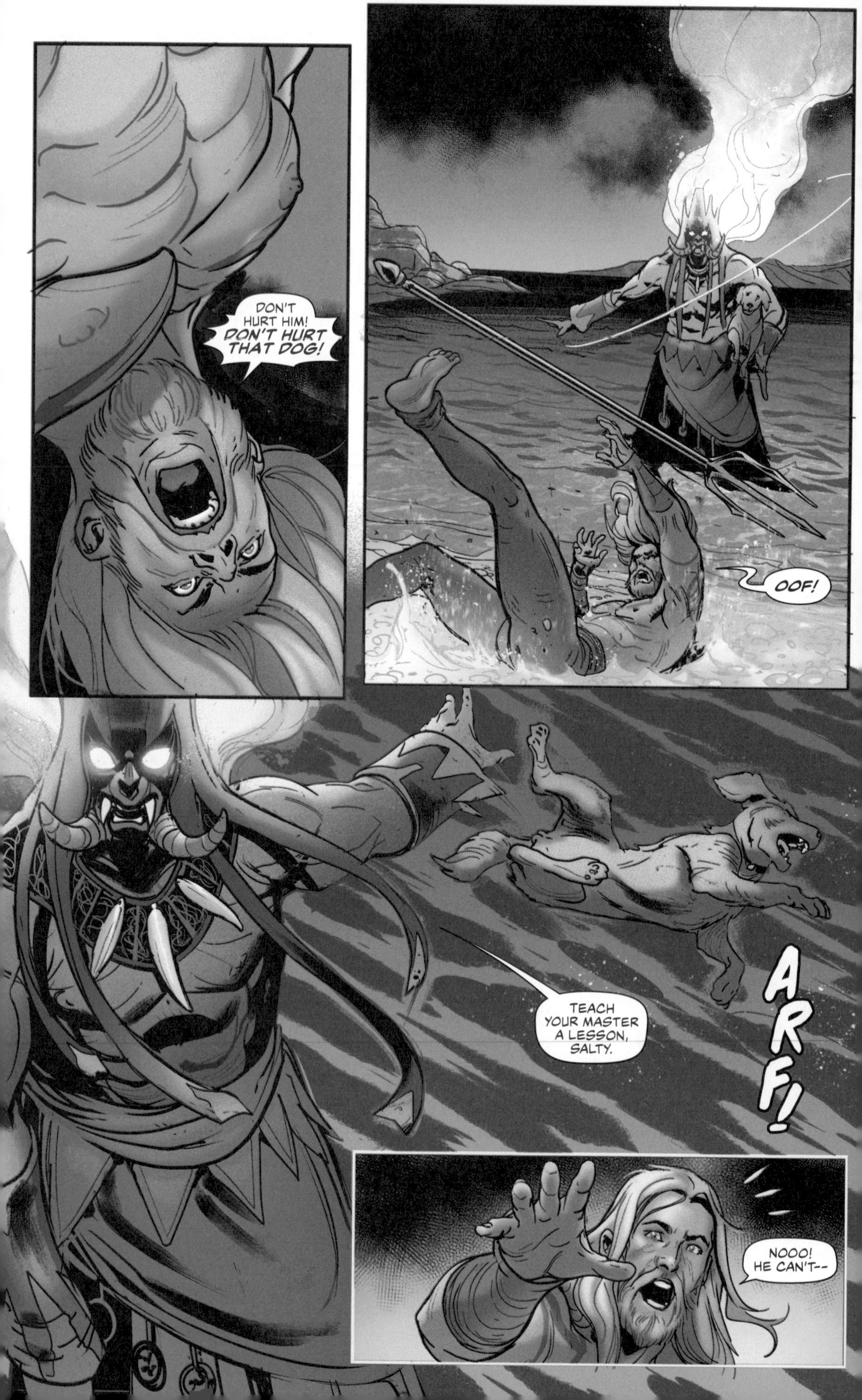
DON'T HURT HIM! DON'T HURT THAT DOG!
OOF!
TEACH YOUR MASTER A LESSON, SALTY.
ARF!
NOOO! HE CAN'T--

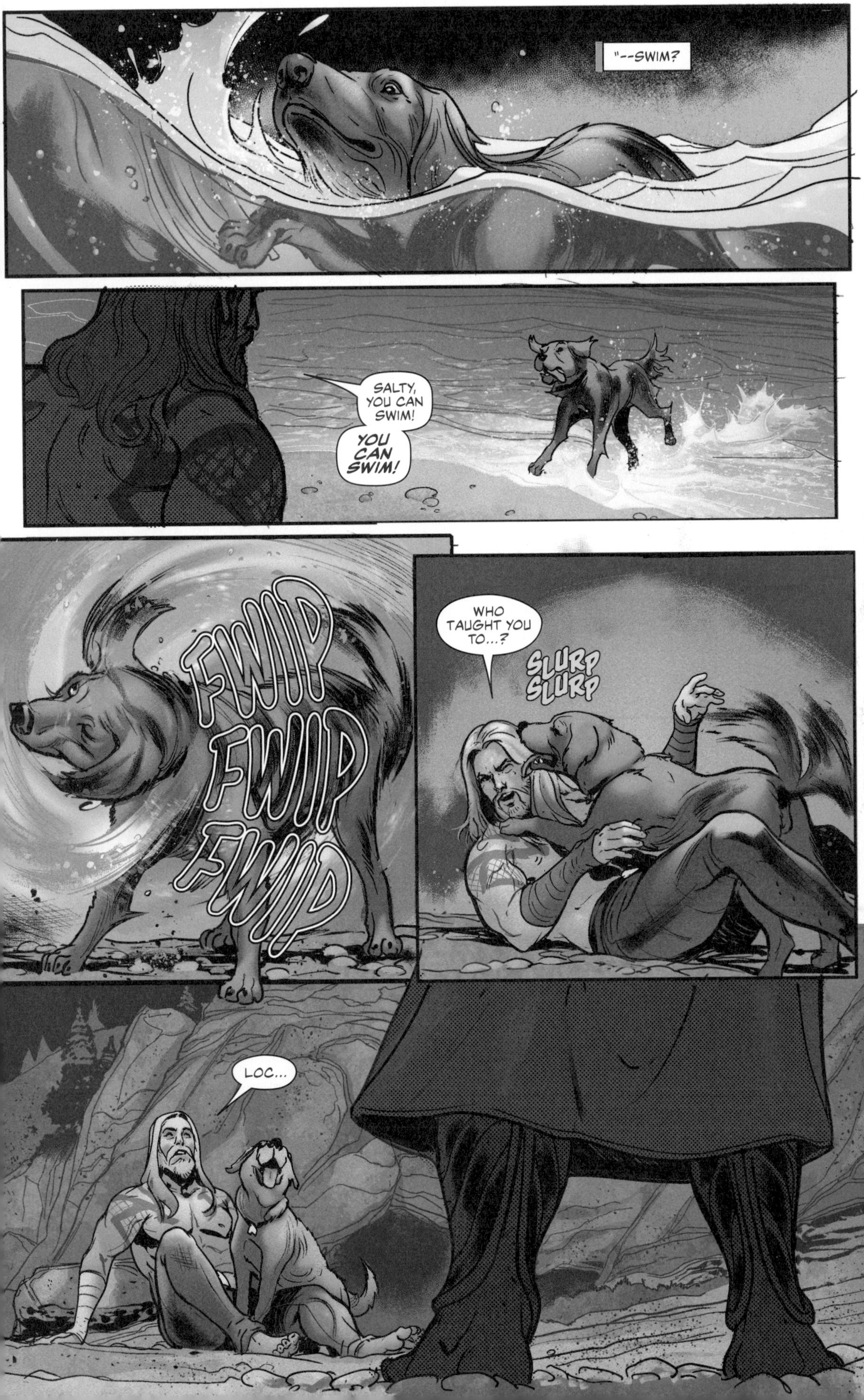
"--SWIM?
SALTY, YOU CAN SWIM!
YOU CAN SWIM!
FWIP FWIP FWIP
WHO TAUGHT YOU TO...?
SLURP SLURP
LOC...

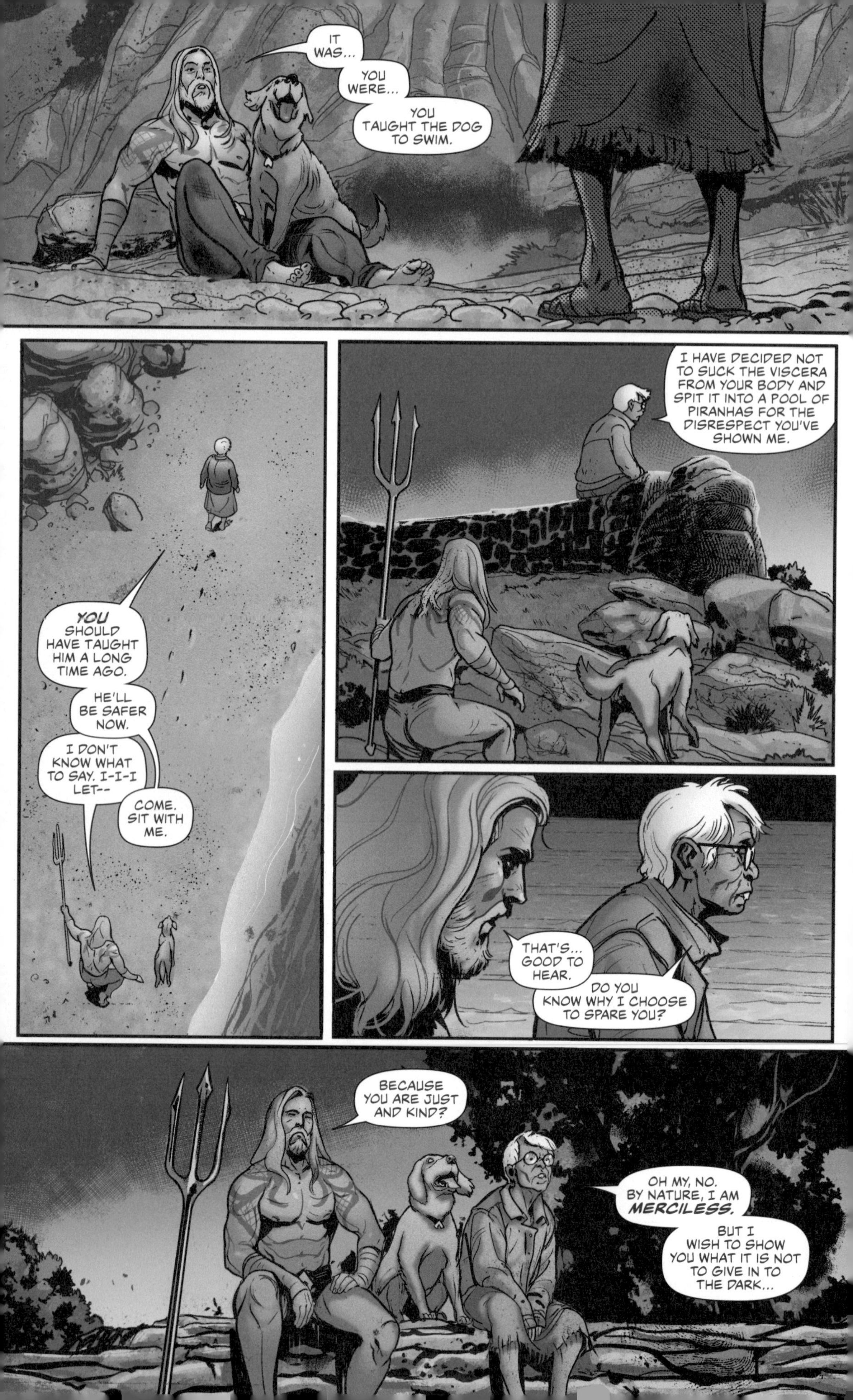
IT WAS...
YOU WERE...
YOU TAUGHT THE DOG TO SWIM.
YOU SHOULD HAVE TAUGHT HIM A LONG TIME AGO.
HE'LL BE SAFER NOW.
I DON'T KNOW WHAT TO SAY. I-I-I LET--
COME. SIT WITH ME.
I HAVE DECIDED NOT TO SUCK THE VISCERA FROM YOUR BODY AND SPIT IT INTO A POOL OF PIRANHAS FOR THE DISRESPECT YOU'VE SHOWN ME.
THAT'S... GOOD TO HEAR.
DO YOU KNOW WHY I CHOOSE TO SPARE YOU?
BECAUSE YOU ARE JUST AND KIND?
OH MY, NO. BY NATURE, I AM ***MERCILESS.***
BUT I WISH TO SHOW YOU WHAT IT IS NOT TO GIVE IN TO THE DARK...

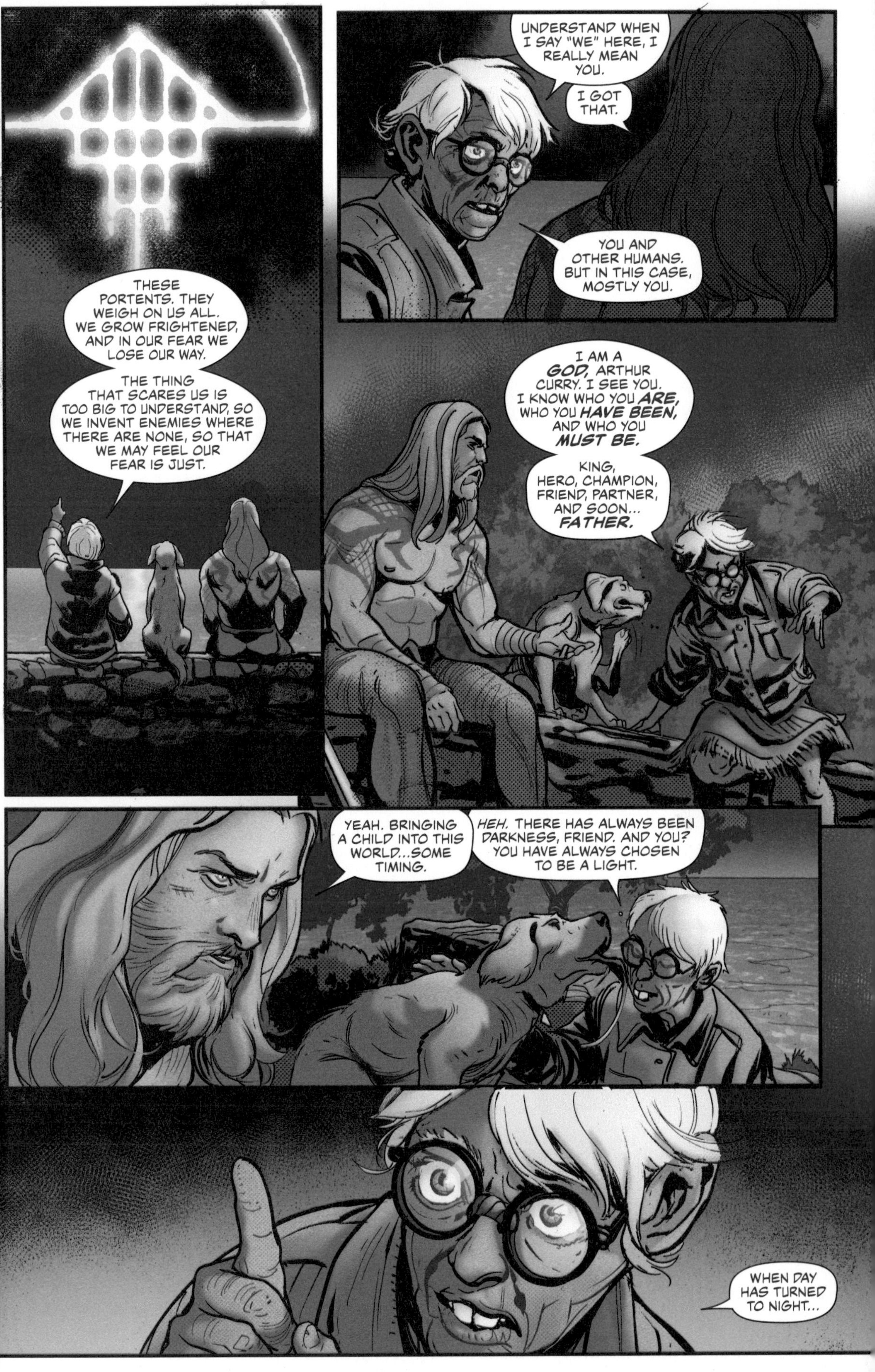
THESE PORTENTS. THEY WEIGH ON US ALL. WE GROW FRIGHTENED, AND IN OUR FEAR WE LOSE OUR WAY.
THE THING THAT SCARES US IS TOO BIG TO UNDERSTAND, SO WE INVENT ENEMIES WHERE THERE ARE NONE, SO THAT WE MAY FEEL OUR FEAR IS JUST.
UNDERSTAND WHEN I SAY "WE" HERE, I REALLY MEAN YOU.
I GOT THAT.
YOU AND OTHER HUMANS. BUT IN THIS CASE, MOSTLY YOU.
I AM A GOD, ARTHUR CURRY. I SEE YOU. I KNOW WHO YOU ARE, WHO YOU HAVE BEEN, AND WHO YOU MUST BE.
KING, HERO, CHAMPION, FRIEND, PARTNER, AND SOON... FATHER.
YEAH. BRINGING A CHILD INTO THIS WORLD...SOME TIMING.
HEH. THERE HAS ALWAYS BEEN DARKNESS, FRIEND. AND YOU? YOU HAVE ALWAYS CHOSEN TO BE A LIGHT.
WHEN DAY HAS TURNED TO NIGHT...

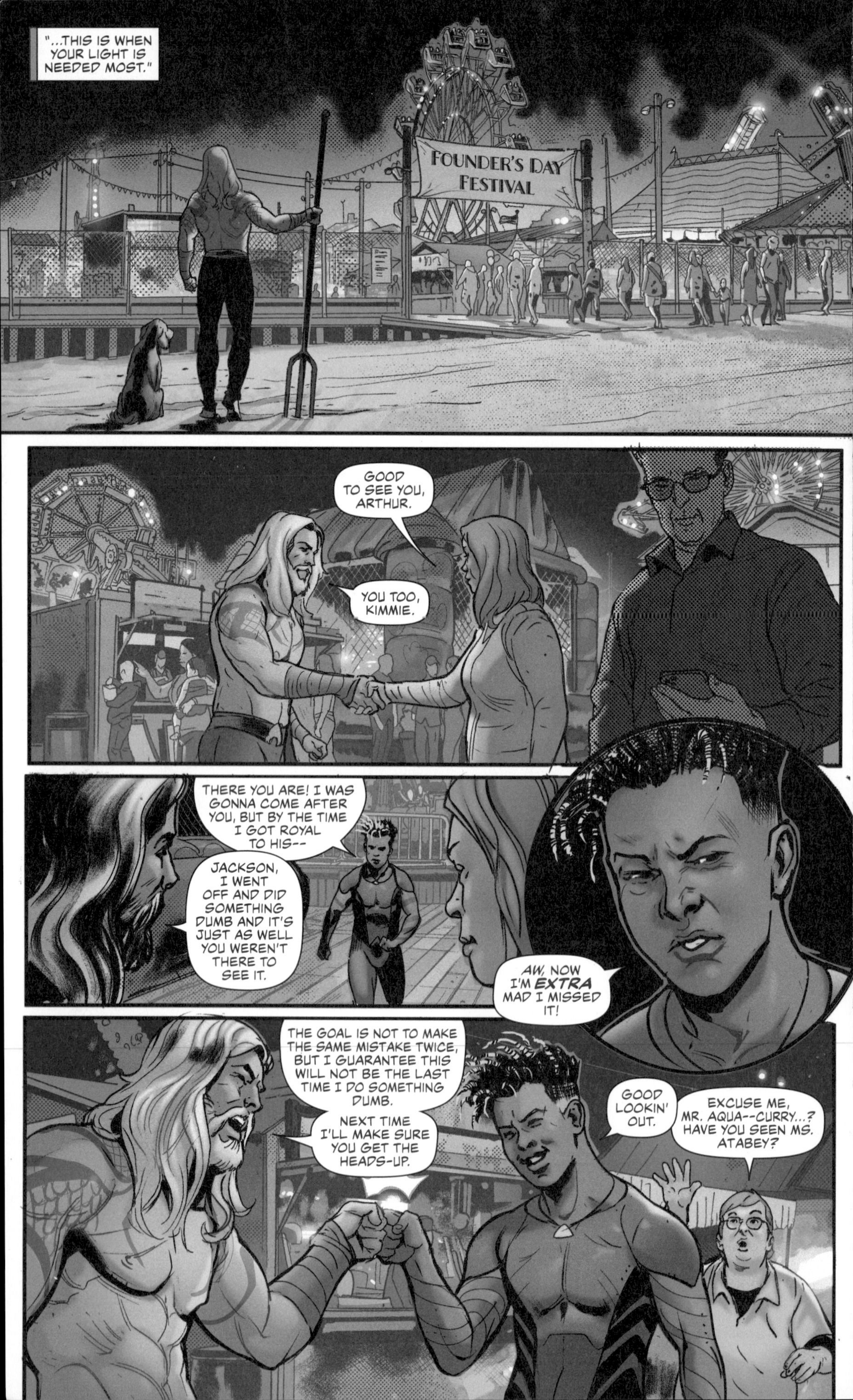
"...THIS IS WHEN YOUR LIGHT IS NEEDED MOST."
FOUNDER'S DAY FESTIVAL
GOOD TO SEE YOU, ARTHUR.
YOU TOO, KIMMIE.
THERE YOU ARE! I WAS GONNA COME AFTER YOU, BUT BY THE TIME I GOT ROYAL TO HIS--
JACKSON, I WENT OFF AND DID SOMETHING DUMB AND IT'S JUST AS WELL YOU WEREN'T THERE TO SEE IT.
AW, NOW I'M *EXTRA* MAD I MISSED IT!
THE GOAL IS NOT TO MAKE THE SAME MISTAKE TWICE, BUT I GUARANTEE THIS WILL NOT BE THE LAST TIME I DO SOMETHING DUMB.
NEXT TIME I'LL MAKE SURE YOU GET THE HEADS-UP.
GOOD LOOKIN' OUT.
EXCUSE ME, MR. AQUA--CURRY...? HAVE YOU SEEN MS. ATABEY?

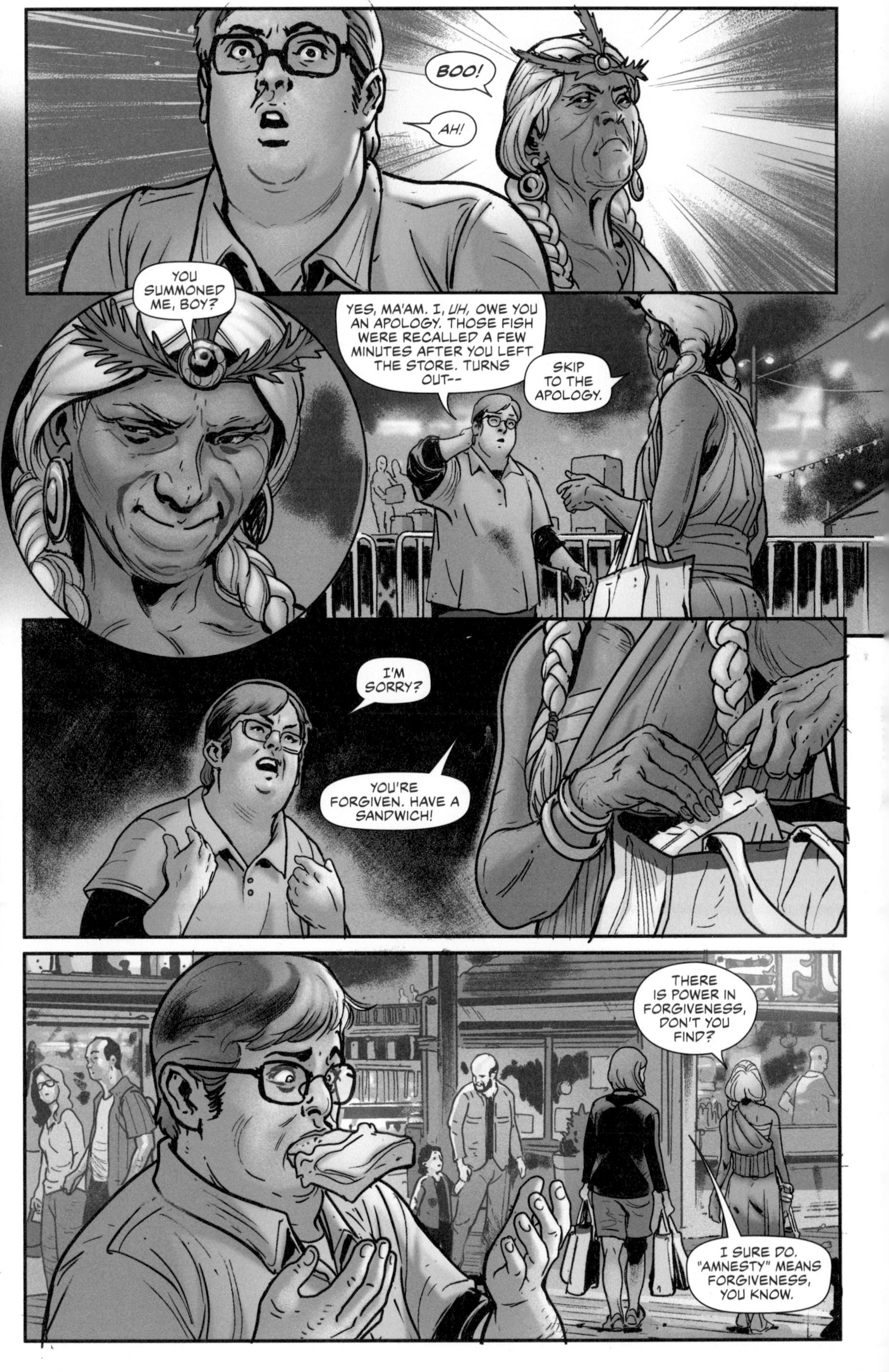
BOO!
AH!
YOU SUMMONED ME, BOY?
YES, MA'AM. I, *UH,* OWE YOU AN APOLOGY. THOSE FISH WERE RECALLED A FEW MINUTES AFTER YOU LEFT THE STORE. TURNS OUT--
SKIP TO THE APOLOGY.
I'M SORRY?
YOU'RE FORGIVEN. HAVE A SANDWICH!
THERE IS POWER IN FORGIVENESS, DON'T YOU FIND?
I SURE DO. "AMNESTY" MEANS FORGIVENESS, YOU KNOW.

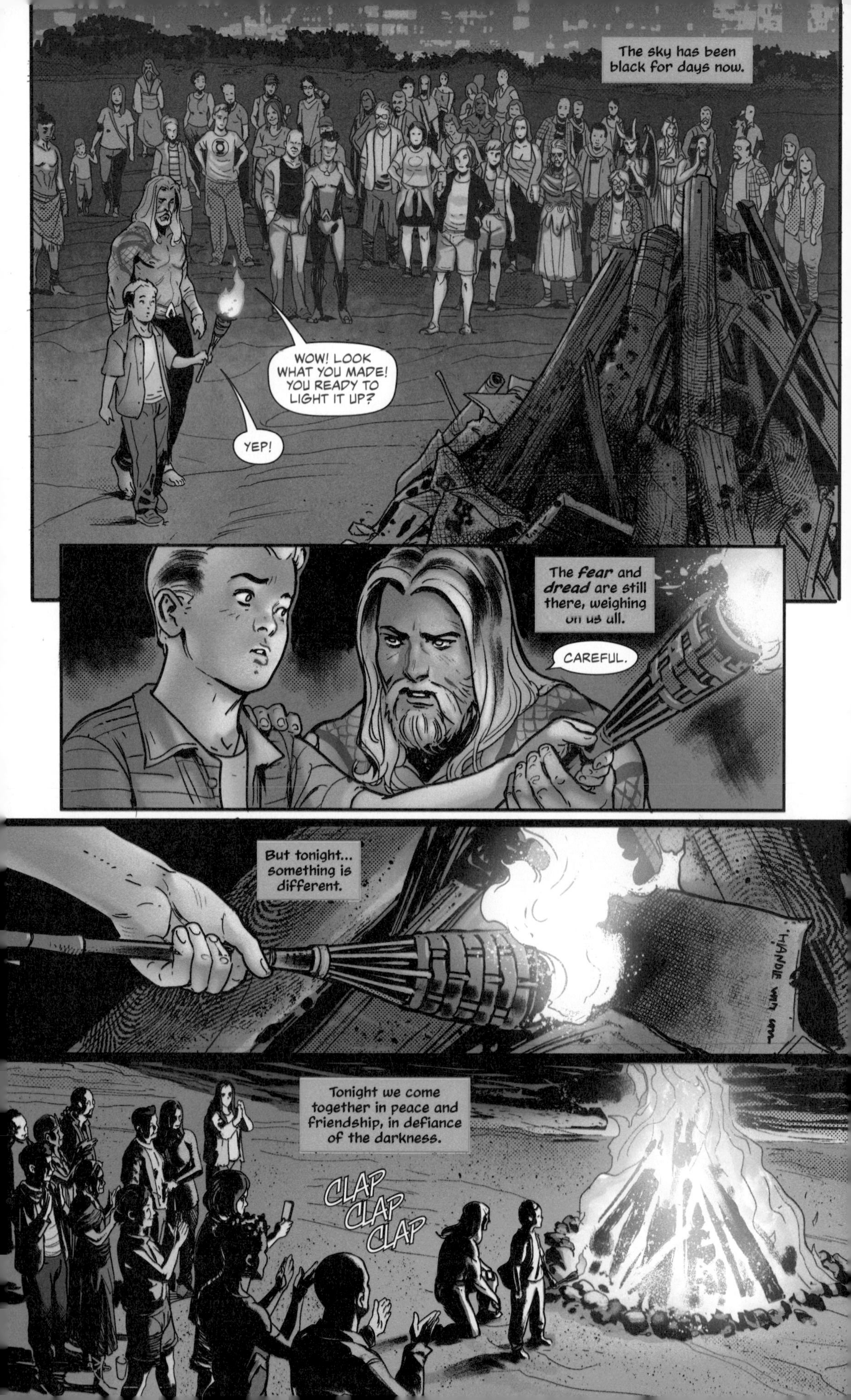
The sky has been black for days now.
WOW! LOOK WHAT YOU MADE! YOU READY TO LIGHT IT UP?
YEP!
The *fear* and *dread* are still there, weighing on us all.
CAREFUL.
But tonight... something is different.
Tonight we come together in peace and friendship, in defiance of the darkness.
CLAP CLAP CLAP

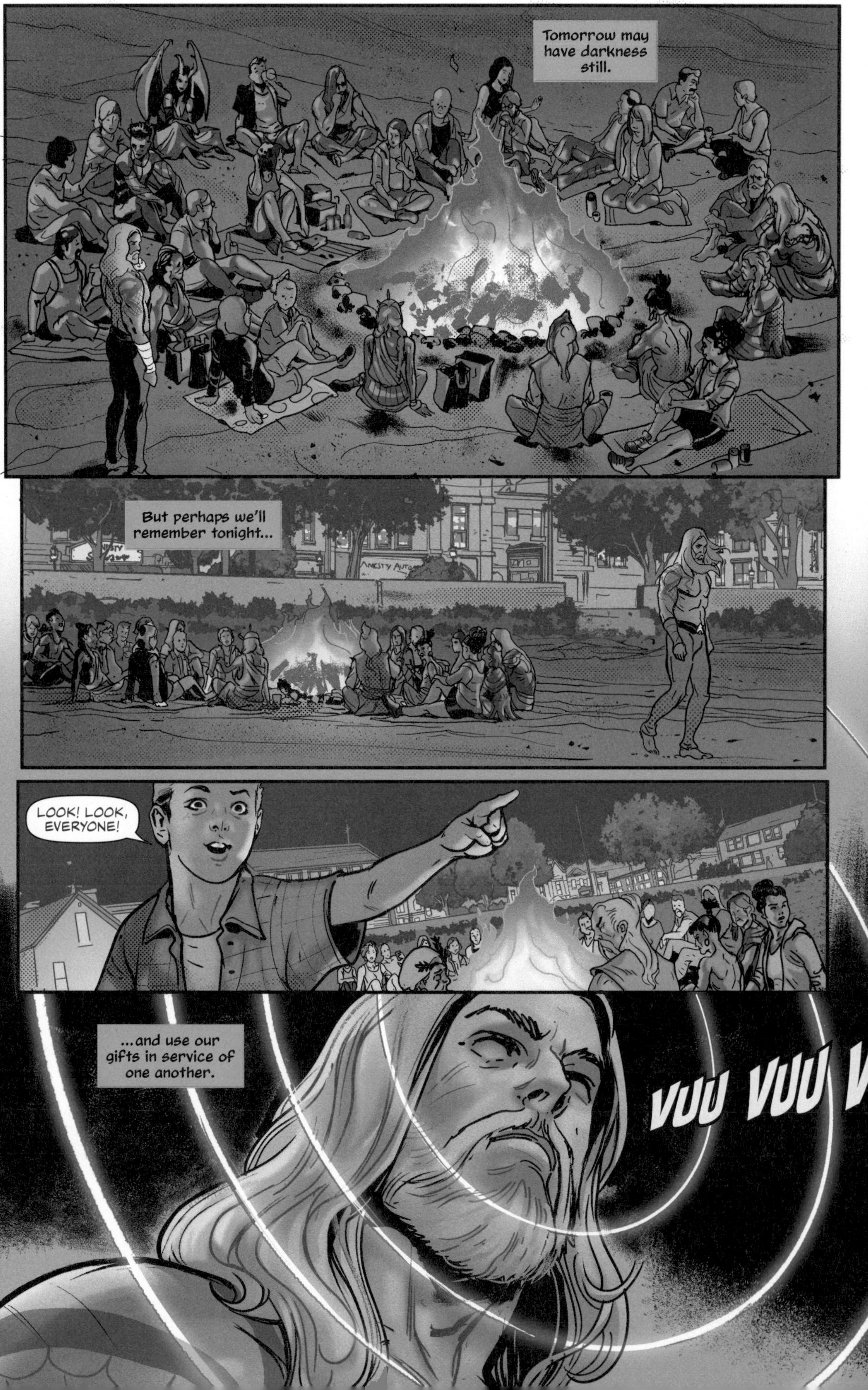
Tomorrow may have darkness still.
But perhaps we'll remember tonight...
LOOK! LOOK, EVERYONE!
...and use our gifts in service of one another.
VUU VUU V

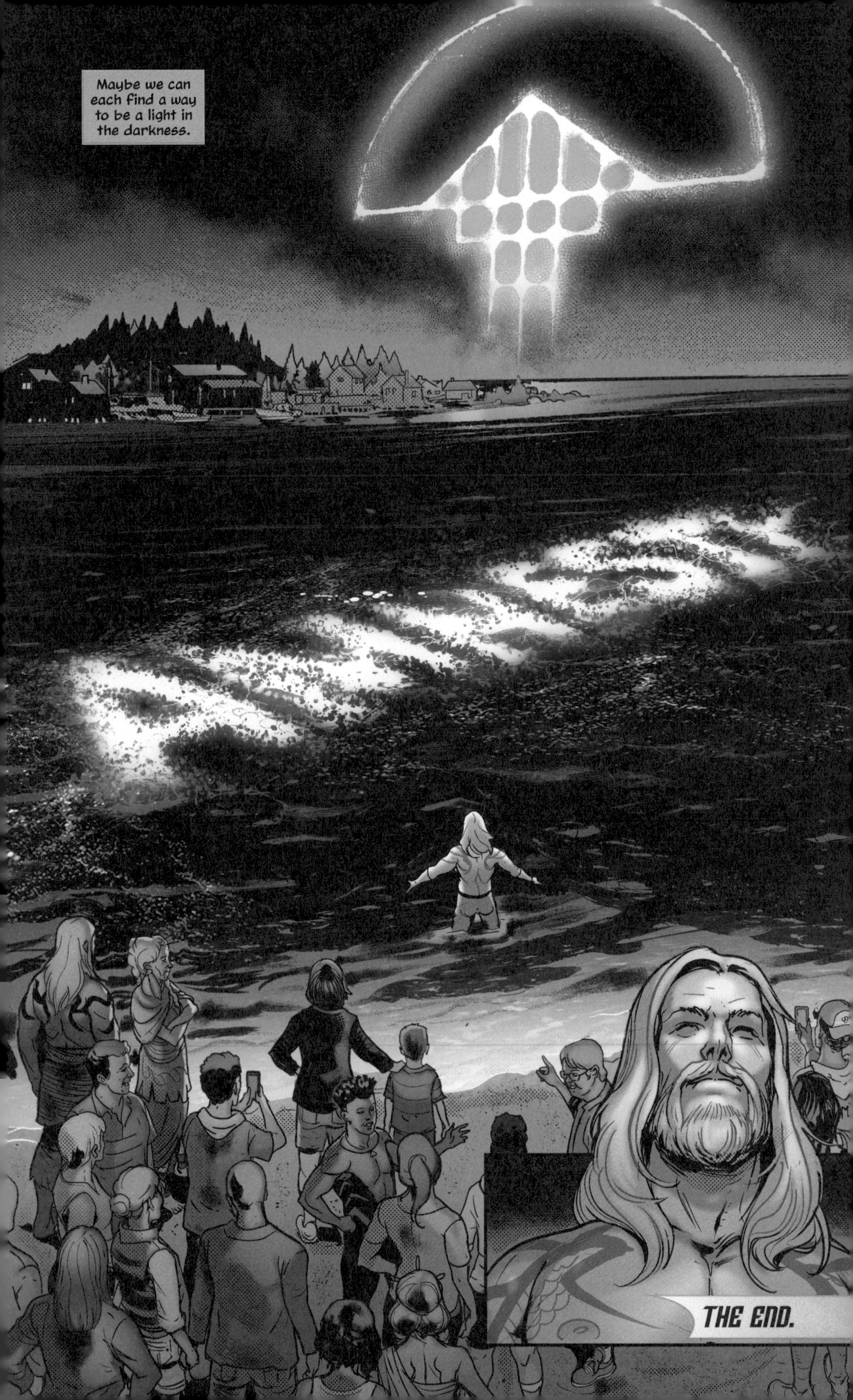
Maybe we can each find a way to be a light in the darkness.
THE END.

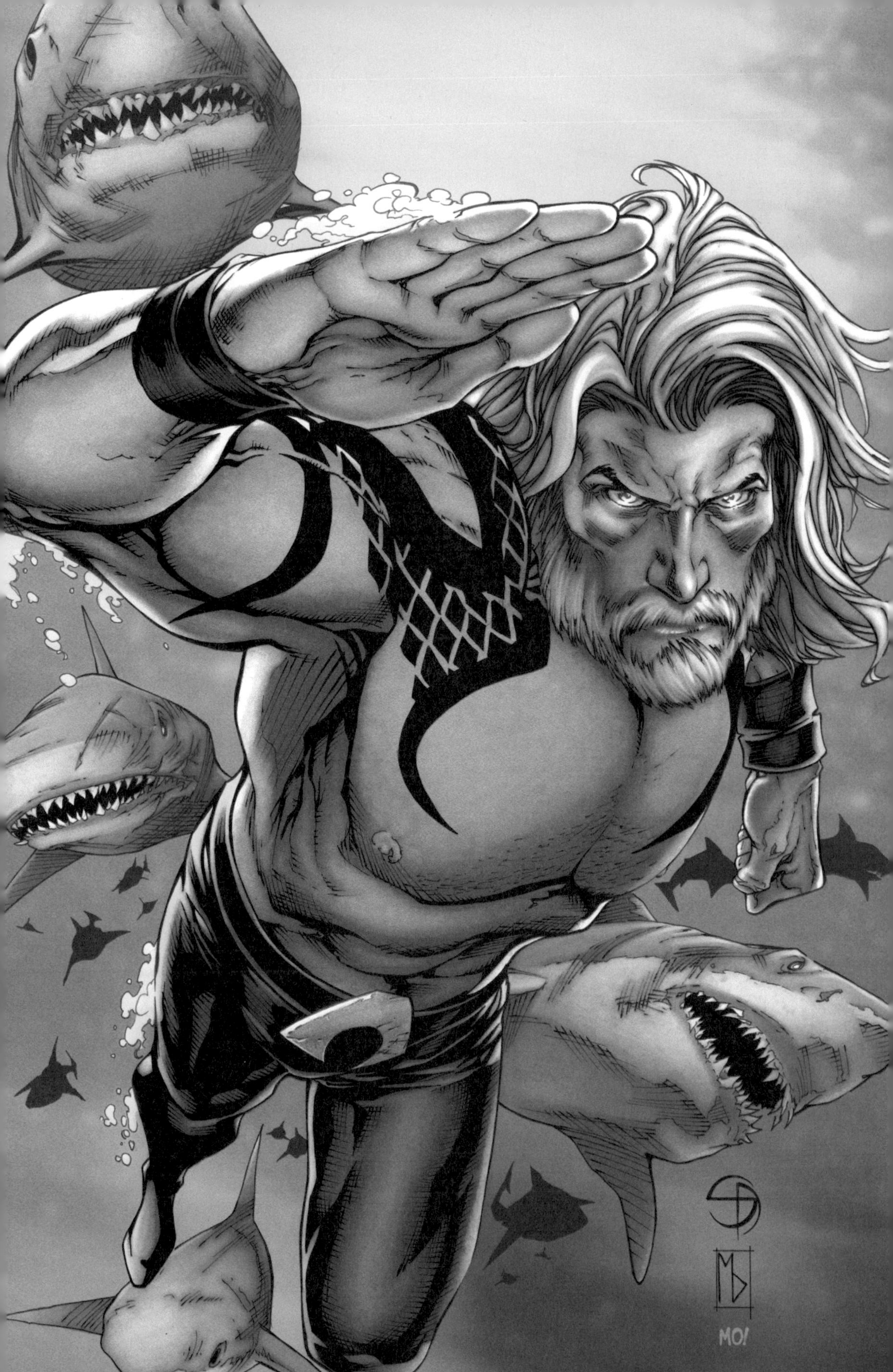
MO!

Aquaman #54 variant cover by
SHANE DAVIS, MICHELLE DELECKI, AND MORRY HOLLOWELL

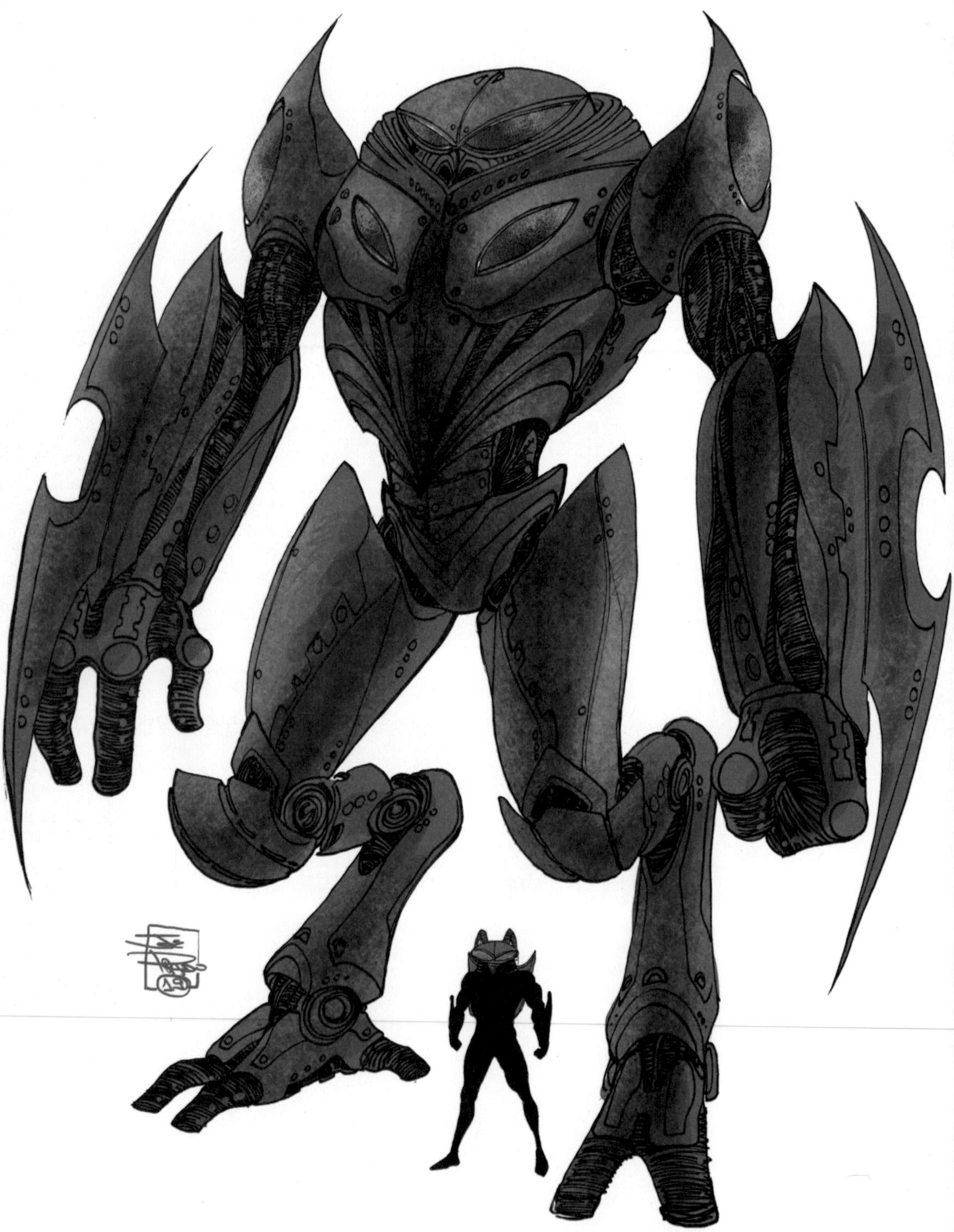

Concept sketch for Mecha Manta by
JOE PRADO

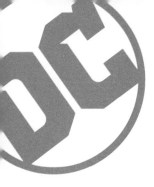

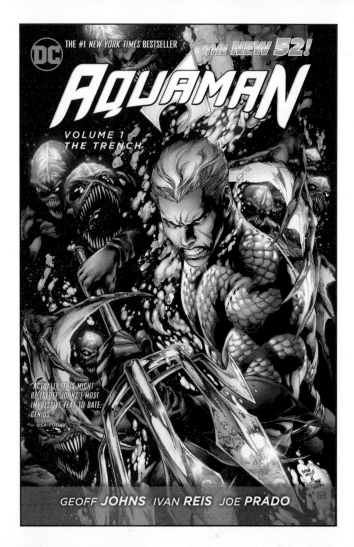

"AQUAMAN has been a rollicking good ride so far… The mythology Johns has been building up here keeps getting teased out at just the right rate, like giving a junkie their fix." **– MTV GEEK**

"With Reis on art and Johns using his full creative juices, AQUAMAN is constantly setting the bar higher and higher."
– CRAVE ONLINE

THE #1 NEW YORK TIMES BESTSELLER
THE NEW 52!
AQUAMAN
VOLUME 1
THE TRENCH
"ACTUALLY, THIS MIGHT BE [GEOFF JOHNS'] MOST IMPRESSIVE FEAT TO DATE. GENIUS."
— USA TODAY
GEOFF JOHNS IVAN REIS JOE PRADO

AQUAMAN

VOL. 1: THE TRENCH

GEOFF JOHNS
with IVAN REIS

THE #1 NEW YORK TIMES BEST-SELLING SERIES
THE NEW 52!
AQUAMAN
VOLUME 2
THE OTHERS
GEOFF JOHNS IVAN REIS JOE PRADO

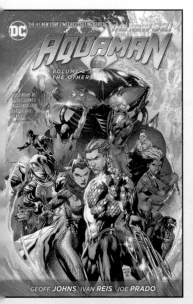

**AQUAMAN VOL. 2:
THE OTHERS**

THE #1 NEW YORK TIMES BEST-SELLING SERIES
THE NEW 52!
AQUAMAN
VOLUME 3
THRONE OF ATLANTIS
"IT'S DRAMATIC, ENGAGING, AND EXPERTLY RENDERED."
GEOFF JOHNS PAUL PELLETIER IVAN REIS

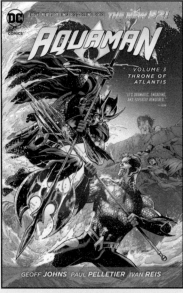

**AQUAMAN VOL. 3:
THRONE OF ATLANTIS**

READ THE ENTIRE EPIC!

AQUAMAN VOL. 4:
DEATH OF A KING

AQUAMAN VOL. 5:
SEA OF STORMS

AQUAMAN VOL. 6:
MAELSTROM

AQUAMAN VOL. 7:
EXILED

AQUAMAN VOL. 8:
OUT OF DARKNESS

Get more DC graphic novels wherever comics and books are sold!